RENEW YOUR LICENSE THE EASY WAY

California's Real Estate License Renewal

7th Edition

Duane Gomer
MBA, BS, CPM, RECI, MLO

Duane Gomer Inc., Real Estate Education Professionals

www.facebook.com./DuaneGomerSeminars   E-mail Duane.G@DuaneGomer.com
Phone 800.439.4909   www.duanegomer.com

This publication is designed to provide accurate and authoritative information in regard to the subject matter covered. It is sold with the understanding that the publisher is not engaged in rendering legal, accounting, or other professional service. If legal advice or other assistance is required, the services of a competent professional person should be sought.

Publisher: **Real Estate Education Unlimited**
Author: **Duane Gomer**
President: **D.J. Gomer**
Editor IN Chief: **Gail Clairmont**
Creative Director: **Miguel Allport**
Consultant: **Leonard Baron**

Student Edition:
ISBN-13:
978-1478281146

ISBN-10:
1478281146

This book includes excerpts form California Civil Codes, Commission Regulations, Business & Professional Code, Equal Credit Opportunity Act, National Association of Realtors Code of Ethics.

© 2013 Real Estate Education Unlimited
Duane Gomer Inc.
23312 Madero, Suite J
Mission Viejo, CA 92691
(949) 457-8930 (800) 439- 4909
www.duanegomer.com

To D.J.

Over the years your understanding, support, compassion, direction and inspiration 24/7 and 365 have been so appreciated. Thanks so much; I am indeed a lucky man.

PREFACE

PROCEDURES

This book is designed to satisfy the requirements for license renewal for all California Real Estate Licenses; one size fits all whether new or old, Broker or Salesperson. It includes the five 3-Hour Courses of Agency, Ethics, Fair Housing, Trust Fund Handling and Risk Management and two 15-Hour Consumer Protection Courses, Property Management Success and Make Money in California Foreclosures, for a total of 45 hours.

You should study each course and when finished follow the instructions at the end of each course to complete practice questions that will help you pass the exams.

Effective March 1, 2008 BRE established a new requirement that you can test on only 15 hours of exams in any 24 hour period. This is all explained on the General Information page that follows. For example, if you are testing all online, when eligible to test, you could test on the five 3-Hour courses in one day, 24 hours later test on one 15-Hour course and the final course 24 hours later.

Many students attend our time saving half-day Optional Review and then receive explicit instructions on how to test on the remaining courses online.

You can take the exams in any order. Follow all requirements in your Student Work Center. To reiterate, when testing be at a computer that can print your certificate. Remember, our mission is to get you renewed as stress-free and quickly as possible.

CALIFORNIA BRE RENEWAL REQUIREMENTS

For complete information on the requirements go to the appendix in this book and read the information there. The Courses presented in this book meet the requirements of any licensee. Some companies will push Survey Courses, etc., but ours is the simple way with no complications.

California BRE Continuing Education began in 1978. Duane Gomer Seminars hold Sponsor #0054, so we are the longest standing private education sponsor. We are proud of our longevity and our reputation, and we will do our best to get you renewed properly and quickly.

DUANE GOMER SEMINARS

HISTORY
Our first courses were presented in 1978 when we presented 45 Hours of Live Continuing Education in 5 days. It has been a pleasure over the years to work with so many outstanding instructors. Some names you might know: Minnie Lush, Noel Seaman, Dennis McKenzie, Gary Watts, Rick Robinson, Hal Morris, Lynn Sewell, Cari Lynn Pace, Maurice Iddings, John Anderson, Sharon Valentino, Joffrey Long, Layne Kulwin, Terry Ward, Jim Eszlinger, Gus Lanatta, Randy Turnquist, Judy Wagner, David Nevin, Sharon Koziel, John Richards, Allan Wallace, Brook Gabrielson, Bob Bruss, Joe De Carlo, Paul Scheper, Kerry Berman, Joel Carlson, Mark Davidson, Craig Young, Warren Doane . . .

Over the years the delivery systems of our courses has changed. Now, we present optional review seminars as well as deliver courses by distance learning using textbooks, CDs and online reading. We did Video Courses in the past and may start again.

PRESENT TIME

We present courses in many areas. These include:

1. Renew an MLO Endorsement
2. Renew a Notary Commission
3. Renew any Real Estate License
4. Qualify to take the exam to become a Real Estate Salesperson, Real Estate Broker, Notary Public, Mortgage Loan Originator, etc.
5. Short Sales, Foreclosures, REO, Property Management, Syndication, Creative Financing, Exchange, Negotiating, etc.

Our courses have been presented by the following Associations and Companies: Arcadia, Bay East, Beverly Hills/Greater L.A., Big Bear, Burbank, California Desert, Central Valley, Citrus Valley, Conejo Simi Moorpark, Contra Costa, Delta, Downey, East San Diego Co., East Valley, Glendale, Greater Antelope Valley, Idyllwild, Inland Valleys, Laguna, Lake, Lassen, Lodi, Madera, Monterey County, Newport Beach, North Bay, North San Diego, Northern Solano Co., Oakland, Orange Belt, Orange County, Pacific Southwest, Pacific West, Pajaro Valley, Palm Springs Regional, Pismo Coast, Placer County, Rancho Southeast, Rim O'The World, Sacramento, San Diego, San Luis Obispo, San Mateo, Santa Barbara, Santa Clara Co., Santa Cruz Co., Santa Maria, Silicon Valley, Solano, South Bay, Southland Regional, Southwest Riverside Co., The Inland Gateway, Tri-Counties, Tulare Co., Ventura Co. Coastal, West San Gabriel, Century 21 Award, Keller Williams, Evergreen, Stratis Financial, Prudential California Realty, Rodeo Realty, Re/Max Olson, All California Mortgage, Princeton Capital, International Mortgage, Regency Real Estate, First Rate Financial, Samuel Scott, Cardinal Pacific Escrow, Coldwell Banker, and more.

More information about our classes is at the back of this book, and you can also check www.DuaneGomer.com, email info@DuaneGomer.com, call 800-439-4909 or text 949-374-3943.

Trying to stay abreast of new changes we have two Facebook pages at www.Facebook.com/DuaneGomerSeminars and www.Facebook.com/Duane.Gomer, starting Twitter at Duane Gomer@Duane_Gomer, our blog at www.DuaneGomer.info. Check out our Interest Groups on our Facebook Fan Page. Also, we send an outstanding, informative, entertaining newsletter (our reader's comments) to anyone who so desires. You can opt-in at www.DuaneGomer.com or email me at Duane@DuaneGomer.com.

Other areas we are considering include Appraisal and Insurance Licensing, Commercial Property Sales, Social Media, and others. See you in a class.

ABOUT THE AUTHOR:

Duane has been a California real estate licensee since 1961, and the owner of Duane Gomer Seminars since 1978. He started as a Real Estate Syndicator and Property Manager in the San Fernando Valley and soon started teaching real estate courses at UCLA to find clients. Duane is still active in course presentations for Real Estate Licensees, Notary Public Commissions and Mortgage Loan Originators. You can read his articles on his BLOG site (Duane's World of Real Estate), Facebook and Twitter.

EDUCATION
- Bachelor of Science – Indiana University with honors
- Masters of Business Administration – UCLA
- Navy Supply Corp. School, Athens, GA
- Naval Officer Candidate School – with honors
- Real Estate Certificate Institute – UCLA
- Certified Property Manager – National Association of Realtors

BUSINESS
- Director of Athletics – 17th Air Force, Germany
- Director of Data Processing – U.S. Exchange Services, Germany
- Director of Property Management – Forest E. Olson
- Founder, Property Management Services – Property Management Syndications, Sales & Court Receiverships
- Founder, Duane Gomer Seminars – Real Estate, Notary, Tax, Mortgage Loan Origination, Foreclosures & Finance Education
- Currently an Approved Sponsor, Vendor and Provider for Education in California

CREDENTIALS
- Teaching Assistant, UCLA
- Instructor, University of Maryland
- Instructor, UCLA Continuing Education
- Author of several textbooks and approved courses
- Realtor, Real Estate Broker, NMLS Mortgage Loan Originator
- Designations: BS, MBA, LTJG, CPM, RECI, MLO, Grandfather

<u>TESTIMONIALS</u>

You guys are a breath of fresh air to a toxic world. I am your biggest fan. I tell everybody about your services. You are the higher standard! D.L.

Just wanted you to know that you are still, by far, the best presenter I have ever seen in this business! I have been selling real estate since 1977 and early on I had to take a crash course for my 45 hours and I bumped into one of your seminars (that YOU were actually doing.) I learned more about real estate in that workshop than I had ever learned from my broker. I have since renewed every time with your system. I even got my notary through Gomer Seminars. It doesn't matter how many friends you have on Facebook, how many blogs you do, how clever your tweets are…in the long run…those referrals that keep coming your way are because YOU are FABULOUS! L.N.

Thanks again for helping me complete my 45 hour home study course. Today, I completed my last test and received 100%. Wow! I have been a "Realtor" (yes I've paid my dues) since 1979. Each time my license comes up for renewal I use your company. Just wanted to let you know to keep up the excellent job! I've attended your live seminars in the past and now find it convenient to test online. BB

I wish I had heard of your company when I last renewed my RE license. With your books I purchased, the tests this time were much easier. Thank you very much. LA

Thank you for your very informative emails. I took your advice and completed my continuing education this month. Using your great materials I was able to pass all of the tests with a very high score. RV

GENERAL INFORMATION PAGE

To be provided to the participant prior to registration/enrollment.

All offerings shall be completed within one year from the date of registration.

COURSE PROVIDER NAME	WEB SITE ADDRESS
Duane Gomer Seminars	www.DuaneGomer.com

BRE SPONSOR ID # (4 DIGITS)	PHONE NUMBER	EMAIL ADDRESS
0054	(800) 439-4909	info@DuaneGomer.com

ADDRESS (STREET, CITY, STATE, ZIP CODE)
23312 Madero #J, Mission Viejo, CA 92691

COURSE NAME
See attached for a complete list of course names

BRIEF COURSE DESCRIPTION
See attached for a complete Course Description. This book includes five 3-Hour and two 15-Hour courses listed on the attachment. The courses are not sold individually.

METHOD OF COURSE PRESENTATION (LIVE, CORRESPONDENCE/INTERNET)	COURSE CATEGORY	CREDIT HOURS
Correspondence delivered by a choice of a textbook, CD or PDF download. Exams are online only.	Agency – Agency; Ethics – Ethics; Trust Fund Handling – Trust Fund Handling; Fair Housing – Fair Housing; Risk Management – Risk Management; Make Money in California Foreclosures – Consumer Protection; Property Management Success – Consumer Protection	Total 45 Hours – Agency, Ethics, Trust Fund Handling, Fair Housing & Risk Management – 3 Hours Each; Property Management Success and Make Money in California Foreclosures – 15 Hours Each

DATES AND LOCATION (FOR LIVE COURSES)

COURSE FEES (INLCUDE ANY SHIPPING AND HANDLING FEES)
Total 45 Hours – Prices subject to change:

Textbook:	$70
CD:	$55
PDF:	$50

TEXTBOOK, WORKBOOK, OR OUTLINE INFORMATION
Title: California's Real Estate License Renewal
Author(s): Duane Gomer
Copyright Date: 2013
Pages: 396
Edition (*if applicable*): 7th

REFUND/CANCELLATION POLICY
If the materials are returned unused (and you have not taken any final exams) within two months of the original purchase date, you will be given a refund less $20.00. If you paid by credit card, your account will be credited and a copy of the credit will be emailed to you. Between two months and twelve months no cash refunds for unused courses, but materials can be returned for a credit towards any of our other courses. After twelve months there are no credits. If you fail to finish the program within one year, you can repurchase for a fee of $40. If you should fail, you can take a second exam at no cost within the one-year period.

FINAL EXAMINATION CRITERIA

NUMBER OF QUESTIONS	TYPES OF QUESTIONS	TIME
Agency, Ethics, Trust Fund Handling, Fair Housing, Risk Management – 20 questions each Property Management Success and Make Money in California Foreclosures – 40 questions each	Multiple Choice	Agency, Ethics, Trust Fund Handling, Fair Housing, Risk Management – 20 minutes each Property Management Success and Make Money in California Foreclosures – 40 minutes each

HOW MANY DIFFERENT FINAL EXAMS ARE OFFERED FOR THIS COURSE (ONE OR TWO)?	MINIMUM PASSING PERCENTAGE
Two	70%

BRE Disclaimer Statement

Prior to the start of the course, the sponsor shall provide participants with the following disclaimer statement: "This course is approved for continuing education credit by the California Bureau of Real Estate. However, this approval does not constitute an endorsement of the views or opinions which are expressed by the course sponsor, instructors, authors, or lecturers."

Attendance Policy

For live courses, students must attend a minimum of 90% of the approved course hours to be eligible to receive BRE continuing education course credit

Live Course Identification Statement

Participants shall present one of the following forms of identification below immediately before admittance to a live presentation of an offering:
A. A current California driver's license.
B. A current identification card described in Section 13000 of the California Vehicle Code
C. Any identification of the participant issued by a governmental agency or a recognized real estate related trade organization within the immediately preceding five years which bears a photograph, signature and identification number of the participant.

Correspondence Course Identification Statement

Participants shall present one of the following forms of identification immediately before the administration of the final examination:
A. A current California driver's license.
B. A current identification card described in Section 13000 of the California Vehicle Code
C. Any identification of the participant issued by a governmental agency or a recognized real estate related trade organization within the immediately preceding five years which bears a photograph, signature and identification number of the participant.

Examination Regulatory Notes

- Participants taking a correspondence offering or package of offerings shall be limited to completion of final examinations for a maximum of fifteen (15) credit hours during any one 24-hour period. A participant shall not be granted access to additional segments of the final examination for offerings or a package of offerings that exceed fifteen (15) credit hours until the appropriate 24-hour period has elapsed.

- An offering may include a provision for one retaking a different final examination by a participant who failed the original examination provided the questions in the re-examination are different questions than those contained in the original examination. A participant who fails the re-examination cannot receive credit for the course. Such a participant is not barred from enrolling and completing the same course, but must retake the course and pass the final examination with a score of 70% or better to receive credit.

- Questions used in a final examination shall not duplicate any more than 10% of questions used in any other quiz or examination utilized during the presentation of the course.

- Final examinations for CE courses consisting only of multiple choice, true/false and/or fill-in the blank questions shall be limited to a maximum of 10% true/false questions.

- Time calculations for a final examination consisting of multiple choice, true/false and/or fill-in the blank questions should be allowed a maximum amount of one (1) minute per question. The minimum number of questions for a continuing education final examination consisting only of multiple choice, true/false and/or fill-in the blank questions is:

1 credit hour = 5	*19-23 credit hours = 50*
2 credit hours = 10	*24-27 credit hours = 60*
3-5 credit hours = 15	*28-31 credit hours = 70*
6-8 credit hours = 20	*32-35 credit hours = 80*
9-11 credit hours = 25	*36-39 credit hours = 90*
12-14 credit hours = 30	*40 credit hours and over = 100 questions*
15-18 credit hours = 40	

Online Evaluation Statement

A course and instructor evaluation is available on the California Bureau of Real Estate (BRE) website at www.bre.ca.gov. Access this form by typing in "RE 318A" in the search box located in the upper right corner of the home page.

Course Names and Brief Course Descriptions

Agency: This 3-Hour course covers Disclosures, Civil Codes, Buyer's Agent, Confirmations, Agency Agreement, Dual Agency, Exclusive Agency, Exclusive Right to Sell, Net Listings, Multiple Listings, Puffing, Implied Authority, Ostensible Authority, Power of Attorneys, Deposit Receipts, Emergencies, Unilateral vs. Bilateral plus a Practice Exam. You have 20 minutes to complete a 20 question multiple-choice exam.

Ethics: This is the first class that was required by the State. It is important. Topics to be discussed in this 3-Hour course include Professional Conduct, Bona Fide Offers, Negotiable Commissions, Franchises, Closing Costs, Deposits, Seller Financing, Changing Contracts, LTV Rules, Square Footage Problems, Zoning, Material Fact Rule, Frivolous Offers, Compensation, Contingencies, Special Relationships, Significant Interest, Loan Broker Code of Ethics, NAR Code, California Business & Professions Code, TDS Statement, Suspensions, Mobile Home Sales, Fraud, Compliance Check List plus a Practice Exam. You have 20 minutes to complete a 20 question multiple-choice exam.

Trust Fund Handling: The following important subjects are presented in this 3-Hour course: Trust vs. Non-Trust Items, Identifying Owners of Funds, Recordkeeping, Disbursements, Advance Fees, Withdrawals, Interest Bearing Accounts, Commingling, Liabilities, Systems, Recording Process, Reconciliation, Documentation, Audits, Broker Supervision, Commissioner Regulations, Violations, Multiple Beneficiaries, Fictitious Names, Retention of Records, Shortages plus a Practice Exam. You have 20 minutes to complete a 20 question multiple-choice exam.

Fair Housing: You will learn in this 3-Hour course about the 1968 Federal Fair Housing Act, 1988 Amendments, Exemptions, Violations, Advertising, Steering/Channeling, Problem Areas, Civil Rights Act of 1866, ADA, California Laws, AIDS, Age Discrimination, Housing Discrimination, Blind & Physically Disabled, Disciplinary Actions, Panic Selling, Business & Professions Code, Partnerships, Home Mortgage Disclosure Act, Equal Credit Opportunity Act, Fair Credit Reporting Act, Do Not Call Registry plus a Practice Exam. You have 20 minutes to complete a 20 question multiple-choice exam.

Risk Management: This additional requirement was effective July 1, 2007. In this 3-Hour course you will receive information on Risk Probability, Standards of Care, Contract Preparation, Property Conditions, Broker Supervision, Trust Fund Handling, Failure to Research or Disclose, Kickbacks, Referrals, Conflicts of Interest, Agency Duties, Disclosures, Advertising, Fair Housing, Employment Issues, Office Management, Predatory Lending, Policies, Consequences of Violations, Responsibilities, Information Access, Statutory Duties, Vicarious Liability, Mediation/Arbitration plus a Practice Exam. You have 20 minutes to complete a 20 question multiple-choice exam,

Property Management Success: This is our premier 15-Hour course and many interesting facts will be disclosed including Selection of Personnel, Rental Policies, Promotion and Advertising, Preparation of the Product, Telephone Techniques, Presentation of the Product, Conversion from Prospects to Applicants, Screening the Applicants, Rental Agreements and Rules, Simplified Accounting Systems, The Slow Rent Payer, Supervision Principles and Methods, Retention of the Good People plus a Practice Exam. You have 40 minutes to complete a 40 question multiple-choice exam.

Make Money in California Foreclosures: Foreclosures are an important area of study for licensees. Our 15-Hour course illustrates Laws and Regulations, Starting in the Field, Buying from the Owner, Junior Lenders, Trustee Sales, Notices of Default, Timelines, Trustee Sales Notices, Beneficiaries/Trustors/Trustees, Trust Deeds, Sale Guarantee Policy, Notice Period, Deeds-in-Lieu, Receiverships, Bankruptcies, Publication, County Recorder Information, Civil Code Section 1695, Cancellation Rights, Price Calculation, Fix-up Costs, Future Value, Senior Lenders, Required Notices, Penalties, Unconscionable Advantage, Foreclosure Consultant plus a Practice Exam. You have 40 minutes to complete a 40 question multiple-choice exam.

TABLE OF CONTENTS

COURSES   **PAGE**

Internet Testing Instructions and Tips   13

Agency √   21

Ethics   45

Trust Fund Handling   73

Fair Housing   99

Risk Management   127

Property Management Success
Chapter 1 – Introduction   155
Chapter 2 – Selection of Personnel   163
Chapter 3 – Rental Policies   181
Chapter 4 – Promotion and Advertising   191
Chapter 5 – Preparation of the Product   199
Chapter 6 – Telephone Techniques   207
Chapter 7 – Presentation of the Product   211
Chapter 8 – Conversion From Prospects to Applicants   219
Chapter 9 – Screening the Applicants   229
Chapter 10 – Rental Agreements and Rules   235
Chapter 11 – Simplified Accounting Systems   245
Chapter 12 – The Slow Rent Payer   257
Chapter 13 – Supervision Principles and Methods   269
Chapter 14 – Retention of the Good People   291

Make Money in California Foreclosures
Chapter 1 – Introduction   303
Chapter 2 – Laws and Regulations   311
Chapter 3 – Starting in the Field   329
Chapter 4 – Buying From the Owner   337
Chapter 5 – Junior Lenders   351
Chapter 6 – Trustee Sales   355
Chapter 7 – Questions, Answers & References   369

INTERNET TESTING INSTRUCTIONS

(For All Continuing Education Courses)

Congratulations on your decision to test online. If you follow these instructions carefully, it will be an easy, simple, timesaving experience. We recommend you test during our office hours so we can assist anyone having difficulties. The vast majority of our students finish the exams with no problems. Our office hours are Monday – Friday, 9 a.m. to 3 p.m., and the best time to call 800-439-4909 is between 9:30 a.m. to 12:30 p.m.

All enrolled students received a unique Student ID and Password at the time you placed your order for those testing online. An e-mail was sent to your email address the same day you ordered your materials. If you are unable to locate your Student ID and Password, please contact our office for further assistance. .

To Log In to take a Final Exam

Go to our home page at www.DuaneGomer.com and click on any link that is titled, "Student Login". This link will take you to the **Student Login** page:

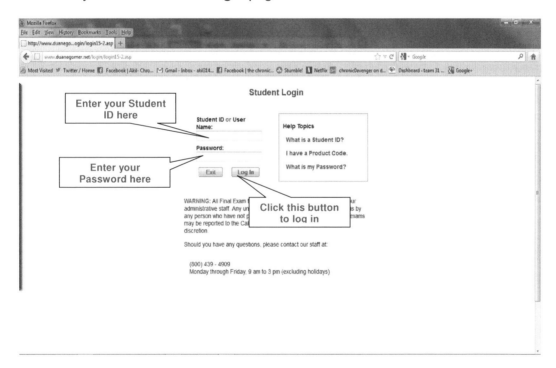

Enter your Student ID and Password in the space provided and then click on the Log In button as noted above. A successful login will take you to the **Identification page**.

Identification Page

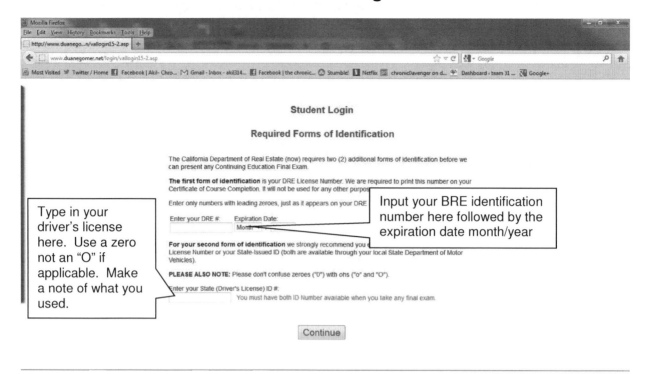

The Student Work Center

The **Student Work Center** is where you take your online final exams. The basic format of this page will look similar to the following:

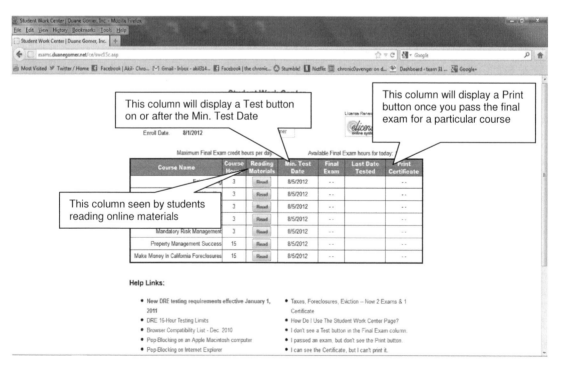

The column labeled **Materials** will only be displayed for students who elected to read their materials online at the time they placed their order. Students with textbooks will not see this column.

In the **Final Exam** column, one *Test* button will appear in each row on or after the Minimum Test Date. The Test button will be removed once you pass the Final Exam for the topic being tested on.

When you click on a *Test* button, you will be taken first to the Verification page.

Verification Page

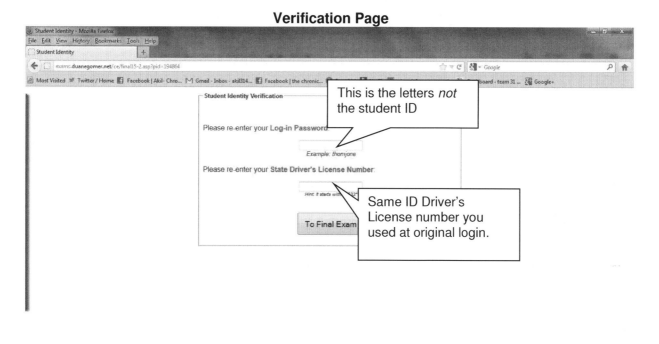

It's important to note that effective March 1, 2008, the maximum number of hours that any student may test on is 15 total credit hours in a 24 hour period. The column labeled **Course Credit** will indicate the credit hours that a course will earn. For more information, click on the link titled "*New BRE testing requirements effective March 1, 2008*" located in the **Help Links**.

In the **Print Certificate** column, when you pass a final exam, a *Print* button will be displayed. Click on the *Print* button to print the certificate for that course.

When you are done, click on the *Logout* button located at the top-right hand corner of your screen.

TO SAVE YOU TIME
INTERNET TESTING TIPS

Some students have problems when they try to test online. Before starting your exam, you should read the following items:

1   Do not use any search engines, such as Yahoo, Google, Alta Vista, etc., to get to our web site. In your Internet Browser Address box, please enter "www.duanegomer.com".

2   When completing your exam, also write your answers on the sample answer sheet form provided. Sometimes students get disconnected by their Internet Service Provider, get interrupted, run out of time, have a malfunction, hit an improper key, etc. **If this happens you have to start the exam over**.

3   We recommend that you test during our service hours of 9 a.m. to 3 p.m. in case you have any questions. The testing procedures are simple and almost all students have no testing problems when they follow the simple instructions. However, computers, servers, software, etc. sometimes have minds of their own. We are here to give you empathetic service and we have no phone menus to negotiate.

4   The Bureau of Real Estate insists that Internet exams cannot be downloaded or printed. You will receive a final score for each course but BRE regulations do not allow us to tell you which questions you missed. When you pass the exam, you must print your certificate immediately. There is a $20.00 charge to replace lost certificates.

5   Save College, Broker, and Statutory Course Certificates forever. You never know when you might need them again. BRE doesn't keep a record of your courses and if a school you used is out of business or can't be found, you would have to take the course again. You need to retain Continuing Education Course Certificate for only 5 years from the date of completion.

SAMPLE ANSWER SHEET

Agency

1	⊂A⊃	⊂B⊃	⊂C⊃	⊂D⊃
2	⊂A⊃	⊂B⊃	⊂C⊃	⊂D⊃
3	⊂A⊃	⊂B⊃	⊂C⊃	⊂D⊃
4	⊂A⊃	⊂B⊃	⊂C⊃	⊂D⊃
5	⊂A⊃	⊂B⊃	⊂C⊃	⊂D⊃
6	⊂A⊃	⊂B⊃	⊂C⊃	⊂D⊃
7	⊂A⊃	⊂B⊃	⊂C⊃	⊂D⊃
8	⊂A⊃	⊂B⊃	⊂C⊃	⊂D⊃
9	⊂A⊃	⊂B⊃	⊂C⊃	⊂D⊃
10	⊂A⊃	⊂B⊃	⊂C⊃	⊂D⊃
11	⊂A⊃	⊂B⊃	⊂C⊃	⊂D⊃
12	⊂A⊃	⊂B⊃	⊂C⊃	⊂D⊃
13	⊂A⊃	⊂B⊃	⊂C⊃	⊂D⊃
14	⊂A⊃	⊂B⊃	⊂C⊃	⊂D⊃
15	⊂A⊃	⊂B⊃	⊂C⊃	⊂D⊃
16	⊂A⊃	⊂B⊃	⊂C⊃	⊂D⊃
17	⊂A⊃	⊂B⊃	⊂C⊃	⊂D⊃
18	⊂A⊃	⊂B⊃	⊂C⊃	⊂D⊃
19	⊂A⊃	⊂B⊃	⊂C⊃	⊂D⊃
20	⊂A⊃	⊂B⊃	⊂C⊃	⊂D⊃

Ethics

1	⊂A⊃	⊂B⊃	⊂C⊃	⊂D⊃
2	⊂A⊃	⊂B⊃	⊂C⊃	⊂D⊃
3	⊂A⊃	⊂B⊃	⊂C⊃	⊂D⊃
4	⊂A⊃	⊂B⊃	⊂C⊃	⊂D⊃
5	⊂A⊃	⊂B⊃	⊂C⊃	⊂D⊃
6	⊂A⊃	⊂B⊃	⊂C⊃	⊂D⊃
7	⊂A⊃	⊂B⊃	⊂C⊃	⊂D⊃
8	⊂A⊃	⊂B⊃	⊂C⊃	⊂D⊃
9	⊂A⊃	⊂B⊃	⊂C⊃	⊂D⊃
10	⊂A⊃	⊂B⊃	⊂C⊃	⊂D⊃
11	⊂A⊃	⊂B⊃	⊂C⊃	⊂D⊃
12	⊂A⊃	⊂B⊃	⊂C⊃	⊂D⊃
13	⊂A⊃	⊂B⊃	⊂C⊃	⊂D⊃
14	⊂A⊃	⊂B⊃	⊂C⊃	⊂D⊃
15	⊂A⊃	⊂B⊃	⊂C⊃	⊂D⊃
16	⊂A⊃	⊂B⊃	⊂C⊃	⊂D⊃
17	⊂A⊃	⊂B⊃	⊂C⊃	⊂D⊃
18	⊂A⊃	⊂B⊃	⊂C⊃	⊂D⊃
19	⊂A⊃	⊂B⊃	⊂C⊃	⊂D⊃
20	⊂A⊃	⊂B⊃	⊂C⊃	⊂D⊃

Trust Fund Handling

1	⊂A⊃	⊂B⊃	⊂C⊃	⊂D⊃
2	⊂A⊃	⊂B⊃	⊂C⊃	⊂D⊃
3	⊂A⊃	⊂B⊃	⊂C⊃	⊂D⊃
4	⊂A⊃	⊂B⊃	⊂C⊃	⊂D⊃
5	⊂A⊃	⊂B⊃	⊂C⊃	⊂D⊃
6	⊂A⊃	⊂B⊃	⊂C⊃	⊂D⊃
7	⊂A⊃	⊂B⊃	⊂C⊃	⊂D⊃
8	⊂A⊃	⊂B⊃	⊂C⊃	⊂D⊃
9	⊂A⊃	⊂B⊃	⊂C⊃	⊂D⊃
10	⊂A⊃	⊂B⊃	⊂C⊃	⊂D⊃
11	⊂A⊃	⊂B⊃	⊂C⊃	⊂D⊃
12	⊂A⊃	⊂B⊃	⊂C⊃	⊂D⊃
13	⊂A⊃	⊂B⊃	⊂C⊃	⊂D⊃
14	⊂A⊃	⊂B⊃	⊂C⊃	⊂D⊃
15	⊂A⊃	⊂B⊃	⊂C⊃	⊂D⊃
16	⊂A⊃	⊂B⊃	⊂C⊃	⊂D⊃
17	⊂A⊃	⊂B⊃	⊂C⊃	⊂D⊃
18	⊂A⊃	⊂B⊃	⊂C⊃	⊂D⊃
19	⊂A⊃	⊂B⊃	⊂C⊃	⊂D⊃
20	⊂A⊃	⊂B⊃	⊂C⊃	⊂D⊃

Fair Housing

1	⊂A⊃	⊂B⊃	⊂C⊃	⊂D⊃
2	⊂A⊃	⊂B⊃	⊂C⊃	⊂D⊃
3	⊂A⊃	⊂B⊃	⊂C⊃	⊂D⊃
4	⊂A⊃	⊂B⊃	⊂C⊃	⊂D⊃
5	⊂A⊃	⊂B⊃	⊂C⊃	⊂D⊃
6	⊂A⊃	⊂B⊃	⊂C⊃	⊂D⊃
7	⊂A⊃	⊂B⊃	⊂C⊃	⊂D⊃
8	⊂A⊃	⊂B⊃	⊂C⊃	⊂D⊃
9	⊂A⊃	⊂B⊃	⊂C⊃	⊂D⊃
10	⊂A⊃	⊂B⊃	⊂C⊃	⊂D⊃
11	⊂A⊃	⊂B⊃	⊂C⊃	⊂D⊃
12	⊂A⊃	⊂B⊃	⊂C⊃	⊂D⊃
13	⊂A⊃	⊂B⊃	⊂C⊃	⊂D⊃
14	⊂A⊃	⊂B⊃	⊂C⊃	⊂D⊃
15	⊂A⊃	⊂B⊃	⊂C⊃	⊂D⊃
16	⊂A⊃	⊂B⊃	⊂C⊃	⊂D⊃
17	⊂A⊃	⊂B⊃	⊂C⊃	⊂D⊃
18	⊂A⊃	⊂B⊃	⊂C⊃	⊂D⊃
19	⊂A⊃	⊂B⊃	⊂C⊃	⊂D⊃
20	⊂A⊃	⊂B⊃	⊂C⊃	⊂D⊃

Risk Management

1	⊂A⊃	⊂B⊃	⊂C⊃	⊂D⊃
2	⊂A⊃	⊂B⊃	⊂C⊃	⊂D⊃
3	⊂A⊃	⊂B⊃	⊂C⊃	⊂D⊃
4	⊂A⊃	⊂B⊃	⊂C⊃	⊂D⊃
5	⊂A⊃	⊂B⊃	⊂C⊃	⊂D⊃
6	⊂A⊃	⊂B⊃	⊂C⊃	⊂D⊃
7	⊂A⊃	⊂B⊃	⊂C⊃	⊂D⊃
8	⊂A⊃	⊂B⊃	⊂C⊃	⊂D⊃
9	⊂A⊃	⊂B⊃	⊂C⊃	⊂D⊃
10	⊂A⊃	⊂B⊃	⊂C⊃	⊂D⊃
11	⊂A⊃	⊂B⊃	⊂C⊃	⊂D⊃
12	⊂A⊃	⊂B⊃	⊂C⊃	⊂D⊃
13	⊂A⊃	⊂B⊃	⊂C⊃	⊂D⊃
14	⊂A⊃	⊂B⊃	⊂C⊃	⊂D⊃
15	⊂A⊃	⊂B⊃	⊂C⊃	⊂D⊃
16	⊂A⊃	⊂B⊃	⊂C⊃	⊂D⊃
17	⊂A⊃	⊂B⊃	⊂C⊃	⊂D⊃
18	⊂A⊃	⊂B⊃	⊂C⊃	⊂D⊃
19	⊂A⊃	⊂B⊃	⊂C⊃	⊂D⊃
20	⊂A⊃	⊂B⊃	⊂C⊃	⊂D⊃

SAMPLE ANSWER SHEET

Property Management Success

1	⊂A⊃	⊂B⊃	⊂C⊃	⊂D⊃
2	⊂A⊃	⊂B⊃	⊂C⊃	⊂D⊃
3	⊂A⊃	⊂B⊃	⊂C⊃	⊂D⊃
4	⊂A⊃	⊂B⊃	⊂C⊃	⊂D⊃
5	⊂A⊃	⊂B⊃	⊂C⊃	⊂D⊃
6	⊂A⊃	⊂B⊃	⊂C⊃	⊂D⊃
7	⊂A⊃	⊂B⊃	⊂C⊃	⊂D⊃
8	⊂A⊃	⊂B⊃	⊂C⊃	⊂D⊃
9	⊂A⊃	⊂B⊃	⊂C⊃	⊂D⊃
10	⊂A⊃	⊂B⊃	⊂C⊃	⊂D⊃
11	⊂A⊃	⊂B⊃	⊂C⊃	⊂D⊃
12	⊂A⊃	⊂B⊃	⊂C⊃	⊂D⊃
13	⊂A⊃	⊂B⊃	⊂C⊃	⊂D⊃
14	⊂A⊃	⊂B⊃	⊂C⊃	⊂D⊃
15	⊂A⊃	⊂B⊃	⊂C⊃	⊂D⊃
16	⊂A⊃	⊂B⊃	⊂C⊃	⊂D⊃
17	⊂A⊃	⊂B⊃	⊂C⊃	⊂D⊃
18	⊂A⊃	⊂B⊃	⊂C⊃	⊂D⊃
19	⊂A⊃	⊂B⊃	⊂C⊃	⊂D⊃
20	⊂A⊃	⊂B⊃	⊂C⊃	⊂D⊃
21	⊂A⊃	⊂B⊃	⊂C⊃	⊂D⊃
22	⊂A⊃	⊂B⊃	⊂C⊃	⊂D⊃
23	⊂A⊃	⊂B⊃	⊂C⊃	⊂D⊃
24	⊂A⊃	⊂B⊃	⊂C⊃	⊂D⊃
25	⊂A⊃	⊂B⊃	⊂C⊃	⊂D⊃
26	⊂A⊃	⊂B⊃	⊂C⊃	⊂D⊃
27	⊂A⊃	⊂B⊃	⊂C⊃	⊂D⊃
28	⊂A⊃	⊂B⊃	⊂C⊃	⊂D⊃
29	⊂A⊃	⊂B⊃	⊂C⊃	⊂D⊃
30	⊂A⊃	⊂B⊃	⊂C⊃	⊂D⊃
31	⊂A⊃	⊂B⊃	⊂C⊃	⊂D⊃
32	⊂A⊃	⊂B⊃	⊂C⊃	⊂D⊃
33	⊂A⊃	⊂B⊃	⊂C⊃	⊂D⊃
34	⊂A⊃	⊂B⊃	⊂C⊃	⊂D⊃
35	⊂A⊃	⊂B⊃	⊂C⊃	⊂D⊃
36	⊂A⊃	⊂B⊃	⊂C⊃	⊂D⊃
37	⊂A⊃	⊂B⊃	⊂C⊃	⊂D⊃
38	⊂A⊃	⊂B⊃	⊂C⊃	⊂D⊃
39	⊂A⊃	⊂B⊃	⊂C⊃	⊂D⊃
40	⊂A⊃	⊂B⊃	⊂C⊃	⊂D⊃

Make Money in California California Foreclosures

1	⊂A⊃	⊂B⊃	⊂C⊃	⊂D⊃
2	⊂A⊃	⊂B⊃	⊂C⊃	⊂D⊃
3	⊂A⊃	⊂B⊃	⊂C⊃	⊂D⊃
4	⊂A⊃	⊂B⊃	⊂C⊃	⊂D⊃
5	⊂A⊃	⊂B⊃	⊂C⊃	⊂D⊃
6	⊂A⊃	⊂B⊃	⊂C⊃	⊂D⊃
7	⊂A⊃	⊂B⊃	⊂C⊃	⊂D⊃
8	⊂A⊃	⊂B⊃	⊂C⊃	⊂D⊃
9	⊂A⊃	⊂B⊃	⊂C⊃	⊂D⊃
10	⊂A⊃	⊂B⊃	⊂C⊃	⊂D⊃
11	⊂A⊃	⊂B⊃	⊂C⊃	⊂D⊃
12	⊂A⊃	⊂B⊃	⊂C⊃	⊂D⊃
13	⊂A⊃	⊂B⊃	⊂C⊃	⊂D⊃
14	⊂A⊃	⊂B⊃	⊂C⊃	⊂D⊃
15	⊂A⊃	⊂B⊃	⊂C⊃	⊂D⊃
16	⊂A⊃	⊂B⊃	⊂C⊃	⊂D⊃
17	⊂A⊃	⊂B⊃	⊂C⊃	⊂D⊃
18	⊂A⊃	⊂B⊃	⊂C⊃	⊂D⊃
19	⊂A⊃	⊂B⊃	⊂C⊃	⊂D⊃
20	⊂A⊃	⊂B⊃	⊂C⊃	⊂D⊃
21	⊂A⊃	⊂B⊃	⊂C⊃	⊂D⊃
22	⊂A⊃	⊂B⊃	⊂C⊃	⊂D⊃
23	⊂A⊃	⊂B⊃	⊂C⊃	⊂D⊃
24	⊂A⊃	⊂B⊃	⊂C⊃	⊂D⊃
25	⊂A⊃	⊂B⊃	⊂C⊃	⊂D⊃
26	⊂A⊃	⊂B⊃	⊂C⊃	⊂D⊃
27	⊂A⊃	⊂B⊃	⊂C⊃	⊂D⊃
28	⊂A⊃	⊂B⊃	⊂C⊃	⊂D⊃
29	⊂A⊃	⊂B⊃	⊂C⊃	⊂D⊃
30	⊂A⊃	⊂B⊃	⊂C⊃	⊂D⊃
31	⊂A⊃	⊂B⊃	⊂C⊃	⊂D⊃
32	⊂A⊃	⊂B⊃	⊂C⊃	⊂D⊃
33	⊂A⊃	⊂B⊃	⊂C⊃	⊂D⊃
34	⊂A⊃	⊂B⊃	⊂C⊃	⊂D⊃
35	⊂A⊃	⊂B⊃	⊂C⊃	⊂D⊃
36	⊂A⊃	⊂B⊃	⊂C⊃	⊂D⊃
37	⊂A⊃	⊂B⊃	⊂C⊃	⊂D⊃
38	⊂A⊃	⊂B⊃	⊂C⊃	⊂D⊃
39	⊂A⊃	⊂B⊃	⊂C⊃	⊂D⊃
40	⊂A⊃	⊂B⊃	⊂C⊃	⊂D⊃

AGENCY

INTRODUCTION

In 1987 a California Civil Code was promulgated concerning Real Estate Licensees and their Agency Relationships. One of the provisions of the Regulation was that you must complete a three-hour class in Agency Law every time you renew your license. That is why you are reading this material and why I am writing it.

You must pass a 20-question, multiple-choice exam with a grade of 70% or more. There are 40 true/false practice questions for assessment with answers included for remediation.

AGENCY DISCLOSURE

Until 1988, 99.999+% of the real estate sales in California were completed under a Sub-Agency Relationship. In short, all Real Estate licensees represented the sellers. If Coldwell-Banker had a listing and Century 21 had the buyer, both companies represented the seller.

The Federal Trade Commission had many complaints from both buyers and sellers. Buyers were amazed that they were not being represented. Sellers were angry that licensees worked as if the buyer was their client, and they would file "Undisclosed Dual Agency" lawsuits.

The Real Estate industry led by the National Association of REALTORS® liked this arrangement. Several Boards of REALTORS® on the Peninsula of California and others were protesting this method so the Federal Trade Commission sent a survey to many buyers across the United States. The major question was, "When you bought your last property, whom did your agent represent?" Over 70% of the respondents said that their agent represented them.

The Trade Commission relayed this information to the National Association of REALTORS®. The FTC's conclusion was that buyers were not being represented in the most important purchase of their lives, and more importantly, they did not know that they were not being represented. The Trade Commission also believed that they could get a jury of the public (i.e. buyers) to rule that buyers should be represented. There was a possibility that a jury could rule that if a licensee in one company listed a property, that company could not sell the property. This would drastically change real estate operations.

In 1987 the California Association of REALTORS® realized something had to be done. A law concerning Agency Relationships was proposed and passed. This Agency Disclosure regulation was placed in the Civil Code and was effective January 1, 1988. A disclosure form was introduced and the Agency Education Requirement that you are completing was mandated as of July 1, 1987.

To purchase copies of the Agency Disclosure, call any Real Estate Board or Association in your area. Be sure to get the latest edition as they change constantly. The best method to learn these regulations is to work with the form itself. Sentences in the disclosure will be highlighted, examined and discussed. Knowing this material might eliminate a lawsuit in your future.

Our company specializes in BRE continuing education and broker courses, Notary Education and other real estate related topics such as foreclosures, short sales, tax, etc. and yearly we have more satisfied students than any other company or Association. The materials you will read have been thoroughly audited by experienced brokers, attorneys, other licensees, and agency experts.

DISCLOSURE REGARDING REAL ESTATE AGENCY RELATIONSHIPS

The official form used is called a "Disclosure." In my classes it is given a different name. "Disclosure" is a word that might scare a client. We call the form a "Handout to Educate the Public about Agency Law." When a purchase contract is signed by a buyer or seller, they must acknowledge the Agency Confirmation that illustrates who is representing whom in the transaction. The disclosure form is designed to give them some general information on the three agency relationships so they can make a decision and approve the relationships listed on a Purchase Contract.

AS REQUIRED BY THE CIVIL CODE

The official name of this Regulation is "Agency Relationships In Residential Real Property Transactions" and is found in the Civil Code. Residential Real Property in California is one to four units of residential properties and mobile homes, and doesn't include commercial, industrial, or apartments over four units, etc. The duties and responsibilities listed on this form apply to all real estate transactions. However, this disclosure form must be given only as provided in the law.

CALIFORNIA ASSOCIATION OF REALTORS® (C.A.R.) STANDARD FORM

The Disclosure Form is copyrighted by the California Association of REALTORS®.
- There is a statement, "This form is available for use by the entire real estate industry. The use of this form is not intended to identify the user as a REALTOR®." So any licensee can purchase and use them.
- The required information on the form is established in the Civil Code.
- Also, there is a statement, "A Real Estate Broker is the person qualified to advise in real estate transactions. If you desire legal or tax advice, consult an appropriate professional." If you are designing your own form, it is recommended that you put a blank line next to this phrase so that all clients can sign that they have read and understand it.

"When you enter into a discussion with a real estate agent regarding a real estate transaction, you should from the outset understand what type of agency relationship or representation you wish to have with the agent in the transaction."
This is the first sentence on the form. Who is "you?" It is obviously the clients.

The clients involved are any owners of 1-4 dwelling residential properties and includes both non-owner occupied and owner-occupied properties. Also, mobile home buyers and sellers are included. Commissions, listing, sale, exchange and installment sales are covered if there is a 1-4 unit involved.

In one of our classes, we were honored to have as a student, Mr. Sam Freshman, Esquire. He took our live classes in Agency and Ethics and Home-Study Classes in Foreclosure and Management. Sam is an outstanding attorney. His Syndication book was the best ever written.

Today, Mr. Freshman has many properties in Ohio. The Department of Real Estate in Ohio watched this law for a few years and then passed an Agency Law. They made one change on who must be given this form. They did not limit the Disclosure to 1-4 units and required that the Disclosure Form be given to all Real Estate clients.

According to Sam, this is a much better rule for Real Estate licensees. It could help eliminate lawsuits for you. In California, the law states that the Disclosure form "must" be given to 1-4 units residential and mobile homes. Sam Freshman and Duane Gomer recommend that you "should" give it to all clients.

"Outset"
When is "outset?" That is when you have to give the form. "Outset" can mean different things to different people. There is one other phrase in the Code. You must give the form when you have more than a "casual relationship." Define that one.

The Code is very specific in that the disclosure form can't be given to a seller after a listing agreement is signed or to a buyer after a purchase contract is signed. The disclosure is an educational handout and should be treated as such. One good rule to remember: It is possible to give it out too late and it is impossible to give it out too early.

The Confirmation step of the transaction is different than the Disclosure step. The Confirmation (who is representing whom?) should be done on the Purchase Contract. Don't confuse the two. If you look at the signature line on the Disclosure, you will see that the client is simply signing that they received a copy of the form.

Huijers vs. De Marsis
This is a Santa Barbara County case where Huijers was doing a Section 1031 Tax Deferred Exchange with DeMarsis. The licensee was working with Huijers as a Buyer and listed DeMarsis' property. DeMarsis signed a contract and wanted to rescind the transaction. His contention was that the agent misrepresented the value and didn't give him the disclosure in a timely fashion.

Huijers sued for damages, and the Superior Court agreed with him and DeMarsis appealed. His property was a landscape nursery but it had a house on it. He was given the disclosure with the offer. First, the appellate court had to decide whether a "mixed use" property qualified for this treatment. They appear to have decided "yes."

Mrs. Larson, the agent, gave the form to the listing client after the listing agreement was signed, so it was too late. The court then stated the penalty for this (since no penalty is mentioned in the Code) was no commission to the agent. The important question of whether a client can rescind a transaction when the disclosure is not received was sent back to Superior Court for another trial.

Legal fees and penalties in the first Superior Court trial were over $150,000. We are now talking big money. There has been a Superior Court trial, Appellate, Superior again, Appellate again and probably State Supreme Court. Whoever loses will probably want to sue his/her agent, who in both instances is (Mrs. Larson) a dual agent. If errors and omissions insurance won't cover the loss, there could be more trials.

Mrs. Larson has been involved in these lengthy lawsuits and could lose a lot of money. Her crime: Giving a Disclosure Form out too late in a 1031 Exchange. It is highly recommended that you give the form out early. Someone says, "Hi" at the shopping center. Give them a form.

"To: the Seller: A Fiduciary duty of utmost care, integrity, honesty and loyalty in dealings with the Seller."
This is the first sentence under the Seller's Agent Section of the Disclosure Form. This section codifies the listing agent's duties to their client. An important word during every real estate transaction is "fiduciary" and CAR capitalized it on this form. Agents should understand it. It is sometimes called the F-word of Real Estate and can get you into lots of trouble. The best word for us to use is "Trustee." You are a Trustee, which is the highest form of any business relationship.

There are four other terms used: "utmost care," "integrity," "honesty" and "loyalty." Perhaps, the law writers could have used words better understood by clients, such as trustworthy, loyal, helpful, friendly, courteous, kind, obedient, cheerful, thrifty, brave, clean and reverent.

Noel Seaman was an outstanding expert in Agency Relationship. He was the Lead Counsel on the California Association of REALTORS® Hot Line for many years. He also taught classes on a contract basis for Duane Gomer Seminars, and his ratings and reviews were excellent. It is so tragic that he passed away so young. In one class, he discussed the duties of an agent to a client. Noel reduced this sentence to one word, "Represents."

When you have a listing, you "represent" the seller. You have to be honest and fair, etc. with others, but you represent only your client. It is a good word to describe your duties.

"To: the Buyer and the Seller
   (a) Diligent exercise of reasonable skill and care in performance of the agent's duties.
   (b) A duty of honest and fair dealing and good faith.
   (c) A duty to disclose all facts known to the agent materially affecting the value or desirability of property that are not known to, or within the diligent attention and observation of, the parties."
Some old-time brokers used to operate under the theory of "Caveat Emptor." If we represented the seller, the buyer "better beware." That theory was reversed forever with the famous "Easton versus Strassburger" case in the early 1980's. In this case, the listing agent did not mention a minor earth slide three years before the purchase plus existing red flags indicating soil problems. The Court held that the Listing Agent had several duties to other parties. This case led to more disclosures by everyone. Now, there is a "Seller's Disclosure Statement" required in residential sales of four or fewer units. This is a change that is good for all licensees. The SDS is called the "Easton Disclosure," in most companies.

There is one word that is interesting in sentence "a." A listing agent owes utmost care to a seller and this sentence states that the listing agent must give "reasonable care" to a buyer. The people who wrote this law must know how to distinguish between reasonable care and utmost care. There must be a line drawn in care that separate the two (utmost and reasonable) but I don't know where it is.

If you ever have to appear in front of a jury concerning a Real Estate transaction, the jury will probably insist on lots of care. It is recommended that you follow the old TV show, "Hill Street Blues." In that show, Michael Conrad would end his briefing of the police officers at the beginning of the show with, "Now, you be careful out there." When any sales meeting ends, the reminder should be made, "Now, you be utmost careful out there."

That Are Not Known to, etc.
The last part of sentence C has this phrase. This points out that all parties must protect their own interest and look around. So many clients do not inspect, check, observe or notice many important items. You should inform buyers and sellers of all facts so that they are responsible for diligent attention and observation.

Materially Affecting
This phrase emphasizes the duty of disclosing all material facts. Many attorneys were called and guidelines of explaining the criteria of a material fact were requested. All of them answered the same. "It depends."

A California Association of REALTORS® report on Disclosure of AIDS and Death had this statement about material facts. The report states:

> Many California cases have held agents and sellers liable for "fraudulent concealment" or "negative fraud" for failure to reveal known material facts affecting the value or desirability of the property. Whether information is "material" depends on all the facts of the particular case. In general, a fact would be considered material if it would affect the decision of a reasonable buyer to buy, or the price and terms on which he or she would be willing to buy, the subject property. For example, Easton vs. Strassburger held that a minor earth slide three years before the purchase, plus existing red flags, indicated soil problems were material facts.

Some other California decisions about the duty to disclose material facts concerned a house constructed on filled land, improvements added without a building permit in violation of zoning regulations, failure to disclose the true lien amount on a property to be acquired, and failure to disclose dual termite reports of considerable variance. In contrast, the California Attorney General has issued opinions that the race of a prospective buyer is not a material fact to be disclosed to the seller, and that a licensed real estate agent is not required to disclose to prospective home buyers that a licensed residential care facility serving six or fewer people is located in the neighborhood.

Value or Desirability
This is a most important phrase. You must disclose any material fact concerning value or desirability. Value is easier to understand. Desirability is difficult to establish. People have widely varied desirability standards.

Some buyers will not consider any houses when:
1. The front door faces North.
2. The front door is in a line with the back door.
3. The front door is in a line with a staircase.
4. Any staircase has a number of steps divisible by 3.
5. A street ends in front of it, (cul-del-sac).
6. A cemetery is next door.
7. Many, many more.

It is impossible to know what is in the mind of a buyer or seller. However, there are some counter-balancing laws concerning what you can disclose to a client. Fair Housing laws limit the answers to some questions. If a seller asks, "Is the buyer of a certain race, creed, religion, handicapped, etc.?" you can't answer. Confidential information that is not a material fact doesn't have to be disclosed.

Some California Civil Codes outline limits on Disclosures. An example is a Code Section on Death and AIDS. Same As Value Above.

What does California Civil Code § 1710.2 provide?
This statute provides in pertinent part that "No cause of action arises against an owner of real property or his or her agent, or any agent of a transferee of real property, for the failure to disclose to the transferee the occurrence of an occupant's death upon the real property or the manner of death where the death has occurred more than three years prior to the date the transferee offers to purchase, lease, or rent the real property, or that an occupant of that property was afflicted with or died from .... (AIDS)."

What types of property are covered under Civil Code § 1710.2?
Civil Code § 1710.2 covers real property, which includes (1) land, (2) that which is affixed to land, and (3) that which is incidental or appurtenant to land. Thus, it appears that real property of every type is covered, including lots, farms, commercial and industrial property, as well as residential property.

Does Civil Code § 1710.2 provide total protection concerning disclosures to an owner or agent?
No. An owner or owner's agent is not protected from intentional misrepresentation in response to a direct question from a transferee or prospective transferee of real property concerning a death on the property.

For example, if a prospective purchaser directly asks an agent if an occupant died on the property and the agent knows that an occupant actually died on the property, the agent cannot answer "no" because that would be an intentional misrepresentation. This is true regardless of whether the death was AIDS-related or not. However, if the agent does not have actual knowledge of a death on the property, then the agent can answer "I don't know" when directly asked about a death. In addition, an owner or agent is not relieved from any obligation to disclose the physical condition of the premises, or any other physical or mental condition or disease (other than AIDS) that may exist and be found to be a material fact.

Must a death or other manner of death, other than AIDS, be disclosed.
It depends. The statute is clear that no cause of action arises for failure to disclose an occupant's death upon the real property or manner of death where the death has occurred more than three years before the transferee's offer on that property. Here, the statute

precludes liability if death precedes the offer by more than three years. The owner's and agent's non-responsibility for disclosing the "manner of death," violent, accidental or natural, is also clear if it occurred more than three years before the offer is made. However, if a death occurred three years or less before the offer to purchase, lease, or rent the real property, the answer depends on whether the occupant's death or manner of death (excluding death by AIDS) is a material fact. If it is a material fact, then it must be disclosed.

Must the affliction with, or death by AIDS, of an occupant of real property be disclosed?
No. The California Legislature specifically declared its intention to regulate disclosures related to AIDS in situations affecting the transfer of real property. Civil Code § 1710.2 provides immunity from liability for failure to disclose that an occupant of a property was "afflicted with or died from" AIDS.

For protection under this statute, must death by AIDS be upon the property?
Probably not, as the statute appears to provide protection without regard to whether a death by AIDS occurred upon or off-site of the subject property.

Does the three-year rule regarding liability for death disclosures apply to AIDS related deaths?
No. AIDS related deaths and/or affliction with AIDS disclosures are protected regardless of when the occupant was afflicted with or died of AIDS. Therefore, an owner and/or agent need not disclose that an occupant was afflicted with or died of AIDS even if it occurred three years or less before the date of the offer.

Must a death, other than by AIDS, which occurs off-site of the subject property be disclosed?
It depends. The disclosure of a death occurring off the property is an unresolved question. The answer would depend on whether the combination of events constituted a material fact.

An agent is not obligated to reveal to either party any confidential information obtained from the other party, which does not involve the affirmative duties set forth above.
There are some facts that a buyer or seller might want to know that would be confidential. One example would be a seller's reason for selling. A buyer might ask, "What is the seller's reason for selling?" It is a normal question. The answer to the question would be confidential if your seller didn't want it revealed. You would not have to answer.

In another circumstance, a seller might want a buyer to know that they are motivated and are making two house payments. A good policy would be to ask your clients their reason for selling. The next question would be, "Do you want me to tell buyers this reason?"

Financial troubles, pending divorce, medical problems, etc are examples of confidential information. A Notice of Default, Short Sale Proposal and a Bankruptcy are different in my opinion. A Notice of Default can affect the wording of a Purchase Contract because of Civil Code Regulations about foreclosures. A Short Sale Purchase Contract must be made subject to lender approval. A sale for a client in Bankruptcy would probably have to be made subject to the Court's approval. All of these areas have many different aspects; therefore, any of your actions should be discussed with your responsible broker. Discuss and then take proper action. More lawsuits come from not disclosing material facts than almost any other causes.

BUYER'S AGENT

The Buyer's Agent section of the Disclosure is almost the same as the Seller's Agent section with the client's names reversed. There is one additional sentence. It is the second sentence.

"In these situations, the agent is not the Seller's agent, even if by agreement the agent may receive compensation for services rendered, either in full or in part from the Seller."
When this regulation was first presented, many licensees said that you worked for who paid you, and it was not possible or legal to work for a buyer and be paid by a seller. This phrase obviously states that you can.

"A real estate agent, either acting directly or through one or more associate licensees, can legally be the agent of both the Seller and the Buyer in a transaction, but only with the knowledge and consent of both the Seller and the Buyer."
This sentence in the Civil Code indicates that the State of California has ruled that you can represent both parties in a transaction. This is Legislative approval of dual agency. The important words are "knowledge and consent." You can be a dual agent if clients know about it and consent to it. In this regulation, consent is called "written confirmation". You check the boxes on the Confirmation Section of the Purchase Agreement to show who is representing whom. When the clients sign the deposit receipt, everything then is known, consented and confirmed.

"In a dual agency situation, the agent has the following affirmative obligations to both the Seller and the Buyer:
(a) A fiduciary duty of utmost care, integrity, honesty and loyalty in the dealings with either the Seller or the Buyer.
(b) Other duties to the Seller and the Buyer as stated above in their respective Sections."
Now, you have a Fiduciary or Trustee Relationship with both Buyer and Seller. This is not easy. One Law book equated Agency Relationships to Horseback Riding. Single Agency is best (one horse (client) and one rider (Agent) riding through the woods). Sub-Agency is the way we worked in California before 1988, (one horse with two riders riding through the woods). This is a little slower and has more problems.

Dual Agency is one company representing both buyer and seller (two horses (clients) with one rider (dual agent) riding through the woods). The agent is standing up with one foot in each saddle. It is possible with skill and cooperation to stay aloft.

However, if the clients want to go in different directions, you can see possible problems.

"In representing both Seller and Buyer, the agent may not, without the express permission of the respective party, disclose to the other party that the Seller will accept a price less than the listing price or that the Buyer will pay a price greater than the price offered."
When this regulation was considered, the authors realized that there would be problems on price questions under dual agency. A buyer will ask, "Will the seller come down?" or the seller will ask, "Will the buyer come up?" They don't know anything about dual agency regulations, and these are normal questions. It is obvious that you answer questions about price differently when you are representing both parties.

Legally you could say, "Civil Code Section 2373 states that I cannot answer your question." That would be legally correct, but not practical in a real estate transaction. What might you say? Our company has had some correspondence with the Bureau of Real Estate on this subject and their deputies approved this example:

Buyer – "Will the seller come down?"
Agent –"The property is listed by our company at _____. However, I will present any reasonable offer you would like to make and here are some Comparable Sales in the area for your information."

Let's say that the buyer asks, "What do you mean by reasonable?"
Agent – "A reasonable offer is any offer that is not patently frivolous."

"The above duties of the agent in a real estate transaction do not relieve a Seller or a Buyer from the responsibility to protect their own interests. You should carefully read all agreements to assure that they adequately express your understanding of the transaction." (The sentences are self-explanatory. They are stressing that clients must protect their own interests.)

"A real estate agent is a person qualified to advise about real estate. If legal or tax advice is desired, consult a competent professional."
Agents should stress to clients that legal and tax advice should be considered. In fact, it would be a good idea to have them put their initials next to this line indicating that they have read it.

"Throughout your real property transaction, you may receive more than one disclosure form, depending upon the number of agents assisting in the transaction. The law requires each agent with whom you have more than a casual relationship to present you with this disclosure form. You should read its contents each time it is presented to you, considering the relationship between you and the real estate agent in your specific transaction."
Some clients might be surprised that they get more than one disclosure during a transaction. On this latest CAR form this subject is addressed by (a) through (d) in the block at the bottom of this form.

"(a) From a Listing Agent to a Seller: Prior to entering into the listing.
(b) From an Agent selling a property he/she has listed to a Buyer: Prior to the Buyer's execution of the offer.
l   From a Selling Agent to a Buyer: Prior to the Buyer's execution of the offer.
(d) From a Selling Agent (in a cooperating real estate firm) to a Seller: Prior to presentation of the offer to the Seller."

"This disclosure form includes the provisions of Article 2.5 of Chapter 2 of Title 9 of Part 4 of Division 3 of the Civil Code set forth on the reverse hereof. Read it carefully."
This sentence means that you must include all the definitions from the Civil Code on the back of your form. The definitions are included at the end of this discussion.

"I/We acknowledge receipt of a copy of this disclosure."
If anyone ever questions the legal significance of this form, show them this phrase. All they are doing is signing that they got a copy. No decision has been made about anything or any relationship or representation.

Also, you should know that there are two times that you can sign the form
1. If the client will not take the form, when you offer it;
2. If the client takes the form, but will not sign that they received it.

You make a statement of the facts and sign yourself. You should also be very careful when dealing with any of these clients. You might even want a witness to sign the form to verify the facts.

AM – PM

The current WINforms Agency Disclosure form has taken the time of day off so write it on. Why CAR did it, I don't understand.

Just a thought – If it is important when this is signed, it could be important when the Purchase Contract and Listing Agreement are signed. Therefore, it might be a good idea to put the Date and Time of Day on these two forms to prevent a future lawsuit over timing.

"It is not necessary or required to confirm an agency relationship using a separate Confirmation form if the agency confirmation portion of the Real Estate Purchase Contract is properly completed in full. However, it is still necessary to use this Disclosure form."
This block was added to the CAR form in early 1994. It is an excellent addition and can be used to better explain the form to clients. Old forms had a written confirmation on the bottom and this was confusing and unnecessary.

You do not need a Separate Confirmation if you use a Purchase Contract with the Confirmation properly completed. Having the Confirmation in the bottom of the Disclosure led to lawsuits when agents did the Confirmation prematurely. Also, clients would ask questions about the Confirmation at the time of Disclosure and this was confusing. Make the decision about the Agency Relationships when the Purchase Contract is completed. An Agency relationship can change from property to property.

CONFIRMATION

A sample of a Confirmation on a Purchase Agreement follows:

1. AGENCY CONFIRMATION: The following agency relationships are hereby confirmed for this transaction:
   Listing Agent: _____(Print Firm Name) is the agent of (check one):
       the Seller exclusively; or   both the Buyer and Seller.
   Selling Agent: _____(Print Firm Name if not same as Listing Agent)
   Is the agent of (check one):
       the Buyer exclusively; or   the Seller exclusively; or   both the Buyer and the Seller.

Your final exam in Confirmation and Agency:
You have a buyer who wants to make an offer on another company's listing. You fill out the Purchase Contract and check the box for the Seller Agent representing Buyer Exclusively on the Agency Confirmation portion. You call the other company but you only get a recording.

My question to you: Should you check the box as to whom the listing agent is representing or should you leave that blank? Think this over before reading on and make a decision. Check the box or not?

Now, I have some further questions for you.
1. There are two boxes for the listing agent to check. The agent can represent the seller exclusively or both seller and buyer. Do you want an agent you don't know representing your client? Do you want another agent being a dual agent when it is unnecessary?
2. If you leave a box or blank open on a form and your client signs, what is the condition of the contract if a blank is filled in after your client has signed? Isn't that a change or alteration? Technically, isn't that a counter offer about the agency relationship from the seller.

After consideration wouldn't it be a better idea to CHECK THE BOX BEFORE YOUR BUYER SIGNS. Be sure to ask your broker what he or she wants you to do. Also, you should consider the remote possibility that sometime an offer will come in on one of your listings where the cooperating agent checks a box to represent your seller. Do you want an outside agent being a sub-agent of your seller? It is legal to be a sub-agent in California today, but if you worked for me, we would recommend to our seller that this is not a good idea. If they have any questions, they should obtain legal advice.

TIMING OF THE CONFIRMATION

The Agency Relationship must be communicated as soon as practicable to clients. The written confirmation must be done prior or coincident with the execution of any purchase contracts. Webster says that coincident means "at the same time."

CALIFORNIA TODAY

The policy on Agency Relationship must be selected by each company by the Responsible Broker. Most companies today represent:
1. Buyers only when we have the offer on another company's listing.
2. Sellers only when we have the listing and another company has the offer.
3. Dual agents when we have both the buyer and the seller.

SOME FINAL THOUGHTS

1. Sub-agency is still legal in California.
2. Any listing agreement in California must be in writing.
3. A gratuitous agent (one working for no commission) still must do all the disclosures.
4. It is still legal to work for the seller exclusively in all transactions, but no one seems to be doing it.
5. Lawsuits are increasing, but it appears that this regulation has eliminated many lawsuits concerning agency.
6. Most of the other States have followed California's example and enacted some form of Agency Regulation.
7. Good Luck in your Real Estate Career. Thanks for using our Company for your education. If we can ever be of service in the future, please call us at once.

DEFINITIONS THAT MUST BE INCLUDED WITH THE DISCLOSURE FORM TO YOUR CLIENTS (These are phrases all on the back of CAR forms and are referenced on the front page of the form.)

Article 25   Agency Relationships in Residential Real Property Transactions.

2079.13   As used in this article, the following terms have the following meanings:

(a) "Agent" means a person acting under provisions of this title in a real property transaction, and includes a person who is licensed as real estate broker under Chapter 3 (commencing with Section 10130) of Part 1 of Division 4 of the Business & Professions Code, and under whose license a listing is executed or an offer to purchase is obtained.

(b) "Associate licensee" means a person who is licensed as a real estate broker or salesperson under Chapter 3 (commencing with Section 10130) of Part 1 of Division 4 of the Business & Professions Code and who is either licensed under a broker or has entered into a written contract with a broker to act as the broker's agent in connection with acts requiring a real estate license and to function under the broker's supervision in the capacity of an associate licensee. The agent in the real property transaction bears responsibility for his or her associate licensees who perform as agents of the agent. When an associate licensee owes a duty to any principal, or to any buyer or seller who is not a principal, in a real property transaction, that duty is equivalent to the duty owed to that party by the broker for whom the associate licensee functions.

I "Buyer" means a transferee in a real property transaction, and includes a person who executes an offer to purchase real property from a seller through an agent, or who seeks the services of an agent in more than a casual, transitory, or preliminary manner, with the object of entering into a real property transaction. "Buyer" includes vendee or lessee.

(d) "Dual agent" means an agent acting, either directly or through an associate licensee, as agent for both the seller and the buyer in a real property transaction.

(e) "Listing agreement" means a contract between an owner of real property and an agent, by which the agent has been authorized to sell the real property or to find or obtain a buyer.

(f) "Listing agent" means a person who has obtained a listing of real property to act as an agent for compensation.

(g) "Listing price" is the amount expressed in dollars specified in the listing for which the seller is willing to sell the real property through the listing agent.

(h) "Offering price" is the amount expressed in dollars specified in an offer to purchase for which the buyer is willing to buy the real property.

(i) "Offer to purchase" means a written contract executed by a buyer acting through a selling agent which becomes the contract for the sale of the real property upon acceptance by the seller.

(j) "Real property" means any estate specified by subdivision (1) or (2) of Section 761 in property which constitutes or is improved with one to four dwelling units, any leasehold in this type of property exceeding one year's duration, and mobile homes, when offered for sale or sold through an agent pursuant to the authority contained in Section 10131.6 of the Business & Professions Code.

(k) "Real property transaction" means a transaction for the sale of real property in which an agent is employed by one or more of the principals to act in that transaction, and includes a listing or an offer to purchase.

(l) "Sell," "sale," or "sold" refers to a transaction for the transfer of real property from the seller to the buyer, and includes exchanges of real property between the seller and buyer, transactions for the creation of a real property sales contract within the meaning of Section 2985, and transactions for the creation of a leasehold exceeding one year's duration.

(m) "Seller" means the transferor in a real property transaction, and includes an owner who lists real property with an agent, whether or not a transfer results, or who received an offer to purchase real property of which he or she is the owner from an agent on behalf of another. "Seller" includes both a vendor and a lessor.

(n) "Selling agent" means a listing agent who acts alone, or an agent who acts in cooperation with a listing agent, and who sells or finds and obtains a buyer for the real property, or an agent who locates property for a buyer for the property for which no listing exists and presents an offer to purchase to the seller.

(o) "Subagent" means a person to whom an agent delegates agency powers as provided in Article 5 (commencing with Section 2349) of Chapter 1. However, "subagent" does not include an associate licensee who is acting under the supervision of an agent in a real property transaction.

2079.14   Listing agents and selling agents shall provide the seller and buyer in a real property transaction with a copy of the disclosure form specified in Section 2375, and, except as provided in subdivision I, shall obtain a signed acknowledgement of receipt from the seller or buyer, except as provided in this section of Section 2374.5, as follows:

     (a)   The listing agent, if any, shall provide the disclosure form to the seller prior to entering into the listing agreement.

     (b)   The selling agent shall provide the disclosure form to the seller as soon as practicable prior to presenting the seller with an offer to purchase, unless the selling agent previously provided the seller with a copy of the disclosure form pursuant to subdivision (a).

     I   Where the selling agent does not deal on a face-to-face basis with the seller, the disclosure form prepared by the selling agent may be furnished to the seller (and acknowledgement of receipt obtained for the selling agent from the seller) by the listing agent, or the selling agent may deliver the disclosure form by certified mail addressed to the seller at his or her last known address, in which case no signed acknowledgement of receipt is required.

     (d)   The selling agent shall provide the disclosure form to the buyer as soon as practicable prior to execution of the buyer's offer to purchase, except that if the offer to purchase is not prepared by the selling agent, the selling agent shall present the disclosure form to the buyer not later than the next business day after the selling agent receives the offer to purchase from the buyer.

2079.15   In any circumstance in which the seller or buyer refuses to sign an acknowledgement of receipt pursuant of Section 2374, the agent, or an associate licensee acting for an agent, shall set forth, sign and date a written declaration of the facts of the refusal.

2079.17   (a)   As soon as practicable, the selling agent shall disclose to the buyer and seller whether the selling agent is acting in the real property transaction exclusively as the buyer's agent, exclusively as the seller's agent, or as a dual agent representing both the buyer and the seller and this relationship shall be confirmed in the contract to purchase and sell real property or in a separate writing executed or acknowledged by the seller, the buyer, and the selling agent prior to or coincident with execution of that contract by the buyer and the seller, respectively.

     (b)   As soon as practicable, the listing agent shall disclose to the seller whether the listing agent is acting in the real property transaction exclusively as the seller's agent, or as a dual agent representing both the buyer and seller and this relationship shall be confirmed in the contract to purchase and sell real property or in a separate writing executed or acknowledged by the seller and the listing agent prior to or coincident with the execution of that contract by the seller.

The concepts of agency and fiduciary duty are quite old, being derived from Common Law. According to Civil Code Section 2295 (enacted in 1872), "An agent is one who represents another, called the principal, in dealings with third persons. Such representation is called agency." In an agency relationship, the principal delegates to the agent the right to act on his or her behalf, and to exercise some degree of discretion while so acting.

A PRINCIPAL AND AGENT CAN CREATE AN AGENCY RELATIONSHIP BY:

- agreement between them;
- by ratification; (Ratification is approval of a transaction that has already taken place)
- by 33stoppels; (33stoppels prohibits a principal from denying that a person is the agent if the principal has mislead another into believing that a person is an agent)
- as the result of the conduct of the parties and the agent's inherent relationship with third parties (i.e., ostensible or implied agency).

ELEMENTS OF AN AGENCY AGREEMENT

An agency agreement/listing typically includes:
1. the names of the parties;
2. effective identification of the property;

3. terms and conditions of the anticipated sale, lease or loan;
4. the amount of commission or other compensation to be paid;
5. the expiration of the agency (An exclusive listing must include a definite, specified date of final and complete termination.); and
6. signatures of the parties to the listing

TYPES OF LISTING AGREEMENTS

The four kinds of listing agreements most commonly used are:
- the open listing
- the exclusive agency listing;
- the exclusive right to sell listing; and
- the net listing.

OPEN LISTING

An open listing is the least restrictive of the four principal kinds of listing agreements, and is distinguished by the fact that the owner retains the right to revoke the listing at any time, to sell the property him or herself, or to list the property with another broker.

EXCLUSIVE AGENCY

An exclusive agency is an agreement by which the owner agrees to employ a particular real estate broker to solicit prospective buyers, tenants/lessees, or lenders. Under an exclusive agency listing, the broker's right to a commission is protected as against other brokers for the duration of the listing agreement. However, under an exclusive agency agreement, the owner retains the right to sell, encumber or rent/lease the property.

EXCLUSIVE RIGHT TO SELL

The exclusive right to sell listing affords a real estate broker the greatest protection and makes him or her the sole agent for the sale of the property. The broker is entitled to a commission provided only that the property is sold during the listing period, regardless of who procures the buyer.

NET LISTING

A net listing is one which contemplates the seller realizing certain net proceeds. The real estate broker's commission is any sum received in excess of the seller's net.

MULTIPLE LISTING

A multiple listing service (MLS) is a means by which information concerning individual listings is distributed all participants and subscribers of the service.

OSTENSIBLE OR IMPLIED AGENCY

An agency relationship can result from the conduct of the parties even though there is no express employment agreement and regardless of the source of compensation. Agency relationships created from the actions or conduct of the parties are known as ostensible or implied agencies.

COMPENSATION

Compensation is not essential to the creation of an agency. One may undertake to act gratuitously as an agent and still be held to certain standards demanded of an agent for compensation. Under the Real Estate Law, one who acts as a gratuitous agent does not need a real estate license. However, in any transaction subject to the Real Estate Law, and where there is an expectation of compensation, regardless of Real Estate Law, and where there is an expectation of compensation, regardless of the form, time, or source of payment, a license is required.

MORE ON DUAL AGENCY

Dual agency arises where the listing broker who is the actual agent of the seller becomes also the actual agent, or ostensible or implied agent of the buyer.

Dual agency also commonly arises when two salespersons associated with the same broker undertake to represent two or more parties to a transaction. The real estate broker is then a dual agent.

Although dual agency is a common practice in California, a real estate broker who represents both parties must act with extreme care.

A form of dual agency which has not been specifically addressed in the disclosure statutes is a broker's presentation of offers on behalf of two different buyers. This can easily happen when a broker is showing the same property to two prospective buyers and both buyers want the broker to write an offer on the property. The situation becomes even more complex if buyer A is in contract and buyer B makes a back-up offer. Buyer A's position is almost certainly weakened and buyer A would have reason to claim that the real estate broker breached fiduciary duties and obligations by participating in the offer by buyer B. A broker should not represent two buyers on the same property without the clear, informed and unequivocal consent of both parties.

DELEGATION OF DUTIES

Agents commonly delegate a certain portion of their duties and their responsibilities to others. Unless specifically forbidden by the principal, the general rule is that such delegation is allowed.

The powers which may be delegated by an agent to others are generally limited to the following:
- purely mechanical acts;
- acts the agent cannot do alone and the subagent can lawfully perform; and

- acts which common practice has established may be delegated or which the principal authorizes to be delegated.

When delegating a power to another, the agent must exercise care in delegating the authority and in choosing and appointing the delegee. Although an agent may not be authorized to assign a *duty of performance* to another, the agent may nevertheless be authorized to delegate the actual performance of such duty to others, and thereby discharge the duty through performance of the delegee. Although most agency agreements do not require the *personal performances* of the original agent, the original agent will typically remain liable for the acts delegated to others.

NO SECRET PROFIT OR UNDISCLOSED COMPENSATION

The courts have unequivocally held that an agent cannot:
- acquire any secret interests adverse to the principal
- make a secret personal profit out of the subject of the agency; or
- conceal the agent's interest in the property being conveyed or encumbered.

If an agent is aware of the amount at which a property may be sold and purchases at a lower amount, reselling and pocketing the difference, the agent will be compelled to disgorge the secret profit.

Claiming or receiving a secret profit or any form of undisclosed compensation is cause for discipline under Business and Professions Code Section 11076(g). The obligation to disclose all compensation regardless of the form, time, or source of payment is imposed upon real estate licensees whether acting in a real property or real property secured transaction.

OBLIGATIONS OF REAL ESTATE SALESPERSON

A real estate salesperson is the agent of a broker and is subject to the same duties and obligations arising out of the fiduciary relationship between the broker and the broker's principal.

A salesperson must disclose to the broker's principal all the information the salesperson has which may affect the principal's decision. Failure to fulfill this obligation could result in disciplinary action against the salesperson's license and may result in disciplinary action against the license of the employing broker. Moreover, a broker will generally be held liable for damages for acts and omissions of the broker's salesperson.

PUFFING

Even in some situations where a licensee honestly believes that representations to the prospective buyer are nothing more than "puffing" or "sales talk" a problem may develop if the impression made upon the buyer is that the representation is one of fact. Persons of limited expertise and sophistication may tend to rely upon such statements and to purchase property as a result of such reliance.

A statement by a licensee that a house was "in perfect shape" while obviously not literally true, has been described by an appellate court as a representation of a material fact.

COMPENSATION-PERFORMANCE REQUIRED UNDER EMPLOYMENT CONTRACT

Generally, to be entitled to a commission in a sale transaction a broker must:
- produce a buyer ready, willing and able to purchase upon the terms and at the price stipulated by the seller; or
- secure from a prospective buyer an offer upon terms and conditions which the seller subsequently accepts.

In the first situation, a real estate broker's right to compensation is based upon the written listing. The listing agreement requires that the broker produce an offer by a buyer ready, willing and able to purchase on the seller's listing terms. A ready and willing buyer denotes one who is prepared to enter into a binding contract while an able buyer is one who has the financial ability to consummate the transaction at the proper time.

From the broker's standpoint, a listing agreement is very much result oriented. The broker's right to a commission is not dependent upon the amount of work put into finding a buyer and negotiating a "meeting of the minds" of buyer and seller. If the broker expends no time and effort on behalf of the principal and yet is able to produce a buyer who is ready and willing to purchase on the terms specified in the listing contract, the broker is the procuring cause and has earned the compensation.

LAWFUL CONDITION

The payment of a commission under a listing contract may be made dependent on any lawful condition. A seller may be relieved from the obligation to pay a commission if it appears from the language of the contract that payment was   contingent upon the happening of a condition that did not occur. The burden is on the broker to establish that he or she has earned a commission. If the fulfillment of a condition is prevented by the fraud or bad faith of the seller, or through collusion between the seller and other parties, the broker may recover compensation even if the condition has not been met.

IF BROKER PERFORMS WITHIN TIME LIMIT BROKER IS ENTITLED TO COMMISSION

Revocation of a broker's authorization cannot operate to deprive the broker of the compensation contracted for, or its equivalent in damages, for nonperformance of the owner's contract if, within the time specified in the listing agreement, the broker has found a buyer ready, willing and able to purchase upon the price and terms in the listing. The principal will not be relieved from liability by a capricious refusal to consummate a sale where the principal's voluntary act precludes the possibility of performance on the principal's part. This is based upon the familiar principle that no one can avail himself or herself of the nonperformance of a condition precedent who has occasioned its nonperformance. It is also well settled that a principal cannot discharge an agent pending negotiations by the agent with a prospective buyer, and then effect a sale to that buyer without liability to the agent.

AGREEMENT BETWEEN BROKERS

An agreement between brokers cooperating in the sale of real property for a division of the commission is not illegal nor against public policy. It will be construed and enforced the same as other contracts not required to be in writing but no partnership or joint venture is created by such an agreement.

LICENSEE ACTING FOR OWN ACCOUNT

A real estate licensee will sometimes act in a real property transaction for his or her own account. Because of professional background and contacts, a licensee is oftentimes more aware than most people of investment and profit opportunities in such transactions. An effort to exploit these opportunities to personal advantage may involve legal or ethical matters to be carefully considered by the licensee.

When acting for his or her own account, a broker or salesperson is obliged to act honestly and fairly, in good faith, and without fraud or deceit. These duties and obligations are expected of all parties to agreements.

In certain fact situations, a broker or salesperson acting as a principal has additional duties to the other party to the transaction. An example is a broker or salesperson acting as a principal in a transaction who is also an arranger of credit pursuant to Civil Code Sections 2956-2957. Licensees who are principals in such transactions must prepare and complete a seller financing disclosure statement to be delivered to the other principal.

UNILATERAL AND BILATERAL AGREEMENTS

An agreement can be classified as either unilateral or bilateral. A unilateral agreement is one in which one party makes a promise to induce some act or performance by the other party, but the latter can act or not act as he chooses. For example, in an open listing the seller agrees to pay compensation to a real estate broker who procures a buyer, but there is no obligation on the part of any broker to do so.

A bilateral agreement is one in which a promise by one party is given in exchange for a promise by the other party. For example, an exclusive right to sell listing includes a broker's promise to use due diligence in attempting to find a buyer. In exchange, the seller promises to pay the broker a commission if the broker is successful.

MULTIPLE LISTING

A multiple listing service (MLS) is a means by which information concerning individual listings is distributed to all participants and subscribers of the service. For example, assume a seller lists property for sale with a broker. Pursuant to the listing, the broker transmits to the MLS information about the property which includes information such as the type of property, its size, location, listed price and other relevant information as well as the compensation offered to other brokers who procure a buyer. The MLS publishes the information in a database and sometimes in book format. Other brokers throughout the region are thereby made aware of the listing and can show the property and contact the listing agent on behalf of prospective buyers.

OSTENSIBLE OR IMPLIED AGENCY

An agency relationship can result from the conduct of the parties even thought there is no express employment agreement and regardless of the source of compensation. Agency relationships created from the actions or conduct of the parties are known as ostensible or implied agencies.

For example, a listing broker can unintentionally become the agent of the other principal to a transaction by leading the buyer to believe they are negotiating on behalf of or advocating the interest of the buyer when presenting the offer to the seller, or when processing the transaction to close of escrow. To act as an undisclosed agent of the other principal (i.e., without the informed consent of both parties), may subject the broker to administrative discipline and/or loss of commission, and may be grounds for rescission of the transaction. {Business and Professional Code Section 10176(a) and (d)}

AUTHORITY OF AGENT

An agent has authority to:
- Do everything necessary, proper or usual in the ordinary course of business to effect the purpose of the agency; and
- Make representations as to facts, not including the terms of the agent's authority, on which the agent's right to use his or her authority depends, and the truth of which cannot be determined by the use of reasonable diligence on the part of the person to whom the representation is being made. (Civil Code Section 2319)

Actual authority is that authority a principal intentionally confers upon the agent, or intentionally, or by want of ordinary care, allows the agent to believe that he or she possesses. (Civil Code Section 2316) Ostensible authority is that authority a principal intentionally, or by want of ordinary care, causes or allows third persons to believe that the agent possesses. (Civil Code Section 2317) Ostensible authority is sometimes referred to as apparent or implied authority.

EXPRESS AUTHORITY

Again, express authority is created by a contract which completely and precisely delineates those activities the agent is authorized to undertake. For example, if the principal authorizes the agent to acquire a particular single-family residence for $100,000, the agent has express authority to do precisely that and nothing else. The agent would not have express authority to purchase the house for $105,000 or to purchase a different house.

IMPLIED AUTHORITY

Implied authority exists because it is often impractical or even impossible for the principal to specifically delineate every aspect of the agent's authority. Implied authority may be derived from express authority and exists to the extent that it is reasonably necessary to accomplish the objectives of the agency. In the example above, the agent had express authority to purchase a particular property at a certain price. The agent might have implied authority to set time limits for performance of the agreement, receive notifications from the seller, waive conditions in the agreement and possibly undertake efforts to obtain financing for the buyer.

Implied authority cannot conflict with express authority but it may exist where there is no relevant grant of express authority. The determination of whether implied authority has been given usually involves determining the custom and practice of the community and whether the specific act was reasonably necessary for achieving the objectives for which the agency relationship was created.

APPARENT AUTHORITY

Apparent authority depends not upon the express or implied agreement between principal and agent, but upon the reasonable expectations of third parties who have been led to believe that the agent is authorized to act on behalf of the principal. Apparent authority is distinctly different from actual or express authority and is sometimes referred to as ostensible authority by estoppel. Ostensible authority by estoppel arises when the principal, by words or contact, leads a third party to believe that another person is his agent.

In other words, apparent or ostensible authority will arise and the principal could be estopped to deny the existence of the agency, or the scope of the agent's authority, when the principal's actions have created the appearance of authority in the agent and a third party reasonably relies, to his/her detriment, upon this authority. The most common causes of questions concerning apparent authority are the principal's placement of a limitation upon the normal and ordinary authority of the agent and failure to communicate this limitation to a third party dealing with the agent.

LIABILITY OF PRINCIPAL TO THIRD PARTIES

The principal is liable to persons who have sustained injury through a reasonable reliance upon the ostensible, whether implied or apparent, authority of an agent. The act of the agent can never alone establish ostensible authority, but silence upon the part of the principal who knows that an agent is holding himself or herself out as vested with certain authority may give rise to liability of the principal.

EMERGENCY BROADENS AUTHORITY

An agent has expanded authority in an emergency, including the power to disobey instructions where it is clearly in the interest of the principal, and where there is no time to obtain instructions from the principal. An example of this authority occurs in the relationship between a property manager and an owner when an immediate repair or replacement is required to protect the property and to provide necessary services to the tenant.

RESTRICTIONS ON AUTHORITY

An agent who is given the power to sell real property for a principal also possesses the power to give the usual covenants of warranty unless there are express restrictions in this regard in the agent's agreement with the principal. Also, an agent can never have authority, either actual or ostensible, to do an act which is known or suspected by the person with whom the agent deals to be fraud upon the principal. Unless specifically authorized an agent has no authority to act in the agent's own name except when it is in the usual course of business for the agent to do so.

An agency to sell property does not carry with it the authority to modify or cancel the contract of sale after it has been made. A limited agency as created between a seller and a real estate broker to sell the property ordinarily empowers the real estate broker to find a buyer, but does not authorize the agent to enter into a contract to convey title to the property on behalf of the principal.

An agent who has authority to collect money on behalf of his or her principal may endorse a negotiable instrument received in payment only where the exercise of this power is necessary for the performance of the agent's duty and where the principal has specifically granted the power to endorse the instrument. Where an agent is expressly authorized to collect money, the agent may accept a valid check and the agent's receipt of the check on behalf of the principal will be considered payment to the principal.

RATIFICATION OF UNAUTHORIZED ACTS

Occasionally, a person may act as agent without authority to do so, or an agent may act beyond the scope of the agent's authority. The alleged principal may not be bound by such acts. A principal may under certain circumstances ratify the acts of the agent and thus become bound. Not only must the principal intend to ratify, but:
1. The agent must have professed to act as a representative of the principal.
2. The principal must have been capable of authorizing the act both at the time of the act and at the time of ratification.
3. The principal must have knowledge of all material facts unless ratification is given with the intention to ratify no matter what the facts are.
4. The principal must ratify the entire act of the agent, accepting the burdens with the benefits.
5. The principal must ratify before the third party withdraws.

Generally, an act may be ratified by any words or conduct showing an intention on the part of the principal to adopt the agent's act as the principal's own. Once ratified, the legal consequences are the same as though the act had been originally authorized.

DUTY TO ASCERTAIN SCOPE OF AGENT'S AUTHORITY

No liability is incurred by the principal for acts of the agent beyond the scope of the agent's actual or ostensible authority. A third party who deals with an agent and knows of the agency is under a duty to ascertain the purpose and scope of the agency.

POWER OF ATTORNEY

A power of attorney is a written instrument giving authority to an agent. The agent acting under such a grant of authority is generally called an "attorney in fact." A special power of attorney authorizes the attorney in fact to do certain prescribed (limited) acts on behalf of the principal. Under a general power of attorney, the agent may transact all of the business of the principal. Powers of attorney are strictly construed and ordinarily where an authority is given partly in general and partly in specific terms, the general authority is limited to acts necessary to accomplish the specific purpose set forth.

AUTHORITY TO RECEIVE DEPOSITS

Virtually all listing agreements now give express authority to the broker to accept an earnest money deposit on behalf of the seller. The authority granted a listing broker also applies to any subagents of the seller. The authority, however, would not apply to a broker who is acting only as an agent of the buyer.

Except for a check to be held uncashed until acceptance of the offer, as discussed below, a broker must place funds accepted on behalf of another into the hands of the owner of the funds, into a neutral escrow depository or into a trust fund account in the name of the broker as trustee at a bank or other financial institution not later than three business days following receipt of the funds buy the broker or the broker's salesperson.

In those cases where a down payment has been paid to the broker and not deposited in escrow, title to such payment vests in the seller when the seller accepts the purchase contract. Further, where an agreement for sale of real property provides that a deposit with the broker is to become a part of the down payment when the seller puts in escrow a deed evidencing good title, the deposit becomes the seller's property when the deed is put in escrow. Similarly, money received by seller's agent under a deposit receipt with a valid liquidated damage clause is generally (in the case of the buyer's breach) not recoverable by the buyer.

The rationale behind this rule is that money received by a broker as agent or subagent for the seller belongs to the seller when the offer has been accepted. In general, the broker may not return the funds to the buyer without the consent of the seller.

DUTIES OWED TO PRINCIPALS

An agency relationship creates a fiduciary duty owed by the agent to the principal within the course and scope of the agency and the authority granted by the principal. The fiduciary duty owed by real estate brokers to their principals has been compared by the courts to the duty owed to the beneficiaries by a trustee under a trust.

Fiduciary duties include: loyalty; confidentiality; the exercise of utmost care (and in certain fact situations, reasonable care); full and complete disclosure of all material facts; the obligation to account to the principal; the obligation to act fairly and honestly and without fraud or deceit; and the duty to "explain" and "counsel" about that which has been disclose, thereby helping the principal make an informed and considered decision to buy, sell, lease, exchange, borrow or lend.

A salesperson owes a duty to the principal equivalent to the duty owed by the real estate broker for whom the salesperson acts.

AGENCY COURSE PRACTICE QUESTIONS:

True or False?

1. Before the Agency Disclosure Regulation was passed almost all sales were completed under a sub-agency relationship. *T*

2. The Agency Disclosure regulation was effective January 1, 1954. *F*

3. The Agency Regulations concerning residential real property transactions are found in the Civil Code. *T*

4. The agency disclosure form can be give to a seller after a listing agreement is signed. *F*

5. A fiduciary duty means utmost care is given to clients. *T*

6. An Agency Disclosure Statement is required in residential sales of up to 16 units. *F*

7. Easton vs. Strassburger held that a minor earth slides three years before the purchase was a material fact. *T*

8. If a client asks is the seller Catholic, you must answer. *F*

9. Civil Code 1710.2 covers death & AIDS on a property. *T*

10. An agent is obligated to reveal any confidential information obtained. *F*

11. A buyer's agent may receive compensation for services rendered from the seller. *T*

12. In a dual agency situation, the agent has obligations to the Seller only. *F*

13. Sellers must protect their own interests. *T*

14. If a client will not take a disclosure form, you must refuse to work with them. *F*

15. An agency relationship can change from property to property. *T*

16. Sub-agency is not legal in California. *F*

17. The term buyer includes vendee or lessee. *T*

18. An agent can be employed by only one principal. *T*

19. The selling agent must provide the disclosure form to the buyer prior to the signing of an offer. *F ?*

20. An agency relationship cannot be created by estoppel.

21. On a net listing the real estate broker's commission is any sum received in excess of the seller's net. *T*

22. Compensation is essential to the creation of an agency. *F*

23. A real estate salesperson is the associate of a broker. *T*

24. The payment of a commission under a listing contract cannot be made dependent on a condition. **F**

25. When acting for his or her own account, a broker or salesperson is obliged to act honestly and fairly. **T**

26. A real estate agreement must be bilateral. **F**

27. Ostensible authority by estoppel arises when the principal leads a third party to believe that another person is his agent. **T**

28. An emergency does not broaden authority. **F**

29. A special power of attorney is a written instrument giving authority to an agent. **T**

30. The broker may return the funds to the buyer without seller consent **F**

31. A real estate broker who is the agent of a principal owes a duty of fair and honest dealings to other parties. **F**

32. The race of the buyer is a material fact and should be disclosed. **F**

33. Most listing agreements allow a broker to accept deposits. **F**

34. The Agency Disclosure Regulations apply to all real estate transactions. **T**

35. A bilateral contract is two promises and binds both parties. **T**

36. In a dual agency relationship the agent can tell the seller a buyer will increase their offer. **F**

37. Buyer means transferee in a real estate transaction. **F**

38. It is legal for an agent to make a secret profit if their broker agrees. **F**

39. No liability is incurred by a principal if the agent acts beyond the scope of their authority and they do not approve the act. **F**

40. The requirement for taking an agency class is only for responsible brokers. **F**

Practice Questions designed to prepare you to pass the final exams are available. New BRE Regulations do not allow us to give the answers to the quizzes in the book so the questions and answers are presented online. This makes the test taking very easy as you get the answers immediately.

To access the practice quizzes please visit http://www.DuaneGomer.com/after . Check on the proper link for the course you desire.

NOTE: Do not use Google, Yahoo, Bing etc. They are Search Engines. You must put the above URL link in your address bar or you won't get there.

You may request the questions by email to info@DuaneGomer.com, fax at 949-455-9931, or phone 800-439-4909. You will receive only the practice questions. You may FAX back your answers to Duane Gomer, Inc., at (949) 455-9931 and we will FAX your results to you within 24 business hours. Our recommendation is find a computer even if it's a friend or relatives it makes everything so easy under the new BRE rules.

ETHICS

INTRODUCTION

This home-study course satisfies the Bureau of Real Estate requirement of a mandatory 3-hour Ethics course.

REASONS FOR THIS CLASS

Real estate agents have never received high credibility marks from the public. In many polls, we have been placed ahead of only one other occupation - car dealers. In the late 1970's, the California Association of REALTORS® and the Bureau of Real Estate promulgated legislation to require Continuing Education for the renewal of licenses. It was hoped that this education requirement would increase the knowledge of agents to protect the public and create a better reputation for our industry.

The initial regulation in 1978 was for 45 hours of education. After a few years, a change was made, and a three-hour Ethics Class became a renewal requirement. This is still in effect today.

When this course was first mandated by the BRE, Commission Regulations had some outstanding sections concerning Professional Conduct. It outlined several standards and level of care that should be followed by Real Estate Licensees.

These sections were eliminated several years ago. Agents are now instructed to know and follow Sections 10176 and 10177 in the California Business and Professional Code. Yes, you should reference those sections whenever you have a question about conduct. However, in my opinion, the eliminated regulations did a better job of explaining required conduct so this course presents them for your educational purposes.

2785. **Professional Conduct.** **In order to enhance the professionalism of the California real estate industry, and maximize protection for members of the public dealing with real estate licensees, whatever their area of practice, the following standards of professional conduct and business practices are adopted.**

    (a) **Unlawful Conduct in Sale, Lease and Exchange Transactions.** **Licensees when performing acts within the meaning of Section 10131 (a) of the Business and Professions Code shall not engage in conduct which would subject the licensee to adverse action, penalty or discipline under Sections 10176 and 10177 of the Business and Professions Code.**

DON'T LIE ABOUT PRICE

(1) <u>Knowingly</u> making a <u>substantial</u> misrepresentation of the likely value of real property:

Two important words are included in this phrase - Knowingly and Substantial. The paragraph heading is "Don't Lie About Price." This is a simplistic explanation of this regulation. The regulation uses the word substantial. The dictionary explains substantial as large, solid, firm, real, etc. Therefore, the rule appears to be, "Don't Lie Large About Price." You shouldn't rely on this explanation. What is large to a hearing deputy or a judge might be real small to you, so "Don't Lie About Price."

Knowingly is another word that you should notice. You might say that you didn't "know" this regulation. However, you passed a license examination that approximately 63% fail. Since you passed this exam, it is assumed that you know the regulations. So let's repeat this thought one more time - "Don't Lie About Price."

TO WHOM CAN'T WE LIE ABOUT PRICE

(A) Its owner either for the purpose of <u>securing a listing or for the purpose of acquiring an interest in the property</u> for the licensee's own account.

(B) A <u>prospective</u> buyer for the purpose of inducing the buyer to make an offer to purchase the real property.

Sentence A says that you can't lie to an owner to secure a listing. This is self-explanatory. The phrase "for the purpose of acquiring an interest" is underlined because it is important. Sometime ago this phrase read, "acquiring an interest while acting as an agent." The phrase "while acting as an agent" has been removed.

What does this mean in street talk? You could lose your license because you bought a property from an owner at too low a price with no brokerage fee involved. You could lose your license even if the transaction had no commission, and you weren't working for any broker at the time. You can't cheat people and keep your license.

Another word needs an explanation, "Prospective" when referring to a buyer. How about this hypothetical situation? You show a buyer a piece of land. The buyer doesn't like you and thinks that you lied about the price. An investigation shows that you recently sold a similar parcel in that area for substantially less. There are other listings in the area priced substantially less. You are "pushing" your overpriced listing onto this buyer. If the facts are as expressed and the buyer complains to the BRE, you could be in big trouble. The buyer did not buy the property, did not make an offer on the property, and didn't suffer any financial loss, and yet you could still lose your license.

BONA FIDE OFFER

(2) Representing to an owner of real property when seeking a listing that the licensee has obtained a <u>bona fide written offer</u> to purchase the property, unless at the time of the representation the licensee has possession of a bona fide written offer to purchase.

The writers of the Regulations were not satisfied with using English words with nebulous meanings. In this regulation, they decided to use a Latin term. Now you have to understand Latin to keep your license. What does "Bona Fide" mean in English? "Bona Fide" translates as "Good Faith". In this usage it means, "If you ever tell someone that you have an offer for them, you better have one".

One of the areas where this problem arises is on expired listings. The sleazy licensee appears at the owner's door immediately after a listing expires. They have an "as-listed offer", but since the listing has expired, they can't submit the offer. The offer expires that day so there is not enough time to relist with the previous broker. Fortunately, the sleazy licensee has a fully completed listing agreement, and by signing this convenient listing agreement, the owner can receive the offer. Many owners do sign the listing to get the offer. The offer is not a legitimate offer. It is from the licensee's friend or associate and includes several contingencies. An example might be a provision for cancellation after an inspection. The offer is cancelled soon after it is signed, and the broker has a new listing for a long time. A complaint with facts like this would lose a license for an agent.

Recommendation - Don't tell anyone that you have an offer unless it is a bona fide (good faith) offer.

Years ago, I received an offer in the mail on an apartment house investment for which I was the general partner. The offer was for a decent price and looked very formal. Our group had no interest in selling and had not talked to anyone about selling. In fact, there would have been some tax problems if we did sell. The broker had worked in the same office with me sometime before. I called him to find out why he sent me the offer. He apologized and said that the address on the tax rolls showed our group's fictitious name or he wouldn't have sent it to me. What was he doing? He would send out formal offers each day to many different owners. The buyer was a phony nominee.

This procedure allowed him to get many listings. Owners would call him to find out what was up? He would get them to discuss the offer. There would always be a reason why his first offer couldn't be accepted, but he could start dialogues that would result in listings. Were his offers bona fide offers? Did his mailing program violate this regulation? Should he keep his license? I believe the Bureau of Real Estate would answer no, yes and no in that order?

NEGOTIABLE COMMISSIONS

(3) Stating or implying to an owner of real property during listing negotiations that the licensee is precluded by law, by regulation, or by the rules of any organization, other than the broker firm seeking the listing, from charging less than the commission or fee quoted to the owner by the licensee.

A Board of REALTORS® in California lost a lawsuit concerning commissions. An investigation discovered that the commissions on every listing in their multiple listing service were 6%. Claims were made to the court that this was price fixing. The Court could not find any instance where the Board or its officers had ever issued any statement on commission fees. However, the verdict was that the Board had never distributed enough information that commissions didn't have to be 6%. The Board was penalized financially.

After this decision, this regulation was added to the Code. Also, the California Association of REALTORS® Listing Agreement added a phrase; "Notice - The amount or rate of real estate commission is not fixed by law. They are set by each Broker individually and may be negotiable between the Seller and Broker". This Regulation is specific in that a licensee can't say that any law, regulation, or association precludes a lower commission. It is believed that licensees used to say, "The commission has to be 6% to go into Multiple," "Everyone has to charge 6%," "No one will work on any property listed lower than 6%," "State Regulation insists on 6%," etc. These statements are all against any Code of Conduct.

However, one part of number (3) states "other than the broker firm seeking the listing." A firm can set a commission and not negotiate. A company could sell all types of properties at one fee and never vary. Also, they could refuse to list any owner's property unless the owner agreed to their fee. This might not be financially prudent, but it is legal.

FRANCHISES, FRANCHISES, FRANCHISES

(4) Knowingly making substantial misrepresentations regarding the licensee's relationship with an individual broker, corporate broker, or franchised brokerage company or that entity's/person's responsibility for the licensee's activities.

This statement expresses the feeling that the public doesn't understand the franchise arrangement of many real estate offices. I agree with this assumption. Licensees understand that a Century 21 office is a separate organization, but the public doesn't. The advertising programs of many Franchise Companies give the illusion that each company is one firm. Homeowners and buyers are puzzled to find out that this is not true and when they have a problem with a local franchisee they can't go after a parent company for damages.

Also, it is believed that in the past some licensees working for a franchise made misrepresentation about their firms. Statements like "List with us, we're all over the country", "We have millions of sales", "We're the largest in the World", etc. caused problems. Franchise licensees are hereby put on notice to stop this behavior.

Most franchises have required a phrase on their business cards that reads something like "Each office is independently owned and operated". This should forewarn owners and buyers that this is a Franchise Office. Maybe someday in a perfect world the public will understand franchising.

CLOSING COSTS

(5) Knowingly underestimating the probable closing costs in a communication to the prospective buyer or seller of real property in order to induce that person to make or to accept an offer to purchase the property.

This regulation is self-explanatory, and I believe everyone knows it. You can't underestimate, but you can, I guess, legally overestimate. However, if you overestimate, you might lose sales, and have different problems. Become an expert and know closing costs.

DEPOSITS

(6) Knowingly making a false or misleading representation to the seller of real property as to the form, amount and/or treatment of a deposit toward the purchase of the property made by an offerer.

In my live classes it is apparent that all the students know this rule. You have to be candid and truthful about the type and amount of any deposit. However, many students fail a verbal test that I give them. "What must you do with a post-dated check when it is given as an earnest money deposit?" The answers that I get vary from:

1. You should never take a post-dated check.
2. You can take a post-dated check, but any acceptance would be conditional and a seller could cancel the contract.
3. Yes, you can take a post-dated check and proceed if you inform the seller.
4. Ask for a promissory note instead of a post-dated check.
5. Ask for cash even if a small amount.
6. Write the offer with no consideration.

You would be amazed how many students say that they wouldn't take a post-dated check and wouldn't write an offer until the buyer gives a good check. This is wrong, wrong, wrong. End-of-story.

Answers 3 through 6 are all correct and can be used. One student had legitimate buyers who didn't have their checkbook or a counter check with them. The offer was on a high-priced home in an exclusive area. The broker took a $1.00 bill and stapled it to the offer. The seller asked, "What is this?" The broker said, "The buyer will have a check tomorrow, but had none today and very little cash. I tried to staple a quarter to the form but it wouldn't work." The seller had a sense of humor and signed.

If the buyer doesn't have a proper check, you could take a post-dated check or no consideration at all. In the book "Real Estate Sales Agreements" on page 34, Erik Jorgensen, explained how to write an offer with a post-dated check. Since Erik is considered an authority in the field, we should agree. He also mentions using a promissory note, a small amount of cash or no consideration at all.

In my opinion, the promissory note is better than the other methods. All of the methods are legally correct, but the promissory note method is the most practical. I believe that sellers would be more apt to accept a promissory note. The public and many agents have trepidations when considering post-dated checks, no consideration deposits and small amounts of cash. You should carry blank promissory notes in your briefcase for use in these cases.

Many agents take checks that they know are no good that exact time. They believe the buyers will make a deposit before it is cashed. If any check bounces in escrow, you could have real problems. If a person gives you a $20,000 check out of their regular account and the check has doggies and kittens on it, I would guess that the account doesn't have that much money and you're betting that they make a deposit.

SELLER FINANCING

(7) Knowingly making a false or misleading representation to a seller of real property, who has agreed to finance all or part of a purchase price by carrying back a loan, about a buyer's ability to repay the loan in accordance with its terms and conditions.

Seller financing is not used often enough in real estate. More property would be sold, more buyers could find properties, less taxes would be paid by sellers and licensees would make more money if seller financing was used more often. Sellers and buyers should be advised about the advantages and disadvantages of seller financing. If you want to make more money, learn more about the advantages and disadvantages.

There are some rules concerning the problems of seller financing. Years ago a phrase called "Creative Finance" became a hot topic in California Real Estate. In its practical usage it meant the sellers carried back financing. Many problems arose because the clients were never told the pitfalls of seller financing. Lawsuits followed.

To help the public and agents a Civil Code Section (C.C. Section 2956-57) was instituted and now real estate licensees must explain the problems of seller financing to their clients in the sale of 1-4 residential units. A disclosure must be made in writing to these clients. The California Association of REALTORS®' form, Seller Financing Disclosure (SFD), accomplishes this disclosure. Become familiar with this outstanding form.

CAR has listed the problems of Seller Financing on their current purchase agreement. The points are so important that they are repeated below.

ADDITIONAL SELLER FINANCING TERMS

The following terms apply only to financing extended by Seller under this agreement. Any promissory note and/or deed of trust given by Buyer to Seller shall contain, but not be limited to, the following additional terms:
1. Request for notice of default on senior loans.
2. Buyer shall execute and pay for a request for notice of delinquency in escrow and any future time if requested by seller.
3. Acceleration Clause Making the Loan due, when permitted by law, at Seller's option, upon the sale or transfer of the property or any interest in it.
4. A late charge of 6.0% of the installment due, or $5.00, whichever is greater, if the installment is not received within 10 days of the date it is due.
5. Title insurance coverage in the form of a joint protection policy shall be provided insuring Seller's deed of trust interest in the Property.
6. A Tax Service shall be obtained and paid for by Buyer to notify Seller if property taxes have not been paid.
7. Buyer shall provide fire and extended coverage insurance during the period of the seller financing, in an amount sufficient to replace all improvements on the Property, or the total encumbrances against the Property, whichever is less, with a loss payable endorsement in favor of Seller.
8. The addition, deletion, or substitution of any person or entity under this agreement, or to title prior to close of escrow, shall require Seller's written consent. Seller may grant or withhold consent in Seller's sole discretion. Any additional or substituted person or

entity shall, if requested by Seller, submit to Seller the same documentation as required for the original named Buyer. Seller and/or Broker(s) may obtain a credit report on any such person or entity.

9. If the Property contains 1 to 4 dwelling units, Buyer and Seller shall execute a Seller Financing Disclosure Statement (C.A.R. Form SFD-14) (Civil Code §§2956-2967), if applicable, as provided by arranger of credit, as soon as practicable prior to execution of security documents.

ADDITIONAL POINTS TO CONSIDER

1. This Regulation is required only on the sale of 1-4 units residential. It is strongly recommended that you use the SFD on all sales with Seller Financing.
2. The ultimate responsibility for the completion of the form is the "arranger of credit." If only one agent is involved, obviously that agent is responsible. If one agent represents the buyer and another agent represents the seller, the agent representing the buyer is by definition the "arranger of credit."
3. There is a note of caution on the SFD about the availability of funds for refinance at the time of the due date. It reads, "If any of the obligations secured by the property calls for a balloon payment, then Seller and Buyer are aware that refinancing of the balloon payment at maturity may be difficult or impossible depending on the conditions in the mortgage marketplace at that time. There are no assurances that new financing or a loan extension will be available when the balloon payment is due."
4. Another note of Caution concerns the use of a Collections Agent: It reads, "The parties are advised to consider designating a neutral third party as the collection agent for receiving Buyer's payments and disbursing them to the payee(s) on the senior encumbrances(s) and to the Seller."

CHANGING CONTRACTS

(8) Making an addition to or modification of the terms of an instrument previously signed or initialed by a party to a transaction without the knowledge and consent of the party. If you have to have this phrase explained, get out of real estate.

"LTV" RULE

(9) A representation made as a principal or agent to a prospective purchaser of a promissory note secured by real property about the market value of the securing property without a reasonable basis for believing the truth and accuracy of the representation.

If you are going to make a statement about LTV (Loan to Value Ratio of Loans on the Property in Relation to its Market Value), know what you are talking about. The code states, "without a reasonable basis." In practical terms, that means you have some documented objective data. Don't depend on hearsay or other people's opinions. You could find yourself in real trouble.

FEATURES OF A PROPERTY

(10) Knowingly making a false or misleading representation or representing, without a reasonable basis for believing its truth, the nature and/or condition of the interior or exterior features of a property when soliciting an offer.

The best way to explain this statement is to present facts from a landmark case, **Krause v. Miller (1956) 154 CA 2d 656,** on this subject.

    a. Cooperating broker failed to tell buyer that lot was filled and actually said it was not filled.

    b. Buyers sued sellers for rescission because of later discovery that lot was filled.

    c. Co-op broker liable to seller for not informing seller of representations made by co-op broker to buyer.

    d. Case says that a broker's statement should have a solid basis in fact as these statements can subject a broker to liability because he or she is presumed to have superior knowledge and what they give as an opinion may be interpreted as a representation of fact.

    e. Recommendation:

        1) Always qualify opinion as such.

        2) Give all reasons for opinion.

        3) Written back-up is advisable.

Example: Buyer asks if the roof leaks, and the agent says that it does not because it does not appear to leak (thinks the licensee). If the licensee says there is no leak, this is a representation, which may not be reasonable. The licensee should say he or she does not know and should check through an inspection or by obtaining additional information from the seller.

Another Example: Stating the second story of a building is original construction when it is an add-on with no permit, and that the foundation is solid when it will not truly support the second floor. Checking for permits, or checking with the seller, would help the licensee make accurate disclosure, so again the answer, "I do not know but I will check and let you know" would be the correct procedure.

SQUARE FOOTAGE, SQUARE FOOTAGE, SQUARE FOOTAGE

(11) Knowingly making a false or misleading representation or representing, without a reasonable basis for believing its truth, the size of a parcel, <u>square footage of improvements</u> or the location of the boundary lines of real property being offered for sale, lease or exchange.

Lawsuits concerning square footage have been around forever and will continue in the future. What to do in this area is confusing. Some Realtor Associations have rules that square footage estimates are never to be used. I believe that the question of square footage is pertinent and is a normal query for buyers. Buyers want to have some idea about what they are buying. Agents must give them an estimate that is proper, based on fact and can be defended if questioned.

To whom do you go to for direction? Your responsible broker should give you guidelines on this topic. They are responsible for your conduct, and you should know what they want you to do. One reputable company lost a lawsuit, and there were three disclaimers in the lawsuit concerning an estimate of square footage. The words were "unmeasured", "approximately" and "per assessor's records." The assessor's records were quoted correctly, but the records were wrong. The moral of this story - "Measure accurately yourself; Check and Double Check."

This same company later had a sale where a buyer was told the home was 3,200 square feet. Later, it was surveyed and found to be 3,600+ square feet. The buyers are claiming damages, as the larger home is not what they wanted. To them it costs more to heat and clean, taxes are more, etc. You never know from where the next complaint will be coming.

ZONING

(12) Knowingly making a false or misleading representation or representing to a prospective buyer or lessee of real property, without a reasonable basis to believe its truth, that the property can be used for certain purposes with the intent of inducing the prospective buyer or lessee to acquire an interest in the real property.

This regulation brings to mind a California case, "Saludin v. Coldwell Banker". A buyer was told that the one-acre plot purchased could be subdivided into two building pads. The lot was 200 square feet short of an acre, and the county wouldn't give a variance for this error of less than .5%. The brokers had to pay. Don't make statements about zoning unless you have documented objective data.

MATERIAL FACT RULE

(13) When acting in the capacity of an agent in a transaction for the sale, lease or exchange of real property, failing to disclose to a prospective purchaser or lessee facts known to the licensee <u>materially affecting the value or desirability of the property,</u> when the licensee has reason to believe that <u>such facts are not known to nor readily observable by a prospective purchaser or lessee.</u>

All clients must be told about any material facts that affect value or desirability. This sentence is probably the important sentence in real estate. The problem is, "What is a material fact?" In the early 80's a case came out of Northern California that in my opinion affects licensees more than any other. This most famous case is, "Easton v. Strassburger". An excerpt from a California Association of Realtor's Legal Department Article explains this case and a few other important facts.

Whether information is "material" depends on all the facts of the particular case. In general, a fact would be considered <u>material</u> if it would affect the desirability of the property. Stated another way, a fact would be considered <u>material</u> if it would affect the decision of a reasonable buyer to buy, or the price and terms on which he or she would be willing to buy, the subject property.

For example, Easton v. Strassburger held that a minor earth slide three years before the purchase plus existing red flags indicating soil problems were material facts. In another case, "Reed v. King", a Superior Court held that a multiple murder 10 years before the offer of sale was a material fact.

Some other California decisions finding material facts together with a duty to disclose concerned a house constructed on filled land, improvements added without a building permit in violation of zoning regulations, failure to disclose the true lien amount on a property to be acquired, and failure to disclose dual termite reports of considerable variance.

In contrast, the California Attorney General has issued opinions that the race of a prospective buyer is not a material fact to be disclosed to the seller, and that a licensed real estate agent is not required to disclose to prospective home buyers that a licensed residential care facility servicing six or fewer people is located in the neighborhood.

There are some other points to discuss about this regulation. The last part of the statement says, "such facts are not known to nor readily observable by a prospective purchaser or lessee". Simply stated, "Buyers and lessees are to protect their own interests." This should be stressed, but as the agent for the seller you can't trust a buyer to "look around". Therefore, you should have your seller list any and all problems (visible or not) on the seller's Transfer Disclosure Statement.

In another part of the regulation are the words "value or desirability." The tricky word is desirability. You may have clients whose ideas of a home are different than in the past. Some buyers will not look at a home where the front door faces north, the front door is in direct line with the back door or a staircase, the number 4 is in the address, a street dead ends into this home's lot, any staircase has a number of steps divisible by the number 3 (9, 12 or 15, etc.). Buyers must be asked some extra questions to find out their "desires".

You must tell buyers any "material facts," but some questions are not to be answered. For example, "confidential information" doesn't have to be relayed to the other party even if you are asked a specific question. The buyer asks, "What is the seller's reason for selling?" That could be confidential.

Also, there are Fair Housing Regulations and other legislation that outlaws certain questions:
1. Is the seller African American?
2. Is the seller Jewish?
3. Are the buyers married?
4. Does the seller have AID's?
5. Questions about Death in a Home are regulated by Civil Code Section 1710.2. A Disclosure of deaths varies due to time of death (3 year rule), manner of death, occupant or not, death from AIDS, etc. For answers to these questions check the Code Section or if you are a member of CAR call them for a copy of their "Disclosure on Death and AID's".

FRIVOLOUS OFFERS

(14) Willfully failing, when acting as a listing agent, to present or cause to be presented to the owner of the property any written offer to purchase received <u>prior to the closing of a sale,</u> unless <u>expressly instructed</u> by the owner not to present such an offer, or unless the offer is <u>patently frivolous.</u>

Our company had a home study course on "Real Estate Sales Agreements" and one practice exam question used to be, "All written offers must be presented promptly". The answer is "False" and an unbelievably high percentage of students answered "True". If a question says all, always, never, every, etc. and there is one exception, the answer is false.

Do all offers have to be submitted promptly? This code section obviously says no. Examples of offers that don't have to be presented at all:
1. Received after the close of escrow.
2. A seller says, "No more."
3. A patently frivolous offer.

Number one item above needs no explanation so I will not bore you with one. You understand that any offer received during an escrow must be forwarded to a seller. The seller can't cancel any existing contract without cause, but extra offers can be taken as legal backup offers with the proper disclosures to all parties.

Number two is self-explanatory, but the details could be cumbersome. Your seller says, "I have enough offers and enough backup offers. So, please no more." The code doesn't state that this instruction has to be in writing, but obviously a written instruction would be better. If you say, "Could I have that instruction in writing?" you are really saying, "I don't trust you to remember you said this". That is not very good for your relationship. You might try saying, "I will fax you a simple form that you can send back stating you want no more offers. This will work great if some outside brokers puts pressure on our office to bother you with another offer".

Another question, "What is a patently frivolous offer?" My explanation is that it is an offer with a patently frivolous price. How do you know it is frivolous? You know because you know value. You are a Real Estate Licensee ordained by the State of California. Some students say, "The seller should decide whether an offer is frivolous or not." I disagree. If you send an offer to an owner that is impossible to be accepted under the current circumstances, because the price is patently frivolous, you will lose credibility with the owners. They will think you are an idiot.

What should you do with a "patently frivolous offer?" In my opinion, you should decide that it is frivolous and tell your owner before you present the offer. Then, still send it on with a statement, "This is for your file". You don't have to send it, but why not do it?

GREATEST COMPENSATION

(15) **When acting as the listing agent, presenting competing written offers to purchase real property to the owner in such a manner as to induce the owner to accept the offer which will provide the greatest compensation to the listing broker without regard to the benefits, advantages and/or disadvantages to the owner.**

The Bureau of Real Estate believes that there are some companies with listings in the state who present offers to their owners and make any offer from their company appear better than an offer from an outside cooperating firms. They hope to earn a higher commission by doing this even though the offer from outside brokers is better. You have now been told in a written code section not to do this, although you already knew it.

CONTINGENCIES

(16) **Failing to explain to the parties or prospective parties to a real estate transaction for whom the licensee is acting as an agent <u>the meaning and probable significance of a contingency</u> in an offer or contract that the licensee knows or reasonable believes may affect the closing date of the transaction, or the timing of the vacating of the property by the seller or its occupancy by the buyer. The explanation for this section is simple. Explain any and all contingencies. Let's move on.**

SPECIAL RELATIONSHIPS

(17) **Failing to disclose to the seller of real property in a transaction in which the licensee is an <u>agent for the seller</u> the nature and extent of any direct or indirect interest that the licensee expects to acquire as a result of the sale. The prospective purchase of the property by a person related to the licensee by blood or marriage, purchase by an entity in which the licensee has an ownership interest, or purchase by any other person with whom the licensee occupies a special relationship where there is a reasonable probability that the licensee could be indirectly acquiring an interest in the property shall be disclosed to the seller.**

An important phrase to note here is "agent for the seller" underlined above. This section applies when your company has a listing, and you also have the buyer. Most companies would call this a dual agency relationship.

If you are buying a direct or indirect interest, tell your seller. In one case a seller was puzzled to see their listing broker in possession of their property six months after the close of escrow. The broker explained that he had made an agreement with the buyer whereby he would buy the property back after six months if the buyer was dissatisfied. This agreement had not been disclosed to the seller.

The Seller complained to the BRE that the broker hadn't told him because the broker believed that a better price would be forthcoming if the seller didn't know that the broker was going to get the property after six months. The broker said he was protecting his buyer. BRE believed the seller. If you sell to a person related to you by blood or marriage, tell the seller. If you sell to a company of which you own part, tell the seller. If you have a <u>special relationship</u> with someone, tell the seller.

In one class a student mentioned that she sold her company's listing to her fiancé and didn't tell the seller. In another case a broker sold her listing to a person with whom she had been living eight years and didn't tell the seller. What do you think about these two cases? How would a BRE hearing officer look at them?

DITTO RULE

(18) **Failing to disclose to the <u>buyer</u> of real property in a transaction in which the licensee is an agent for the buyer the nature and extent of a licensee's direct or indirect ownership interest in the property by a person related to the licensee by blood or marriage, by an entity in which the licensee has an ownership interest,**

or by any other person with whom the licensee occupies a special relationship shall be disclosed to the buyer. This section is exactly the same as the prior section except the word buyer is substituted for seller.

SIGNIFICANT INTEREST

(19) Failing to disclose to a principal for whom the licensee is acting as an agent <u>any significant interest</u> the licensee has in a particular entity when the licensee recommends the use of the services or products of such entity.

You can recommend a company to a client. You can recommend a company of which you own an interest to a client. This rule states that when you own part of a recommended company you must tell the client. The question is, "What is a significant interest?" Going again to our trusty dictionary, the meaning is noteworthy, meaningful, consequential, etc. The problem again is that your opinion of noteworthy and a BRE hearing officer's opinion of significant could be different. I recommend that you tell a client of your ownership even if the percentage is low. In my opinion, significant interest means "any interest".

IN JUNE 1990 BRE ESTABLISHED A CODE OF ETHICS FOR LOAN BROKERS. THE SECTION FOLLOWS BELOW. IT IS PRESENTED FOR YOUR INFORMATION AND CONSIDERATION.

(b) Unlawful Conduct When Soliciting, Negotiating or Arranging a Loan Secured by Real Property or the Sale of a Promissory Note Secured by Real Property. Licensees when performing acts within the meaning of subdivision (d) or (e) of Section 10131 of the Business and Professions Code shall not violate any of the applicable provisions of subdivision (a), or act in a manner which would subject the licensee to adverse action, penalty or discipline under Sections 10176 or 10177 of the Business and Professions Code including, but not limited to, the following acts and omissions:

(1) Knowingly misrepresenting to a prospective borrower of a loan to be secured by real property or to an assignor/endorser of a promissory note secured by real property that there is an existing lender willing to make the loan or that there is a purchaser for the note, for the purpose of inducing the borrower or assignor/endorser to utilize the services of the licensee.

(2) (a) Knowingly making a false or misleading representation to a prospective lender or purchaser of a loan secured directly or collaterally by real property about a borrower's ability to repay the loan in accordance with its terms and conditions.
(b) Failing to disclose to a prospective lender or note purchaser information about the prospective borrower's identity, occupation, employment, income and credit data as represented to the broker by the prospective borrower:
(c) Failing to disclose information known to the broker relative to the ability of the borrower to meet his or her potential or existing contractual obligations under the note or contract including information known about the note is in default or the borrower is in bankruptcy.

(3) Knowingly underestimating the probable closing costs in a communication to a prospective borrower or lender of a loan to be secured by a lien on real property for the purpose of inducing the borrower or lender to enter into the loan transaction.

(4) When soliciting a prospective lender to make a loan to be secured by real property, falsely representing or representing with a reasonable basis to believe its truth, the priority of the security, as a lien against the real property securing the loan, i.e., a first, second or third deed of trust.

(5) Knowingly misrepresenting in any transaction that a specific service is free when the licensee knows or has a reasonable basis to know that it is covered by a fee to be charged as part of the transaction.

(6) Knowingly making a false or misleading representation to a lender or assignee/endorsee of a lender of a loan secured directly or collaterally by a lien on real property about the amount and

treatment of loan payments, including loan payoffs, and the failure to account to the lender or assignee/endorsee of a lender as to the disposition of such payments.

(7) When acting as a licensee in a transaction for the purpose of obtaining a loan, and in receipt of an "advance fee" from the borrower for this purpose, the failure to account to the borrower for the disposition of the "advance fee".

(8) Knowingly making false or misleading representation about the terms and conditions of a loan to be secured by a lien on real property when soliciting a borrower or negotiating the loan.

(9) Knowingly making a false or misleading representation or representing, without a reasonable basis for believing its truth, when soliciting a lender or negotiating a loan to be secured by a lien on real property about the market value of the securing real property, the nature and/or condition of the interior or exterior features of the securing real property, its size or the square footage of any improvements on the securing real property.

Also, the National Association of REALTORS® has another Code of Ethics with hundreds of important explanations, case studies and antidotes. You should understand and follow their recommendations at all times. Let's all be careful out there, as our California Agency Disclosure reminds us, let's be "utmost" careful out there.

Ethics is a most important subject for real estate licensees. For many years it has been a mandatory course for license renewal.

To give you the best information, this section will be devoted to the outstanding National Association of REALTORS® Code of Ethics and the Business and Professions Code Sections 10176 and 10177 that control license discipline. If you follow these guidelines, you will be ethical.

Code of Ethics and Standards of Practice of the NATIONAL ASSOCIATION OF REALTORS®:

Where the word REALTORS® is used in this Code and Preamble, it shall be deemed to include REALTOR-ASSOCIATE® s.

While the Code of Ethics establishes obligations that may be higher than those mandated by law, in any instance where the Code of Ethics and the law conflict, the obligations of the law must take precedence.

Preamble

Under all is the land. Upon its wise utilization and widely allocated ownership depend the survival and growth of free institutions and of our civilization. REALTORS® should recognize that the interests of the nation and its citizens require the highest and best use of the land and the widest distribution of land ownership. They require the creation of adequate housing, the building of functioning cities, the development of productive industries and farms, and the preservation of a healthful environment. Such interests impose obligations beyond those of ordinary commerce. They impose grave social responsibility and a patriotic duty to which REALTORS® should dedicate themselves, and for which they should be diligent in preparing themselves. REALTORS®, therefore, are zealous to maintain and improve the standards of their calling and share with their fellow REALTORS® a common responsibility for its integrity and honor.

In recognition and appreciation of their obligations to clients, customers, the public, and each other, REALTORS® continuously strive to become and remain informed on issues affecting real estate and, as knowledgeable professionals, they willingly share the fruit of their experience and study with others. They identify and take steps, through enforcement of this Code of Ethics and by assisting appropriate regulatory bodies, to eliminate practices which may damage the public or which might discredit or bring dishonor to the real estate profession.

Realizing that cooperation with other real estate professionals promotes the best interests of those who utilize their services, REALTORS® urge exclusive representation of clients; do not attempt to gain any unfair advantage over their competitors; and they refrain from making unsolicited comments about other practitioners. In instances where their opinion is sought, or where REALTORS® believe that comment is necessary, their opinion is offered in an objective, professional manner, uninfluenced by any personal motivation or potential advantage or gain.

The term REALTORS® has come to connote competency, fairness, and high integrity resulting from adherence to a lofty ideal of moral conduct in business relations. No inducement of profit and no instruction from clients ever can justify departure from this ideal.

In the interpretation of this obligation, REALTORS® can take no safer guide than that which has been handed down through the centuries, embodied in the Golden Rule, "Whatsoever ye would that others should do to you, do ye even so to them." Accepting this standard as their own, REALTORS® pledge to observe its spirit in all of their activities and to conduct their business in accordance with the tenets set forth below.

Article 1
When representing a buyer, seller, landlord, tenant, or other client as an agent, REALTORS® pledge themselves to protect and promote the interests of their client. This obligation of absolute fidelity to the client's interests is primary, but it does not relieve REALTORS® of their obligation to treat all parties honestly. When serving a buyer, seller, landlord, tenant or other party in a non-agency capacity, REALTORS® remain obligated to treat all parties honestly.

Article 2
REALTORS® shall avoid exaggeration, misrepresentation, or concealment of pertinent facts relating to the property or the transaction. REALTORS® shall not, however, be obligated to discover latent defects in the property, to advise on matters outside the scope of their real estate license, or to disclose facts which are confidential under the scope of agency duties owed to their clients.

Article 3
REALTORS® shall cooperate with other brokers except when cooperation is not in the client's best interest. The obligation to cooperate does not include the obligation to share commissions, fees, or to otherwise compensate another broker.

Article 4
REALTORS® shall not acquire an interest in or buy or present offers from themselves, any member of their immediate families, their firms or any member thereof, or any entities in which they have any ownership interest, any real property without making their true position known to the owner or the owner's agent. In selling property they own, or in which they have any interest, REALTORS® shall reveal their ownership or interest in writing to the purchaser or the purchaser's representative.

Article 5
REALTORS® shall not undertake to provide professional services concerning a property or its value where they have a present or contemplated interest unless such interest is specifically disclosed to all affected parties.

Article 6
REALTORS® shall not accept any commission, rebate, or profit on expenditures made for their client, without the client's knowledge and consent. When recommending real estate products or services (e.g., homeowner's insurance, warranty programs, mortgage financing, title insurance, etc.), REALTORS® shall disclose to the client or customer to whom the recommendation is made any

financial benefits or fees, other than real estate referral fees, the REALTOR® or REALTORS® firm may receive as a direct result of such recommendation.

Article 7

In a transaction, REALTORS® shall not accept compensation from more than one party, even if permitted by law, without disclosure to all parties and the informed consent of the REALTORS® client or clients.

Article 8

REALTORS® shall keep in a special account in an appropriate financial institution, separated from their own funds, monies coming into their possession in trust for other persons, such as escrows, trust funds, clients' monies, and other like items.

Article 9

REALTORS®, for the protection of all parties, shall assure whenever possible that agreements shall be in writing, and shall be in clear and understandable language expressing the specific terms, conditions, obligations and commitments of the parties. A copy of each agreement shall be furnished to each party upon their signing or initialing.

Article 10

REALTORS® shall not deny equal professional services to any person for reasons of race, color, religion, sex, handicap, familial status, or national origin. REALTORS® shall not be parties to any plan or agreement to discriminate against a person or persons on the basis of race, color, religion, sex, handicap, familial status, or national origin.

Article 11

The services which REALTORS® provide to their clients and customers shall conform to the standards of practice and competence which are reasonably expected in the specific real estate disciplines in which they engage; specifically, residential real estate brokerage, real property management, commercial and industrial real estate brokerage, real estate appraisal, real estate counseling, real estate syndication, real estate auction, and international real estate.

REALTORS® shall not undertake to provide specialized professional services concerning a type of property or service that is outside their field of competence unless they engage the assistance of one who is competent on such types of property or service, or unless the facts are fully disclosed to the client. Any persons engaged to provide such assistance shall be so identified to the client and their contribution to the assignment should be set forth.

Article 12

REALTORS® shall be careful at all times to present a true picture in their advertising and representations to the public. REALTORS® shall also ensure that their professional status (e.g., broker, appraiser, property manager, etc.) or status as REALTORS® is clearly identifiable in any such advertising.

Article 13

REALTORS® shall not engage in activities that constitute the unauthorized practice of law and shall recommend that legal counsel be obtained when the interest of any party to the transaction requires it.

Article 14

If charged with unethical practice or asked to present evidence or to cooperate in any other way, in any professional standards proceeding or investigation, REALTORS® shall place all pertinent facts before the proper tribunals of the Member Board or affiliated institute, society, or council in which membership is held and shall take no action to disrupt or obstruct such processes.

Article 15

REALTORS® shall not knowingly or recklessly make false or misleading statements about competitors, their businesses, or their business practices.

Article 16

REALTORS® shall not engage in any practice or take any action inconsistent with the agency or other exclusive relationship recognized by law that other REALTORS® have with clients. (Amended 1/98)

Article 17

In the event of contractual disputes or specific non-contractual disputes as defined in Standard of Practice 17-4 between REALTORS® associated with different firms, arising out of their relationship as REALTORS®, the REALTORS® shall submit the dispute to arbitration in accordance with the regulations of their Board or Boards rather than litigate the matter.

In the event clients of REALTORS® wish to arbitrate contractual disputes arising out of real estate transactions, REALTORS® shall arbitrate those disputes in accordance with the regulations of their Board, provided the clients agree to be bound by the decision.

California Business and Professions Code, Grounds for Revocation or Suspension:

The commissioner may, upon his own motion, and shall, upon the verified complaint in writing of any person, investigate the actions of any person engaged in the business or acting in the capacity of a real estate licensee within this state, and he may temporarily suspend or permanently revoke a real estate license at any time where the licensee, while a real estate licensee, in performing or attempting to perform any of the acts within the scope of this chapter has been guilty of any of the following:

Making any substantial misrepresentation.

Making any false promises of a character likely to influence, persuade or induce.

A continued and flagrant course of misrepresentation or making of false promises through real estate agents or salesmen.

Acting for more than one party in a transaction without the knowledge or consent of all parties thereto.

Commingling with his own money or property the money or other property of others which is received and held by him.

Claiming, demanding, or receiving a fee, compensation or commission under any exclusive agreement authorizing or employing a licensee to perform any acts set forth in Section 10131 for compensation or commission where such agreement does not contain a definite, specified date of final and complete termination.

The claiming or taking by a licensee of any secret or undisclosed amount of compensation, commission or profit or the failure of a licensee to reveal to the employer of such licensee the full amount of such licensee's compensation, commission or profit under any agreement authorizing or employing such licensee to do any acts for which a license is required under this chapter for compensation or commission prior to or coincident with the signing of an agreement evidencing the meeting of the minds of the contracting parties, regardless of the form of such agreement, whether evidenced by documents in an escrow or by any other or different procedure.

The use by a licensee of any provision allowing the licensee an option to purchase in an agreement authorizing or employing such licensee to sell, buy, or exchange real estate or a business opportunity for compensation or commission, except when such licensee prior to or coincident with election to exercise such option to purchase reveals in writing to the employer the full amount of licensee's profit and obtains the written consent of the employer approving the amount of such profit.

Any other conduct, whether of the same or a different character than specified in this section, which constitutes fraud or dishonest dealing.

Obtaining the signature of a prospective purchaser to an agreement which provides that such prospective purchaser shall either transact the purchasing, leasing, renting or exchanging of a business opportunity property through the broker obtaining such signature, or pay a compensation to such broker if such property is purchased, leased, rented or exchanged without the broker first having obtained the written authorization of the owner of the property concerned to offer such property for sale, lease, exchange or rent.

REAL ESTATE TRANSFER DISCLOSURE STATEMENT VIOLATIONS
10176.5. *(there are no sections 10176.2, 10176.3 or 10176.4)*

The commissioner may, upon his or her own motion, and shall upon receiving a verified complaint in writing from any person, investigate an alleged violation of Article 1.5 (commencing with Section 1102) of Chapter 2 of Title 4 of Part 4 of Division 2 of the Civil Code by any real estate licensee within this state. The commissioner may suspend or revoke a licensee's license if the licensee acting under the license has willfully or repeatedly violated any of the provisions of Article 1.5 (commencing with Section 1102) of Chapter 2 of Title 4 of Part 4 of Division 2 of the Civil Code.
(b) Notwithstanding any other provision of Article 1.5 (commencing with Section 1102) of Chapter 2 of Title 4 of Part 4 of Division 2 of the Civil Code, and in lieu of any other civil remedy, subdivision (a) of this section is the only remedy available for violations of Section 1102.6b of the Civil Code by any real estate licensee within this state.

FURTHER GROUNDS FOR DISCIPLINARY ACTION 10177

The commissioner may suspend or revoke the license of any real estate licensee, or may deny the issuance of a license to an applicant, who has done, or may suspend or revoke the license of, or deny the issuance of a license to, a corporate applicant if an officer, director, or person owning or controlling 10 percent or more of the corporation's stock has done, any of the following:

Procured, or attempted to procure, a real estate license or license renewal, for himself or herself or any salesperson, by fraud, misrepresentation or deceit, or by making any material misstatement of fact in an application for a real estate license, license renewal or reinstatement.

Entered a plea of guilty or nolo contendere to, or been found guilty of, or been convicted of, a felony or a crime involving moral turpitude, and the time for appeal has elapsed or the judgment of conviction has been affirmed on appeal, irrespective of an order granting probation following that conviction, suspending the imposition of sentence, or of a subsequent order under Section 1203.4 of the Penal Code allowing that licensee to withdraw his or her plea of guilty and to enter a plea of not guilty, or dismissing the accusation or information.

Knowingly authorized, directed, connived at, or aided in, the publication, advertisement, distribution, or circulation of any material false statement or representation concerning his or her business, or any business opportunity or any land or subdivision (as defined in Chapter 1 (commencing with Section 11000) of Part 2) offered for sale.

Willfully disregarded or violated the Real Estate Law (Part 1 (commencing with Section 10000)) or Chapter 1 (commencing with Section 11000) of Part 2 or the rules and regulations of the commissioner for the administration and enforcement of the Real Estate Law and Chapter 1 (commencing with Section 11000) of Part 2.

Willfully used the term "realtor" or any trade name or insignia of membership in any real estate organization of which the licensee is not a member.

Acted or conducted himself or herself in a manner which would have warranted the denial of his or her application for a real estate license, or has either had a license denied or a license issued by another agency of this state, another state, or the federal government, revoked or suspended for acts which if done by a real estate licensee would be grounds for the suspension or revocation of a California real estate license, if the action of denial, revocation, or suspension by the other agency or entity was taken only after giving the licensee or applicant fair notice of the charges, an opportunity for a hearing, and other due process protections comparable to the Administrative Procedure Act (Chapter 3.5 (commencing with Section 11340), Chapter 4 (commencing with Section 11370), and Chapter 5 (commencing with Section 11500) of Part 1 of Division 3 of Title 2 of the Government Code), and only upon an express finding of a violation of law by the agency or entity.

Demonstrated negligence or incompetence in performing any act for which he or she is required to hold a license.

As a broker licensee, failed to exercise reasonable supervision over the activities of his or her salespersons, or, as the officer designated by a corporate broker licensee, failed to exercise reasonable supervision and control of the activities of the corporation for which a real estate license is required.

Has used his or her employment by a governmental agency in a capacity giving access to records, other than public records, in such manner as to violate the confidential nature of the records.

Engaged in any other conduct, whether of the same or a different character than specified in this section, which constitutes fraud or dishonest dealing.

Violated any of the terms, conditions, restrictions, and limitations contained in any order granting a restricted license.

Solicited or induced the sale, lease, or the listing for sale or lease, of residential property on the ground, wholly or in part, of loss of value, increase in crime, or decline of the quality of the schools, due to the present or prospective entry into the neighborhood of a person or persons of another race, color, religion, ancestry, or national origin.

Violated the Franchise Investment Law (Division 5 (commencing with Section 31000) of Title 4 of the Corporations Code) or regulations of the Commissioner of Corporations pertaining thereto.

Violated the Corporations Code or the regulations of the Commissioner of Corporations relating to securities as specified in Section 25206 of the Corporations Code.

Failed to disclose to the buyer of real property in a transaction in which the licensee is an agent for the buyer, the nature and extent of a licensee's direct or indirect ownership interest in that real property. The direct or indirect ownership in the property by a person related to the licensee by blood or marriage, by an entity in which the licensee has an ownership interest, or by any other person with whom the licensee occupies a special relationship shall be disclosed to the buyer.

The commissioner may not deny or suspend the license of a corporate real estate broker if the offending officer, director, or stockholder has been completely disassociated from any affiliation or ownership in the corporation.

SUSPENSION WITHOUT HEARING FOR FRAUD, ETC., IN OBTAINING A LICENSE 10177.1

The commissioner may, without a hearing, suspend the license of any person who procured the issuance of the license to himself by fraud, misrepresentation, deceit, or by the making of any material misstatement of fact in his application for such license.

The power of the commissioner under this section to order a suspension of a license shall expire 90 days after the date of issuance of said license and the suspension itself shall remain in effect only until the effective date of a decision of the commissioner after a hearing conducted pursuant to Section 10100 and the provisions of this section.

A statement of issues as defined in Section 11504 of the Government Code shall be filed and served upon the respondent with the order of suspension. Service by certified or registered mail directed to the respondent's current address of record on file with the commissioner shall be effective service.

The respondent shall have 30 days after service of the order of suspension and statement of issues in which to file with the commissioner a written request for hearing on the statement of issues filed against him. The commissioner shall hold a hearing within 30 days after receipt of the request therefore unless the respondent shall request or agree to a continuance thereof. If a hearing is not commenced within 30 days after receipt of the request for hearing or on the date to which continued with the agreement of respondent, or if the decision of the commissioner is not rendered within 30 days after completion of the hearing, the order of suspension shall be vacated and set aside.

A hearing conducted under this section shall in all respects, except as otherwise expressly provided herein, conform to the substantive and procedural provisions of Chapter 5 (commencing with Section 11500) of Part 1 of Division 3 of Title 2 of the Government Code applicable to a hearing on a statement of issues.

GROUNDS FOR DISCIPLINARY ACTION – MOBILE HOME SALES VIOLATIONS 10177.2

The commissioner may, upon his or her own motion, and shall, upon the verified complaint in writing of any person, investigate the actions of any licensee, and he or she may suspend or revoke a real estate license at any time where the licensee in performing or attempting to perform any of the acts within the scope of Section 10131.6 has been guilty of any of the following acts:

(a) Has used a false or fictitious name, knowingly made any false statement, or knowingly concealed any material fact, in any application for the registration of a mobile home, or otherwise committed a fraud in that application.
(b) Failed to provide for the delivery of a properly endorsed certificate of ownership or certificate of title of a mobile home from the seller to the buyer thereof.
(c) Has knowingly participated in the purchase, sale, or other acquisition or disposal of a stolen mobile home.
(d) Has submitted a check, draft, or money order to the Department of Housing and Community Development for any obligation or fee due the state and it is thereafter dishonored or refused payment upon presentation.

REFERRAL OF CUSTOMERS FOR COMPENSATION 10177.4 (There is no section 10177.3)

Notwithstanding any other provision of law, the commissioner may, after hearing in accordance with this part relating to hearings, suspend or revoke the license of a real estate licensee who claims, demands, or receives a commission, fee, or other consideration, as compensation or inducement, for referral of customers to any escrow agent, structural pest control firm, home protection company, title insurer, controlled escrow company, or underwritten title company. A licensee may not be disciplined under any provision of this part for reporting to the commissioner violations of this section by another licensee, unless the licensee making the report had guilty knowledge of, or committed or participated in, the violation of this section.

(b) The term "other consideration" as used in this section does not include any of the following: Bona fide payments for goods or facilities actually furnished by a licensee or for services actually performed by a licensee, provided these payments are reasonably related to the value of the goods, facilities, or services furnished;

Furnishing of documents, services, information, advertising, educational materials, or items of a like nature that are customary in the real estate business and that relate to the product or services of the furnisher and that are available on a similar and essentially equal basis to all customers or the agents of the customers of the furnisher.

Moderate expenses for food, meals, beverages, and similar items furnished to individual licensees or groups or associations of licensees within a context of customary business, educational, or promotional practices pertaining to the business of the furnisher.

Items of a character and magnitude similar to those in paragraphs (2) and (3) that are promotional of the furnisher's business customary in the real estate business, and available on a similar and essentially equal basis to all customers, or the agents of the customers, of the furnisher.

Nothing in this section shall relieve any licensee of the obligation of disclosure otherwise required by this part.

FRAUD IN A CIVIL ACTION 10177.5

When a final judgment is obtained in a civil action against any real estate licensee upon grounds of fraud, misrepresentation, or deceit with reference to any transaction for which a license is required under this division, the commissioner may, after hearing in accordance with the provisions of this part relating to hearings, suspend or revoke the license of such real estate licensee.

The California Bureau of Real Estate has an outstanding information source on their website at www.bre.ca.gov. It is called the "Broker Compliance Evaluation Manual." This manual and the companion Form RE540 compliance check list. Some important exceptions follow:

Does the broker have a written broker-salesperson agreement with each of his/her salespersons?
Each broker must have a written agreement with each of his/her salespersons, whether licensed as a salesperson or as a broker under a broker-salesperson arrangement. The agreement shall be dated and signed by the parties and shall cover material aspects of the relationship between the parties, including supervision of licensed activities, duties and compensation.

Is the broker properly supervising?
A broker shall exercise reasonable supervision over the activities of his or her salespersons. Reasonable supervision includes, as appropriate, the establishment of policies, rules, procedures and systems to review, oversee, inspect and manage.
1. Transactions requiring a real estate license.
2. Documents which may have a material effect upon the rights or obligations of a party to the transaction.
3. Filing, storage and maintenance or such documents.
4. The handling of trust funds.
5. Advertising of any service for which a license is required.
6. Familiarizing salespersons with the requirements of federal and state laws relating to the prohibition of discrimination.
7. Regular and consistent reports of licensed activities of salespersons.

The form and extent of such policies, rules, procedures and systems shall take into consideration the number of salespersons employed and the number and location of branch offices.

A broker shall establish a system for monitoring compliance with such policies, rules, procedures and systems. A broker may use the services of brokers and salespersons to assist in administering the provisions of this section so long as the broker does not relinquish overall responsibility for supervision of the acts of salespersons licensed to the broker.

Does the broker retain copies of all documents?
A licensed broker must retain for 3 years copies of all listings, deposit receipts, canceled checks, trust account records, and other documents executed by him or her or obtained by

him or her in connection with any transaction for which a broker's license is required. The retention period shall run from the date of the closing of the transaction or from the date of the listing if the transaction is not consummated. After reasonable notice, the books, accounts and records shall be made available for audit, examination, inspection and copying by a Bureau representative during regular business hours.

Do the documents disclose the negotiability of commissions?

Any printed or form agreement which initially establishes, or is intended to establish, or alters the terms of any agreement which previously established a right to compensation to be paid to a licensee for the sale of residential real property containing not more than four residential units, or for the sale of a mobile home, shall contain the following statement in not less than 10-point boldface type immediately preceding any provision of such agreement relating to compensation of the licensee:

Notice: The amount of rate of real estate commissions is not fixed by law. They are set by each broker individually and may be negotiable between the seller and broker.

As used above "alters the terms of any agreement which previously established a right to compensation" means an increase in the rate of compensation, or the amount of compensation if initially established as a flat fee, from the agreement which previously established a right to compensation.

The broker must make certain that his/her agreements and forms are not preprinted with any amount of rate of compensation.

Does the broker have a license for each business location?

A broker is authorized to conduct business only at the address listed on his/her license. If the broker maintains more than one place of business within the State, he/she shall apply for and procure an additional license for each branch office so maintained. The application for a branch office license must state the name of the person and the location of the place or places of business for which the license is desired.

COMPLIANCE CHECKLIST

This checklist is designed to assist you in conducting a self-evaluation of your residential real estate business activities. The checklist covers the most common violations found during BRE broker office surveys. Copies of the cited code sections are attached for your reference. You should refer to your *Real Estate Law* book for the complete set of laws and regulations administered by the Bureau of Real Estate which affect your licensed real estate operation.

Before you begin answering the questions on this checklist, you should review the Bureau's licensing records. The following information is available on BRE's Web site **www.bre.ca.gov** or may be requested from any District Office: current main address, branch office locations, authorized fictitious business names, corporate affiliations, and list of salespersons sponsored under your broker's license.

Licensing Compliance

1. Do you have a branch office license for each location from which you conduct business? (B&P 10163)
   You may only operate your business from the main office address printed on your license certificate unless you have a branch office license for other locations.

2. Are you operating with an unlawful fictitious business name? (Reg. 2731)
   You may only use a fictitious business name if it is approved by BRE. The fictitious business name must appear on the face of a license in your possession as issued by the Bureau.

3. Are you employing salespersons without BRE notification? (Reg. 2752) .
   A broker has five days to notify BRE whenever a salesperson is hired or terminated.

4. Are you employing expired/unlicensed salespersons? (B&P 10137) .
   A broker may not pay an expired licensee or an unlicensed person for an act requiring a license. (B&P 10131) You should keep current original licenses for all salespersons licensed to you (B&P 10160) and consider setting up a system to monitor expiration dates.

5. Are you employing salespersons without contracts? (Reg. 2726) .
   Written employment agreements are required for each salesperson or broker working for you as sales agents. Both you and the sales agent should sign, date and retain a copy of this agreement for three years from the date employment is terminated.

Trust Account Compliance

1. Is a record maintained of funds not placed in trust account? (Reg. 2831)
   Uncashed checks made out to escrow companies, appraisers, sellers, etc. are considered trust funds and you must keep records of all trust funds not placed in your trust account as specified in the Regulations.

2. Is a record maintained of funds deposited in trust account? (Reg. 2831)
   A general trust fund control record must be maintained of all trust funds placed in your trust account. These records must contain the information specified in this Regulation.

3. Are separate records maintained? (Reg. 2831.1)
   In addition to the general trust fund control records required by Regulation 2831, you must keep separate trust account records for each beneficiary or transaction. By adding the total of all these separate records, your total should equal the balance of your general trust fund control record. A separate record should be maintained for any broker funds (not to exceed $200) required to service the account.

4. Are trust funds being held too long? (Reg. 2832)
   Regulations normally require that you place funds accepted on behalf of another person into the hands of that person, into a neutral escrow depository or into your trust account no later than three business days following the receipt of the funds.

5. Are there unexplained overages in the trust account? (Reg. 2831.1)
   You must keep a separate record of these trust account overages and the funds must remain in a trust account and be reconciled on a monthly basis.

6. Is the trust account a designated trust account in your name as trustee? (Reg. 2832)
A trust account may be in the name of your fictitious business name as trustee if you are the holder of a license bearing the fictitious name.

7. Is the trust account interest bearing? (B&P 10145)
You may not keep interest earned on trust funds and must have written authorization from the owner of the trust funds to set up an interest bearing trust account. There must be a separate interest bearing account set up for each beneficiary.

8. Unlawful signatory to trust account? (Reg. 2834)
In order for someone to sign on your trust account, they must be a salesperson licensed to you, a broker working under contract with you or an unlicensed person who is bonded to the maximum amount of trust funds he/she has access to.

9. Do you place general or payroll account funds in an account with trust funds? (B&P 10176(e))
This is commingling and must be avoided.

10. Do you ever get NSF trust account checks?
This is an obvious red flag that there is trouble with the trust account.

11. Do you perform monthly reconciliation of trust account records? (Reg. 2831.2)
Once a month, you must be sure that the total of all separate beneficiary records balances with both your general trust account control records and with your trust account bank statement.

Supervision

1. Do you exercise reasonable supervision over the activities of your salespersons? (Reg. 2725)
Reasonable supervision includes the establishment of polices and procedures to (1) review and manage all transactions requiring a license, (2) documents which may have a material effect on the parties, (3) filing and maintaining these documents, (4) handling of trust funds, (5) advertising, (6) familiarizing salespersons with laws relating to prohibition of discrimination, and (7) regular reports of activities of salespersons.

2. Can you describe your system to monitor compliance with established policies and procedures? (Reg. 2725)
A broker may use the services of brokers and salespersons to assist in supervision, as long as the broker does not relinquish overall responsibility.

Required Disclosures

1. Do you keep receipts for delivery of pest control documents? (Reg. 2905)
Records should be kept as evidence that you delivered pest control inspection reports, certifications, completion notices or otherwise informed the buyer of his/her rights under Civil Code Section 1099.

2. Are definite termination dates included in exclusive listings? (B&P 10176(f))
You cannot claim, demand or receive a commission if your exclusive listing does not contain a definite termination date.

3. Are negotiability of commission disclosures provided? (B&P 10147.5)
   Any agreement that establishes your right to compensation for licensed acts must contain a notice that commission rates are negotiable and not established by law.

4. Are Real Estate Transfer Disclosure Statements provided? (B&P 10176.5)
   Willful or repeated failure to provide buyers with a Real Estate Transfer Disclosure Statement is a violation of law.

Record Keeping

1. Do you keep all listings, deposit receipts, canceled checks, trust account records, employment agreements, and other material documents obtained or executed in connection with your real estate transactions for three years?
   These records are to be retained for three years and made available to the Commissioner for inspection and copying upon request.

ETHICS PRACTICE QUESTIONS:

True or False?

1. Agents are instructed to know Sections 10176 and 10177 in the California Business and Professional Code. T

2. Knowingly making a substantial misrepresentation of the likely value of real property is recommended. F

3. "Bona Fide" translates as "Good Faith". T

4. A commission set by their association is proper. F

5. A firm can set a commission and not negotiate. T

6. Post-dated checks are never acceptable. F

7. Seller financing has many advantages. T

8. A request for notice of default is never recommended.

9. Making an addition to the terms of an instrument previously without their knowledge could be a license losing move. T

10. You do not have to be concerned about LTV when offering a note for sale. F

11. Lawsuits concerning square footage have been around forever. T

12. Easton vs. Strassburger held that a minor earth slide three years before the purchase was not a material fact. F

13. Confidential information doesn't have to be relayed to the other party even if you are asked a specific question. T

14. Frivolous offers must always be presented. F

15. Explaining any and all contingencies is a good practice. T

16. A sale to your brother-in-law does not quality as a special relationship. F

17. You can recommend a company you own to a client if you tell the client. T

18. Loan brokers do not have to follow BRE directives. F

19. An outstanding Code of Ethics to follow was developed by the National Association of Realtors. T

20. Realtors do not urge exclusive representation of clients. F

21. The obligation to cooperate does not include the obligation to share commission.

22. Realtors can discriminate because of a person's religion. F

23. Realtors shall not engage in activities that constitute the unauthorized practice of law. T

24. Realtors cannot use arbitration to settle disputes at any time. F

25. The claiming or taking by a licensee of any secret or undisclosed amount of compensation is grounds for revocation. T

26. The Commissioner will investigate verbal complaints made by a consumer. F

27. The benchmark for percentage of ownership of a company for suspension of an officer is 10%. F

28. A salesperson must exercise reasonable supervision over their associates. T

29. The power of the commissioner to order a suspension of a license shall expire 90 days after the date of issuance. F

30. Mobile sale violations are not covered by the Code of Ethics. F

31. Fraud in a civil action could lose someone their real estate license. T

32. Brokers need a written agreement only with broker associates. F

33. Brokers shall exercise supervision over trust funds. T

34. Brokers must retain copies of all listings for 10 years. F 3 years

35. Listing Agreements need a notice of commission negotiability in 10 pt. type. T

36. Brokers need only one main office license. F

37. A broker has five days to notify BRE if a salesperson is hired. T

38. A broker can hold trust funds only 24 hours. F

39. Trust funds must be reconciled on a monthly basis if there is activity in the account. T

40. Exclusive listings can have an indefinite expiration date. F

Practice Questions designed to prepare you to pass the final exams are available. New BRE Regulations do not allow us to give the answers to the quizzes in the book so the questions and answers are presented online. This makes the test taking very easy as you get the answers immediately.

To access the practice quizzes please visit http://www.DuaneGomer.com/after . Check on the proper link for the course you desire.

NOTE: Do not use Google, Yahoo, Bing etc. They are Search Engines. You must put the above URL link in your address bar or you won't get there.

You may request the questions by email to info@DuaneGomer.com, fax at 949-455-9931, or phone 800-439-4909. You will receive only the practice questions. You may FAX back your answers to Duane Gomer, Inc., at (949) 455-9931 and we will FAX your results to you within 24 business hours. Our recommendation is find a computer even if it's a friend or relatives it makes everything so easy under the new BRE rules.

TRUST FUND HANDLING

GOALS OF THIS COURSE

This Trust Fund Handling Course will provide the student with knowledge of the legal requirements for receiving and handling trust funds in real estate transactions, as set forth in the Real Estate Law and the Regulation of the Real Estate Commissioner. This course will describe the requisites for maintaining a trust fund account. Further, this course will explain and illustrate trust fund record keeping requirements. Trust Fund Courses may be individually tailored for specific areas of real estate activity, but this course is approved for all licensees. In the area of mortgage loan brokerage, there are additional legal and regulatory requirements for trust fund handling, which should be covered in a course that is specific to that area.

TRUST FUNDS VS. NON-TRUST FUNDS

- Trust funds are money or other things of value that are received and held for others in the performance of real estate licensed acts.
- Examples of trust fund items - cash, purchase deposit check (made payable to broker or escrow or title company), personal note, pink slip to a car, bicycle, etc.
- Examples of non-trust fund items - commission, operating funds, broker owned rental income, etc. These funds are not to be commingled with trust fund monies.
- Non-trust funds are not subject to these laws, but BRE does have the jurisdiction to audit a broker's private accounts.

TRUST FUND HANDLING REQUIREMENTS

- You have a fiduciary responsibility when handling any owner's funds.
- Can only be used for authorized purposes and according to existing laws.
- Accurate, complete and up-to-date accounting of funds must be maintained.
- Funds received must be placed with the owners, neutral escrow or a proper trust fund not later than the third business day following receipt. Trust funds must be deposited into a neutral escrow depository, into the hands of the principal or into the broker's trust fund account not later than three business days following their receipt by the broker or the broker's salesperson. However, the regulation still provides that if a check received from a buyer is held uncashed by the broker until acceptance, it must be deposited into escrow or the trust fund account, or given to the principal, no later than the 3rd business day following acceptance, unless there is written authorization from a seller to continue to hold it.

- Checks may be held uncashed until acceptance if:
  1. The check is not negotiable by its terms.
  2. Offeror has given written instructions checks shall not be deposited or cashed until acceptance.
  3. Offeree is informed that the check is being so held before or at the time of presentation of the offer for acceptance.

- After acceptance, brokers can hold these checks only with the offeror's written authorization.
- Trust Funds-Regulation 2831 allows trust fund records to be maintained on computers. Brokers need not keep trust fund records for checks which are written by a principal and given to the broker and made payable to third parties for provision of services when the total amount of such checks for any transaction from that principal does not exceed $1,000. The broker must keep a receipt given for such checks for at least three years.
- According to Business and Professions Code Section 10145, a real estate salesperson who accepts trust funds on behalf of the broker under whom he or she is licensed must immediately deliver the funds to the broker or, if directed by the broker, place the funds into the hands of the broker's principal or into a neutral escrow depository, or deposit the funds into the broker's trust fund bank account.
- A *neutral escrow depository*, as used in Business and Professions Code Section 10145, means an escrow business conducted by a person licensed under Division 6 (commencing with Section 17000) of the Financial Code or by any person described in subdivisions (a) and (c) of Section 17006.

IDENTIFYING THE OWNERS OF TRUST FUNDS

- All funds must be identified as to who owns them and can be disposed of only with their authorization.
- Owners of funds may or may not be the original giver.
- Ownership of funds may change after certain events in a transaction.
- For example, acceptance of an offer to lease could change fund ownership from the prospective leasee to the landlord.
- Prior to offer acceptance, an offeror may give instruction on handling of the funds and the funds are maintained for their benefit until acceptance.
- After acceptance of the offer, however, the funds shall be handled according to instructions from the offeror and the offeree as follows:
  1. An offeror's check held uncashed by the broker before acceptance of the offer may continue to be held uncashed after the acceptance of the offer, only upon written authorization from the offeree.
  2. The offeror's check may be given to the offeree only if the offeror and offeree expressly so provide in writing {Commissioner's Regulation 2832 (d)}.
  3. All or part of an offeror purchase money deposit in a real estate sales transaction shall not be refunded by an agent or subagent of the seller without the ***express written permission*** of the offeree to make the refund.

ADVANCE FEE TRUST ACCOUNTS

RECORD KEEPING REQUIREMENT

- Definition - Business and Professions Code 10026. The term "advance fee" as used in this part is a fee claimed, demanded, charged, received, collected or contracted for a listing, advertisement or offer to sell or lease property, other than in a newspaper of general circulation, issued primarily for the purpose of promoting the sale or lease of business opportunities or real estate or for referral to real estate brokers or salesmen, or soliciting borrowers or lenders for, or to negotiate loans on, business opportunities or real estate.
- Any real estate broker who contracts for or collects advance fees from a principal must deposit the funds into a trust account. Advance fees are trust funds and not the broker's funds. When advance fees are not handled by the brokers in accordance with Real Estate Law, it shall be presumed that the broker has violated Penal Code Sections 506 and 506a, and strict penalties and fines may be levied against the broker.
- *Exception:* The Bureau does not treat as advance fees, funds collected in advance for appraisal and credit reports as long as the broker collects as near as possible the exact amount(s) necessary, and refunds any excess as soon as it is identified to the principal. However, even though these funds are not treated as advance fees, they are still principals' funds and, therefore, like advance fees they must be deposited into a trust account.

DISBURSEMENT DISCLOSURE REQUIREMENTS

- Agents must be familiar with all Disclosure Requirements for Advance Fees.
- Business and Professions Code includes this statement concerning Advance Fees: Licensees when performing acts within the meaning of subdivision (d) or (e) of Section 10131 of the Business and Professions Code shall not violate any of the applicable provisions of subdivision (a), or act in a manner which would subject the licensee to adverse action, penalty or discipline under Sections 10176 and 10177 of the Business and Professions Code including, but not limited to, the following acts and omissions: When acting as a licensee in a transaction for the purpose of obtaining a loan, and in receipt of an "advance fee" from the borrower for this purpose, the failure to account to the borrower for the disposition of the "advance fee."

APPROVAL OF ADVANCE FEE AGREEMENT

- Advance fees may, however, only be collected pursuant to an advance fee agreement approved by the Bureau of Real Estate prior to the use of the agreement and the collection of any such fees. All advertising materials used in conjunction with advance fees must also be submitted to the Bureau for prior approval before use. (See Business and Professions Code Section 10085.)

TRUST FUND BANK ACCOUNTS

GENERAL REQUIREMENTS (B & P Code 10145 and Commissioner's Regulation 2830.1) – A copy of this and other regulations are included at the back of this material.

- A Trust Fund must be:
  1. Designated as a trust account in the name of the broker as trustee.
  2. Maintained with a bank or recognized depository located in California; and
  3. Not an interest-bearing account for which prior written notice can by law or regulation be required by the financial institution as a condition to withdraw the funds, except as noted in the following discussion of "Interest Bearing Accounts."

TRUST ACCOUNT WITHDRAWAL

- Withdrawals may be made by signature of one or more of the following:
  1. The broker in whose name the account is maintained; or
  2. The designated broker-officer if the account is in the name of a corporate broker; or
  3. If specifically authorized in writing by the broker, a salesperson licensed to the broker; or
  4. If specifically authorized in writing by the broker, an unlicensed employee of the broker covered by a fidelity bond at least equal to the maximum amount of the trust fund to which the employee has access at any time.

Any arrangement under which a person named in items 3 or 4 is authorized to make withdrawals from a broker's trust fund account does not relieve an individual broker or the broker-officer of a corporate broker licensee from responsibility or liability as provided by law in handling trust funds in the broker's custody. The fact of an employee's irresponsibility or negligence also does not relieve the broker of compliance with the law.

Brokers or broker-officers of corporations are responsible and liable for any irresponsibility or negligence of person named in 3 and 4 above.

INTEREST BEARING ACCOUNTS

- Accounts are normally not interest bearing.
- By authorization from proper owners or principal brokers may use interest-bearing accounts if all of the following requirements are met:
  1. The account is in the name of the broker as trustee for a specified beneficiary or specified principal of a transaction or a series of transactions;
  2. All of the funds in the account are covered by insurance provided by an agency of the federal government;
  3. The funds in the account are kept separate, distinct, and apart from funds belonging to the broker or to any other person for whom the broker holds funds in trust; and
  4. The broker discloses the following information to the person from whom the trust funds are received and to any beneficiary whose identity is known to the broker at the time of establishing the account:
     - The nature of the account;
     - How the interest will be calculated and paid under various circumstances;
     - Whether service charges will be paid to the depository and by whom; and

- Possible notice requirements or penalties for withdrawal of funds from the account.

5. No interest earned on funds in the account shall inure directly or indirectly to the benefit of the broker or to any person licensed to the broker. Even authorization by the funds' owners *shall not* legally permit the broker to collect the earned interest on trust funds.

6. In an executory sale, lease, or loan transaction in which the broker accepts funds in trust to be applied to the purchase, lease, or loan, the parties to the contract shall have specified in the contract or by collateral written agreement the person to whom interest earned on the funds is to be paid or credited.

- The only other situation where a real estate broker is allowed to deposit trust funds into an interest bearing account is when the broker is acting as an agent for a financial institution that is the beneficiary of a loan. In this case the broker may, pursuant to Commissioner's Regulation 2830.1, deposit and maintain funds received from or for the account of an obligor (or borrower) into an interest bearing trust account in a bank or savings and loan association in order to pay interest on an impound account to the obligor in accordance with Section 2954.8 of the Civil Code, as long as the following requirements are met:

1. The funds received from or for the account of the obligor are for the future payment of property taxes, assessments or insurance relating only to a property containing a one-to-four-family residence;

2. The account is in the name of the broker as trustee;

3. All of the funds in the account are covered by insurance provided by an agency of the federal government;

4. All of the funds in the account are funds held in trust by the broker for others;

5. The broker discloses to the obligor how interest will be calculated and paid; and

6. No interest earned on the trust funds shall inure directly or indirectly to the benefit of the broker or to any person licensed to the broker.

WHY A TRUST ACCOUNT?

- Better control of funds.
- Trust funds are not "frozen" pending litigation against a broker or during probate of broker's death.
- Each client with funds deposited in a trust account maintained with a federally insured bank is insured by the FDIC up to $100,000, as opposed to just $100,000 for the entire account, as long as the regulatory requirements are met.

COMMINGLING PROHIBITED

- Funds belonging to the licensee may not be commingled with trust funds. Commingling is strictly prohibited by the Real Estate Law. It is grounds for the revocation or suspension of a real estate license pursuant to Business and Professions Code Section 10176 (e).
- Commingling occurs when:
1. Personal or company funds are deposited into the trust fund bank account. This is a violation of the law even if separate records are kept.

2. Trust funds are deposited into the licensee's general or personal bank account rather than into the trust fund account. In this case the violation is not only commingling, but also handling trust funds contrary to Business and Professions Code Section 10145. It is also grounds for suspension or revocation of a license under Business and Professions Code Section 10177 (d).
3. Commissions, fees or other income earned by the broker and collectible from the trust account are left in the trust account for more than 25 days from the date they were earned.

- Other examples of commingling:
  1. Depositing monies from broker-owned properties into trust account.
  2. Paying broker's mortgage payment from account even if broker plans to reimburse and does reimburse.
  3. Conducting personal business with trust funds.

- Funds may be commingled:
  1. Up to $200 can be kept in account for check charges, etc. (Broker could have their bank debit their own account for these charges.)
  2. Commissions, etc. earned by broker may remain there for up to 25 days.

- An example of commingling would be property management fees. It is difficult to remove management fees every time a rent deposit is made, but removals must be done in a timely fashion.
- Brokers can't pay personal fees from this income. A check must be written to the broker with documentation for the income earned from this account.

TRUST FUND LIABILITY

- Liability increases and decreases with the different transactions.
- "Positive balance" - Is the total due to trust fund beneficiaries.
- "Trust fund shortage" - Account balance is less than "Positive Balance."
- "Trust fund overage" - Account balance is greater than "Positive Balance." After three years of an overage, the money is sent to the California Secretary of State.
- Shortages and overages must be investigated immediately and be corrected. These are serious violations and one of the biggest reasons for loss of a broker's license.
- "Conversion" is converting funds to your own use (stealing).
- To stay on the straight and narrow -
  1. Deposit intact and in a timely manner to the trust account all funds that are not forwarded to escrow or to the funds' owner(s) or which are not held uncashed as authorized. A licensee is accountable for all trust funds received whether or not they are deposited. Bureau auditors have seen numerous cases where trust funds received were properly recorded on the books, but were never deposited to the bank.
  2. Maintain adequate supporting papers for any disbursement from the trust account, and accurately record the disbursement both in the Bank Account Record and in the Separate Beneficiary Record. The Broker must be able to account for all disbursements of trust funds.
  3. Disburse funds against a beneficiary's account only when the disbursement will not result in a negative or deficit balance (negative accountability) to the account.

Many trust fund shortages are caused by the broker making disbursements for a beneficiary in excess of funds received from or for account of that beneficiary. The over-disbursements are, in effect, paid out of funds belonging to other beneficiaries with positive balances. A shortage occurs because the balance of trust fund bank account, even if it is a positive balance, is less than the broker's liability to those other beneficiaries.

4. Ensure that a check deposited to the trust fund account has cleared before disbursing funds against that check. This applies, for example, when a broker after depositing an earnest money deposit check for a purchase transaction has to return the funds to the buyer because the offer is rejected by the seller. A trust fund shortage will result if the broker issues the buyer a trust account check and the buyer's deposit check bounces or for some reason fails to clear the bank.

5. Keep accurate, current and complete records of the trust account and the corresponding beneficiary accounts.

6. Reconcile the cash record with the bank statement and with the separate record for each beneficiary or transaction. Monthly if there is activity in the account.

MAINTAINING TRUST ACCOUNT INTEGRITY

- In summary, to maintain the integrity of the trust fund bank account, a broker must ensure that:
  1. His/her personal or general operating funds are not commingled with trust funds;
  2. The balance of the trust fund account is equal to the broker's trust fund liability to all owners of the funds; and
  3. The trust fund records are in an acceptable form and are current complete, and accurate.

ACCOUNTING RECORDS

RECORD KEEPING SYSTEMS

- Three choices of systems:
  1. Columnar records prescribed by CR2831 and 2831.1.
  2. Generally accepted accounting practices.
  3. Regulation 2831 now allows all records to be maintained on computers.

- Systems must show:
  1. All trust fund receipts and disbursements with pertinent details presented in chronological sequence;
  2. The balance of each trust fund account calculated based on recorded transactions;
  3. All receipts and disbursements exclusively affecting each beneficiary's account presented in chronological sequence; and
  4. The balance owing to each beneficiary or for each transaction, such balance calculated based on recorded transactions.

- Records can be:
  1. Manual or computer-produced.
  2. Factors should be business nature, number of clients, volume, reports will determine proper system.

- Columnar Records are:
  1. Columnar Record of All Trust Funds Received and Paid-Out-Trust Fund Bank Account (BRE form RE 4522).
  2. Separate Record for Each Beneficiary or Transaction (BRE form RE 4523).
  3. Record of Trust Funds Received but not Deposited to the Trust Fund.

- The first two records are required when trust funds are received and deposited or supposed to be deposited to the trust fund bank account. The third record is required when trust funds received are not deposited to the bank account, but are forwarded to escrow or to the owner of the funds.
- If the trust fund account involves clients' funds from rental properties managed by the broker, the Separate Record for Each Property Managed. (BRE form RE 4525) may be used in lieu of the Separate Record for Each Beneficiary or Transaction.

RECORDING PROCESS

- Record all Trust Funds Received and Disbursed - #RE 4522
  1. Used to journalize all transactions
  2. Minimum information
     - Date received or paid out and amounts
     - Names of parties
     - Check number and date
     - Daily balance
  3. Transactions are in chronological sequence
     - All transactions affecting the bank account are entered in chronological sequence on this record regardless of payee, payor or beneficiary. If there is more than one trust fund bank account, a separate record must be maintained for each account, pursuant to Commissioner's Regulation 2831

- Separate Record for Each Beneficiary or Transaction
  1. To keep records per each party
  2. Minimum information is same as #RE 4522 above
  3. A separate record must be maintained for each beneficiary or transaction from which the broker received funds that were deposited to the trust fund bank account. If the broker has more than one trust fund account, each account must have its own set of separate beneficiary records so that they can be reconciled with the individual trust fund bank account record required under Commissioner's Regulation 2831

- Record of Trust Funds Received But Not Deposited to the Trust Fund Bank Account
  1. To track funds received and not put in trust account
  2. Regulation 2831 provides that brokers no longer need to keep these detailed trust fund records for trust fund checks they have received during a transaction which are made payable to third party service providers such as escrow, credit or appraisal services, if the total amount of such checks received in that transaction is $1,000 or less. Brokers must still keep for three years copies of receipts given or obtained in connection with such third party checks and must account to the principal or the BRE for the receipt and distribution. These checks are still considered trust funds.

3. It must show the date funds were received, the form of payment (check, note, etc.), amount received, description of property, identity of the person to whom funds were forwarded, and date of disposition.
4. Trust fund receipts are recorded in chronological sequence, while their disposition is recorded in the same line where the corresponding receipt is recorded.
5. Transaction folders usually maintained by a broker for each real estate sales transaction showing the receipt and disposition of undeposited checks are *not* acceptable alternatives to the Record of Trust Funds Received But Not Deposited to the Trust Fund Bank Account.

- Separate Record for Each Property Managed
  1. This record is similar to and serves the same purpose as the Separate Record for Each Beneficiary or Transaction. It does not have to be maintained if the Separate Record is already used for a property owner's account.
  2. The Separate Record for Each Property Managed is useful when the broker wants to show some detailed information about a specific property being managed.

- Non-Columnar records must
  1. Be prescribed by CR 2831 and 2831.1.
  2. In accordance with generally accepted accounting practices.
  3. Include the following records:
     - Detailed journals in chronological sequence
     - Cash ledger
     - Beneficiaries' ledgers for each account
  4. Regulations definitely allow computer records, but it is highly recommended that you receive proper accounting advice before starting any accounts.

- Follow specific procedures
  1. Record daily
  2. Use the same specific source document consistently
  3. Calculate all account balances at time entries are made
  4. Reconcile all accounts monthly
  5. Keep a separate set of records for each account

RECONCILIATION OF RECORDS

PURPOSE

- To keep accurate records for your clients
- Accuracy can be verified by reconciliation
- Reconciliation should be done monthly if there is activity in the account

RECONCILIATION

- "Definition" - Process of comparing two or more sets of records to see if their balances agree
- Verifies accuracy of records
- Two reconciliations must be made each month

- Your account balance with separate beneficiary or transaction records:
  1. Required by BRE
  2. To substantiate that all transactions of the account were placed on the correct individual records
  3. Differences in balance must be located and corrected
  4. Must be done monthly unless there has been no activity
  5. Reconciliation records must be maintained
  6. Records should identify:
     - Account name and number
     - Date of reconciliation
     - Names of principals, beneficiaries and transactions and liability to each
     - Your account balance with the bank statement
       a. Discloses any errors by you or the bank
       b. Adjustments for outstanding checks, deposits in transit, and other transactions that haven't reached bank
       c. Not required by law, but it is an essential part of any good accounting system

- Before reconciling records:
  1. Record all transactions to cut-off date
  2. Use balances from same cut-off date
  3. For the bank account reconciliation, calculate the adjusted bank balance both from the bank statement and from the bank account record. (Trust account audits made by the Bureau of Real Estate have revealed that licensees commonly err by calculating the adjusted bank balance based solely on the bank statement but not on the bank account record. While they may know the correct account balances, they may not realize their records are incomplete or erroneous.)
  4. Keep a record of the two reconciliations performed at the end of each month along with the supporting schedules.
  5. Locate any difference between the three sets of accounting records in a timely manner. A difference can be caused by any of the following: not recording a transaction, recording an incorrect figure, erroneous calculations of entries used to arrive at account balances, missing beneficiary records, and bank errors.

DOCUMENTATION REQUIREMENTS

TRANSACTIONS AND RELATED DOCUMENTS

TRANSACTIONS AND RELATED DOCUMENTS

Type of Transaction	Documents Needed
1. Receiving trust funds in the form of:	
a. Purchase deposits from buyers	☐ Real estate purchase contract and receipt, signed by the buyer
b. Rents and security deposits from tenants	☐ Collection receipts
c. Other receipts	☐ Collection receipts
2. Depositing trust funds	☐ Bank deposit slips
3. Forwarding buyers' check to escrow	☐ Receipt from title company and copy of check
4. Returning buyers' check	☐ Copy of buyers' check signed and dated by buyer signifying he received his check back
5. Disbursing trust funds	☐ Checked issued
	☐ Supporting papers for the checks, such as invoices, escrow statements, billings, receipts, etc.
6. Receiving offers and counter-offers from buyers and sellers	☐ Real estate purchase contract and receipt for deposit, signed by respective parties
7. Collecting management fees from the trust fund bank account	☐ Cancelled checks
8. Reconciling bank account records with separate beneficiary records	☐ Record of reconciliation

PERSON SIGNING CONTRACT TO BE GIVEN COPY

- Under Business and Professions Code Section 10142, any time a licensee prepares or has prepared an agreement authorizing or employing that licensee to perform any acts for which a real estate license is required or when the licensee obtains the signature of any person to any contract pertaining to such services or transaction, the licensee must deliver a copy of the agreement to the person signing it at the time the signature is obtained. Examples of such documents are listing agreements, real estate purchase contract and receipt for deposit forms, addendums to contracts, and property management agreements.

BROKER REQUIRED TO SUPERVISE

- Regulation 2725 lists a number of elements, which constitute an acceptable minimum level of supervision, including the obligation to "review, oversee, inspect and manage documents which may have a material effect upon the rights or obligations of a party to the transaction." Brokers also have a duty to review or manage transactions, document filing, handling of trust funds, advertising, regular reports of salesperson activities and familiarizing salespersons with anti-discriminating laws. This regulation allows brokers the flexibility to design and structure the method and manner by which they exercise their duty to supervise by taking into consideration various factors, such as the number of salespersons employed and the number of branch offices maintained. Brokers will be expected in addition to establishing policies, rules, procedures and systems to affect their duty to supervise, to have in place systems, which monitor compliance with these policies and rules.
- The consequences of trust fund conversion are varied and costly to licensees. Trust fund violations can result in loss of license, receivership, civil liability and criminal sanctions.

AUDITS AND EXAMINATIONS

- Because of the importance of trust fund handling, the Commissioner has an ongoing statewide program of examining brokers' records. Licensees audited will be made aware of trust fund handling and record keeping requirements where necessary. If during the course of an audit or examination, actual trust fund imbalances are uncovered or money-handling procedures pose a potential monetary loss situation, even if a loss has not yet occurred, appropriate disciplinary proceedings will be initiated.
- Section 10148 of the Business and Professions Code provides that a licensed real estate broker shall retain for three years copies of all listings, deposit receipts, canceled checks, trust records, and other documents executed by or obtained by the broker in connection with any transaction for which a real estate broker license is required.
- The retention period shall run from the date of the closing of the transaction or from the date of the listing if the transaction is not consummated.
- After giving notice, such books, accounts and records shall be made available for examination and inspection by the commissioner or his designated representative during regular business hours, and shall, upon the appearance of sufficient cause, be subject to audit without further notice, except that such audit shall not be harassing in nature.

QUESTIONS AND ANSWERS ON TRUST FUND REQUIREMENTS AND RECORD KEEPING

Q. Are security deposits on rental units the property of the owner or should they be held in trust by the broker for the tenant?

A. *They are trust funds. As such, control and disbursement of the security deposits are at the instruction of the property owner.*

Q. Am I permitted to wait until checks deposited to my trust account have cleared before I would issue a trust check to fund a customer's check?

A. *Although the Real Estate Law is silent on this, good business practice dictates that you wait until a customer's check deposited to your trust account has cleared prior to the issuing of your trust check as a refund.*

Q. How should I handle an earnest money check, which is to be deposited into escrow upon acceptance of the offer?

A. *Such a check may be held until the offer is accepted and then placed in escrow, but only when directed to do so by the buyer and the fact the check is being held in uncashed form is specifically disclosed to the seller. In such cases, it is good practice to include such a provision in the deposit receipt. You must keep a columnar record of the receipt of the check, the name of the escrow company and the date the check was forwarded to the escrow.*

Q. As a broker-owner of rentals, do I have to put security deposit monies in a trust account?   NO

A. *Monies you receive on your own property would be monies received as a principal, not as an agent. As such, these are not trust funds and should not be placed in the trust account.*

Q. Must I keep a deposit receipt signed only by the buyer and rejected by the seller?

A. *Yes. Such a record must be maintained for the three-year period.*

Q. May I maintain one trust fund account for both collections from my property management business and deposits on real estate sales transactions?

A. *Since property management funds usually involve multiple receipt of funds and several monthly disbursements, it is suggested that separate trust fund accounts be maintained for property management funds and earnest money deposits; however, all trust funds can be placed in the same trust fund account as long as separate records for each trust fund deposit disbursement are maintained properly.*

Q. If the buyer and seller decide to go directly to escrow and the buyer makes out a check to the escrow company and hands it directly to the escrow clerk, do I have to maintain any records of this check?

A. *No. You must maintain records only of trust funds, which pass through your hands for the benefit of a third party.*

Q. How long must I keep deposit receipts?

A. *Deposit receipts must be maintained for three years.*

IN SUMMARY

Trust fund violations cause the most problems for Bureau of Real Estate Audit and Enforcement staff. It is a quick and easy way to lose your license.

Some recommendations from Duane Gomer:
- Try to have deposit checks made payable to a Title or Escrow Company and deposit them there. This eliminates some accounting problems. Sometimes, buyers want their deposit money back and sellers don't want to "release" the funds. This can cause you extensive problems if the money is in your trust fund.
- Be sure to make it definite in the Purchase Contract if checks are to be held until acceptance or some other future date.
- Don't allow the same associate to be responsible for deposits and withdrawals and bank reconciliations. One embezzlement is one too many and it could prove fatal to your real estate career.
- Don't make withdrawals until checks have "cleared" your bank. Enough said. It happened to me with a very "large" check from a very "established, long-line" mortgage company.
- If you do property management, solicit professional accounting advise about your systems before starting. As a Certified Property Manager who has made many mistakes, I recommend that you consider having a bank account for each owner. This addresses many future problems and although there are many accounts to reconcile, in the long run it could be less trouble.
- Try to make an arrangement with your bank to have the expenses to the account charged to you directly. You then would not have to maintain an amount in the account to handle bank charges, etc.
- Some accountants recommend that you maintain your trust fund account at a different bank than your business accounts.
- Have your accountant or someone else come to your office yearly and "audit" your procedures.
- If you don't have enough time to do your trust fund accounting in a timely fashion, you may have a lot of time later when your name appears on the page in the BRE bulletin that lists suspensions or revocations of license. Good luck.

COMMISSIONER'S REGULATIONS

The Bureau of Real Estate has many outstanding research articles to help you stay out of trouble. A partial list of the items available at www.bre.ca.gov under the Publications Tab:
- Business & Professions Code 10145 – Handling of Trust Funds – Interest-Bearing Accounts – Neutral Escrow Defined
- Broker Self-Evaluation – Compliance Checklist (Outstanding)
- Trust Funds (45 pages) – A Guide for Real Estate Brokers and Salespersons
- Brokers (16 pages) – Compliance Evaluation Manual (Thorough, a must read)

There are two other important articles on the site. These are so important that we have included here any reference to trust fund problems in these articles for your study and review.

Most Common Enforcement Violations

Trust Fund Record Keeping Violations

Trust fund handling and record keeping is one of the most common problem areas. We see case after case in which brokers handle trust monies on behalf of others and either convert the monies to their own use, or do not have the expertise to maintain proper accounting records and end up with shortages in their trust accounts. To avoid problems in this area, all real estate brokers should be familiar with the following laws and regulations that govern the handling of trust funds by real estate brokers.

Section 10145 - General statute governing the handing of trusts funds.
Regulation 2831 - Maintaining columnar records of trust funds received.
Regulation 2831.1 - Maintaining separate records for each beneficiary.
Regulation 2831.2 - Performing monthly reconciliation of trust fund accounts.
Regulation 2834 - Allowing unlicensed and unbonded signatories on a trust account.

Remedy

Deficiencies in the area of trust fund records usually stem from one of two common deficiencies by real estate brokers.

The most common problem found among brokers who maintain poor trust fund records is a lack of knowledge of what the law requires in the area of trust fund record keeping and a lack of basic bookkeeping or accounting skills. Brokers often attempt to handle large amounts of trust funds without any specific training in the area. This often results in a trust fund disaster.

Brokers should understand that simply because they are able to handle large amounts of trust funds by virtue of their license, it doesn't necessarily follow that they should. Before accepting any trust funds, brokers should make sure that they have the proper knowledge and skills necessary to handle and account for the trust funds that are received in their business operations. The level of knowledge and skill that is necessary will vary with the type of operation and the amount of trust funds that are handled. Brokers must be able to recognize the limitations of their knowledge and skills as their business operations expand and either get further training or hire professionals with appropriate training.

A second common problem found among brokers who maintain poor trust fund records is a general lack of supervision over their trust fund operations. It is common to find brokerage operations where the responsible broker has simply turned this aspect of the operation over to office personnel. A broker must always exercise vigilant and consistent oversight of the trust fund operation to ensure that there is compliance with the law.

The Real Estate Law is very specific as to how trust fund monies are to be handled and how records are to be maintained. Real estate brokers who handle trust fund monies have a responsibility to become knowledgeable in this area. A good place to start is by reviewing the BRE's publication entitled Trust Funds which is available on our Web site.

Trust Fund Shortage Violations

Section 10145 - General statute governing the handling of trust funds.
Regulation 2832 - Trust fund handling.
Regulation 2832.1 - Trust fund shortages.

Remedy

Often, trust fund shortages in brokerage operations are caused by poor record keeping and lack of control on the part of the responsible broker. The remedies to this problem were previously discussed.

Of even more concern than poor record keeping, are trust fund shortages resulting from the deliberate conversion of trust funds for personal use by the broker or by employees of the broker. When this occurs, it is taken very seriously. Real estate brokers who are found to have converted trust funds can be assured that disciplinary action will be taken against their license. Also, the potential for criminal prosecution exists.

Ten Most Common Violations Found in BRE Audits

The real estate industry has moved into a new millennium. New things pop up everyday changing the way we do business. New terms, such as E-Loans, Internet Marketing, and E-Form have become jargons of the trade. Yet, certain things have not changed - the most common violations found in BRE Audits. In this regard, the top ten common violations are listed below. The purpose of this article is to call your attention to these common deficiencies and to provide you with procedures that you can follow to ensure compliance with these laws and regulations.

B & P Code Section 10148 - Retention of Records
Business and Professions Code Section 10148(a) states that a real estate broker shall retain for three years copies of all listings, deposit slips, canceled checks, trust records, and other documents executed by him or her or obtained by him or her in connection with any transactions for which a real estate license is required. This section requires that, after notice, the books, accounts, and records shall be made available for examination, inspection, and copying by the commissioner or his or her designated representative during regular business hours; and shall, upon the appearance of sufficient cause, be subject to audit without further notice, except that the audit shall not be harassing in nature.

A broker who fails to keep transaction files, canceled checks, deposit slips or other records prepared or obtained for a period of three years may be cited for violation of this section. Some brokers cited for violation of this section have simply failed to provide records after reasonable attempts by the Bureau to examine them. Other brokers cited have lost control of or destroyed records that should have been maintained. Formal legal action can result from a broker's failure to provide records. You should review the record retention policies for your office to make sure you are in compliance with this code section.

Regulation 2731 - Use of False or Fictitious Name
Commissioner's Regulation 2731 states that a licensee shall not use a fictitious name in the conduct of any activity for which a license is required under the Real Estate Law unless the licensee is the holder of a license bearing the fictitious name. Brokers should periodically check their license status with the Bureau to be sure that their license bears the fictitious name(s) they are using. Many brokers cited for violation of this regulation believed that having the dba registered with the county was sufficient to allow them to use it in their real estate business. Other brokers who are cited for this violation state that they had the fictitious name on their license at one time but may have had their license lapse for a brief period of time and failed to add the dba back on to their license.

Regulation 2831 - Trust Fund Records To Be Maintained

This regulation requires the broker to maintain, in columnar form, a record of all trust funds received and deposited by the broker. At a minimum, the following information must be indicated in columnar form in chronological order: date funds were received; name of payee or payor; amount received; date of deposit; amount paid out; check number and date; and the daily running balance of the trust account. If any of these columns are not present, then there is a violation of Regulation 2831. The accurate use of BRE form RE 4522 fully complies with this regulation.

When we cite this regulation, most of the time it is for one or more of the following reasons:
- The broker did not maintain any trust fund records.
- If trust fund records were maintained, they were either not in columnar form or a column (noted above) was missing. We have seen many brokers utilize a standard checkbook as trust fund records. These records do not comply with Regulation 2831.
- In some instances, columnar records were maintained by a licensee but he/she was still cited because the items posted were not accurate, e.g., when posting a check, it was the wrong amount; or, for a deposit, "the amount" was wrong and/or "the date of deposit" was the wrong date.
- A broker maintaining columnar records can still be cited if a daily running balance is not maintained or is inaccurate. Brokers must always keep a daily running balance of the aggregate amount of trust funds in their bank accounts.

(For trust funds not deposited into a trust account, the columnar record should show the date trust funds were received, the form of the trust funds, amount received, description of the property, identity of the person to whom funds were forwarded, and date of disposition. The accurate use of BRE form RE 4524 fully complies with this part of the regulation.)

It should be noted that records maintained under an automated data processing system in accordance with generally accepted accounting principles should be in compliance as long as they contain the elements previously noted.

Regulation 2831.1 - Separate Record for Each Beneficiary or Transaction

This regulation requires the broker to maintain, in columnar form, a separate record of trust funds for each beneficiary or transaction accounting for all funds which have been deposited into a trust account. This record identifies which beneficiary has funds in the trust account. This record must indicate the following in chronological order and in columnar form: date of deposit, amount of deposit, name of payee or payor, check number, date and amount, and running balance of the separate record after each transaction on any date.
- This regulation is cited mostly due to one or more of the following reasons:
- The broker did not maintain separate records for each beneficiary.
- Separate records were maintained, but the broker was cited because information was missing.
- Separate records were maintained, but the broker was cited because the items posted were not accurate, e.g., when posting a check, it was the wrong amount; or, for a deposit, "the amount" was wrong and/or "the date of deposit" was the wrong date.
- Separate records were maintained, but a daily running balance for each record was not maintained or it was not accurate. Brokers must always keep a daily balance for each separate record.

It should be noted that records maintained under an automated data processing system in accordance with generally accepted accounting principles should be in compliance as long as they contain the elements previously noted.

Regulation 2831.2 - Trust Account Reconciliation

Regulation 2831.2 requires that the total of all Separate Beneficiary or Transaction Records maintained pursuant to Regulation 2831.1 be reconciled with the balance of the Record of All Trust Funds Received and Paid Out required by Regulation 2831, at least once a month except when the bank account did not have any activities. The requirement is that the accounting records be reconciled to each other. This is not only a legal requirement; this is also part of a sound internal control for trust fund handling.

In order for this procedure to have a reliable result, the Record of All Trust Funds Received and Paid Out must be reconciled first with the bank account statements as of a certain cut-off date. This procedure is commonly known as bank reconciliation and is performed basically to determine the accuracy of the records. A cut-off date is the calendar date (usually end of the month), when no transaction or activity thereafter is considered. This process is completed once all adjustments and corrections of any reconciling items have been made to the ending balance on each record to arrive at an adjusted cash balance. In other words, the balance of the record of all trust funds received and paid out has to equal the adjusted cash balance.

The next step is to compare and reconcile the total of all beneficiary or transaction records with the adjusted cash balance as of the cut-off date of the bank reconciliation. The main objective of this procedure is to determine, based on the records, whether all trust funds held on behalf of others are on deposit in the corresponding trust account. Another purpose of this procedure is to ascertain that there is no unidentified overage or broker's funds in excess of $200 in the trust account. Any discrepancy must be corrected accordingly. The broker is required to maintain a record of the trust account reconciliation showing the name of the bank account and number, date of the reconciliation, account number or name of the principals, beneficiaries or transactions and the amount of trust funds held by the broker for each of the principals, beneficiaries or transactions. Failure to comply with this Regulation could result in substantial loss of trust funds and disciplinary action against the broker by the Bureau.

Regulation 2832.1 - Trust Fund Handling for Multiple Beneficiaries (Trust Fund Shortage)

Regulation 2832.1 requires the real estate broker to obtain written consent from every owner of the trust funds in the bank account prior to each disbursement if the disbursement will reduce the balance of the funds in the bank account to an amount less than the existing trust fund liability of the broker to all owners of the funds. A trust fund shortage therefore exists when the following conditions are present:
1. The balance of the bank account is less that the total trust fund liability of the broker to all owners of the funds; and
2. There is no written authorization from all owners of the trust funds allowing this.

The most obvious reason for a trust fund shortage is the intentional misuse (conversion) of trust funds. However, simple record keeping errors that remain undetected could result in trust fund shortages and an actual loss of funds. Failure to record a disbursement, or understating the amount of a check disbursed, or overstating the amount of a deposit on the beneficiary ledger/record will cause the beneficiary ledger to show a balance that is larger than the true amount owed to the individual beneficiary. This overstated balance on the ledger is more likely to be paid and, consequently, the beneficiary will be paid more than what is due. The end result is a trust fund shortage.

Performing the proper trust account reconciliation pursuant to Regulation 2831.2 should enable the broker to detect such causes of a trust fund shortage.

Regulation 2832 - Trust Fund Handling
The most common violations of this section found in audits relate to Commissioner's Regulation 2832(a), which requires that a broker place funds accepted on behalf of another into the hands of the owner of the funds, into a neutral escrow depository or into a trust fund account in the name of the broker, or in a fictitious name if the broker is the holder of a license bearing such fictitious name, as trustee at a bank or other financial institution not later than three business days following receipt of the funds by the broker or by the broker's salesperson. Two of the most common problems related to this regulation are:
1. A broker's failure to designate accounts receiving trust funds as trust fund accounts in the name of the broker or broker's dba as trustee; and
2. Failure to deposit trust funds received by a broker or broker's employee into a trust fund account within three business days of receipt.

B & P Code Section 10240 - Written Disclosure Statement
Another often-cited violation is Section 10240 of the code which requires brokers to provide a borrower with a mortgage loan disclosure statement within three business days after receipt of a completed loan application or before the borrower becomes obligated on the note, whichever is earlier. Real estate brokers often fail to provide the Mortgage Loan Disclosure Statement (Borrower) or, in a federally regulated residential mortgage loan transaction, fail to comply with Section 10240(c). Other brokers fail to maintain completed copies for their files.

In conclusion, as you race to keep up with the ever-changing opportunities that present themselves in business today, take a moment to stop and ensure that your business is operating in compliance with these and other important real estate laws.

There are some other very important Commissioner Regulations that you should know. Some chosen excerpts follow:

2830.1. Interest Bearing Trust Account
A real estate broker, when acting as agent for a financial institution as beneficiary of a loan, may deposit and maintain funds from or for the account of an obligor for the future payment of property taxes, assessments or insurance relating to real property containing only a one-to-four family residence, in an interest-bearing trust account in a bank or savings and loan association in order to pay interest to the obligor in accordance with Section 2954.8 of the Civil Code if the following requirements are met:
a) The account is in the name of the broker as trustee.
b) All of the funds in the account are covered by insurance provided by an agency of the federal government.
c) All of the funds in the account are funds held in trust by the broker for others.
d) The broker discloses to the obligor how interest will be calculated and paid.
e) No interest earned on the funds shall inure directly or indirectly to the benefit of the broker nor to any person licensed to the broker.

2831. Trust Fund Records To Be Maintained
a) Every broker shall keep a record of all trust funds received, including uncashed checks held pursuant to instructions of his or her principal. This record, including records maintained under an automated date processing system, shall set forth in chronological sequence the following information in columnar form:

1. Date trust funds received.
2. From whom trust funds received.
3. Amount received.
4. With respect to funds deposited in an account, date of said deposit.
5. With respect to trust funds previously deposited to an account, check number and date of related disbursement.
6. With respect to trust funds not deposited in an account, identity of other depository and date funds were forwarded.
7. Daily balance of said account.

b) For each bank account which contains trust funds, a record of all trust funds received and disbursed shall be maintained in accordance with subdivision (a) or (c).

c) Maintenance of journals of account cash receipts and disbursements, or similar records, or automated data processing systems, including computer systems and electronic storage and manipulation of information and documents in accordance with generally accepted accounting principles, shall constitute compliance with subdivision (a) provided that such journals, records, or systems contain the elements required by subdivision (a) and that such elements are maintained in a format that will readily enable tracing and reconciliation in accordance with Section 2831.2.

d) Nothing in this section shall be construed to permit a violation of Section 10145 of the Code.

e) A broker is not required to keep records pursuant to this section of checks which are written by a principal, given to the broker and made payable to third parties for the provision of services including but not limited to escrow, credit and appraisal services, when the total amount of such checks for any transaction from that principal does not exceed $1,000. Upon request of the Bureau or the maker of such checks, a broker shall account for the receipt and distribution of such checks. A broker shall retain for three years copies of receipts issued or obtained in connection with the receipt and distribution of such checks.

2831.1   Separate Record for Each Beneficiary or Transaction

a) A broker shall keep a separate record for each beneficiary or transaction, accounting for all funds which have been deposited to the broker's trust bank account and interest, if any, earned on the funds on deposit. This record shall include information sufficient to identify the transaction and the parties to the transaction. Each record shall set forth in chronological sequence the following information in columnar form:
1. Date of deposit.
2. Amount of deposit.
3. Date of each related disbursement.
4. Check number of each related disbursement.
5. Amount of each related disbursement.
6. If applicable, dates and amounts of interest earned and credited to the account.
7. Balance after posting transactions on any date.

b) Maintenance of trust ledgers of separate beneficiaries or transactions, or similar records, or automated data processing systems, including computer systems and electronic storage and manipulation of information and documents, in accordance with generally accepted accounting principles will constitute compliance with subdivision (a), provided that such ledgers, records, or systems contain the elements required by subdivision (a) and that such elements are maintained in a format that will readily enable tracing and reconciliation in accordance with section 2831.2.

2831.2. Trust Account Reconciliation

The balance of all separate beneficiary or transaction records maintained pursuant to the provisions of Section 2831.1 must be reconciled with the record of all trust funds received and disbursed required by Section 2831, at least once a month, except in those months when the bank account did not have any activities. A record of the reconciliation must be maintained, and it must identify the bank account name and number, the date of the reconciliation, the account number or name of the principals or beneficiaries or transactions, and the trust fund liabilities of the broker to each of the principals, beneficiaries or transactions.

2832. Trust Fund Handling

a) Compliance with Section 10145 of the Code requires that the broker place funds accepted on behalf of another into the hands of the owner of the funds, into a neutral escrow depository or into a trust fund account in the name of the broker, or in a fictitious name if the broker is the holder of a license bearing such fictitious name, as trustee at a bank or other financial institution not later than three business days following receipt of the funds by the broker or by the broker's salesperson.

b) Except as expressly provided by subdivision (d) of Section 10145 of the code or by a regulation in this article, the account into which the trust fund are deposited shall not be an interest-bearing account for which prior written notice can by law or regulation be required by the financial institution as a condition to the withdrawal of funds.

c) A check received from the offeror may be held uncashed by the broker until acceptance of the offer if:

   1. The check by its terms is not negotiable by the broker or if the offeror has given written instructions that the check shall not be deposited not cashed until acceptance of the offer and,

   2. The offeree is informed that the check is being so held before or at the time the offer is presented for acceptance.

d) In these circumstances if the offeror's check was held by the broker in accordance with subdivision (c) until acceptance of the offer, the check shall be placed into a neutral escrow depository or the trust fund account, or into the hands of the offeree if offeror and offeree expressly so provide in writing, not later than three business days following acceptance of the offer unless the broker receives written authorization from the offeree to continue to hold the check.

e) Notwithstanding the provisions of subdivisions (a) and (d), a real estate broker who is not licensed under the Escrow Law (Section 17000, et seq., of the Financial Code) when acting in the capacity of an escrow holder in a real estate purchase and sale, exchange or loan transaction in which the broker is performing acts for which a real estate license is required shall place all funds accepted on behalf of another into the hands of the owner of the funds, into a neutral escrow depository or into a trust fund account in the name of the broker, or in a fictitious name if the broker is the holder of a license bearing such fictitious name, as trustee at a bank or other financial institution not later than the next business day following receipt of the funds by the broker or by the broker's salesperson.

2832.1 Trust Fund Handling for Multiple Beneficiaries

The written consent of every principal who is an owner of the funds in the account shall be obtained by a real estate broker prior to each disbursement if such a disbursement will reduce the balance of funds in the account to an amount less than the existing aggregate trust fund liability of the broker to all owners of the funds.

COMMINGLING (INCLUDES CODE SECTION 2835)

Commingling occurs when:
1. Personal or company funds are deposited into the trust fund bank account. **Except for what is provided in Section 2835 of the Commissioner's Regulations as noted below, this** is a violation of the law even if separate records are kept.
2. Trust funds are deposited into the licensee's general or personal bank account rather than into the trust fund account. In this case the violation is not only commingling, but also handling trust funds contrary to Business and Professions Code Section 10145. It is also grounds for suspension or revocation of a license under Business and Professions Code Section 10177(d).
3. Commissions, fees, or other income earned by the broker and collectible from the trust account are left in the trust account for more than 25 days from the date they were earned.

A common example of commingling is depositing rents and security deposits on broker-owned properties into the trust account. As these funds relate to the broker's properties, they are not trust funds and, therefore, may not be deposited into the trust fund bank account. Likewise, the broker may not make mortgage payments and other payments on broker-owned properties from the trust account even if the broker reimburses the account for such payments. Conducting personal business through the trust account is strictly prohibited and is a violation of the Real Estate Law.

Commissioner's Regulation 2835 provides that the following situations do not constitute "commingling" for purposes of Business and Professions Code Section 10176(e):
(a) The deposit into a trust account of reasonably sufficient funds, not to exceed $200, to pay service charges or fees levied or assessed against the account by the bank or financial institution where the account is maintained.
(b) The deposit into a trust account maintained in compliance with item (d) below of funds belonging in part to the broker's principal and in part to the broker when it is not reasonably practicable to separate such funds, provided the part of the funds belonging to the broker is disbursed not later than 25 days after the deposit and there is no dispute between the broker and the broker's principal as to the broker's portion of the funds. When the right of a broker to receive a portion of trust funds is disputed by the broker's principal, the disputed portion shall not be withdrawn until the dispute is settled.
(c) The deposit into a trust account of broker-owned funds in connection with mortgage loan activities as defined in subdivision (d) or (e) of Section 10131 of the Business and Professions Code or when making, collecting payments on, or servicing a loan which is subject to the provisions of Section 10240 of the Business and Professions Code provided:
(1) The broker meets the criteria of Section 10232 of the Business and Professions Code.
(2) All funds in the account which are owned by the broker are identified at all times in a separate record which is distinct from any separate record maintained for a beneficiary.
(3) All broker-owned funds deposited into the account are disbursed from the account not later than 25 days after their deposit.
(4) The funds are deposited and maintained in compliance with item (d) below.
(5) For this purpose, a broker shall be deemed to be subject to the provisions of Section 10240 of the Business and Professions Code if the broker delivers the statement to the borrower required by Section 10240.

(d) The trust fund account into which the funds are deposited is maintained in accordance with the provisions of Section 10145 of the Business and Professions Code, the Commissioner's Regulations, and the provisions of Title 10, California Code of Regulations, Section 260.105.30.

To summarize, a real estate broker's personal funds may be in the trust account in the following two specific instances:

1. Up to $200 to cover checking account service fees and other bank charges such as check printing charges and service fees on returned checks. Trust funds may not be used to pay for these expenses. (The preferred practice, however, is for the broker to have the bank debit his/her own *personal* account for any trust account fees and charges.)

2. Commissions, fees, and other income earned by a broker and collectible from trust funds may remain in the trust account for a period not to exceed 25 days. Regulation 2835 recognizes that it may not always be practical to disburse the earned income immediately upon receipt. For instance, a property management company may find it too burdensome to collect its management fee every time a rent check is received and deposited to the trust account. Therefore, as long as the broker disburses the fee from the trust account within 25 days after deposit there is no commingling violation. Note, however, that income earned *shall not* be taken from trust funds received *before* depositing such funds into the trust bank account. Also, under no circumstances may the broker pay personal obligations from the trust fund bank account even if such payments are a draw against commissions or other income. The broker must issue a trust account check to himself/herself for the total amount of the income earned, adequately documenting such payment, and then pay personal obligations from the proceeds of that check.

TRUST FUND HANDLING PRACTICE QUESTIONS:

True or False?

1. The BRE has the jurisdiction to audit a broker's private accounts if they have a trust fund. **T**

2. Brokers can never hold checks uncashed. **F**

3. An acceptance of an offer to lease could change fund ownership from the prospective lessee to the landlord. **T**

4. Advance fees can never be collected. **F**

5. If specifically authorized in writing by the broker, a salesperson licensed to the broker can sign checks. **T**

6. Trust funds can never be put in an interest earning account. **F**

7. An example of commingling is depositing monies from broker-owned properties into a trust account. **T**

8. After ten years of an overage, the money is sent to the California Secretary of State. **F** *3 years*

9. If there is activity in the account, trust funds must be reconciled monthly. **T**

10. Records can never be computer-produced. **F**

11. All transactions affecting a trust fund account are entered in chronological sequence. **T**

12. Separate records for each property managed are not recommended. **F**

13. It is best to record transactions once a month. **F** *daily*

14. When reconciling records, use balances from the same cut-off date. **T**

15. The consequences of trust fund conversion can be costly to licensees. **T**

16. A broker must keep trust fund records for ten years. *? 3 ?*

17. Control of security deposits is at the instruction of the property owner. **T**

18. Trust fund violations cause very few problems for the Bureau of Real Estate. **F**

19. You could try to make arrangements with your bank to have expenses charged to you directly. **F**

20. Trust fund violations are rare. **F**

21. The BRE website at www.dre.ca.gov is invaluable. **T**

22. Brokers should attempt to establish large trust account balances. **F**

23. BRE audits turn up many problems. **T**

24. Fictitious names are never allowed. **F**

25. Trust funds not deposited in a trust account must still be recorded. F

26. Accounts do not need to be reconciled according to Regulation 2831.2. F

27. The most obvious reason for a trust fund shortage is conversion by a broker. T

28. The broker is not allowed to deposit funds into a neutral escrow company.

29. An unlicensed employee must be bonded to make withdrawals. T

30. Funds can never be in an interest bearing account. F

31. Maintenance of journals must be in accordance with generally accepted accounting principles. T

32. A broker has six business days to deposit funds. F

33. A trust fund check may be held uncashed if the check is postdated. T

34. Personal funds are never deposited into a trust by a broker. T

35. A broker can keep up to $200 in an account for services charges, etc. T

36. All broker-owned funds must be disbursed one day after deposit. F

37. A preferred way for a broker to pay bank charges is to have his personal account debited. F

Review Questions

38. Real estate brokers have few problems with supervision. F

39. Brokers must keep records for three years. T

40. Brokers making loans have 30 days to give disclosures. F

Practice Questions designed to prepare you to pass the final exams are available. New BRE Regulations do not allow us to give the answers to the quizzes in the book so the questions and answers are presented online. This makes the test taking very easy as you get the answers immediately.

To access the practice quizzes please visit http://www.DuaneGomer.com/after . Check on the proper link for the course you desire.

NOTE: Do not use Google, Yahoo, Bing etc. They are Search Engines. You must put the above URL link in your address bar or you won't get there.

You may request the questions by email to info@DuaneGomer.com, fax at 949-455-9931, or phone 800-439-4909. You will receive only the practice questions. You may FAX back your answers to Duane Gomer, Inc., at (949) 455-9931 and we will FAX your results to you within 24 business hours. Our recommendation is find a computer even if it's a friend or relatives it makes everything so easy under the new BRE rules.

FAIR HOUSING

FEDERAL FAIR HOUSING ACT (TITLE VIII OF U.S. CIVIL RIGHTS ACT OF 1968 AND THE 1988 AMENDMENTS

This act prohibits discrimination in the sale or rental of housing on the basis of race, color, religion, sex, handicap, familial status, or national origin.

- Refusing to sell or rent after a bona fide offer has been made.
- Discriminating in the terms, conditions or privileges of a sale or lease or in providing services or facilities.
- Indicating any preference in advertising or statements, oral or written.
- False representations as to the availability of a dwelling unit including "channeling" and "steering" to particular neighborhoods.
- Attempting to persuade owners to sell or rent dwellings by making representations about the entry into the neighborhood of certain classes of people.

In 1988 the act was amended to include familial status and handicapped as protected categories. Most of the familial status actions involve discrimination against children. Before any owner makes any Building Rules to limit the renting to children, they should check with a local real estate attorney. Children are people too and if you allow three people to live in a one-bedroom apartment, you can't make a rule that a couple with one child can't live there. Other forms of discrimination would include making renters with children pay more rent or larger deposits.

Handicapped people include not only the ones of which we are aware (blind, crippled, deaf, etc.) but also people afflicted with AIDS and alcoholics. People who are addicted to illegal substances are not protected under this regulation.

These rules apply not only to renting, selling and leasing of property but also to financing transactions. Lenders, loan brokers, etc. come under the same regulations.

EXEMPTIONS:

- Religious organizations and private clubs may limit to their members any transactions other than commercial purposes.
  1. No brokers can be involved.
  2. Must apply to 100% of members.

- Housing for Older Persons does not have to adhere to familial status provisions.

- Individuals who own four or less single family homes are exempt for one transaction in any twenty-four month period. (Provided no broker is involved.)
- Individuals may rent rooms or units in a dwelling containing four units or less, without regard to fair housing laws, if they live in the dwelling. (Individuals owning property must follow State laws and this provision applies only if no broker is involved.)
- Parties exempt above have to follow discriminatory advertising rules.

CONSEQUENCES OF VIOLATION OF THIS LAW

- Who may seek remedies?
  1. Department of Housing and Urban Development
  2. U.S. Attorney General
  3. Private parties
  4. State agencies when assigned by HUD

- Proceedings
  1. Administrative complaint by HUD (Intention of government to be a quick and inexpensive alternative)
  2. Lawsuit in Federal Court
  3. All of the above

- Penalties – You Better Follow the Rules
  1. If HUD brought action Civil Penalties
     - Up to $10,000 for first-timer
     - Up to $25,000 for repeaters within 5 years
     - Up to $50,000 for three actions within 7 years
     - For natural persons (not firm or corporation) sanctions may be used without regard to 5 & 7 year rules
     - Injunctive relief
     - Attorney fees
  2. If Attorney General brought action
     - Damages
     - Up to $50,000 Civil Penalties for first-timers
     - Up to $100,000 for any subsequent violations
     - Injunctive relief
     - Attorney fees
  3. If action brought by private parties
     - Actual and punitive damages
     - Injunctive relief
     - Attorney fees

UNLAWFUL TO DISCRIMINATE IN ADVERTISING

- Because of race, color, religion, sex, handicap, familial status, or national origin
- Written and oral communication and telemarketing covered
- Publishers are also liable
- Human models should be selected carefully
- Affirmative duty to display Equal Housing Opportunity Logos, Statement
- Slogans, etc.

- Brokers are responsible for salespersons
- Direct mail is very vulnerable to complaints. Check the lists that you use.
- Phrases to critique - Adult or Executive Home, Perfect for Couple, Family Home, Bachelor Pad

STEERING OR CHANELLING

- Steering is any statement or conduct by a real estate seller that, in effect, discourages someone from considering a particular location, home or apartment, and encourages them to consider another location or property because of their race, color, religion, national origin, family status or handicap.
- Steering can be accomplished through the use of selective listing and showing of properties, limited and selective advertising, a discriminatory tenant assignment policy, the maintenance of separate waiting lists, or the failure to notify eligible people of color on a waiting list of vacancies in other predominantly white buildings managed by the same firm or landlord.
- Evidence of racial steering is often gathered through the use of testers, and the testers often bring suits challenging alleged racial steering themselves or the fair housing organization that employs them.
- Preventing steering:
  1. Run ads in the general media to ensure your property is made available to everyone.
  2. Use direct mail only as a secondary source of prospects. Direct mail advertising is vulnerable to discrimination complaints. If you use direct mail, you should be able to prove a legitimate business purpose for your targeting criteria, such as income, distance to your site, and desired housing type. Define your market carefully, using strict demographic data, preferably from a commercial data service.
  3. Be careful if someone wants you to restrict his housing choices for him. You should never encourage or discourage a prospect from renting or buying a property because of the racial, ethnic, or religious make-up of a building or neighborhood. If a prospect asks you to restrict his or her housing search based on race, color, religion, sex, national origin, handicap, or family status, be clear about your commitment to the requirements of the fair housing laws.
  4. Review your written materials to see if you send a message that only one race is welcome in your community.

OTHER PROBLEM AREAS

- Deed Restrictions cannot be contrary to Discrimination Regulations.
- Appraisers must not use discriminatory practices in estimating value.
- Redlining - Licensees should be aware that effective January 1, 1978, the California Housing Financial Discrimination Act prohibits state financial institutions from engaging in blanket refusals to lend money in neighborhoods of faded property values. Redlining is where such refusals are due in whole or in part to conditions, trends, or characteristics in the neighborhood or geographic areas surrounding the housing accommodations, unless the lender can demonstrate that in a particular case it would be unsafe or unsound business practice to do so. Lenders must consider credit worthiness of borrowers desiring loans in these neighborhoods, without discriminating due to composition of neighborhood in regard to race, color, ancestry, sex, religion,

marital status or national origin. Also, Commissioner's Regulation 2780 sets out discriminatory conduct by a licensee as the basis for disciplinary action.
- Civil Rights Clause - On the California Association of Realtors Listing Agreement Clause #15 - "Equal Housing Opportunity: "The property is offered in compliance with federal, state and local anti-discrimination laws." This is a necessary clause in your listing agreement.

THE CIVIL RIGHTS ACT OF 1866

The Civil Rights Act of 1866 established the concept of "Fair Housing". It provided for equal housing opportunity by prohibiting discrimination on "racial grounds" in contracts.
- Applies to race only
- Applies to all types of property transactions (inheritance, purchase, lease, sale, and convey);
- Applies to both real property and personal property.

Unlike later acts, which applied to residential property only, this act was not limited to residential property.

Passed by a Reconstruction Congress shortly after the end of the Civil War, the Civil Rights Act of 1866 stated: "all citizens of the United States shall have the same rights in every state and territory as is enjoyed by white citizens thereof to inherit, purchase, lease, sell, hold and convey real and personal property."

The Civil Rights Act of 1866 could be enforced through a civil lawsuit by the party discriminated against. Remedies include:
- an injunction (an order to cease and desist);
- actual damages (compensation); and
- punitive damages (to punish the wrongdoer)

President Andrew Johnson was a moderate presiding in a radical nation. President Johnson felt that the Civil Rights Act of 1866 was an unconstitutional extension of federal powers, because it had not been covered in the constitution. President Johnson considered civil rights to be a matter for the states. Therefore, he vetoed the Civil Rights Act of 1866. The veto was overridden. Congress was angry with President Johnson, not just for his veto of the 1866 Act, but for his moderate views toward punishing the South. This led to the impeachment of President of Andrew Johnson by the House of Representatives.

The act provides that all persons have the same right to make and enforce contracts to the full and equal benefit of all laws and proceedings for the security of person's properties.

This act has been upheld in many court rulings. It has been used when there has been racially motivated opposition to the construction of low-income housing in a neighborhood, refusal to sell lots to African-Americans, racially based steering, etc. Victims of discrimination can file lawsuits for violation of their "Civil Rights" due to race only. Also, HUD and other agencies can assist in filing of the lawsuits. Private parties can sue for damages and attorney's fees.

AMERICANS WITH DISABILITIES ACT

Q. Does the Act include handicapped persons as a protected class?

A. *Yes. The Act added physically and mentally handicapped persons to the classes of people protected under Federal fair housing laws. Previously, Federal law did not prohibit discrimination against handicapped persons. Since 1987 California has prohibited discrimination against persons based on blindness or physical disability and they are also protected under the Act.*

Q. How is "handicap" defined by the Act?

A. *Handicap is defined as a physical or mental impairment, which substantially limits one or more of a person's major life activities. Such activities would include caring for one's self, performing manual tasks, walking, seeing, hearing, speaking, breathing, learning and working. Persons with a record of such an impairment are also protected under the Act.*

Q. Are drug users within the definition of physically or mentally handicapped?

A. *No. The Act does not protect the fair housing rights of drug users and the term handicap does not include illegal use of or addiction to a controlled substance (as defined by law). If an otherwise handicapped individual takes a controlled substance under the care of a physician, it would not be an illegal use and the handicapped person cannot be denied housing because of drug use.*

Q. Must housing be made available to every person whose handicap comes within the Act's definition of handicap?

A. *No. The Act does not require that housing be made available to individuals whose tenancy would be a direct threat to the health or safety of others or would result in substantial physical damage to the property of others. It is anticipated that HUD regulations will require objective evidence of the direct threat (i.e., the housing provider must have reason to know the particular individual will constitute a direct threat to property or others).*

Q. Must landlords make modifications to existing housing to accommodate handicapped persons?

A. *No. Landlords are not required to make modifications. However, they must permit handicapped tenants to make reasonable modifications at the tenant's own expense if such modifications are necessary to provide the tenant with full enjoyment of the premises. Such modifications may include, but are not limited to, the installation of hand bars in shower stalls, the lowering of light switches and other environmental controls. The landlord may also reasonably require that the tenant return the premises to its original state at the tenant's expense.*

Q. Must a landlord modify the rules and policies of a rental complex to accommodate handicapped persons?

A. *Yes, reasonable modifications must be made in the rules, policies and practices, or services when such accommodations may be necessary to allow the handicapped person to use and enjoy the dwelling. For example, allowing a guide dog, even though there is a "no pets" policy or providing a reserved, convenient parking place, if possible, for a wheelchair tenant would be reasonable accommodations.*

Q. What requirements exist for new housing projects to meet the needs of handicapped persons?

A. *This Act provides that new multifamily buildings, including rental, cooperatives and condominiums with four or more units that are ready for occupancy after March 1991 must be constructed to allow access and use by handicapped persons.*

There must be routes accessible by wheelchair to and through each dwelling location. Bathroom walls must be reinforced to support grab bars. Bathrooms and kitchens must be designed to accommodate a wheelchair. If a multifamily dwelling of four or more units has no elevators, access must be provided to handicapped tenants only on the ground floor.

Compliance with the Act is satisfied when a builder meets the requirements of the American National Standard for buildings and facilities for the handicapped or when there is compliance with State laws that incorporate the Act's handicapped standards.

Individuals or HUD may file complaints against builders who do not comply. In addition, state and local governments are encouraged (but not obligated) to enforce the requirements as a part of their review and approval of newly constructed multifamily dwellings.

CALIFORNIA FAIR HOUSING
DISCRIMINATION PROHIBITED BY STATE LAW

The Unruh Civil Rights Act (Civil Code Section 51, et seq.) declares: "All persons within the jurisdiction of this State are free and equal, and no matter what their sex, race, color, religion, ancestry, or national origin are entitled to full and equal accommodations, etc."

The validity of the act has been tested and applies to real estate activities. Thus, real estate brokers who unlawfully deny full and equal accommodations, advantages, facilities, privileges and services of their business establishment on grounds of race or color are in violation of the act.

Its intent is to give all persons full and equal accommodations, advantages, facilities, privileges, or services in all business establishments of every kind whatsoever and prohibits them from discriminating based on essentially the same classes as the Federal Fair Housing Act.

Civil Code Section 52 further states, "Whoever denies, or who aids, or incites such denial, or whoever makes any discrimination, distinction or restriction on account of sex, color, race, religion, ancestry, or national origin is liable for each and every such offense for three times the actual damages, but in no case less than one thousand dollars ($1000) in addition thereto, and any attorney's fees suffered by any person denied the rights provided in this California code."

AIDS
§ 1710.2. Occupant of property afflicted with or who died from AIDS; failure to disclose to transferee; no cause of action; state preemption of AIDS disclosure

(a) No cause of action arises against an owner of real property or his or her agent, or any agent of a transferee of real property, for the failure to disclose to the transferee the occurrence of an occupant's death upon the real property or the manner of death where the death has occurred more than three years prior to the date the transferee offers to purchase, lease, or rent the real property, or that an occupant of that property was afflicted with or died from Human T-Lymphotropic Virus Type III/Lymphadenopathy-Associated Virus. As used in this section, "agent" includes any person licensed pursuant to Part 1 (commencing with Section 10000) of Division 4 of the Business and Professions Code. As used in this section, "transferee" includes a purchaser, lessee, or renter of real property.

(b)   It is the intention of the Legislature to occupy the field of regulation of disclosure related to deaths occurring upon real property and of AIDS in situations affecting the transfer of real property or any estate or interest in real property.

(c)   This section shall not be construed to alter the law relating to disclosure pertaining to any other physical or mental condition or disease, and this section shall not relieve any owner or agent of any obligations to disclose the physical condition of the premises.

(d)   Nothing in this section shall be construed to immunize an owner or his or her agent from making an intentional misrepresentation in response to a direct inquiry from a transferee or a prospective transferee of real property, concerning deaths on the real property.

AGE DISCRIMINATION - SENIOR CITIZEN HOUSING

The Unruh Civil Rights Act has been held to apply to age discrimination in apartment rentals and condominium properties because they are considered to be businesses subject to this act.

In 1984 the Legislature enacted Civil Code Section 51.2 to clarify the holdings in the California Supreme Court cases dealing with the scope of the applicability of the Unruh Civil Rights Act. In the same bill it enacted Civil Code Section 51.3 to establish and preserve specially designed accessible housing for senior citizens.

Section 51.2 says that: "Section 51 shall be construed to prohibit a business establishment from discriminating in the sale or rental of housing based upon age. Where accommodations are designed to meet the physical and social needs of senior citizens, a business establishment may establish and preserve such housing for senior citizens, pursuant to Section 51.3 of the Civil Code."

Section 51.3 defines the senior citizen accommodations referred to in Section 51.2 as/for:
*   Senior citizens are persons 62 years or older or one 55 years or older in a senior citizen housing development.

The definition of a senior citizen housing development varies, depending on its location. If it is in a standard metropolitan statistical area (SMSA), it must consist of 150 or more units. If it is not in a SMSA, then it must consist of 35 or more units. In either case, the project must be developed for or substantially renovated for senior citizens. The law does not apply to mobile home developments. The law contains several conditions required for senior citizen housing developments. The restrictions cannot limit occupancy more strictly than to limit it to senior citizen residents and a younger spouse or cohabitant or, as an alternative to a spouse, any person who provides primary physical or financial support to the senior citizen. In either case, the lower age limit is 45 years.

The restrictions must allow for temporary residency of any person for not less than 60 days per calendar year, and if the senior citizen dies, is absent for a prolonged period, or there is dissolution of a marriage, the remaining permanent resident is entitled to continue in residence.

The project must have been developed for and initially put to use as senior citizen housing or substantially renovated and immediately put to use as senior citizen housing.

The existing age restrictions or policies will be enforceable until December 1986, after which they will be enforceable only to the extent authorized by Section 51.3. Any person who has a right to reside in housing subject to this section on January 1, 1985 is allowed to continue in residence.

Federal Regulations call the elderly "senior persons" and fall under the Federal Fair Housing Act (Title VIII). The regulations are not as severe or restrictive as California Regulations, so in California the Unruh Act and Section 12900 will apply on age rental rules.

HOUSING DISCRIMINATION

The Fair Employment and Housing Act (Government Code Section 12900 et seq.) has many ramifications applying as it does to owners of specified types of property, to real estate brokers and salespersons, to other agents and to financial institutions. Sections 12955 and 12980-12988 specifically cover housing discrimination.

The law prohibits discrimination in supplying housing accommodations because of race, color, religion, sex, marital status, national origin or ancestry. Housing accommodations as used in the law means improved or unimproved real property used or intended to be used as a residence by the owner and which consists of not more than four dwelling units. The definition also includes four or fewer owner occupied housing units that secure a home improvement loan. It forbids such discrimination in the sale, rental, lease or financing of practically all types of housing, and establishes methods of investigating, preventing and remedying violations.

Housing discrimination complaints directed to the Department of Fair Employment and Housing are investigated by its staff. If the Department decides that the law has been violated, and if the person accused of violating the law cannot be persuaded to correct the violation, the department may file an accusation or bring an action in the Superior Court for an injunction. If the Commission of Fair Employment and Housing, after hearing, finds a violation of the law, it may order the sale or rental of the accommodation or like accommodations, if available. It may order financial assistance terms, conditions or privileges previously denied. In addition, it may order payment of punitive damages not to exceed $1,000 adjusted annually in accordance with the consumer price index and the payment of actual damages. The department is required to do a compliance review to determine whether its order is being carried out.

As stated above, Sections 12900 et seq. of the Government Code expand the application of the Rumford Act in the prohibition of discrimination in housing in making it apply to all housing accommodations, including single-family houses, except it will not apply to renting or leasing to a roomer or boarder in a single-family house provided that no more than one roomer or boarder is to live within the household.

The term "discrimination" includes refusal to sell, rent, or lease properties including misrepresentation as to availability, inferior terms, cancellations, etc. For sale or rent advertisements containing discriminatory information are prohibited.

State laws and the Real Estate Commissioner's Regulations concerning discrimination include:

1. *The Housing Financial Discrimination Act of 1977 also known as the Holden Act (Part 6 of Division 24 of Health and Safety Code Section 35800 et seq.)* which prohibits financial institutions (banks, savings and loan associations, or other financial institutions, including mortgage loan brokers, mortgage bankers and public agencies) which regularly make, arrange, or purchase loans for the purchase, construction rehabilitation, improvement, or refinancing of real property housing accommodations (used as an owner-occupied residence of not more than four dwelling units) from engaging in discriminatory loan practices.

   No financial institution shall discriminate in their financial assistance wholly or partly on the basis of consideration of race, color, religion, sex, marital status, national origin, or ancestry. Nor will it consider the racial, ethnic, religious, or national origin composition of trends in a neighborhood or geographic areas surrounding a housing accommodation. The foregoing is qualified by permitting the lender a demonstration that such consideration in the particular case is required to avoid an unsound business practice.

   The Secretary of the Business, Transportation and Housing Agency has issued rules, regulations and guidelines for enforcement of the act and is empowered to investigate lending patterns and practices, and to attempt to conciliate complaints. Investigation of complaints has been delegated to the state agency, which regulates the particular financial institution involved. If a violation of the Act is found to have occurred, the Secretary can order that the loan be made on nondiscriminatory terms or impose a fine of up to $1,000.

   The Secretary shall annually report to the Legislature on the activities of the appropriate regulatory agencies and departments in complying with this part. The report shall include a description of any actions taken by the Secretary or the Secretary's designee to remedy patterns or practices the secretary determines are in violation of the Act. Financial institutions are required to notify loan applicants of the existence of the act.

2. *Expanded Business and Professions Code Section 125.6* contains disciplinary provisions for discriminatory acts by any person licensed under the provisions of the Business and Professions Code.

3. *Article 10, Commissioner's Rules and Regulations 2780, 2781, and Business & Professions Code Section 10177(l),* sets forth in detail the discriminatory conduct which, if practiced by real estate licensees, will be the basis for disciplinary action:

   Commissioner's Regulation 2780: Discriminatory conduct by Real Estate Licensees is basis for disciplinary action.

   Commissioner's Regulation 2781: Panic selling is basis for disciplinary action.

   Business & Professions Code Section 10177(l): Solicited or induced the sale, lease, on the listing for sale or lease, of residential property on the ground, wholly or in part, of loss of value, increase in crime, or decline of the quality of the schools, due to the present or prospective entry into the neighborhood of a person or persons of another race, color, religion, ancestry, or national origin.

(m) Violated the Franchise Investment Law (Division 5 (commencing with Section 31000) of Title 4 of the Corporations Code) or regulations of the Commissioner of Corporations pertaining thereto.

4. There are other protections against discrimination written into the law and regulations, including:

- Business and Professions Code Section 10177 (l), which was added to the Code in 1964 to include the practice of "block busting" (aka panic selling) as a cause for discipline of a real estate licensee.
- Commissioner's Regulation Section 2792.25 adopted in 1976 to prevent use of the "right of first refusal" as a means of discrimination against prospective buyers of common interest subdivision interests.

CALIFORNIA CIVIL CODE 54-55.1 BLIND AND OTHER PHYSICALLY DISABLED PERSONS

This Code Section states that individuals with disabilities are entitled to the same rights as the general public to the full and free use of public places. A disability is a physical or mental impairment that substantially limits one or more of the major life activities of someone.

This Code covers housing as well as many other aspects of life. Also, owners can't discriminate against guide dogs. Damages can be as much as three times actual damages but no less than $1,000 plus attorney's fees.

Owners can't refuse any reasonable accommodations to afford equal use. Also, owners can't refuse to allow tenants to make reasonable modifications if they will restore the premises to their original condition upon movement.

CALIFORNIA BUREAU OF REAL ESTATE COMMISSIONER'S REGULATIONS #2780 – 2781

2780. DISCRIMINATORY CONDUCT AS THE BASIS FOR DISCIPLINARY ACTION.

Prohibited discriminatory conduct by a real estate licensee based upon race, color, sex, religion, ancestry, physical handicap, marital status or national origin includes, but is not limited to, the following:

(a) Refusing to negotiate for the sale, rental or financing of the purchase of real property or otherwise making unavailable or denying real property to any person because of such person's race, color, sex, religion, ancestry, physical handicap, marital status or national origin.

(b) Refusing or failing to show, rent, sell or finance the purchase of real property to any person or refusing or failing to provide or volunteer information to any person about real property, or channeling or steering any person away from real property, because of that person's race, color, sex, religion, ancestry, physical handicap, marital status or national origin or because of the racial, religious, or ethnic composition of any occupants of the area in which the real property is located.

(c) Discriminating because of race, color, sex, religion, ancestry, physical handicap, marital status or national origin against any person in the sale or purchase or negotiation or solicitation of the sale or purchase or the collection of payment or the performance of services in connection with contracts for the sale of real property or in connection with loans secured directly or collaterally by liens on real property or on a business opportunity. It shall not constitute discrimination under this subdivision for a real estate licensee to refuse or fail to show, rent, sell or finance the purchase of real property to any person having a physical handicap because of the presence of hazardous conditions or architectural barriers to the physically handicapped which conform to applicable state or local building codes and regulations.

Prohibited discriminatory conduct by a real estate licensee under this subdivision does not include acts based on a person's marital status which are reasonably taken in recognition of the community property laws of this state as to the acquiring, financing, holding or transferring of real property.

(d) Discriminating because of race, color, sex, religion, ancestry, physical handicap, marital status or national origin against any person in the terms, conditions or privileges of sale, rental or financing of the purchase of real property.

This subdivision does not prohibit the sale price, rent or terms of a housing accommodation containing facilities for the physically handicapped to differ reasonably from a housing accommodation not containing such facilities.

(e) Discriminating because of race, color, sex, religion, ancestry, physical handicap, marital status or national origin against any person in providing services or facilities in connection with sale, rental or financing of the purchase of real property, including but not limited to: processing applications differently, referring prospects to other licensees because of the prospects' race, color, sex, religion, ancestry, physical handicap, marital status or national origin, using with discriminatory intent or effect, codes or other means of identifying minority prospects, or assigning real estate licensees on the basis of a prospective client's race, color, sex, religion, ancestry, physical handicap, marital status or national origin.

Prohibited discriminatory conduct by a real estate licensee under this subdivision does not include acts based on a person's marital status which are reasonably taken in recognition of the community property laws of this state as to the acquiring, financing, holding or transferring of real property.

(f) Representing to any person because of his or her race, color, sex, religion, ancestry, physical handicap, marital status or national origin that real property is not available for inspection, sale or rental when such real property is in fact available.

(g) Processing an application more slowly or otherwise acting to delay, hinder or avoid the sale, rental or financing of the purchase of real property on account of the race,color, sex, religion, ancestry, physical handicap, marital status or national origin of a potential owner or occupant.

(h) Making any effort to encourage discrimination against persons because of their race, color, sex, religion, ancestry, physical handicap, marital status or national origin in the showing, sale lease or financing of the purchase of real property.

(i)   Refusing or failing to cooperate with or refusing or failing to assist another real estate licensee in negotiating the sale, rental or financing of the purchase of real property because of the race, color, sex, religion, ancestry, physical handicap, marital status or national origin of any prospective purchaser or tenant.

(j)   Making any effort to obstruct, retard or discourage the purchase, lease or financing of the purchase of real property by persons whose race, color, sex, religion, ancestry, physical handicap, marital status or national origin differs from that of the majority of persons now residing in a structural improvement of real property or in an area in which the real property is located.

(k)   Performing any acts, making any notation, asking any questions or making or circulating any written or oral statement which when taken in context, expresses or implies a limitation, preference or discrimination based upon race, color, sex, religion, ancestry, physical handicap, marital status or national origin; provided, however, that nothing herein shall limit the administering of forms or the making of a notation required by a federal, state or local agency for data collection or civil rights enforcement purposes; or in the case of a physically handicapped person, making notation, asking questions or circulating any written or oral statement in order to serve the needs of such a person.

(l)   Making any effort to coerce, intimidate, threaten or interfere with any person in the exercise or enjoyment of, or on account of such persons having exercised or enjoyed, or on account of such persons having aided or encouraged any other person in the exercise or enjoyment of any right granted or protected by a federal or state law, including but not limited to: assisting in any effort to coerce any person because of his or her race, color, sex, religion, ancestry, physical handicap, marital status or national origin to move from, or to not move into, a particular area; punishing or penalizing real estate licensees for their refusal to discriminate in the sale or rental of housing because of the race, color, sex, religion, ancestry, physical handicap, marital status or national origin of a prospective purchaser or lessee; or evicting or taking other retaliatory action against any person for having filed a fair housing complaint or for having undertaken other lawful efforts to promote fair housing.

(m)   Soliciting of sales, rentals or listings of real estate from any person, but not from another person within the same area because of differences in the race, color, sex, religion, ancestry, physical handicap, marital status or national origin of such persons.

(n)   Discriminating because of race, color, sex, religion, ancestry, physical handicap, marital status or national origin in informing persons of the existence of waiting lists or other procedures with respect to the future availability of real property for purchase or lease.

(o)   Making any effort to discourage or prevent the rental, sale or financing of the purchase of real property because of the presence or absence of occupants of a particular race, color, sex, religion, ancestry, physical handicap, marital status or national origin, or on the basis of the future presence or absence of a particular race, color, sex, religion, ancestry, physical handicap, marital status or national origin, whether actual, alleged or implied.

(p) Making any effort to discourage or prevent any person from renting, purchasing or financing the purchase of real property through any representations of actual or alleged community opposition based upon race, color, sex, religion, ancestry, physical handicap, marital status or national origin.

(q) Providing information or advice to any person concerning the desirability of particular real property or a particular residential area(s) which is different from information or advice given to any other person with respect to the same property or area because of differences in the race, color, sex, religion, ancestry, physical handicap, marital status or national origin of such persons.

This subdivision does not limit the giving of information or advice to physically handicapped persons for the purpose of calling to the attention of such persons the existence or absence of housing accommodation services or housing accommodations for the physically handicapped.

(r) Refusing to accept a rental or sales listing or application for financing of the purchase of real property because of the owner's race, color, sex, religion, ancestry, physical handicap, marital status or national origin or because of the race, color, sex, religion, ancestry, physical handicap, marital status or national origin of any of the occupants in the area in which the real property is located.

(s) Entering into an agreement, or carrying out any instructions of another, explicit or understood, not to show, lease, sell or finance the purchase of real property because of race, color, sex, religion, ancestry, physical handicap, marital status or national origin.

(t) Making, printing or publishing, or causing to be made, printed or published, any notice, statement or advertisement concerning the sale, rental or financing of the purchase of real property that indicated any preference, limitation or discrimination because of race, color, sex, religion, ancestry, physical handicap, marital status or national origin, or any intention to make such preference, limitation or discrimination.

This subdivision does not prohibit advertising directed to physically handicapped persons for the purpose of calling to the attention of such persons the existence or absence of housing accommodation services or housing accommodations for the physically handicapped.

(u) Using any word, phrases, sentences, descriptions or visual aids in any notice, statement or advertisement describing real property or the area in which real property is located which indicates any preference, limitation or discrimination because of race, color, sex, religion, ancestry, physical handicap, marital status or national origin.

(v) Selectively using, placing or designing any notice, statement or advertisement having to do with the sale, rental or financing of the purchase of real property in such a manner as to cause or increase discrimination by restricting or enhancing the exposure or appeal to persons of a particular race, color, sex, ancestry, physical handicap, marital status or national origin.

This subdivision does not limit in any way the use of an affirmative marketing program designed to attract persons of a particular race, color, sex, religion, ancestry, physical handicap, marital status or national origin who would not otherwise be attracted to the real property or to the area.

(w) Quoting or charging a price, rent or cleaning or security deposit for a particular real property to any person which is different from the price, rent or security deposit quoted or charged to any other person because of differences in the race, color, sex, religion, ancestry, physical handicap, marital status or national origin of such persons.

This subdivision does not prohibit the quoting or charging of a price, rent or cleaning or security deposit for a housing accommodation containing facilities for the physically handicapped to differ reasonably from a housing accommodation not containing such facilities.

(x) Discriminating against any person because of race, color, sex, religion, ancestry, physical handicap, marital status or national origin in performing any acts in connection with the making of any determination of financial ability or in the processing of any application for the financing or refinancing of real property.

Nothing herein shall limit the administering of forms or the making of a notation required by a federal, state or local agency for data collection or civil rights enforcement purposes. In any evaluation or determination as to whether, and under what terms and conditions, a particular lender or lenders would be likely to grant a loan, licensees shall proceed as though the lender or lenders are in compliance with Sections 35800 through 35833 of the California Health and Safety Code (The Housing Financial Discrimination Act of 1977).

Prohibited discriminatory conduct by a real estate licensee under this subdivision does not include acts based on a person's marital status which are reasonably taken in recognition of the community property laws of this state as to the acquiring, financing, holding or transferring of real property.

(y) Advising a person of the price or value of real property on the basis of factors related to the race, color, sex, religion, ancestry, physical handicap, marital status or national origin of residents of an area or of residents or potential residents of the area in which the property is located.

(z) Discriminating in the treatment of, or services provided to, occupants of any real property in the course of providing management services for the real property because of the race, color, sex, religion, ancestry, physical handicap, marital status or national origin of said occupants.

This subdivision does not prohibit differing treatment or services to a physically handicapped person because of the physical handicap in the course of providing management services for a housing accommodation.

(aa) Discriminating against the owners or occupants of real property because of the race, color, sex, religion, ancestry, physical handicap, marital status or national origin of their guests, visitors or invitees.

(bb) Making any effort to instruct or encourage, expressly or implied, by either word or acts, licensees or their employees, or other agents to engage in any discriminatory act in violation of a federal or state fair housing law.

(cc) Establishing or implementing rules that have the effect of limiting the opportunity for any person because of his or her race, color, sex, religion, ancestry, physical handicap, marital status or national origin to secure real property through a multiple listing or other real estate service.

(dd) Assisting or aiding in any way, any person in the sale, rental or financing of the purchase of real property where there are reasonable grounds to believe that such person intends to discriminate because of race, color, sex, religion, ancestry, physical handicap, marital status or national origin.

2781. PANIC SELLING AS THE BASIS FOR DISCIPLINARY ACTION

Prohibited discriminatory conduct includes, but is not limited to, soliciting sales or rental listings, making written or oral statements creating fear or alarm, transmitting written or oral warnings or threats, or acting in any other manner so as to induce or attempt to induce the sale or lease of real property through any representation, express or implied, regarding the present or prospective entry of one or more persons of another race, color, sex, religion, ancestry, marital status or national origin into an area or neighborhood.

BUSINESS & PROFESSIONS CODE SECTION 10177(L)

A broker licensee shall take reasonable steps to become aware of and to be familiar with and to familiarize his or her salespersons with the requirements of federal and state laws and regulations relating to the prohibition of discrimination in the sale, rental or financing of the purchase of real property. Such laws and regulations include but are not limited to the current provisions and any amendments thereto of:

(a) Sections 12900 through 12996 of the California Government Code

(b) Sections 51 and 52 of the California Civil Code (Unruh Civil Rights Act)

BE GOOD OR ELSE

Violation of any of these acts and regulations could result in disciplinary action by the Commissioner. The BRE treats complaints against licensees very seriously. Also, HUD and other groups are using more and more testers to check property owners and licensees.

Be warned. It is not only for the public good that you should follow these rules, but it is good for your real estate career. If you are unsure about anything, call the proper agency. Don't rely on office experts.

Brokers are responsible for adherence to the Fair Housing laws. They must supervise their associates closely and be sure that they know the rules and follow the rules.

FAIR HOUSING PARTNERSHIP RESOLUTION

The best method to present this information is to give you the pertinent passages from the resolution concerning the principles involved.

NOW, THEREFORE, BE IT RESOLVED that the National Association of Realtors and the U.S. Department of Housing and Urban Development reaffirm their commitment and hereby formulate a partnership to promote fair housing in all communities across our nation. BE IT FURTHER RESOLVED that such partnership is based on the following principles;

1. All participants in our nation's housing market share a responsibility for the achievement of fair housing.
2. HUD and NAR (the partnership) will, on an ongoing basis, jointly identify fair housing issues and concerns, which need be addressed.
3. The partnership will develop measurable strategies and actions to address identified issues and concerns.
4. The partnership will evaluate the results of the actions taken to determine future strategies and actions.
5. The partnership is national in scope but will be implemented both on the local community level and national level.
6. Realtors are encouraged to adopt a fair housing declaration outlining their commitment fair housing.
7. Also, Realtors must submit an affirmative fair housing marketing plan in order to do certain business with HUD. A model plan follows:

I agree to:

- Provide equal professional service without regard to the race, color, religion, sex, handicap, familial status, or national origin of any prospective client, customer, or the residents of any community.
- Keep informed about fair housing law and practices, improving my clients' and customers' opportunities and my business.
- Develop advertising that indicates that everyone is welcome and no one is excluded; expanding my client's and customer's opportunities to see, buy, or lease property.
- Inform my clients and customers about their rights and responsibilities under the fair housing laws by providing brochures and other information.
- Document my efforts to provide professional service, which will assist me in becoming a more responsive and successful REALTOR®.
- Refuse to tolerate non-compliance.
- Learn about those who are different from me and celebrate those differences.
- Take a positive approach to fair housing practices and aspire to follow the spirit as well as the letter of the law.
- Develop and implement fair housing practices for my firm to carry out the spirit of this declaration.

HOME MORTGAGE DISCLOSURE ACT (HMDA) – CALIFORNIA HEALTH & SAFETY CODE 35815-35816

The Federal Home Mortgage Disclosure Act, covered under HMDA, includes requirements for lenders that meet specified criteria to report loans made by census tract number. The student will also learn that lenders who are in the business of originating residential loans while operating under State licenses must report their lending activities to the State agency under whose jurisdiction they operate.

TEN STEPS TO HELP ILLUSTRATE THAT YOU ARE FOLLOWING PROPER PROCEDURES

1. Include the official fair housing and equal opportunity slogan or logo in all advertising. The slogan or logo is not necessary in classified advertising when the publisher's notice appears on the lead page of the newspaper's advertising section, or if the ad is less than six column inches.
2. Display the equal housing slogan or logo in a prominent place in all direct mail advertising brochures, circulars, and billboards. This logo or slogan should also be used on signs and other advertising if it does not add significantly to the cost.
3. When human models are used to illustrate any display advertising, the selection of models should be such to indicate that the advertised housing is available to all persons regardless of race, color, religion, sex, national origin, familial status or handicap.
4. Display the Fair Housing poster at your firm. This poster was developed by HUD and N.A.R. and includes N.A.R.'s code of Equal Opportunity in Housing, adopted in May 1972.
5. Make the N.A.R. *Affirmative Marketing Handbook* available to all your associates. Encourage them to become familiar with the guidelines, and urge them to attend and participate in available educational programs.
6. Conduct an information program for sales personnel, agents, and employees, telling them of their responsibilities and each member should also encourage his/her associates to comply with the Fair Housing Partnership Resolution and any other Fair Housing Laws.
7. Adopt, implement and monitor specific office management procedures to achieve objectives of the Fair Housing Partnership Resolution. The local Boards should develop suggested procedures, make them available to their members, and recommend implementation. Procedures should:
    * Make prospective buyers and renters aware of available choices within their price and interest range.
    * Provide complete and accurate information to all prospective purchasers and renters.
    * Elicit suggestions from buyers/renters for improvement of the program.
8. Recruit salaried employees and real estate professionals of all religions, sexes, races, and ethnic background with and without disabilities through advertising using the equal opportunity slogan. Develop programs, such as C.A.R.'s Real Estate Internship program, likely to produce candidates from all backgrounds for employment.
9. Encourage all associates to distribute copies of the booklet entitled, *What Everyone Should Know About Equal Opportunity in Housing,* to all sellers at the time the listing contract is signed. The booklet will make sellers aware of the requirements under the fair housing law and equal housing opportunity policy.
10. Become a fair housing leader in your community. Invite and encourage community participation in Board fair housing activities.

EQUAL CREDIT OPPORTUNITY ACT (15 U.S. CODE 1691, ET SEQ.)

This act became effective on October 28, 1975 and it prohibits discrimination on the basis of race, color, religion, national origin, sex, marital status, or on the ground of receipt of income from a public assistance program. The law also requires that a lender/creditor who denies an application for credit must provide the applicant with a statement of reasons or a written notification of the applicant's right to obtain a statement of reasons.

In addition to the foregoing Federal law, state law regulates the issuance of consumer credit reports, access by the consumer to such reports, and the obligations of credit reporting agencies. Also, users of consumer credit reports are subject to the requirements of State law and must provide notice to the consumer when credit is denied. This law is found in California Civil Code Section 1785.1 et seq.

SOME IMPORTANT FACTS ABOUT ECOA
EQUAL CREDIT OPPORTUNITY ACT, REGULATION B

1. Available credit to all without regard to race, color, religion, national origin, sex, marital status, or age (provided the applicant has the capacity to contract); to the fact that all or part of the applicant's income derives from a public assistance program; or to the fact that the applicant has in good faith exercised any right under the Consumer Credit Protection Act.
   - The regulation prohibits creditor practices that discriminate on the basis of any of these factors.
   - The regulation also requires creditors to notify applicants of action taken on their applications.
   - To report credit history in the names of both spouses on an account.
   - To retain records of credit applications.
   - To collect information about the applicant's race and other personal characteristics in applications for certain dwelling-related loans.
   - To provide applicants with copies of appraisal reports used in connection with credit transactions.

2. Creditor:
   - Creditor means a person who, in the ordinary course of business, regularly participates in a credit decision, including setting the terms of the credit. The term creditor includes a creditor's assignee, transferee, or subrogee who so participates. For purposes of § 202.4 (a) and (b), the term creditor also includes a person who, in the ordinary course of business regularly refers applicants or prospective applicants to creditors, or selects or offers to select creditors to whom requests for credit may be made.

3. Elderly:
   - Elderly means age 62 or over.

4. Good Faith:
   - Good faith (bona fide) means honesty in fact.

5. Unmarried:
   - Unmarried includes singles, divorced, or widowed.

6. Person:
   - Person means a natural person, corporation, government or governmental subdivision or agency, trust, estate, partnership, cooperative, or association.

7. Discouragement:
   - A creditor shall not make any oral or written statement, in advertising or otherwise, to applicants or prospective applicants that would discourage on a prohibited basis a reasonable person from making or pursuing an application.

8. Foreign-Language Disclosures:
   - Disclosures may be made in languages other than English, provided they are available in English upon request.

9. Self-test:
   - A creditor may inquire about the race, color, religion, national origin, or sex of an applicant or any other person in connection with a credit transaction for the purpose of conducting a self-test. A creditor that makes such an inquiry shall disclose orally or in writing, at the time the information is requested, that
     - The applicant will not be required to provide the information.
     - The creditor is requesting the information to monitor its compliance with the federal Equal Credit Opportunity Act.
     - Federal law prohibits the creditor from discriminating on the basis of this information, or on the basis of an applicant's decision not to furnish the information; and
     - If applicable, certain information will be collected based on visual observation or surname if not provided by the applicant or other person.

10. Sex:
    - An applicant may be requested to designate a title on an application form (such as Ms., Miss, Mr., or Mrs.) if the form discloses that the designation of a title is optional. An application form shall otherwise use only terms that are neutral as to sex.

11. Information about a spouse or former spouse:
    - General rule: Except as permitted in this paragraph, a creditor may not request any information concerning the spouse or former spouse of an applicant.

12. Permissible inquires:
    - A creditor may request any information concerning an applicant's spouse (or former spouse) that may be requested about the applicant if:
      - The spouse will be permitted to use the account;
      - The spouse will be contractually liable on the account;
      - The applicant is relying on the spouse's income as a basis for repayment of the credit requested;
      - The applicant resides in a community property state or is relying on property located in such a state as a basis for repayment of the credit requested; or
      - The applicant is relying on alimony, child support, or separate maintenance payments from a spouse or former spouse as a basis for repayment of the credit requested.

13. Other accounts of the applicant:
    - A creditor may request that an applicant list any account on which the applicant is contractually liable and to provide the name and address of the person in whose

name the account is held. A creditor may also ask an applicant to list the names in which the applicant has previously received credit.

14. Other limitations on information requests:
   - Marital status: If an applicant applies for individual unsecured credit, a creditor shall not inquire about the applicant's marital status unless the applicant resides in a community property state or is relying on property located in such a state as a basis for repayment of the credit requested. If an application is for other than individual unsecured credit, a creditor may inquire about the applicant's marital status, but shall use only the terms married, unmarried, and separated. A creditor may explain that the category unmarried includes single, divorced, and widowed persons.
   - Disclosure about income from alimony, child support, or separate maintenance: A creditor shall not inquire whether income stated in an application is derived from alimony, child support, or separate maintenance payments unless the creditor discloses to the applicant that such income need not be revealed if the applicant does not want the creditor to consider it in determining the applicant's creditworthiness.
   - Childbearing, childrearing: A creditor shall not inquire about birth control practices, intentions concerning the bearing or rearing of children, or capability to bear children. A creditor may inquire about the number and ages of an applicant's dependents or about dependent-related financial obligations or expenditures, provided such information is requested without regard to sex, marital status, or any other prohibited basis.
   - Permanent residency and immigration status: A creditor may inquire about the permanent residency and immigration status of an applicant or any other person in connection with a credit transaction.

15. Age, receipt of public assistance:
   - Except as permitted in this paragraph, a creditor shall not take into account an applicant's age (provided that the applicant has the capacity to enter into a binding contract) or whether an applicant's income derives from any public assistance program.
   - In an empirically derived, demonstrably and statistically sound, credit scoring system, a creditor may use an applicant's age as a predictive variable, provided that the age of an elderly applicant is not assigned a negative factor or value.
   - In a judgmental system of evaluating creditworthiness, a creditor may consider an applicant's age or whether an applicant's income derives from any public assistance program only for the purpose of determining a pertinent element of creditworthiness.
   - In any system of evaluating creditworthiness, a creditor may consider the age of an elderly applicant when such age is used to favor the elderly applicant in extending credit.

16. Childbearing, childrearing:
   - In evaluating creditworthiness, a creditor shall not make assumptions or use aggregate statistics relating to the likelihood that any category of persons will bear or rear children or will, for that reason, receive diminished or interrupted income in the future.

17. Telephone listing:

- A creditor shall not take into account whether there is a telephone listing in the name of an applicant for consumer credit, but may take into account whether there is a telephone in the applicant's residence.

18. Income:
    - A creditor shall not discount or exclude from consideration the income of an applicant or the spouse of an applicant because of a prohibited basis or because the income is derived from part-time employment or is an annuity, pension, or other retirement benefit; a creditor may consider the amount and probable continuance of any income in evaluating an applicant's creditworthiness. When an applicant relies on alimony, child support, or separate maintenance payments in applying for credit, the creditor shall consider such payments as income to the extent that they are likely to be consistently made.

19. Credit history:
    - To the extent that a creditor considers credit history in evaluating the creditworthiness of similarly qualified applicants for a similar type and amount of credit, in evaluating an applicant's creditworthiness a creditor shall consider:
        a. The credit history, when available, of accounts designated as accounts that the applicant and the applicant's spouse are permitted to use or for which both are contractually liable.
        b. On the applicant's request, any information the applicant may present that tends to indicate that the credit history being considered by the creditor does not accurately reflect the applicant's creditworthiness; and
        c. On the applicant's request, the credit history, when available, of any account reported in the name of the applicant's spouse or former spouse that the applicant can demonstrate accurately reflects the applicant's creditworthiness.

20. Immigration status:
    - A creditor may consider the applicant's immigration status or status as a permanent resident of the United States, and any additional information that may be necessary to ascertain the creditor's rights and remedies regarding repayment.

21. Marital status:
    - Except as otherwise permitted or required by law, a creditor shall evaluate married and unmarried applicants by the same standards; and in evaluating joint applicants, a creditor shall not treat applicants differently based on the existence, absence, or likelihood of a marital relationship between the parties.

22. Race, color, religion, national origin, sex:
    - Except as otherwise permitted or required by law, a creditor shall not consider race, color, religion, national origin, or sex (or an applicant's or other person's decision not to provide the information) in any aspect of a credit transaction.

23. State property laws:
    - A creditor's consideration or application of state property laws directly or indirectly affecting creditworthiness does not constitute unlawful discrimination for the purposes of the Act or this regulation.

24. Notifications:
    - Notification of action taken, ECOA notice, and statement of specific reasons. When notification is required: A creditor shall notify an applicant of action taken within:

a. 30 days after receiving a completed application concerning the creditor's approval of, counteroffer to, or adverse action on the application;
b. 30 days after taking adverse action on an incomplete application;
c. 30 days after taking adverse action on an existing account; or
d. 90 days after notifying the applicant of a counteroffer if the applicant does not expressly accept or use the credit offered.

25. Content of notification when adverse action is taken:
   - A notification given to an applicant when adverse action is taken shall be in writing and shall contain a statement of the action taken; the name and address of the creditor; a statement of the provisions of § 701(a) of the Act; the name and address of the federal agency that administers compliance with respect to the creditor; and either:
   a. A statement of specific reasons for the action taken; or
   b. A disclosure of the applicant's right to a statement of specific reasons within 30 days, if the statement is requested within 60 days of the creditor's notification. The disclosure shall include the name, address, and telephone number of the person or office from which the statement of reasons can be obtained. If the creditor chooses to provide the reasons orally, the creditor shall also disclose the applicant's right to have them confirmed in writing within 30 days of receiving the applicant's written request for confirmation.

26. Inconsistent state laws:
   - Except as otherwise provided in this section, this regulation alters, affects or preempts only those state laws that are inconsistent with the Act and this regulation and then only to the extent of the inconsistency. A state law is not inconsistent if it is more protective of an applicant.

27. Preempted provisions of state law:
   - A state law is deemed to be inconsistent with the requirements of the Act and this regulation and less protective of an applicant within the meaning of the Act to the extent that the law:
   a. Requires or permits a practice or act prohibited by the Act or this regulation;
   b. Prohibits the individual extension of consumer credit to both parties to a marriage if each spouse individually and voluntarily applies for such credit;
   c. Prohibits inquiries or collection of data required to comply with the Act or this regulation;
   d. Prohibits asking about or considering age in an empirically derived, demonstrably and statistically sound, credit scoring system to determine a pertinent element of creditworthiness or to favor an elderly applicant; or
   e. Prohibits inquiries necessary to establish or administer a special purpose credit program.

28. Rules on providing appraisal reports:
   - Providing Appraisals. A creditor shall provide a copy of an appraisal report used in connection with an application for credit that is to be secured by a lien on a dwelling.
   - Routine Delivery. A creditor may routinely provide a copy of an appraisal report to an applicant (whether credit is granted or denied or the application is withdrawn).
   - Upon Request. A creditor that does not routinely provide appraisal reports shall provide a copy upon an applicant's written request.

- Notice. A creditor that provides appraisal reports only upon request shall notify an applicant in writing of the right to receive a copy of an appraisal report. The notice may be given at any time during the application process but no later than when the creditor provides notice of action. The notice shall specify that the applicant's request must be in writing, give the creditor's mailing address, and state the time for making the request.
- Delivery. A creditor shall mail or deliver a copy of the appraisal report promptly (generally within 30 days) after the creditor receives an applicant's request, receives the report, or receives reimbursement from the applicant for the report, whichever is last to occur. A creditor need not provide a copy when the applicant's request is received more than 90 days after the creditor has provided notice of action taken on the application or 90 days after the application is withdrawn.
- Credit Unions. A creditor that is subject to the regulations of the National Credit Union Administration on making copies of appraisal reports available is not subject to this section.
- Definitions. The term dwelling means a residential structure that contains one to four units whether or not that structure is attached to real property. The term includes, but is not limited to, an individual condominium or cooperative unit, and a mobile or other manufactured home. The term appraisal report means the document(s) relied upon by a creditor in evaluating the value of the dwelling.

29. Incentives for self-testing and self-correction:
    - General rules
      a. Voluntary self-testing and correction. The report or results of the self-test that a creditor voluntarily conducts (or authorizes) are privileged as provided in this section. Data collection required by law or by any governmental authority is not a voluntary self-test.
      b. Corrective action required. The privilege in this section applies only if the creditor has taken or is taking appropriate corrective action.
      c. Other privileges. The privilege created by this section does not preclude the assertion of any other privilege that may also apply.
      d. Self-test defined. Definition: A self-test is any program, practice, or study that:
      e. Is designed and used specifically to determine the extent or effectiveness of a creditor's compliance with the Act or this regulation; and
      f. Creates data or factual information that is not available and cannot be derived from loan or application files or other records related to credit transactions.

Two important acts for Real Estate Agents to know are the Fair Credit Reporting Act and the National Do Not Call Registry. Information about these two acts follows:

Fair Credit Reporting Act (FCRA)
Regulation V, the Fair Credit Reporting Act is a federal law supervised by the Federal Trade Commission (FTC) that deals with the granting of credit, access to credit information, the rights of debtors, and the responsibilities of creditors. FCRA:
- Gives consumers access to the same information about themselves that lenders use when making credit decisions.
- Allows consumers to seek damages for violations of their rights.
- Provides additional rights for identity theft victims and active duty military personnel.

Consumer Rights: Copy of Consumer Credit File
Consumers are entitled to a free copy of their credit file under these circumstances.

- Information in a credit report resulted in adverse action. Adverse action requires the creditor to provide the consumer with the name, address, and phone number of the agency that provided the information. The requirements under FCRA differ somewhat from those under the ECOA, although both laws can be satisfied with a single Adverse Action Notice (sometimes called a Statement of Credit Denial).
- The consumer was a victim of identify theft and a fraud alert was inserted in credit file.
- The credit file contains inaccurate information as a result of fraud.
- The consumer is on public assistance or is unemployed.

Other Consumer Rights
- **Request a Credit Score.** Although it is not free, consumers have the right to ask for a credit score from any consumer reporting agency that creates or distributes scores used in residential real property loans.
- **Dispute Incomplete or Inaccurate Information.** Consumers have the right to dispute any incomplete or inaccurate information that they find in their credit report. The consumer reporting agency must correct or delete inaccurate, incomplete, or unverifiable information.
- **Limit Prescreened Offers.** Consumers may choose to limit "prescreened" offers of credit and insurance based on information in their credit report. Unsolicited prescreened offers for credit and insurance must include a toll-free phone number to call to be removed from the lists on which these offers are based.

Consumer Reporting Agency Obligations
Under the Fair Credit Reporting Act, consumer reporting agencies:
- May not report outdated negative information. In most cases, a consumer reporting agency will not report negative credit information that is more than seven (7) years old or bankruptcies that are more than ten (10) years. There is no time limit on the reporting of criminal convictions.
- Must limit access to a credit file. A consumer reporting agency may provide information to people with a valid need-usually to consider an application with a creditor, insurer, employer, landlord, or other business. The FCRA specifies those with a valid need for access.
- May not give out consumer credit information to an employer, or a potential employer, without written consent given to the employer by the consumer.

Other Information from FACTA Act in 2003 which amended FCRA
Access to Credit Reports
- Requires that consumers applying for credit receive the Home Loan Applicant Credit Score Information Disclosure notice, which explains their rights.
- Allows consumers to obtain a free copy of their credit report once every twelve (12) months from each of the three credit bureaus: Equifax, Experian, and TransUnion by contacting a centralized website, maintained in cooperation with the Federal Trade Commission: www.annualcreditreport.com

Truncation of Credit and Debit Card Numbers
FACTA also prohibits business from printing more than five digits of any customer's card number or card expiration date on any receipt provided to the cardholder at the point of sale or transaction. The provision excludes receipts that are handwritten or imprinted, if that is the only method of recording the credit card number.

Security and Disposal

Requires businesses to take measures to responsibly secure and dispose of sensitive personal information that is found in a consumer's credit report. Reasonable methods for security and disposal include:

- Burning or shredding papers that contain consumer report information so that information cannot be reconstructed.
- Destroying or erasing electronic files or media so that information cannot be recovered or reconstructed.
- Placing all pending loan documents in locked desks, cabinets, or storage rooms at the end of the work day.

The National Do Not Call Registry

- A provision of the federal telemarketing sales rule, the Do Not Call Registry is managed by the Federal Trade Commission (FTC), the nation's consumer protection agency and enforced by the FTC, the Federal Communications Commission (FCC), and state law enforcement officials.
- Applies to any plan, program, or campaign to sell goods or services through interstate phone calls. This includes telemarketers who solicit consumers, often on behalf of third party sellers. It also includes sellers who provide, offer to provide, or arrange to provide goods or services to consumers in exchange for payment. The National Do Not Call Registry does not limit calls by political organizations, charities, or telephone surveyors.
- Requires companies to maintain national and internal lists of customers and prospects and keep them updated regularly (national list every three months).
- Prohibits calls to consumers no later than 31 days after consumer asks to be included on the registry.
- Allows consumers who receive a telemarketing call despite being on the registry to file a complaint with the FTC. Violators could be fined up to $16,000 per incident.

Established Business Relationship

A telemarketer or seller may call a consumer with whom it has an established business relationship (EBR) for up to eighteen (18) months after the consumer's last purchase, delivery, or payment, even if the consumer's number is on the National Do Not Call Registry. In addition, a company may call a consumer for up to three (3) months after the company makes an inquiry or submits an application to the company. Obtaining the name, phone number, and signature from a consumer provides written consent that does not expire until rescinded.

One warning: If a consumer has asked to be put on the company's internal do not call list, the company may not call, even if there is an EBR.

FAIR HOUSING PRACTICE QUESTIONS:

True or False?

1. Our current Civil Rights Act was promulgated in 1968. *F*

2. HUD is disallowed from seeking remedies for violations. *F*

3. It is unlawful to select discriminatory direct mail lists. *T*

4. Redlining is allowed for California lenders. *F*

5. The first Civil Rights Act was established in 1866. *T*

6. A mental impairment is not considered a handicap under ADA. *F*

7. Rules must be modified for reasonable changes for handicapped person *T*

8. The Unruh Act does not apply to real estate activities. *F*

9. California Civil Codes Section 1710.2 addresses AIDs. *T*

10. In senior citizen housing the lowest age of a younger spouse is 27. *F*

11. The Unruh Act is more restrictive than Federal Law so it will apply in California. *F*

12. The Holden Act does not prohibit sex discrimination. *F*

13. Panic selling is illegal. *T*

14. "Block busting" is permitted by licensees. *F*

15. Community property laws can be considered in marital status questions. *T*

16. Processing applications slowly is permissible in ancestry questions. *F*

17. It is permissible to ask questions about race, color or sex when such data is required by Federal Agencies. *T*

18. Discussion of the future presence of a particular race in a neighborhood can be used to discourage rentals. *F*

19. State law does not prohibit advertising directed to physically handicapped persons for the purpose of calling to their attention the existence of certain housing accommodations. *T*

20. State law limits the use of an affirmative marketing program designed to attract persons of a particular race to the area. *T*

21. State law does not prohibit differing treatment to a physically handicapped person in the course of providing management services. *F*

22. The BRE does not become involved with licensee violations of these fair housing laws. *F*

23. The Fair Housing Partnership was developed by NAR and HUD. *X*

24. The ECOA Act was effective in 1866. F *1975*

25. When human models are used to illustrate any display advertising, the selection of models should be such as to indicate that the advertised housing is available to all persons. T

26. Elderly means age 62 or over. T

27. Disclosures may not be made in languages other than English. F

28. An application form shall use only terms that are neutral as to sex. T

29. A creditor may not inquire about the immigration status of an applicant. F

30. A creditor may consider the age of an elderly applicant when such age is used to favor the elderly applicant. T

31. A creditor's consideration of state property laws affecting creditworthiness does constitute unlawful discrimination. F

32. A state law is not inconsistent if it is more protective of an applicant. T

33. A creditor shall not mail or deliver a copy of the appraisal report after the creditor receives an applicant's request. F

34. The term dwelling includes a mobile or other manufactured home. F

35. The Fair Credit Reporting Act is a Federal Law. T

36. A customer has the right to a free credit report and a free credit score. F

37. Businesses can only print up to 5 digits of a credit card number. T

38. A violator of the National-Do-Not-Call list can be fined up to $100,000 per incident. F *16,000*

39. After a purchase a seller can call a consumer up to 18 months. T

40. The National-Do-Not-Call List is managed by the California BRE. F *Fed. Trade Comm.*

Practice Questions designed to prepare you to pass the final exams are available. New BRE Regulations do not allow us to give the answers to the quizzes in the book so the questions and answers are presented online. This makes the test taking very easy as you get the answers immediately.

To access the practice quizzes please visit http://www.DuaneGomer.com/after . Check on the proper link for the course you desire.

NOTE: Do not use Google, Yahoo, Bing etc. They are Search Engines. You must put the above URL link in your address bar or you won't get there.

You may request the questions by email to info@DuaneGomer.com, fax at 949-455-9931, or phone 800-439-4909. You will receive only the practice questions. You may FAX back your answers to Duane Gomer, Inc., at (949) 455-9931 and we will FAX your results to you within 24 business hours. Our recommendation is find a computer even if it's a friend or relatives it makes everything so easy under the new BRE rules.

RISK MANAGEMENT

UNDERSTANDING THE BASIC CONCEPTS OF RISK MANAGEMENT

TERMS AND DEFINITION

Risk management is a crucial topic in the real estate industry and becoming more and more important with each passing day. With this in mind the California State Legislature passed a requirement requiring mandatory education on this topic for all persons renewing a California Bureau of Real Estate License.

This addition to the continuing education requirements is in Business and Professions Code 10170.5 (a) (5). It reads in part: Required is a three hour course in Risk Management that shall include but need not be limited to principle, practice and procedures of real estate license activities. This new law will be effective for licensees renewing a license after July 1, 2007.

What does the term Risk Management mean? For a comprehensive definition we will use "Webster's Encyclopedic Unabridged Dictionary."

Risk is: Exposure to the chance of injury or loss; a hazard or dangerous chance. Synonym: peril, jeopardy, and hazard.

Management is: The act or manner of managing: handling, direction or control. Synonym: Administration, care, guidance, superintendence, conduct.

Combining the two definitions indicate that Real Estate Licensees are exposed to chaos, peril and jeopardy and they better manage and control their activities in their real estate endeavors or they will face a chance of injury and loss of their money, time and license.

Is there risk involved in being a real estate licensee? As you know, that is obviously a rhetorical question. There is a chance for loss from the time you are licensed till the day you die. (Some violations have a very long statute of limitations.)

What could you lose?
   1. You could lose your license or have your license severely restricted. Remember the BRE bulletins that we used to receive? There in clear printed form were the names of licensees who were investigated and disciplined. Incidentally, those bulletins we all loved to receive so that we could check to see if we knew any of the fallen are now available on-line. Make sure your name never appears there.

2. You could lose money at a trial or in a settlement. There are words like treble damages, punitive damages, and prevailing attorney fees in the regulations.
3. You could lose large amounts of time fighting lawsuits or investigations. This is true even if you believe that the accusations are frivolous, ridiculous, or without merit.
4. You could lose even more time if a criminal court ruled that you should be a guest of the state in a penitentiary for an extended period of time.

THE PROBABILITY OF RISK

What is the probability of risk? To understand what is happening in real estate become a subscriber to the Bureau of Real Estate monthly report #149. You will be amazed at the increase in the number of licensees and in the number of investigations.

Are we becoming more or less of a litigious culture? TV shows like Law & Order, Boston Legal, Convictions, Cold Case, etc. are showing the public more creative ways to sue. If something goes wrong, a vast majority of clients believe that somebody or everybody should be sued. As a successful businessperson with a successful broker, you are front and center in their mind. You are like the largest chocolate bunny at an Easter Egg Hunt. Does the phrase "deep pockets" mean anything to you?

STANDARDS OF CARE

To what standard of care will you be judged? Are there any guidelines in writing for you to observe? Let's check the extremely valuable California Civil Code. You should have your own copy of these regulations because so many sections apply to real estate. These Codes discuss lending, property management, foreclosure, agency disclosures, trust fund handling, common interest developments, civil rights, senior citizen housing and much, much more.

How do you find these valuable Civil Code guidelines? You can purchase the Real Estate Law book from the Bureau of Real Estate, or you can go online and view the California Real Estate Commissioner's Regulations at www.bre.ca.gov. Also, you can check the Business and Professions Code and the California Civil Code at www.leginfo.ca.gov.

We were discussing "Standard of Care Issues." Civil Code Section 2079 reads as follows: (a) It is the duty of a real estate broker or salesperson, licensed under Division 4 (commencing with Section 10000) of the Business and Professions Code, to a prospective purchaser of residential real property comprising one to four dwelling units, or a manufactured home as defined in Section 18007 of the Health and Safety Code, to conduct a reasonably competent and diligent visual inspection of the property offered for sale and to disclose to that prospective purchaser all facts materially affecting the value or desirability of the property that an investigation would reveal, if that broker has a written contract with the seller to find or obtain a buyer or is a broker who acts in cooperation with that broker to find and obtain a buyer. (b) It is the duty of a real estate broker or salesperson licensed under Division 4 (commencing with Section 10000) of the Business and Professions Code to comply with this section and any regulations imposing standards of professional conduct adopted pursuant to Section 10080 of the Business and Professions Code with reference to Sections 10176 and 10177 of the Business and Professions Code.

Section 10080 referred to in the above paragraph says that the Real Estate Commissioner can change the rules of the game at any time so you must keep up to date on all changes.

It reads in part: the Commissioner may adopt, amend, or repeal such rules and regulations as are reasonably necessary for the enforcement of the provisions of this part and of Chapter 1 (commencing with Section 11000) of Part 2 of this division. Such rules and regulations shall be adopted, amended, or repealed in accordance with the provisions of the Administrative Procedure Act.

Another reference that discusses Standard of Care is Civil Code Section 2079.2 which reads as follows: The standard of care owed by a broker under this article is the degree of care that a reasonably prudent real estate licensee would exercise and is measured by the degree of knowledge through education, experience, and examination, required to obtain a license under Division 4 (commencing with Section 10000) of the Business and Professions Code.

The most important guidelines for licensees are Section 10176-10177 of the Business and Professions Code. They are so important that a recap of them is included here.

Recap of Section 10176:
The commissioner may, upon his own motion, and shall, upon the verified complaint in writing of any person, investigate the actions of any person engaged in the business of acting in the capacity of a real estate licensee within this state, and he may temporarily suspend or permanently revoke a real estate license at any time where the licensee, while a real estate licensee, in performing or attempting to perform any of the acts within the scope of this chapter has been guilty of any of the following:

1. Making any substantial misrepresentation.
2. Making any false promises.
3. A continued and flagrant course of misrepresentation.
4. Acting for more than one party in a transaction without the knowledge or consent of all parties thereto.
5. Commingling with his own money or property the money or other property of others, which is received and held by him.
6. Preparing listing agreements with no termination date.
7. Receiving secret compensation without disclosure.
8. Secret profits on options.
9. Fraud or dishonest dealings.
10. Doing contracts before getting signed listing on business opportunities.
11. Failing to disburse funds properly.
12. Intentionally delaying a closing.

Recap of Section 10177:
The Commissioner may take action when there is:
1. Fraud or misstatement to get a license.
2. A felony or moral turpitude crime.
3. False advertising.
4. Violation of Real Estate Law Section 10000.
5. Use of the term Realtor when licensee is not a Realtor.
6. Loss of license from California or other States.
7. Negligence or incompetence.
8. Failure to supervise.
9. Improper use of government records.
10. Fraud or dishonest dealing.
11. Violation of terms of a restricted license.

12. Violation of Fair Housing Regulations.
13. Violation of the Franchise Investment Act or Commissioner of Corporation's regulations.
14. Violation of the Corporate Securities Law.
15. Non-disclosure of any special relationships.

COMMON AREAS OF RISK

CONTRACT PREPARATION

The topic of Risk Management is so complex that it is impossible to cover all the areas of residential sales, commercial or industrial sales, loan brokerage, property management and business opportunities in a three-hour course. This program is individually tailored to focus on the vast problems in the field of residential sales. Almost all of the material will be applicable to the other specialties, but sales activities will be stressed.

Contract preparation is so important because when you are preparing or discussing a contract with a client your risk begins immediately. In many cases, you are working with the client's most important contract of his or her life. Their expectations are huge and the chance for errors whether intentional or unintentional are vast.

The benchmark contract in California is from the California Association of Realtors. It is the California Residential Purchase Agreement and Joint Escrow Instructions. Also, many large companies & Realtor Associations have their own agreements. Study your contract. Read it over. Keep up-to-date on any changes. Someday, someplace, somewhere, or somehow, you will be so happy that you did.

Become the lead expert on contracts in your office. Go to education sessions to learn even more. Want to become even more of an expert? Teach a class at your local community college or adult education school. When you know that you are going to make a presentation at a seminar, you will study and know all your lines. I have always found it valuable to have guest speakers at my classes. You will learn from your guests and will learn even more from your students.

As a real estate licensee you can fill in contracts under the theory that you are functioning as an inscriber or scribe. You cannot practice law, therefore, be careful not to create any long amendments or contract changes without getting legal advice.

If you are dispensing legal advice on any topic such as how to hold title, tax law, legal questions, comprehensive handwritten phrases, original addendums, etc, you could be accused of the unauthorized practice of law. You should learn all that you can about real estate law, regulations, court cases and other matters. This will allow you to avoid an accusation of practicing law.

Tips on how to prepare a contract properly:
1. Use a recognized form that is understood by California practitioners.
2. Take advantage of classes that the REALTOR® Associations present on this subject. Purchase the California Association of REALTORS'® Sample Forms Book; it changes twice a year and you need a copy.

3. Join your local Association of REALTORS®, National Association of Realtors and the California Association of REALTORS®. Pay the extra money to be a member of the California Legal Hotline and buy their Risk Management package.
4. Purchase books on contract law from the California Association of REALTORS® (i.e. Your Guide To The California Residential Purchase Agreement).

PROPERTY CONDITIONS: PROPERTY OWNERSHIP

As a licensee you have certain responsibilities when doing visual inspections. This is spelled out in Civil Code 2079. There is a standard of care listed in this article that was discussed beginning on page three of this booklet.

You should investigate properties to make sure there are no apparent problems with ownership. Sources for information on this subject would be County Recorder Records, Title Companies, and other research firms.

TRUST FUND HANDLING

If you study the past history of license revocations in BRE Bulletins, you will discover a large percentage of them are due to trust fund handling errors. Every licensee learns the word commingling. Don't do it. Even worse don't convert the funds to your use.

You have the responsibility of treating the funds of any person like a trustee. This is the highest form of a business relationship. Are there risks involved in doing this? Is another rhetorical question?

Many extremely honest licensees have been penalized for their trust fund maintenance. You must be ethical, capable, and competent. You must be detailed in your handling of this money and you also must be certain anyone involved is trustworthy, loyal, helpful, friendly, courteous, kind, obedient, cheerful, thrifty, brave, clean and reverent.

BROKER SUPERVISON

You will hear many theories and tips from lectures and other pundits on how a broker should supervise licensees. However, when you go to a court or to a Bureau of Real Estate hearing, the important people in your legal life (those who can take your money and license etc.) will refer to the Real Estate Commissioner's Regulations among other codes.

Commissioner's Regulation 2725
A broker shall exercise reasonable supervision which includes, as appropriate, the establishment of policies, rules, procedures and systems to review, oversee, inspect and manage:
1. Transactions requiring a real estate license.
2. Documents that may have a material effect upon the rights or obligations of a party to the transaction.
3. Filing, storage, maintenance and disposal of such documents.
4. The handling of trusts funds.
5. Advertising of any service for which a license is required.

6. Familiarizing salespersons with the requirements of federal and state laws relating to the prohibition of discrimination.
7. Regular and consistent reports of licensed activities of salespersons.

The form and extent of such policies, rules, procedures and systems shall take into consideration the number of salespersons employed and the number and location of branch offices. A broker shall establish a system for monitoring compliance with such policies, rules, procedures and systems. A broker may use the services of brokers and salespersons to assist in administering the provisions of this section so long as the broker does not relinquish overall responsibility for supervision of the acts of salespersons licensed to the broker. That's the law, so you now know what to do when you have your own company, so do it.

FAILURE TO RESEARCH, INVESTIGATE AND DISCLOSE MATERIAL FACTS

The requirement of a broker to perform a competent diligent visual inspection was mentioned earlier. There are some other items that must be disclosed according to State Law.

Any inspection to be performed does not include or involve an inspection of areas that are reasonably and normally inaccessible to such an inspection nor an affirmative inspection of areas off the site of the subject property or public records or permits concerning the title or use of the property, and, if the property comprises a unit in a planned development as defined in Section 11003 of the Business and Professions Code, a condominium as defined in Section 783, or a stock cooperative as defined in Section 783, or a stock cooperative as defined in section 11003.2 of the Business and Professions Code, does not include an inspection of more than the unit offered for sale, if the seller or the broker complies with the provisions of Section 1368.

In no event, shall the time for commencement of legal action for breach of duty imposed by this article exceed two years from the date of possession, which means the date of recordation, the date of close of escrow, or the date of occupancy whichever occurs first. Nothing in this article relieves a buyer or prospective buyer of the duty to exercise reasonable care to protect himself or herself, including those facts which are known to or within the diligent attention and observation of the buyer or prospective buyer.

Let's discuss another subject. If a consumer information booklet described in Section 10084.1 of the Business and Professions Code is delivered to a transferee in connection with the transfer of real property, including property specified in Section 1102 of the Civil Code, or manufactured housing, as defined in Section 18007 of the Health and Safety Code, a seller or broker is not required to provide additional information concerning, and the information shall be deemed to be adequate to inform the transferee regarding, common environmental hazards, as described in the booklet, that can affect real property.

If a Homeowner's Guide to Earthquake Safety described in Section 10149 of the Business and Professions Code is delivered to a transferee in connection with the transfer of real property, including property specified in Section 1102 or under Chapter 7.5 (commencing with Section 2621) of Division 2 of the Public Resources Code, a seller or broker is not required to provide additional information concerning, and the information shall be deemed to be adequate to inform the transferee regarding, geologic and seismic hazards, in general, as described in the guide, that may affect real property and mitigating measures that the transferee or seller might consider.

If the informational booklet published pursuant to Section 2079.9 of the California Civil Code, concerning the statewide Home Energy Rating Program adopted pursuant to Section 25942 of the Public Resources Code, is delivered to a transferee in connection with the transfer of real property, including, but not limited to, property specified in Section 1102 manufactured homes as defined in Section 18007 of the Health and Safety Code, and property subject to Chapter 7.5 (commencing with Section 2621) of Division 2 of the Public Resources Code, the seller or broker is not required to provide information additional to that contained in the booklet concerning home energy ratings, and the information in the booklet shall be deemed to be adequate to inform the transferee about the existence of a statewide home energy rating program.

KICKBACKS; RESPA VIOLATIONS

The Real Estate Settlement Procedures Act (RESPA) is a federal law passed by Congress in 1974. It requires lenders to disclose information about closing costs to loan applicants. RESPA applies to most federally related loans. A loan is federally related if it meets all of the following criteria:
1. It will be used to finance the purchase of real property.
2. It is secured by a first trust deed (or mortgage) on residential property (one to four units); and
3. The lender is federally regulated, has federally insured accounts, makes loans in connection with a federal program, sells loans to FNMA, GNMA or FHLMC, or makes more than $1 million per year in real estate loans. In short, the act applies to almost all institutional lenders and to most residential loans. It would be a good rule to always follow RESPA rules.

RESPA has four basic requirements:
1. The lender must give a copy of the booklet "Settlement Procedures and You" (prepared by HUD, the Department of Housing and Urban Development) to each loan applicant within three days of receiving a written loan application.
2. The lender must give the applicant a good faith estimate of settlement costs within three days of receiving the loan application.
3. The lender must itemize all loan settlement charges on a Uniform Settlement statement.
4. The lender may not pay kickbacks or referral fees to anyone for referring customers for any transactions involving a federally related loan.

REFERRALS TO VENDORS AND THIRD PARTIES AND NEGLIGENT ADVICE

You will be asked many times for referrals concerning vendors, title, services, insurance, etc. etc. etc. You will also be asked for advice about offers, income tax, property taxes, exchange, etc.

Be careful. You can recommend vendors or other third party suppliers but you cannot insist that they be used. If your broker owns a percentage of a company, you can recommend the company if you disclose the ownership interest. When you recommend an entity, you should consider recommending more than one and let the client make their selection after talking to the people. This would help you in court. If you will receive any referral fee, it should be disclosed to your client.

For a pertinent discussion of referrals you should check Business and Professions Code 10177.4, which reads:

(a) Notwithstanding any other provision of law, the commissioner may, after hearing in accordance with this part relating to hearings, suspend or revoke the license of a real estate licensee who claims, demands, or receives a commission, fee, or other consideration, as compensation or inducement, for referral of customers to any escrow agent, structural pest control firm, home protection company, title insurer, controlled escrow company, or underwritten title company. A licensee may not be disciplined under any provision of this part for reporting to the commissioner violations of this section by another licensee, unless the licensee making the report had guilty knowledge of, or committed or participated in, the violation of this section.

(b) The term "other consideration" as used in this section does not include any of the following:

(1) Bona fide payments for goods or facilities actually furnished by a licensee or for services actually performed by a licensee, provided these payments are reasonably related to the value of the goods, facilities, or services furnished.

(2) Furnishing of documents, services, information, advertising, educational materials, or items of a like nature that are customary in the real estate business and that relate to the product or services of the furnisher and that are available on a similar and essentially equal basis to all customers or the agents of the furnisher.

(3) Moderate expenses for food, meals, beverages, and similar items furnished to individual licensees or groups of associations of licensees within a context of customary business, education or promotional practices pertaining to the business of the furnisher.

(4) Items of a character and magnitude similar to those in paragraphs (2) and (3) that are promotional of the furnisher's business customary in the real estate business, and available on a similar and essentially equal basis to all customers or the agents of the furnisher.

(c) Nothing in this section shall relieve any licensee of the obligation of disclosure otherwise required by this part.

Some anecdotes from actual experiences:

1. A well-known CPA with a great local reputation became an accommodator for 1031 Exchanges. He did free seminars and built a strong following with licensees who referred many clients. The accommodator disappeared with a whole bunch of money. The clients lost their money and could not complete their upleg exchanges. They lost their money and still had to pay income taxes on the gain. Were they angry?

2. A friend of mine was lucky. A painter he referred to many clients had his five minutes of fame. He murdered a young woman in Orange County & kept the body in a freezer for years until it was discovered in a Dewey, Arizona housing project where my in-laws reside. Fortunately, there were no problems on my friend's referrals.

3. Early in my career a new property manager made an "arrangement" with a gardener where he maintained two lawns for a certain fee and the fee also included the maintenance of the manager's lawn. When I removed the manager, she hadn't even realized she was doing anything unethical. She thought she was being a prudent businessperson and that I was discriminating against her because she was a woman.

CONFLICTS OF INTEREST

We already discussed the problem of kickbacks and referral fees in a previous section. There are a couple other possible risk areas that I would like to discuss. One is when a licensee has a special relationship with a client. The best treatment on this subject is from a superseded Real Estate Commissioner's Regulation from some years ago.

It reads in part:
"Failing to disclose to the seller of real property in a transaction in which the licensee is an agent for the seller the nature and extent of any direct or indirect interest that the licensee expects to acquire as a result of the sale. The prospective purchase of the property by a person related to the licensee by blood or marriage, purchase by an entity in which the licensee has an ownership interest, or purchase by any other person with whom the licensee occupies a special relationship where there is a reasonable probability that the licensee could be indirectly acquiring an interest in the property shall be disclosed to the seller."

The same theories prevail if a licensee is an agent for the buyer and the licensee owns any part of a property or someone with whom they have a special relationship owns any part. Disclose, disclose, disclose.

Also, our agency disclosure forms states that an agent can be a dual agent if the parties have knowledge of that part and that they consent to the Dual Agency. Dual agency is now rampart in California. Before 1988 we were all agents or sub-agents of the seller. Times have changed.

In the opinion of many attorneys, judges, and Duane Gomer, it is impossible to be a perfect dual agent. You can't serve two masters. What can you do? Disclose, disclose, disclose and then disclose some more.

For example, have you ever read this item on the Agency Disclosure? "In representing both seller and buyer, the agent may not without the express permission of the respective party, disclose to the other party that the seller will accept a price less than the listing price or that the buyer will pay a price greater than the price offered."

Another misunderstood passage, "An agent is not obligated to reveal to either party any confidential information obtained from the other party that does not involve the affirmative duties set forth above." You must know every phrase on all of the Disclosures.

LICENSEE ACTIVITIES LIKELY TO CONTRIBUTE TO RISK

AGENCY DUTIES

The Agency Disclosure form was required after January 1, 1988. This form was designed because of the decision in the infamous Easton versus Strassburger decision. Why? Civil Code Section 2079.12 (a) sentences one through three makes a strong statement.

Legislature's Findings and Intent Regarding Agent's Duty to Inspect.
1. That the imprecision of terms in the opinion rendered in Easton V. Strassburger, 152 Cal. App. 3d 90, and the absence of a comprehensive declaration of duties, standards and exceptions has caused insurers to modify professional liability coverage of real estate licensees and has caused confusion among real estate licensees as to the manner of performing the duty ascribed to them by the court.
2. That it is necessary to resolve and make precise these issues in an expeditious manner.
3. That it is desirable to facilitate the issuance of professional liability insurance as a resource for aggrieved members of the public.

This section also establishes some rules for agents to follow. For example:
1. When you are representing a client exclusively, you owe them a fiduciary duty of utmost care, integrity, honesty and loyalty.
2. If you are representing one party exclusively, you owe the other party these duties:
    a. Diligent exercise of reasonable skill and care in the performance of the agent's duties.
    b. A duty of honest and fair dealing and good faith.
    c. A duty to disclose all facts known to the agent materially affecting the value or desirability of the property that are not known to or within the diligent attention and observation of the parties.
3. When you are a dual agent you owe both parties a fiduciary relationship.

Also, you will have some other duties arise when you list a property. Some of the items you agree to do are:
1. Exercise reasonable effort and due diligence to achieve the purpose of this listing agreement. This means that you have agreed to work hard and if you don't, you have violated your contract and a seller might sue for damages.
2. Unless the seller gives the Broker written instructions to the contrary, the Broker is authorized to order reports and disclosure as appropriate or necessary. This means that you better know all the disclosures necessary.
3. Advertise and market the property by any method and in any medium selected by the broker including multiple listings and the internet and to the extent permitted by these media, control the dissemination of the information submitted to any medium. You can be sued for not advertising or marketing. If you don't understand this phrase, ask your responsible broker, as they must supervise your marketing and advertising efforts. If you are a broker and don't understand this phrase, see a good reliable, honest real estate attorney who understands agency. Search hard for this person. Your career could depend on it.

DISCLOSURE

Many facts of disclosure law have already been discussed. Some other thoughts. If you are puzzled about whether to disclose something or not disclose, talk to your responsible broker or manager. If they can't be reached and you are ambivalent, you might be better to disclose.

You need to disclose so many things:
1. The different opportunities of Agency Representation from the Agency Disclosure and your Company's Policies about Agency
2. Any Special Relationships
3. Inspections
4. Environmental Hazards
5. Earthquake Safety
6. Home Energy Rating Program and Water Conservation
7. Megan's Law Data Base and any New Changes
8. The Seller's Transfer Disclosure Statement
9. Termite Problems
10. Local Option Disclosures
11. Mellos-Roos
12. Smoke Detection
13. Lead Based Paint
14. Ordinance Location
15. Flood Hazards
16. City and County Ordinance Regulations
17. Foreign Investment in Real Property
18. State Tax Withholding
19. Controlling Documents, Financial Statements of a Common Interest Development
20. Advisability of Title Insurance
21. Seller Financial Disclosure Statement (Carry-back financing)
22. Water Heating Bracing
23. Multiple Representation
24. Estoppel Certificates in Rentals

CONTRACT FAMILIARITY

In their guidelines for this course, the Bureau of Real Estate stated that you should know the following segments of a contract: preparation, formation, interpretation, performance and termination.

How do you accomplish this? Read all of the facets of the contract. If you don't understand any phrase well enough to discuss it thoroughly with a client and answer their questions, don't do a contract until you do understand. Some of the most misunderstood phrases in the California Association of Realtor's Contracts include:
1. The word contingency that is in bold print.
2. The increased deposit in section 2B. Explain why this is there and why a seller and the brokers want this extra deposit.
3. Seller carry-back financing and the form that is required when this happens. It is three pages long and is comprehensive.
4. Tenant-occupied properties have different rules of occupancy than owner occupied properties.

5. Planned unit developments.
6. The buyer's seventeen-day right to cancel.
7. Liquidated damages.
8. Mediation vs. arbitration.
9. Joint escrow instructions.
10. Confirmation of acceptance.

The termination of a contract should be clearly stated. The California Association of Realtor's form has a separate "Expiration of Offer" phrase, as do almost all contracts in use. This should be duly noted by all parties. You might have the buyer initial this phrase when he or she signs the offer and have any seller initial the phrase when they first read the offer.

This initialing is used by car rental companies, hotels and motels. They have you initial rates, etc. Car rental companies have you initial three times. There must be a reason for doing this. Perhaps you should consider having clients initial different phrases. By the way, another item you should have clients initial is a phrase on the Agency Disclosure. It states that, "If legal or tax advice is desired, consult a competent professional." We mentioned this earlier.

ADVERTISING

In Business and Professions Code Section 10177 discussed before, the regulations against false advertising are listed. This section includes subdivision sales as well as general property sales.

Another good guideline for licensees is an article from the National Association of Realtors Code of Ethics. It states, "Realtors shall be careful at all times to present a true picture in their advertising and representations to the public. Realtors should also ensure that their professional status (e.g. broker, appraiser, property manager, etc. or status as Realtors) is clearly identifiable in any such advertising."

There is one other important source for advertising. It is a booklet created by the Newspaper Publishers Association. Call your local newspaper and ask them for a copy of their guide for advertising to meet Fair Housing Regulations. You will be happy you did.

Some of the phrases that you should not use are "Great for Kids," "Near St. Joseph's Church," "Next to ABC County Club," etc. Discriminatory advertising will attract the attention of Fair Housing Administration staff and testers.

Want some more information on advertising? Check "Fair Housing Advertising Regulations" Federal Register Vol.54. No.13, Monday January 23, 1989, Rules and Regulations. Check www.fha.gov.

Some phrases from this Regulation: Statements such as Whites Only, Hispanic Neighborhood, Christian Home, Adults Only, Adults Preferred or Older Neighborhood, Singles, No Children, Walking Distance to the Synagogue, One Block from the Italian Club, Parish Schools are considered discriminatory. It is permissible to say in-law quarters, family room, walk to bus stop, bachelor pad, great view or wheelchair ramp. These are federal guidelines, so be sure to also consult any state references as well.

FAIR HOUSING

This is the area where there is the biggest potential for risk. You have to know the Fair Housing Laws completely and keep up-to-date on all changes.

Most of you have taken a three hour Fair Housing Course when you renewed your license for the first time. If not, you will have to take it when you do your first four-year renewal.

You have to study the Federal Fair Housing Act Of 1968. This act prohibits discrimination in the sale or rental of housing on the basis of race, color, religion, sex, or national origin. Discrimination includes:
1. Refusing to sell or rent after a bona fide offer has been made.
2. Changing the terms, conditions or privileges of a sale or lease or in providing services or facilities.
3. Indicating any preference in advertising or statements, oral or written.
4. False representations as to the availability of a dwelling unit including "channeling" and "steering" to particular neighborhoods.
5. Attempting to persuade owners to sell or rent dwellings by making representations about the entry into the neighborhood of certain classes of people. This is Panic Selling or Blockbusting.

In 1988 the act was amended to include familial status and handicapped as protected categories. Most of the familial status actions involve discrimination against children. Before any owner makes any building rules to limit the renting to children, they should check with a local real estate attorney. Children are people too and if you allow three people to live in a one-bedroom apartment, you can't make a rule that a couple with one child can't live there. Other forms of discrimination would include making renters with children pay more rent or larger deposits.

Handicapped people include not only the ones of which we are aware (blind, crippled, deaf, etc.) but also people afflicted with AIDS and alcoholics. People who are addicted to illegal substances are not protected under this regulation.

The most comprehensive study of the subject is in the Real Estate Commissioner's Regulations, Section 2780 and 2781. Section 2780 is about six pages of small legal print so it is not included here but you can download it from the Internet and read it. Section 2781 is interesting as it addresses the subject of Panic Selling and reads as follows: Prohibited discriminatory conduct includes, but is not limited to, soliciting sales or rental listings, making written or oral statements creating fear or alarm, transmitting written or oral warnings or threats, or acting in any other manner so as to induce or attempt to induce the sale or lease of real property through any representation express or implied, regarding the present or prospective entry of one or more persons of another race, color, sex, religion, ancestry, marital status or national origin into an area or neighborhood.

EMPLOYMENT ISSUES AND OFFICE MANAGEMENT

Brokers must exercise supervision over their associates in accordance with Bureau of Real Estate Regulations. Systems, procedures, policies and staffing must be established to accomplish this supervision.

First and most importantly there must be a comprehensive employment agreement between the parties. This establishes the rules for employment and must be kept by each party. The California Association of Realtors has an excellent form for this. However, it is in excess of five pages with small type size so it is not included here, but study it.

The topics that need to be addressed in a contract are:
1. License status
2. Independent contractor relationship including workmen's compensation
3. License activities
4. Property information
5. Supervision
6. Trust Fund Policies
7. Compensation
8. Termination
9. Handling of Disputes
10. Automobile insurance (Coverage required)
11. Assistants (Who pays and how)
12. Office policy manual
13. Indemnity
14. Definition
15. Attorney fees
16. Space for extra provisions

TRUST FUND HANDLING

This is another area that has a large possibility of risk. Many brokers in an attempt to minimize their risk have as many deposit checks as possible made payable to an Escrow or Title Company.

Even with this policy, brokers must maintain a trust fund register to list the checks when they are received by an agent, forwarded to another entity or returned to the buyer. This procedure is forgotten by so many licensees. Practical examples of other violations of Trust Fund Handling will be covered in a later section of this booklet.

PRIVACY ISSUES

More and more the public is insisting on the right to privacy. They don't want to be subjected to a constant barrage of solicitations. In response to this groundswell, politicians at many levels are passing legislation to attempt to stem this tide. Some of the areas of consideration are bulk mailing, phone calls, faxes, emails and direct contact.

Spam is now a very common word in business jargon. Incidentally, many people attribute the word to the Monty Python Comedy Group. True, one of their famous sketches illustrated the word, but senior citizens can tell you that the word was used in an unflattering tone to describe the canned food the U.S. Military consumed during World War II. Either way, the public does not want to be spammed and they are fighting back.

Real estate licensees must use the government guidelines and not send email blasts of unwanted advertisements to their prospective clients. Make sure you send your emails to proper databases. When you ask people visiting your web site or calling your office for their email address, be specific that they are giving you permission to send them emails. Also, spend some time and produce a Privacy Policy for your web site emails, faxes, snail mail and phone prospecting. Put this privacy policy on your web site and reference it when sending email. When you produce a privacy policy, follow it and insist that all associates follow it. Don't sell or release your data.

Before doing this research, investigate the privacy statements of some major web sites. On one sports oriented web site their carefully worded privacy policy sounds good to a web visitor but a closer reading indicates that the web site will distribute your email address to just about anyone who has even a minimal interest. Do you think that they might be selling your address?

Anti-spam software now eliminates many emails based on key words and other criteria. Be sure to leave XXX, sexy, free, etc. out of your subject lines. Always, have an apology on bulk emails and a clear message on how recipients can be removed from any future mailings.

In California there are strict rules concerning unsolicited fax transmissions. The dollar penalties are severe, and you should know the rules about how to remove people from your database and rules about using improper fax number lists.

Also, there is now a national do-not-call list. You are supposed to be aware of the names on the list. Remember that you can call someone on the list for one year if you have had a business transaction with them and ninety days if they have requested information. It is poor business planning to spend time calling people who don't want to be called. For you will suffer somehow in the end.

Bulk mail is still legal. Some licensees say that snail mail is worthless and should never be used. If this is so, why do I get so many mailers from AOL, AT&T, CompUSA, etc? Snail mail has strong advocates even among the computer intelligent. Many web site promotion companies recommend using bulk mail to increase trips to your site. However, use snail mail properly. Have an "opt-out" phrase on your bulk mail even if this is not required by law. Not everyone wants new recipes, law updates, your success stories, etc. You could be antagonizing people who don't want your mail, and you are spending money to antagonize them.

A couple tips on mailing: Before you use any database, have it "scrubbed" by one of the address correction companies. If you are mailing regularly to some spheres of influence, periodically mail them a regular size postcard. If the address is out-dated, the postcard will be returned and you can remove their address. If you always mail the popular 8.5 x 6.5 inch post card at bulk rates and the address is wrong, it is thrown away by mail carriers. You could be using many addresses that are not reliable. That costs money.

PRACTICAL EXAMPLES OF HIGH RISK AREAS

TRUST FUND HANDLING

Trust Fund Handling has an abundant amount of areas for improper behavior, both intentional and unintentional. The California Commissioner's Regulations from 2820 to 2835 cover this topic in minute detail. Every broker with a trust fund or contemplating starting a trust fund should really study these statutes closely.

Whenever anyone has read the BRE bulletins in the past, many of the license violations involved Trust Fund Violations. Now, for sure some of the violations were for brokers commingling their funds and even worse using the Trust Fund as their own piggy bank hoping that there would be no audit until they returned their "loans".

Some areas of specialization have a higher propensity of violations. This is so apparent that one regulation for Trust Fund Continuing Education is that a course sponsor can design their three-hour mandatory course for one specialty. Some of the trust fund problem areas are Property Management, Loan Brokering, Advance Fees, and Affiliated Escrow Companies.

There are many violations that might occur:
1. An employee embezzling funds.
2. Leaving rents from management activities in the account too long.
3. Taking some of the interest earned.
4. Receiving a check from a beneficiary and then paying their bills based on that advance and the client's check bounces.
5. Paying out deposit funds without getting approval.
6. Being lax on the required bank reconciliations.
7. Just downright poor record keeping.
8. Not keeping good records of uncashed checks, as they must be logged when received and a note made when they are returned to the client.
9. Not depositing funds in a timely fashion.
10. Allowing unapproved employees to make withdrawals.
11. Etc. etc. etc.
12. Many, many, many more.

MISREPRESENTATION OF VALUE OR PROPERTY CONDITION

Licensees are instructed to maintain a fiduciary relationship with their clients. A fiduciary relationship is the highest form of business relationships. You are like a trustee for your client's wishes. As such, you are to evaluate their property properly as to fair market value, so they receive the most benefits. Prices for listing should be set to benefit the owner not the broker. Setting a price substantially below market for a naïve seller is a license violation. A statement by an agent that "the client was happy with that price" will not eliminate the legal problems of an agent. The agent was either not being fair with their seller or didn't know the proper market value or didn't research the matter. Setting a price too high so you can get a listing could lead to a lawsuit.

Any of these acts will get licensees in trouble. I would much rather be the plaintiff's attorney in a lawsuit on the subject instead of the attorney for the agent defendant in these cases.

The same fiduciary relationship applies when you are advising a buyer on an offer and more importantly it applies for both parties when you are a dual agent. One definition of your relationship is that you are supposed to feel that "you are walking in the client's moccasins." Buyers and sellers both start thinking about attorneys when they feel they have been wronged on price.

You want to know about a lawsuit waiting to happen. You use a net listing with a seller where you agree to pay them a certain price and anything above that price will go to you. If the property sells for too much, your seller is angry. If an offer is too low and you would receive little or no commission, you might not want to present the offer. Both instances are bad and lead to lawsuits.

CONCEALMENT OF MATERIAL FACTS OR CONDITION

In the past the California Association of Realtors and the Bureau of Real Estate have cooperated and made many inspections and disclosures mandatory. Still many violations occur.

1. Does the word mold bring fear to your heart? It should. Some licensees don't understand the problem.
2. The words "as is" do not remove all chance of liability from sellers and brokers.
3. Failure to disclose that commissions are negotiable.
4. Rules on pest control in Civil Code Section 1099 must be followed.
5. Not using a Seller Financing Disclosure Statement. This disclosure includes so many material facts. This form must be used, when a broker is an "arranger of credit." So many licensees have never heard about this form. Check it out on Win-Forms before recommending seller-assisted financing.
6. Not disclosing to an equity seller in foreclosure that the buyer is an investor, not showing them your real estate license and a bond and not using the forms for a five-day right to cancel and the Notice Required by California Law.

PROVIDING FALSE OR MISLEADING ADVERTISING

The official code section about false advertising is Business and Professions Code Section 10176 (a) It was listed previously in this booklet. There is Section 10140 (b) (c) that pertains to land and subdivision sales that should be noted. Also, Section 10140.5 and 10140.6 mentions advertising. All areas of advertising must be monitored and supervised such as newsletters, press releases, brochures, videos, yellow pages, outdoor advertising, etc.

BASIC AREAS OF POSSIBLE CONSPIRACY

The outcome of any trial will depend entirely on what the judge or jury believed took place. As a result, compliance programs are concerned, as much with avoiding conduct that creates the appearance of a conspiracy in restraint of trade, as with conduct that actually constitutes such a conspiracy. Nowhere is the opportunity greater to create appearances that real estate brokers are conspiring to restrain competition than in sales associate's dealings with actual and potential clients and customers. The keys to avoid vulnerability based upon the fees a broker establishes for professional services rendered to a client are to:

1. Establish the fees unilaterally without consultation or discussion with persons affiliated with any other competing firm.
2. Ensure that when the company's brokers or salespeople discuss fees with actual or potential clients they use words that clearly convey to the listener the fact that the company does, in fact, price its services independently.

Conspiracies could be charged on other policies such as type of listings accepted, length of listings, etc. Brokers must establish company policies and train salespeople to explain them in the "language of competition." Phrases not to use include: "This is what all brokers do," or "No one will cooperate unless you do this."

As in medicine, the cause of a disease must be determined before a cure can be sought or preventative measures undertaken. The same is true with legal liability in general and liability in particular. Brokers and salespeople who can identify the sources of potential vulnerability will be able to take measures to ensure that their conduct complies with dictates of the anti-trust laws. A National Association of Realtor's Guide offers advice on the structure of an anti-trust compliance program for real estate firms and sales associates.

An anti-trust compliance program is a business necessity for several reasons. Brokers must institute an office compliance program because they will be held responsible for the conduct of their sales associates. A brokerage firm cannot avoid anti-trust liability simply because it did not authorize the price-fixing scheme undertaken by its sales associates and sales associates from another firm. Ignorance is never an excuse for any violation of the law. Therefore, continuous education and training of sales associates is essential.

But more importantly, anti-trust education and compliance can lead to confidence and freedom to pursue vigorously legitimate business activity. There are some other phrases to avoid so there is no appearance of a conspiracy.
1. "I'd like to lower the commission rate but our board has a rule."
2. "This is the rate that everyone charges."
3. "The MLS will not accept less than a 120-day listing."
4. "Before you list with XYZ Realty, you should know that nobody works on their listings."
5. "If John Doe was really professional or ethical, he would have joined the board."
6. "The board requires all REALTORS® to insist their salespeople join."
7. "The best way to deal with John Doe is to boycott him."
8. "If you valued your services as a professional, you wouldn't cut your commission."
9. "No board member will accept a listing for less than ninety days."
10. "Let them stay in their own market. This is our territory."
11. "If he/she were really professional, they wouldn't use part-timers."

PREDATORY LENDING

As a licensee you must be careful to avoid claims of predatory lending or avoid referring clients to companies who are predators. Are there any predators? Household Finance and Ameriquest are companies that just paid nine digit dollar amounts to settle claims against them and there will be others to follow.

Regulation Z and the Truth in Lending Act (TILA) must be followed for all federal loans. Some examples of predatory lending to sub prime clients include:
1. Charging them higher fees.
2. Not explaining the effect of teaser rates.
3. Processing loans that clients will not be able to afford.
4. Using stated income figures instead of using complete applications.
5. Intimidating clients to sign.
6. Prospecting for sub prime borrowers exclusively.

RISK REDUCTION

ESTABLISH POLICY

It is important to remember that like stress, risk can never be completely eliminated. As a licensee you must learn to recognize possible problem areas and try to avoid them. If you can't avoid risk areas, you must strive to manage the perils of risk and strive to control them.

Even if you are the most intelligent, honest, hard working, organized and loyal licensee and you exhibit utmost care at all times, you can still be sued. How can we reduce the possibilities and sleep better and longer?

It always starts with the broker. The broker must establish official risk policies that address company procedures. The goals of risk management should be clearly stated to all licensees and employees and be understood by them. These policies should be available for all clients and other pertinent people to read.

A positive written mission statement for your company would be valuable for risk management and marketing purposes. Put in writing what you believe. Clients have much more faith in the written word than in the spoken word and it would help you in court.

Some of the items to be covered in the Policy Manual:
1. The Office Policy
2. Valid Real Estate License
3. Independent Contractor/Employee Status
4. Terms
5. Compensation
6. Tax Reporting
7. Insurance
8. Proprietary Information/Confidentiality
9. Personal Assistants
10. Transaction Coordinators
11. Office Hours
12. Holiday Hours
13. After Hours
14. Broker-Supplied Items
15. Office Meetings
16. Caravans
17. Smoking Policy
18. Alcoholic Beverages
19. Drug and Substance Abuse
20. Sexual And Other Harassment

A good opening statement should include a purpose such as: "This Office is committed to providing the highest quality service to our clients and the professionals with whom we work. It is the policy of this office to strive to conduct ourselves at all times in the highest ethical, professional, and competent manner when dealing with our clients, associates and employees of this office, other REALTORS and other professionals."

The purposes of a policy and procedure manual is to:

1. Establish a uniform system of daily conduct when dealing with other members of the office, our clients and members of the public.
2. Provide policies and guidelines to help avoid disputes with and liability to others.
3. Provide an orderly system of conflict resolution.
4. Explain that failure to comply with the policies and procedures within this manual may result in your termination from this office.

The following items are to be incorporated into this manual whether or not the items are attached:
1. California Real Estate Laws.
2. The Bylaws, Rules, and Regulations of the National, State, and Local Associations of REALTORS of which this office is a member, including the REALTOR Code of Ethics.
3. The Bylaws, Rules, and Regulations of the Multiple Listing Service (S) for which this office is a member.

Also, the policy manual should include reference materials that would explain different procedures. Furthermore, the policy manual should be updated regularly. Before initial implementation, it should be examined by professionals, such as an Attorney, Certified Public Accountant, Escrow Officer, Title Officer or others.

In today's real estate climate it would be beneficial to have another policy manual for assistants and transaction coordinators. These people have different problems that do not apply to licensees. There are two areas where there is substantial risk.
1. Method of payments.
   a. Who will pay them?
   b. Independent contractors or employees.
2. Different rules for licensed and unlicensed assistants. Before anyone in a company hires an unlicensed assistant the Guidelines for Unlicensed Assistants from should be studied.

It is recommended that there be a contract between the Associate-Assistant and another three-way contract between the Associate-Assistant-Broker. Do you think that any assistants have ever sued an associate for violation of the Minimum Wage Law and also sued the broker? There is a Deep Pockets mentality in all people who believe that they have been wronged and they will always go after the Broker.

RISK MINIMIZATION BY MANAGEMENT

As previously mentioned you need an up-to-date policy manual that addresses the areas of risk. Broker associate contracts should be reviewed regularly and they should be updated regularly. After planning, the troops must be trained. This would involve education and follow-up to the education. A three-hour required risk management course is a start but only a start. The more education and follow-up completed makes the next step of supervision easier.

It is my belief that the most important decision that any Broker makes concerning Risk Management is the decision about their hiring policies. A broker can minimize risk by being more selective in the hiring process. Granted, people should always be given a second chance when warranted, but do your due diligence when hiring. Check them out. At least use the BRE Status Sheet to see if there are any disciplinary actions listed for the applicant.

RESPONSIBILITY OF BROKERS, OFFICE MANAGERS, AND SUPERVISORS

There is a Latin term in our business law and property management textbooks. It is respondent superior. It means the superior person will be held liable. Many brokers learn that every year. If you are responsible, you by regulation must supervise.

There is an excellent and valuable Bureau of Real Estate booklet that would apply in part to this section. The title is "Broker Compliance Evaluation Manual." Get a copy yesterday if you are a licensee, broker or salesperson.

Topics covered are:
1. Properly licensed salespersons
2. Hiring and termination of salespersons
3. Written broker-salesperson agreements
4. Broker supervision
5. Retention of documents
6. Negotiability of commissions
7. Branch office licenses
8. Use of fictitious business name
9. Real Estate Transfer Disclosure Statement
10. Pest control documentation
11. Broker escrows
12. Broker as trustee
13. Interest-bearing accounts
14. Control records
15. Separate records
16. Monthly reconciliation
17. Timely deposit of funds
18. Authorized signatories
19. Commingling and Conversion

CONSEQUENCES OF ILLEGAL OR UNETHICAL BEHAVIOR

This section can be covered in a succinct and pithy fashion. There are consequences to people who misbehave. As stated before, you can lose:
1. Your job with the broker.
2. Your affiliation in different Associations.
3. Your reputation.
4. Your money including legal fees and punitive damages.
5. Your time to prepare to settle a claim or go to court.
6. Your time by going to jail.

Also, licensees have lost marriages, friends, relatives, houses, investments, elected offices, health, sleep and many other items too numerous to mention. Stay current because risk is ongoing.

The laws and regulations for licensees are forever changing. You must stay current. Read important changes and learn when to research questions. Some sources are BRE, California Association of Realtors, libraries, seminars and home-study courses.

Companies should follow the polices established by BRE. One last point: If someone violates a policy, there must be some form of enforcement. Many times the most frequent violators of policies are the top producers in a company. Brokers don't want to discipline them for fear they will leave the company. Cut your losses and just do it now.

RISK MANAGEMENT AND THE CONSUMER

ACCESS TO INFORMATION

In today's market many clients are more computer literate than the licensees. Clients now have access to so much information that they can easily check and verify information given to them by associates and brokers.

With this added information, they can quickly discover when misleading facts are given to them or when material facts are not disclosed. This situation increases a licensee's liability because lawsuits, complaints to BRE and complaints to brokers associations are much easier to research and file.

CONSUMER'S DEMAND FOR GREATER VALUES

In the past, agents controlled the information about all listings. There were large binders of MLS listings, and they were confidential. Today, most of this information is online or readily available in other formats.

Clients calling agents have probably done extensive research of listings, did virtual tours, Zillowed the neighborhood, checked property tax records, etc. They believe that they have done most of an agent's job so why should they pay such a large commission? Agents have to do a better job of informing clients of their services and the value of those services.

Clients, who have visited real estate web sites make faster decisions, visit fewer properties and are "pre-qualified" on an area and on a home. Agents have to be ready to give complete service and discuss with their client reasons why they should be compensated. What do web clients want? Emails answered quickly.

CUSTODIANS OF PUBLIC TRUST AND FIDUCIARY RESPONSIBILITY

As you realize from this material, businesses have to walk a straight and narrow path. We previously discussed your levels of care. In transactions you are held to standards of care based on your experience and length of licensure.

Your responsibilities are large. We must complete ethics and agency classes. Many times you will wish that clients also had to adhere to certain standards and to complete ethics classes. However, you must be like Caesar's wife. Above reproach.

Judges and jurors consider licensees "superior knowledge persons" and must conduct their affairs at a higher level. The more experienced you become, the more care you must exhibit.

LEGAL RESPONSIBILITY

VICARIOUS LIABILITY

What exactly does vicarious mean? Again, let's go to our Webster's Encyclopedic Unabridged Dictionary. The most pertinent definition is "taking the place of another, to substitute for someone." Yes, you could be standing on the sidelines and be considered fair game for liability by a plaintiff.

A possible time could be when a responsible broker or designated manager is being considered liable for the actions of an associate. Two examples of this responsibility shift happened to people I know. One was a broker of an extremely large company. He assumed that a successful agent had renewed his license after completing the required continuing education. The agent procrastinated or plain forgot or just ignored the renewal like many "entitled" people believe they can. The agent sold several properties and a legal problem arose on one transaction. The adversarial attorney checked BRE license status, such an easy thing to do, and discovered there was no license at time of sale. Bingo – severe consequences for the agent and responsible broker.

Another highly placed CAR Realtor was a broker and went to work for a company owned by a salesperson. The broker was to be the company manager and signed with the BRE as the responsible broker. He had no operational control of the petty cash fund and the "owner" used it as his personal piggy bank. License restriction and humiliation from the bulletin posting happened to the guiltless but naïve broker. Be careful in your actions at all times. You could be the substituted party.

STATUTORY DUTIES

An agent has many duties and responsibilities. The statutory duties arise from Laws of the Land. A California agent must know and follow all the statutes, (Federal, State, City, County, etc.)

On a recent trip to Sacramento, in my function as a company owner in California, I had to visit the State Bureau of Real Estate, The Secretary of State, Bureau of Private and Post Secondary Schools, Franchise Tax Board, Board of Equalization, Workmen's Compensation and the Commissioner of Corporations. These were fact finding sojourns to hopefully avoid future trouble and settle existing problems.

Go into lending and you will become aware of HUD, FHA, and many others. Property managers need to follow Fair Housing Orders, State Employment Board and Rent Control Agencies, etc. Developers will be discussing problems with Inspectors, Planning Commissioners, City Councils, and many, many, more.

MEDIATION, ARBITRATION OR LAWSUIT

In recent years, if you have visited a doctor's office or HMO, you are familiar with agreements to arbitrate. We sign them or we don't get treated. Why do all these agencies and individuals do this? It must be cost and time effective. There must be a reason why this most litigated profession takes these measures. We probably should follow their lead and try to arbitrate confrontations instead of going to court.

It is my impression that in California cases will have to mediate before moving on to arbitration or to a court. The phrase I hear is, "Even if not agreed to ahead of time, mediation will be mandatory."

Some old-timers will say, "I want my day in court." No, you don't. That may be your right and privilege but it is an expensive right and privilege. California has the highest number of licensed attorneys per capita of any State. Check the yellow pages for lawyers or listen to late night television. Attorneys are advertising their wares and promising "Aggressive Representation," "We Fight and Win," "The Tenant's Friend in Need," etc.

The Commissioner's Regulations will give you the information to follow if you are investigated. Remember, BRE can investigate, restrict, and revoke, but you can be heard along the way. The best way to handle an investigation is not to do anything wrong.

SELF-REGULATIONS

The Realtor's Associations at the local level will review grievances and make rulings after hearing the evidence. The Associations are constantly updating their procedures and educating the volunteer personnel who conduct the hearings. They are really trying to improve this process and they are succeeding.

If you have a problem with another Realtor, first try to settle it with a simple conference. If that is impossible, go to your Realtor's Association before going to attorneys and courts. Remember another fact. At most times the number of licensees who are members of any Association of Realtors varies between 30% to 40%. Therefore, the majority of licensees are not Realtors, so threatening them with Realtor justice is not a big threat. If the Realtor's major penalty is expulsion from the Association that does not mean much to a person who is not a member.

CONCLUSIONS

What are some steps to controlling your risk?
1. Education – This course or any other course is a beginning but only a beginning. Keep up to date. An idea – Appoint a Risk Management Advisor in your group and have them try to keep your people up to date on new rules and problems that other firms have encountered.
2. Establish systems and procedures if you are a leader and request them if you are not. Give your troops exams about Real Estate Regulations. Several examples are on our web site at www.duanegomer.com. Make it a game with prizes. Have regular regulatory meetings and ask questions, role-play and keep an open door for communication. Informal mediation costs nothing and could save your company time and money.
3. Insist everyone follow these systems and if they don't, do some practical timely enforcement.
4. Substitute your own vicarious risk holder – I mean get Errors and Omissions Insurance. Get the best coverage. You get what you pay for is a truism in the field of Real Estate Licensure.

5. If you have a possible problem arising, move fast. Take your own action before agencies take their action. Show the investigators that you are concerned and are moving to correct any inadequacies in your systems.

6. Get good legal and professional advice in all areas. You should not have a good attorney. You should have several good attorneys. If you have a claim pending for Minimum Wages for a Manager and you have no time sheets, you don't want an attorney who specializes in 1031 Exchanges.

Use common sense at all times, and act ethically, professionally, and with compassion and your name will never appear in the BRE bulletins.

RISK MANAGEMENT PRACTICE QUESTIONS:

True or False?

1. The BRE required Risk Management Course is for three hours.

2. Severe regulation violations can result in fines or suspension but never prison time.

3. Section 10080 of the Business and Professional Code allows the Commissioner to adopt, amend or repeal regulations.

4. Section 10176 & 10177 of the Business and Professions Code apply only to salespersons not brokers.

5. An important area of risk is contract preparation.

6. It is a waste of time and money to join any association.

7. Regulation 2725 states a responsible broker shall exercise <u>reasonable</u> supervision.

8. The statute of limitations for commencing a legal action for breach of duty concerning inspections is ten years.

9. It is a good policy to give buyers a copy of "The Homeowner's Guide to Earthquake Safety."

10. The federal law requiring lenders to disclose closing costs is the Safe Act.

11. Moderate expenses for food, etc. are allowed to be paid by a lender to a licensee and not be considered other considerations.

12. If you are listing and selling a property owned by your sister, you do not have to disclose this fact to buyers.

13. Confidential information does not have to be disclosed.

14. If you are representing a seller exclusively, you have no duties to the buyer.

15. You need to disclose the different opportunities of Agency Representation.

16. It is recommended that contingencies not be explained.

17. It is not permissible to advertise a rental as being in a Hispanic neighborhood.

18. The Federal Fair Housing Act was passed in 2008.

19. A comprehensive employment agreement should be used between brokers and associates.

20. Spam is a good business technique.

21. You should be aware of the provisions of the National-do-not-call list.

22. Embezzling never happens in trust fund handling.

23. The words "as-is" do not remove all chances of liability.

24. Commissions should be established by conferring with other companies in your area.

25. A phrase to avoid is "MLS will not accept less than a six month listing."

26. By using proper procedures, all your risk can be eliminated.

27. One purpose of a policy manual is to provide an orderly system of conflict resolution.

28. A policy manual should be inflexible and updated rarely.

29. Respondent superior literally means the superior person will be held liable.

30. With information much more readily available for clients in today's culture, liability risk for agents drops.

31. Clients today have researched many properties before they call, and they want e-mails and texts answered quickly.

32. Vicarious liability means no liability.

33. BRE can investigate, restrict and revoke.

34. One attorney should be handling all of your problems.

Review Questions

35. Panic selling and blockbusting are violations of the Federal Fair Housing Act.

36. Preparing your own long addendums, amendments and other changes to contracts is recommended.

37. Risk according to Webster is "exposure to the chance of injury or loss."

38. It is a waste of time to arbitrate or mediate any conflicts.

39. When you are representing a client exclusively, you owe them a fiduciary duty.

40. The Truth in Lending Act does not apply to real estate licensees.

Practice Questions designed to prepare you to pass the final exams are available. New BRE Regulations do not allow us to give the answers to the quizzes in the book so the questions and answers are presented online. This makes the test taking very easy as you get the answers immediately.

To access the practice quizzes please visit http://www.DuaneGomer.com/after . Check on the proper link for the course you desire.

NOTE: Do not use Google, Yahoo, Bing etc. They are Search Engines. You must put the above URL link in your address bar or you won't get there.

You may request the questions by email to info@DuaneGomer.com, fax at 949-455-9931, or phone 800-439-4909. You will receive only the practice questions. You may FAX back your answers to Duane Gomer, Inc., at (949) 455-9931 and we will FAX your results to you within 24 business hours. Our recommendation is find a computer even if it's a friend or relatives it makes everything so easy under the new BRE rules.

PROPERTY MANAGEMENT SUCCESS

Chapter 1
Introduction

During the past years it has been a pleasure for me to discuss real estate management in classes in California, Nevada, Arizona, Massachusetts, New Hampshire, Wisconsin, Mexico, Hawaii, Germany, Thailand and Japan. After these discussions people have asked me if I would recommend a book about managing apartment buildings and residences.

While there are a few excellent books on the subject of apartment house management, many of them are written for the large owner or larger management company. The problems outlined include the handling of supervisors, on-site managers, assistant managers, rental or leasing agents, maintenance executives, maintenance workers, gardeners, janitors, recreation directors, bookkeepers, etc. What do you do if it is just you and a manager or just you against the world? To help you, I wrote this book.

MY BACKGROUND

For many years I owned a property management company. At one time, over 3,700 apartment units in over 100 locations were under our control. We managed everything from 300+ unit buildings to single family homes.

During this time I earned the designation of Certified Property Manager from the National Association of Realtors. My academic background includes a Bachelor's of Science Degree in Management from Indiana University and an MBA in Management from UCLA. I have taught classes in management at UCLA, University of Maryland, various California State Universities, Associations of Realtors, and Property Management Associations.

Managing apartment units of all sizes, shapes and forms has been an enlightening experience. Many of the properties were distressed buildings and were in trouble when management control was assumed. The clients of my management company included Savings and Loans, banks, real estate owned departments of different lenders, court-appointed receiverships, syndicated properties, partnerships, corporate owners, private parties, attorneys, partnerships, investment trusts, pension plans, and many others.

Hours have been spent in developing operations procedures, streamlining accounting systems, preparing and revising forms, hiring and firing, handling complaints, establishing supervision standards, training, improving communications between all parties and performing the other functions of ownership and management. I do not believe that I am more intelligent than any reader; however, being exposed for so many years to the field of property management has helped me to formulate many "tried and true" ideas and suggestions.

In addition, many recommendations have been learned at seminars and by reading available materials on management. Therefore, it is my belief that you will benefit by evaluating and adapting some of the ideas presented. Many of the topics in this book may not concern you, but if you learn just one new cost saving or timesaving method your reading time will be worthwhile.

This book will not be an intellectual or pontifical treatment of the subject. The approach will be pragmatic at a "nuts and bolts" level. There are recommended procedures, policies, forms and ideas to improve any operations and save you time and money. There are chapters of value to owners, property management company executives, supervisors, attorneys, prospective investors, managers, assistant managers, tenants and anyone interested in the field.

REAL ESTATE INVESTING IS A GOOD IDEA

Real estate has always been an extraordinary investment in the long run. Grover Cleveland said, "No investment on earth is so safe, so sure, so certain to enrich its owner as real estate" and who are we to argue with Grover Cleveland.

There are many advantages of investing in real estate when compared to other possible investments of stocks, gold, commodities, etc.

1. Cash Flow – There can be some cash return on your investment when your rental income exceeds your expenses. However, you should realize that many knowledgeable investors buy properties that earn no cash and might even have a negative cash flow. They do this when other return factors outweigh this negative aspect.

2. Equity Growth – This is a term used to describe the benefit to you that occurs as your loans on the property are paid down each month. You can buy real estate with low down payments. This process of using other people's money is called leverage. To illustrate the use of leverage, let's take a simple sample investment. You find a building worth $1,000,000.00 and the return after the payment of all of your expenses is $120,000.00 or 12%. If you bought the building for all cash, your situation would be:

Loan	Your Investment	Interest Cost	Yearly Return	Return on Investment
0	1,000,000	0	$120,000	12%

If you borrow $750,000 from a savings and loan at 9% interest, your situation would be:

Loan	Your Investment	Interest Cost	Yearly Return	Return on Investment
$750,000	$250,000	$67,500	$52,500	21%

If you received the same primary loan and convinced the seller to give you secondary financing of $150,000 at 9% interest, your situation would be:

Loan	Your Investment	Interest Cost	Yearly Return	Return on Investment
$900,000	$100,000	$81,000	$39,000	39%

The ability to use other people's money at a rate of interest lower than the net percentage of return on your building increases your return significantly. However, remember that the interest costs do not include all of your loan costs because your loan constant (percentage of total loan payment in relation to the amount of the loan) is higher than 9%. Therefore, as you borrow more money, your chance of having a negative cash flow increases. This example illustrated a building with a 12% return rate (capitalization rate) and a 9% loan interest rate. Buildings with a true 3% differential between these two rates are difficult to find, to say the least. (I gave this example to show the possible advantage of buying with a lower down payment and to illustrate how the return on your investment increases when you do.)

You might be more conservative and want more of a margin for error. That is fine, but consider this: If the economy continues on an inflationary ascent and apartments flourish, your return will be higher due to leverage with just a 10% position in this building. Likewise, if the economy goes bad and you lose the building, would you rather have 10% or 100% in the building? Don't invest your last dollar in any building and consider the benefits of a lower down payment.

Many sophisticated real estate investors try to borrow as much as possible and buy with nothing down if they can. One investment book has an illustration showing that the author had bought a $500,000 building that had a first loan against it of $300,000 and a second loan of $150,000. The seller was desperate and agreed to take a third loan for $45,000. The buyer put up $5,000, borrowed from his bank on a 36-month payment plan. *That* is leverage. Each year he had to advance a large sum of cash to meet his payments, but there were other advantages to his ownership and he was elated. This illustrates the theory that "You own tomorrow – what you owe today." (But only "if you meet all of the payments.") So –get yourself in debt in real estate as deeply as you possibly can. It is risky, and you might not sleep some nights, but when it works, it really works.

Let me illustrate a more conservative and over-simplified example of equity growth. If a young couple invests $30,000 in a $300,000 rental home when they are 25 years old, they can probably get a 20-year loan for the $270,000 difference. When they are 45 years of age they will own this building free and clear. If they bought in a good area, it will, in all likelihood, be worth more than they paid. If we still use a $300,000 value, let's assume that they find a building worth $3,000,000, trade for it and get another 20-year loan. If they meet the payments again, they will have $3,000,000 in equity in the building when they are 65 years old. This example assumed no appreciation, no cash flow and no tax benefits. Here, we have one investment of $30,000 and a trade in 20 years and the couple will have millions of dollars for their retirement. Realistically, we know that most investors would trade up sooner than 20 years and this would pyramid their return even more.

Incidentally, it is the Savings and Loan companies that should be concerned because they have much more money in most buildings than the owners do. Someone asked me recently when I bought my new home, "Aren't you worried about buying a bigger home at your age?" I had only 10% in the property and the lender had 90% in the property. They should be really worried.

TAX BENEFITS

The "tax shelter" aspects of real estate ownership are discussed all the time. Owning real estate can lower the amount of your income taxes considerably. Many millionaires pay little or no taxes due to their investments.

Consider a simple illustration. If you bought a $120,000 rental home (with $100,000 considered an improvement and $20,000 considered land) you would use a 27.5-year Straight Line Depreciation Rate on the improvement. That would give you $3,636.00 of depreciation write-off. If your building had no cash flow income (you broke even) and no equity growth (interest-only loans), that amount would be used to lower your active income under most circumstances. As an active-passive owner, you can write off up to $25,000 in losses if your income is under $100,000 per year. This saves you tax dollars.

APPRECIATION

Appreciation is the increase in value while you own an investment. The value of apartment houses is tied into the inflationary spiral, whereas a $300,000 insurance annuity is still worth $300,000 when you get it years later.

Another inherent advantage in real estate is that you control large amounts of property with low down payments. The inflation rates work on the value of the buildings, not on your down payment amounts. This is like buying stocks on a high-margin arrangement.

OTHER RETURNS

Owning real estate can give a person a pride of ownership and a strong sense of worth. Also, it is a great investment for someone who "wants something to do." A retired person can still own real estate and operate it. There is no mandatory retirement age for apartment managers and owners. There is no discrimination due to race, creed, color, national origin, sex, marital status, age, or physical handicap. If you can save some money, you can own an apartment house.

APARTMENT HOUSE INVESTMENT

In my opinion, apartments are the best real estate investment. Some reasons are:

1. You can buy with a lower down payment percentage than other improved properties.

2. More properties are available and it is easier to determine a correct value on an apartment house. You can also find your investment quicker and sell your investment faster.

3. You can start on a smaller scale with less money.

4. Vacancy rates can be more severe in industrial and commercial projects when new projects are built nearby.

5. Many investors find that the "trouble-free" commercial and industrial buildings are anything but trouble-free.

6. Depreciation rates are higher on apartment houses with more of your property depreciable.

7. Financing rates are more attractive.

If you want to find out what lenders think of properties, go to a lender and ask about their rates for apartments and then ask for their rates on a similar size commercial or industrial building. You will find that they will lend you a higher percentage of value on apartments with a lower interest rate for a longer term with less loan charges. This always proves to me that most lenders believe that apartments are more stable.

TOPICS TO BE COVERED IN THIS BOOK

As in any business, the most important ingredient for successful apartment operation is superior personnel. Therefore, one chapter will discuss how to recruit, interview, select, train and pay a manager. To many tenants, the manager is their only contact with the ownership side of the business. In surveys conducted among tenants, one of the most important considerations given for renting or remaining in a building is the attitude of the manager. It is crucial that a good manager be selected.

The most critical function of a manager is to rent to qualified tenants who will remain for a reasonable period of time. Therefore, other chapters will deal with promotion and advertising for tenants, showing and closing techniques, preparation of the property, phone courtesy, qualification and screening of prospects.

Accounting and paperwork should be kept to a minimum. The amount of accounting needed must satisfy you as an investor and the government. Simplified approaches and timesaving steps will be outlined.

It is impossible to account for money until it is received. The late-payer or non-payer must be disciplined. Courts are so tenant-oriented that extreme care must be taken when attempting to eject a bad tenant. Some proven methods for handling "deadbeats" are listed.

Other subjects include the tenant's desire for a secure building; noise factors in a building, control of keys, and embezzling by employees. Policies concerning children, pets and rent raises are evaluated.

POSITIVE ATTITUDE

Managers, owners and tenants must cooperate to accomplish the highest degree of satisfaction for everyone. It would be stress free to have apartment houses with no tenants or managers. However, our philosophy must be that tenants are not a necessary evil, but rather they are the reason for the existence of our business.

Therefore, let's approach our problems with a positive attitude. In management situations there are always alternatives. Evaluate your alternatives and make good decisions. After a period of good decisions, you will find that the alternatives available to you become more attractive all the time.

THERE ARE PROBLEMS

The apartment industry is fantastic. The opportunities have been outstanding and will continue to be good. That is not to say that there are not problems. Government agencies are constantly harassing owners and managers with increased taxes, rent control proposals, minimum wage law enforcement, free legal aid to deadbeats, decreased tax benefits, and so on. Tenants are forming unions or committees, starting rent strikes, exhibiting disrespect for rules and regulations and causing unwarranted damage, etc. Suppliers and repairmen are raising prices and lowering service every day. Some Lenders are not helping us to solve loan problems.

In the many years that I have managed buildings, I have encountered most of the possible problems. Managers have disappeared with the rent money, a manager chased a carpet-layer with a gun, and a young woman committed suicide while she was a manager. A male manager made improper advances towards women tenants, while a female manager turned out to be a nymphomaniac.

Maintenance problems covered a wide range of situations. A sewer system for 132 units stopped on a Sunday, all electricity has gone out, pipes have burst under the concrete, rains have started when roofers had a roof completely off, etc. Buildings have developed problems that were caused by external factors, such as thefts in an area, murders outside a project, and one building lost many tenants because someone in the neighborhood was starting fires in cars.

A property manager soon meets inspectors and officials of every type: the Health Department, Fire Department, Building and Safety Inspectors, Fair Labor Practices, Fair Housing, Legal Aid, Police Narcotics Units, Workman's Compensation Auditors, State and Federal Tax Authorities, and the Internal Revenue Service to name just a few.

This book is the result of many years of regulations, notices and letters to tenants and managers and has many recommendations and ideas to make management more profitable and less troublesome. Reading management materials, attending seminars and having a general willingness to improve will help you stay ahead of the competition. Good luck to all of you, and I hope that the apartment industry is better to you than it has been to me and it has been good to me.

Chapter 2
Selection of Personnel

The most important decision that you will make concerning your investment will be the selection of personnel. The most important decision that you will make concerning your investment will be the selection of personnel. The most important decision that you will make concerning your investment will be the selection of personnel. This statement is so important that I repeated it 3 times.

Owners can design the greatest procedures, manuals and forms, but if they hire someone incompetent to manage, they will have problems. If you visit different buildings run by the same owner or management company, you will notice that some buildings are operated better than others. A resident manager can make a real difference in performance.

Do not treat this selection process lightly. Take enough time and thought to pick the best person available. You might even have to design a sales pitch to convince great applicants to work for you.

JOB DESCRIPTION

One of the first steps is to prepare a job description for your apartment. When you want to hire someone to manage, he or she will want to know what is expected. Having the future duties listed eliminates many possibilities for misunderstanding and proves helpful in hiring, training and supervising a manager.

The job description explains what the manager will do. You will notice on the sample form at the end of this chapter that this manager is not responsible for interior apartment cleaning, painting or gardening. It has been my experience that many people can both manage and do extensive maintenance. However, we achieved more success when the manager just managed, and we hired outside contractors to do the other functions. The complaints and problems in a building always seemed to increase when the manager spent excessive hours painting or cleaning. Whether the tenants were ignored, or the managers were short-tempered due to working many hours or no one was visible, overburdened managers can cause problems.

In addition, we found that problems arose when we gave the manager money for these other functions. Sometimes, the manager is outstanding as a manager and terrible as a pool cleaner. Now, you have to make a decision to either hire another manager or get a pool cleaner and leave the manager's salary the same. The first alternative will antagonize the manager, and the second will cost you more money.

In a larger building it is difficult to arrive at suitable compensation for a combination manager/maintenance worker. During one month with many move-outs the manager may be overworked with painting and fix-up, and apartments may be idle. During the next month the manager may not have enough to do to keep busy.

If you still insist on using your manager for painting, apartment cleaning, pool cleaning, gardening, and maintenance, I recommend that you set a fee for each of these jobs, just as if the manager were an outside contractor. You will both be happier in the long run.

JOB SPECIFICATIONS

After you have described a job, you must next decide what type of person you want. You should make a list specifying the characteristics needed to best suit your managerial needs. In human resource departments this list is called a "job specification" or a "job profile".

My opinion is that in most cases the renting ability of the person is paramount. Some might argue that maintenance ability is most critical. However, a manager who has the ability to qualify, screen and close rental prospects is invaluable. In a 50-unit building a $10 a month increase in the rent is $500 a month more income. That can pay for a lot of maintenance. A good manager can easily keep rents $10 higher a month than a poor manager. When you go to sell your building, the $500 a month in extra income will be worth close to $50,000 in added price. Because this increase in income is realized without any increase in expenditures, it is pure profit.

Another important consideration is that the manager must fit into the building as a tenant. You cannot, in most instances, put an uneducated young couple with children in an expensive high-rise with older, wealthy tenants. An elderly retired couple may be out of place in a building filled with young married couples. There are exceptions to every rule, but be sure that you consider the tenants' lifestyles when deciding which type of person you select as your manager.

LIST OF CHARACTERISTICS

Make a list of what you want in a manager for your sample building. Our job description will be the sample at the end of the chapter. Our building is a 50-unit apartment house, all adults, in a fine suburb. The average age of our tenants is 30 to 50 years with lower middle class incomes. Most of them are married with both husband and wife working. There are no pets and all of the apartments are two bedrooms, unfurnished. Many of the tenants have lived there for a long time, and there are problems of excessive maintenance requests and a lack of discipline on the part of some tenants. Several new apartments have opened in the area and vacancies are not being rented as quickly as they have been in past years.

Some characteristics that you might want a manager to possess:

1. Ability to show apartments, screen and qualify prospects and close good tenants.

2. Honesty and loyalty to our apartment.

3. Some minor maintenance capability.

4. Basic bookkeeping talent.

5. Well-kept appearance, both in person and in their apartment.

6. Social skills necessary to both sell our apartment and deal with tenant problems pleasantly, yet firmly.

7. Previous experience in a building of this type.

8. A nice smile, friendly voice, enthusiasm.

9. No excessive habits such as wild parties.

I would like to note that while we may want a couple about the same age as the tenants, due to age discrimination laws now in effect we cannot exclude any age bracket. However, a young couple might not be happy to stay around the project long enough to suit us, and they might not be mature enough to handle these tenants. In addition, they cannot have any friends or pets living with them.

Now that you have decided what you want someone to do and what characteristics you want someone to have, we must go find our manager. Remember, there is no such thing as a perfect manager. Your final choice may be outstanding, but you will have to compromise with some of the listed characteristics. Also, you are limited in your search by the amount of money that you can pay. Traditionally, apartment management is a low-paying occupation.

Another point to consider is that you can have more trouble if you hire someone with whom you have a personal relationship. I know that many buildings are run in an outstanding manner by mothers-in-law, brothers, children, close friends, mistresses, etc. However, one of the worst problems that I ever encountered in management occurred when an owner and his wife gave me a building to manage and told me to fire the manager, who was the wife's mother. Hiring a mother-in-law or mother could be a problem.

Some relatives or friends make outstanding managers because they take their appointment seriously as the owner's agent, and there are no hidden conflicts. Just be sure to consider all of the possibilities before doing anything of this kind, for all manner of problems may develop, and it is difficult to fire unsatisfactory managers when they are friends or relatives.

RECRUITING

The following sources should be evaluated:

1. Previous or present employees.

2. Referrals or contacts.

3. Managers in nearby successful buildings.

4. Present tenants in our building.

5. Newspaper ads.

6. Agencies or apartment associations.

7. State Department of Employment.

8. Sign placed on property.

If you have an employee ready for promotion or reassignment, this would probably be your best choice. You know the couple and their performance, and they know and like working for you. Keep in mind though, that they may not like the new building or their projected living quarters.

If you have no one available, you can ask for referrals. If people know that you need someone, you might get recommendations. If you trust the person who is doing the recommending, this can be a good source.

One of the most outstanding managers that I have ever known was a coffee shop waitress when I first saw her. She was so overwhelmingly cheerful, personable and well liked that I mentioned this to the person with whom I was eating. A few weeks later, another acquaintance of mine referred this girl to me as a possible apartment manager. I hired her immediately and put her into a 30-unit building. Shortly thereafter, she took over another 30-unit building next door. She managed the 60 units, rented them at top-dollar rents in a vacancy-prone area and still had free time. She continued managing the units and became my full-time office receptionist and assistant. She started her own company managing high-rise office buildings and retired a very wealthy person.

You can get in your car and drive through the area. You might spot a building that appears to be well managed. It is not illegal for you to offer the managers of this building a chance to improve themselves. This source is excellent, as you can actually see what kind of job they are doing in your competitive market. Also, the manager knows your area. This is also an excellent way to find a top-notch gardener or pool cleaner in an area where you do not know anyone.

Present tenants in your building could be considered. The advantages of this selection are that the couple already knows the building, want to run it, and you have some background on them because of their occupancy in your project. There may be disadvantages. Anyone given this type of assignment will probably have friends as well as enemies in the building. It could make control difficult. In a tight rental market you have given yourself a vacancy.

Advertising fills a large percentage of manager vacancies. This includes classified advertising, display ads, bulletin board ads in markets, mail-outs to real estate offices, etc. The advantage of this approach is that you gain exposure to the largest number of people, and you might come up with a real gem. It is work to write an ad, screen callers, interview prospects, check references and make a decision. But keep in mind that a thorough and knowledgeable decision at this time can save you much trouble later on.

Other resources to check out include employment agencies, apartment associations and other groups. In California, these places have never proved very fruitful to me. Some people have found success by putting a sign saying "Manager Needed" on the building and others have called the local sheriff, police and fire departments for candidates. Police and fire persons make excellent managers. They are trained to handle many types of situations. Control and discipline are strong virtues. I strongly recommend considering police and fire persons for buildings in which they would be suitable.

EXAMPLE OF AN ADVERTISEMENT

There are times you will be deluged with calls when you advertise for a manager. Other times it may be impossible to get any response. Our small sample building is in a fine suburb. It has 50 units, so we should get a good response. To eliminate many obviously unqualified candidates, you should put some concrete information in your ad.

The following is a sample ad to be placed in the "Apartment Managers Wanted" section of the Classifieds:

> "Mature manager, 50 units, salary plus 2 bedroom unfurnished apartment, (name of city located), non-smoker, no pets, good closer, enthusiasm required, experience preferred but not necessary. References will be checked. Phone Mr. Gomer, 888-6523 between 1:00 p.m. and 5:00 p.m., or e-mail Manager@DuaneGomer.com or fax resume to 888-6524. More information about this building and our job description can be found on our Website at www.DuaneGomer.com under Employment Opportunity."

You have told prospects the size of the apartment and its general location.

The exact salary is not listed, as the amount will vary depending on the qualifications of the applicants. The address of the building is not given, as you do not want the residents and the present manager disturbed. You have further qualified the position by telling applicants that they cannot have pets or smoke. You have let them know that an experienced manager is desired, but you will not rule out the inexperienced.

An important note on experience: If a couple is presently managing a building, you can readily and conclusively form some opinion of their qualities. If a couple has managed in the past, they know the problems of managing and are coming back for more. Their references can easily be checked.

Conversely, some people with experience may be dogmatic and established in their procedures. You might correct them, and they will tell you that this is the way the famous "ABC" Management Company works, and you will have a constant battle in changing them.

Ten years' worth of experience can mean that they had one day's experience multiplied by 3,650, and they have never progressed. Generally, if a manager has experience, it is good. However, it is better to take an outstanding prospect with no experience and train them in your professional procedures than to hire a mediocre experienced manager.

You stated that you want a good closer to rule out the introverted and those who do not like showing apartments. Deadbeats and flakes will not bother you if they know beforehand that you will check their references.

Your phone number is given and a time to call is listed. If you do not list any calling time restrictions, you will get calls at all hours of the day and night, especially if it is a choice job. We do not use any P.O. Box numbers or ask managers to write to us. Very few employers do this, and the best prospects will not take the time to write. Today, you put your fax number and e-mail address in any ad.

Keep in mind that your advertising approach will be tempered by whether your current manager knows about the change in managers. I believe that it is best to fire the existing manager before going into a hiring cycle. If you don't, you can end up with all kinds of problems. When you advertise, your manager might read your ad. When people come by to look at the property, your "on-the-way-out" manager will corner them and tell them all of the shortcomings that you didn't realize you had. You can ask some tenant to "hold the fort" for a few days during the changeover. In cases where managers are leaving with good feelings, there should be no problems if you tell them not to get involved with the prospects because you want to answer their questions.

THE TELEPHONE RINGS

In any selling situation the use of the telephone is important. Be ready to do a thorough job with the phone callers. You are looking for the most outstanding manager and he or she can be particular about where they want to go. You might "sell them." At the point of the initial phone call you don't know who that person might be, so you have to "sell" all of the qualified applicants.

The person calling will want to have some idea of the salary and the apartment, what is expected of the manager and for whom they will be working. The call might go something like this:

"Hello, Duane Gomer speaking."

"I'm calling about the ad for the 50-unit manager's job."

"Yes, that is still open. My name is Duane Gomer. What is yours?"

"My name is Jane Brown. What is the salary?"

"Jane, before we cover that, could I ask you a few questions?"

Such as:
- Do you have any pets?
- Can you furnish local references?
- Have you ever lived in an apartment complex?
- Do you own your own furniture?
- Have you ever managed before?
- How long have you been in the area?

From these questions you can form an initial opinion. Their answers to certain questions will bring to mind more penetrating questions. At the end of these basic questions you can rule out certain callers. They obviously do not qualify because of smoking, pets, lack of references, experience, etc. You can let these people down kindly and tell them you believe they wouldn't qualify.

Once the caller has answered the basic questions, you can give them a quick rundown of the duties, stressing there will be no cleaning, painting, gardening, pool work, etc. You can give them an idea of the possible salary or even ask them what they expect based on their experience. Stress that this is negotiable. Tell them that prior to an interview you would like them to visit the apartment building. You can waste a lot of time talking to people who have not seen the living quarters. Tell them that a copy of the building job description is at the property, but they are not to bother the current manager or any of the tenants. At the apartment, you can leave both manager applications and a rental application (requiring other personal information) for each applicant to fill out. Then, they should call you to set up an interview.

When they call, establish a time to meet them. And although you may have many appointments, follow through to the bitter end. Once, I was advertising for a manager for a 32-unit family building. It was during a time of high unemployment and an even higher vacancy factor. I stated in my ad that calls would be taken on one afternoon from 1:00 p.m. to 5:00 p.m. During that time I got almost 60 calls. At about 5:15 p.m. I picked up the phone mentally exhausted and said, "We don't need anymore. I have already talked to 60 people." The caller, a young man who proved later to be about 23 years of age said, "But you haven't talked to the best one. That's me. I have been trying to call, but your line has been busy. All you have to do is drive by the 16-unit building that I am now managing at this address, talk to the owner who is sorry to lose me, and I believe that you will want me."

He was right and proved to be an outstanding closer. He was just starting work in the insurance business. He filled up the building quickly. He became a very successful businessman. It was good timing for both of us.

THE INTERVIEW

Let us say that fifteen people answered the ad, went to the building and called for an appointment. For some unexplained reason, about half of these people will not come to see you at the set time. They will not call. They just won't show up.

You will now have about seven people to interview. Interviewing and making a decision are tough jobs. There is no sure-fire way to pick one out of seven and be right every time.

Many times, the person that you disregard will prove to be an outstanding manager for you later or for someone else.

A couple is sitting across from you in your office. They look nice and refined. They loved the building and would like the job. You read their application and there is nothing that disqualifies them. Now, you have to ask some questions. Keep in mind that you are also on display. Be friendly, courteous, and enthusiastic and everything you want them to be.

There are many different questions that you can ask. When you do ask a question, let them talk. This will give you time to think and it allows them a chance to add anything that might come to their mind about your last question.

In my experience, a couple may look perfect in an interview and when hired, they become sloppy. I believe it is because I didn't ask the proper questions. Again, it is important to make the best choice possible, because getting rid of a poor choice is a headache.

Some sample questions that you should ask:

1. Why do you want to leave your present job? *Or,* Why did you leave your previous job?

2. Why do you want to manage?

3. In what type of property are you currently living?

4. What are your 5 and 10-year goals?

5. What are your hobbies, clubs, outside interests, activities in school, service or community?

6. Do you have any special qualifications for this job?

7. What education or courses have you completed?

8. Where did you go to high school?

9. What are some of the latest books you have read?

10. What other type of work have you done?

11. What is the one thing that you have done of which you are most proud?

12. Give a three-adjective description of yourself.

13. What part of your last job did you most like?

14. What part of your last job did you most dislike?

15. What qualities do you like in a boss?

16. What qualities do you dislike in a boss?

17. Do you have any questions or comments?

You can set up a role-playing sequence with you being a rental prospect or a tenant with a problem and see how they handle it. You can also ask some maintenance questions or have a test maintenance problem available.

Other questions will be suggested by their answers to your questions or from their applications. If you are interviewing a couple, don't let one person dominate the conversation. If the wife is going to be the person at home, her personality and renting ability are important. Draw her out.

You may get some interesting answers to your questions. Once, an answer to "What is the one thing of which you are most proud?" was that during the past three weeks they had won the dance contest at the local Country Western Club. This was quite an accomplishment, but we didn't need dancers.

Another time, a couple used the word "fuzz" in referring to a policeman who had stopped them. At that time, people who had been confined in a prison system typically used that term. We checked with the police, and the man was out on parole.

Another time an associate of mine hired someone who had worked for management company "ABC". She checked with his ex-supervisor and the company owner and got rave reviews. Later, he was arrested at our building for burglary. The ex-supervisor turned out to be his accomplice and had told the previous owner lies about the manager's abilities. (It is a problem when your assistant manager is marched out of your building in handcuffs.)

CHECK REFERENCES

After interviewing everyone, you will need to check references. Do a thorough job of this. A present owner might give a strong reference just to get rid of a poor manager. Any personal reference given is going to be good or the reference wouldn't have been listed. If a person gives out-of-state references, call them. Other people interviewing them might not do that. You should ask their previous supervisor questions like, "What is their best characteristic? What is their worst? Would you rehire them?" etc.

Now, let's assume you have settled on one couple. Many times you will wish that you could combine Mrs. Green with Mr. Brown or some other combination. One final evaluation that I have used hundreds of times is to go to their residence unannounced and see how they live. If they pass this test, I will ask them to manage my building. If they fail, I tell them that I am sorry, but I have hired someone else.

You have to "live" with the couple. Their personality must be compatible to yours. I might consider appearance less than others and value enthusiasm higher. You might opt for experience, whereas, I might seek a past history of success in other fields. You might want a stable, older couple, but I might want someone who in five years will want my job. It is beneficial if you have another person talk to them and compare opinions. When we had a large company, two people interviewed each of the callbacks, and I would interview the best from their recommendations. We would then compare notes. We still made errors, but we were trying.

THEY'RE HIRED

First, make certain that they complete a management contract. Any association in your area should have copies for sale. You can look at a bond application to find some questions that should be answered. While I do not believe in bonding employees, I do have prospects fill out this form due to the information it requests. Also, the unbondable person might balk at filling it out.

A management contract outlines their compensation and other important rules. It allows for immediate vacating of the apartment and lists the number of days notice that is required for quitting or firing. In most states, if you do not have any written contract and you dismiss a manager in a building with monthly rentals, you must give the manager a thirty-day notice because you are changing terms of the rental. The typical thirty-day notice might be too long if you want to get rid of someone. Fifteen days or even seven days might work better. Decide what works best for you and include it in your written contract.

Stating definite work hours is important because of minimum wage laws. Other problems of this law will be discussed in a later chapter.

You must add the couple to your Workmen's Compensation Insurance Policy and get payroll forms from them noting their dependants and social security information. You must also give them the pertinent information on the building:

1. Petty cash fund balance, forms and instructions.

2. Telephone numbers of all suppliers, repairmen, etc.

3. Tenant rental information, bank stamps, deposit slips and a written procedure for cash handling.

4. Information on all utility shutoffs.

5. Keys and recommendations on their handling.

6. Written policy letter on rentals including standards, deposits required, etc.

7. Forms and an explanation of their use.

8. Maintenance records.

9. Copies of active rental agreements.

10. Companies from whom to purchase supplies.

11. Fair Housing Instructions (DON'T DISCRIMINATE).

Our policy on running a building is to have as much work done at the lowest employment level. This is why we have the managers buy petty cash items and use charge accounts for many purchases. They make the bank deposits, maintain tenant account cards and a file of the rental agreements. If there is a question on any of these subjects, it can be checked quickly at the building and duplicate records are not necessary.

GENERAL INSTRUCTIONS TO MANAGERS

The job description, employment contract, rental policy letter and other written procedures constitute a large portion of our instructions to a new manager. We also talk to them about other ideas and concepts.

You must stress the importance of their personal appearance, the building's appearance, and the appearance of their apartment. Some managers have a poor concept of suitable standards of appearance. One manager dressed her entire family from their sofa. This sofa was never empty of clothes. When I entered their unit, I had the impression that I should tie a rope to the front door and hang on so that I could find my way out.

GUIDE FOR MANAGERS

Here is a sample of a behavior guide for managers:

1. Keep smiling. A smile says, "I like you. You please me. I'm glad to see you." It almost always wins a smile in return. Put a mirror on your desk to make sure you are smiling when you are talking on the phone.

2. Speak with a friendly voice. This is especially important on the telephone where you do most of your business and where callers judge you solely by voice.

3. Call people by name. People's names are to them the sweetest and most important words they ever hear. Politicians know that remembering names is a way to win votes. You can enhance your success by using the same techniques and learn names and use them.

4. Take an interest in whatever interests an occupant. There is no surer way to make people like you than to pay them the compliment of interest in their hobbies, experiences, and opinions. Bring it up the next time that you meet them, and they expand like flowers in the sun. How you listen and respond has much to do with how people talk to you. Sometimes by paying attention to small talk, you can be forewarned of trouble before it happens.

5. Show pleasure at every opportunity to help an occupant. If he or she asks for something or complains, show that you are eager to hear about it and eager to do whatever you can to help. Never let a tenant feel that you think they are a nuisance. They will consider themselves a valued tenant if you show that you understand their problem and really care.

6. Show appreciation for people around you. Watch for chances to thank them and praise them. "What a pleasure it is to have a satisfied tenant such as you," or "a resident who takes such good care of his home." You also need to lavish praise and appreciation on employees, tradesmen and others around you – especially the disagreeable ones. An old saying warns, "There are no little enemies." Don't give anyone cause to make a career of getting even with you.

SOME OTHER GENERAL TIPS WORTH MENTIONING

1. Be regular in your office hours.

2. Keep organized records.

3. If you have questions or suggestions, write them down.

4. Attend any important neighborhood meetings.

5. Meet with other managers at association meetings in your area.

6. Write up plans and schedules for your building.

7. Read books available on our industry.

8. Attend any possible classes, lectures and seminars on management.

9. Do not be afraid to make a decision.

10. Be prompt on completing maintenance requests.

11. Like people and let them know it.

12. Be alert and observant.

13. Remember some of the fringe benefits of apartment managing work, such as partially tax-free income on apartment value portion, no commuting to work, no expensive wardrobe to maintain, you can eat at home at a low cost, etc.

14. Plan your day before you go to bed the night before.

15. Learn your area and keep a map near your phone.

16. Treat everyone with consistency; don't show favoritism or bias.

17. Carry out any promises that you make.

18. Listen to tenants with complete attention.

19. Don't include any bad comments or gossip about the owner. Your job is an extension of the owner so show them loyalty or look for another job.

20. If a service request will be delayed, notify the tenant.

COMPENSATION

Should a manager be paid a salary or a commission tied to rental income? Some people believe that giving managers a commission based on rentals motivates them to rent more. My contention is that a good manager is motivated to keep the apartments full, regardless. He or she is motivated to get full occupancy so that they can put up a "full" sign, and not be bothered. Have you ever come upon a motel late in the evening in a small town and rented the last room? The relief on the manager's face as they stand there in their robe and pajamas and flip on the "No Vacancy" sign is readily apparent.

A manager on commission may start renting to bad prospects just to stay full. Another firm used to pay a manager money for each rental and when this manager would get low on cash she would literally provoke turnovers by arguing with tenants. Rentals can depend on factors not at all under the control of the manager. Area vacancy, no prospects, a high rental scale and other factors could mean a low income for an outstanding manager.

It might happen that conditions are good for a while, and a manager becomes used to a higher pay scale. The manager could be getting paid more than he or she is worth. Then, if commissions decline, you will have a disgruntled employee. You should establish a good salary and pay the managers what they deserve.

RULE OF THUMB

It is difficult to establish a rule of thumb on compensation for different areas. After talking to a few applicants, you can start to notice a scale. Apartment management compensation can be based on so much salary per unit or a percentage of the total income. In certain areas, for an "average" building, the salary might be about $50 per unit or 5% of the income. Using this scale, our sample 50-unit manager would receive about $2,500 in total benefits. We would give them a $1,000 apartment free and a $1,500 salary. Expensive apartments might pay more per unit but less a percentage of income. Children or family buildings normally pay less in comparison to adult buildings. This is a simple rule of supply and demand. There are so many families with children who want to manage, even though buildings with children create more problems. Furnished units due to the number of turnovers demand a higher payroll.

One idea worth considering is that it might be more profitable to establish a pay schedule and let the managers pay their own utilities. In this way, they will be careful and keep their costs down. They could be good managers and be wasteful on gas, light, heat and air conditioning. Having them pay their own utilities relieves you of yet another possible area of conflict.

If your building does not require a business phone, you could have the managers list the phone in their name. You would pay them the monthly rate, plus calls charged that were your responsibility. In this manner, you could avoid the problem of them skipping out after making calls all over the world and charging them to you. The telephone company is not very understanding when the phone is listed in your name and phone bills of thousands of dollars have occurred.

MINIMUM WAGE PROBLEMS

There are problems to consider about minimum wage laws. There is a national minimum wage law, and some states have higher rates. There are exceptions for minors, etc. but minors don't normally apply for apartment manager jobs. The manager can't work more hours than the law allows. You must calculate how many hours the manager can work for pay. The apartment agreement must list this amount. The apartment value can only be included at a certain percentage with a minimum limit. It is important that you understand how your state calculates compensation.

PAYROLL RECORDS IMPORTANT

You must keep complete time and payroll records on your managers. Insist on a time sheet before paying them and keep records for five years. Periodically check time sheets to determine accuracy. Be sure that the figures listed genuinely reflect the hours worked. State agencies have ruled in the favor of ex-managers when the forms were filled out with the same hours every day. For example, your manager puts down the same hours every day, month after month. Some auditors believe that this does not reflect the true hours and will rule against the owner when the manager says that they worked additional hours.

You can own buildings for years and never have a problem. However, when a problem does arise, you will wish that you had proper records. Ex-managers will appear, claim that they were on duty twenty-four hours a day and want to be paid for overtime at time and a half. They will produce a diary that shows all of the hours "worked" and it is unbelievable how much they were "on-call." You thought that they worked about two hours a week, and they claim that they worked twenty-four hours a day. Unfortunately, many commission auditors will agree with them.

By having accurate time sheets on your managers you can protect yourself from possible loss. If you have any questions, call your State Labor Agency. I have a couple of recommendations concerning these laws. For example, have your tenants realize that your manager's office hours are from 9:00 a.m. to 10:00 a.m. and 5:00 p.m. to 6:00 p.m. except in case of emergencies. This means the managers can show apartments, do cleaning, handle emergencies, etc. at other times, but they are not on call at all times. Their time sheets will have to reflect what they did during the unscheduled time. A slot in the manager's door can be used for receiving written maintenance requests and rental payments. Post the agreed upon schedule in a laundry room or on the manager's front door.

NO SET SALARY PLAN

Another method for payment is to establish no set monthly salary amount. Establish an hourly rate for the manager and pay them accordingly at the end of the pay period. You credit them with the value of the apartment in accordance with the wage laws. The manager's pay might vary, but he or she will be paid for exactly how many hours they worked.

BONUS TIME

You should give your manager a good salary. This is an area where trying to save a few dollars could lose you a lot of money. You get what you pay for. Apartment managers are underpaid. Dissatisfaction is sure to arise if a manager believes she or he is extremely underpaid and overworked.

If managers do additional work such as painting, cleaning, carpet cleaning or comprehensive repair work, you should have an agreement beforehand on how they will be paid. Remember, the money earned should be included in their payroll, and deductions should be taken unless they qualify as an outside contractor or have a separate business.

The manager's compensation should be reviewed periodically and discussed with them. They should be given raises, time off and vacations like any other employees. It is easy to tie pay increases into rent increases. For example, if your rents were increased by 5%, your manager's pay would be increased by 5%. If you do this, you will probably get much more cooperation on rent increases from your managers. If they know that their pay will go up at the same time and at the same general percentage of any rent raises, they will be eager to raise rents. They probably know the market better than you do, and they might even recommend a larger rent increase than you thought possible.

SHOW APPRECIATION

There are many other ways to show appreciation for good work. Our company used to select a "Manager of the Month." We would write them a flowery letter of commendation and give them a certificate for dinner at a top restaurant. We did not do this every month, but whenever there was a deserving recipient. We got a lot of value out of these selections as the managers commented on how appreciated they felt.

If managers do something outstanding, give them a gift at once. Immediate action is very impressive. We once had a building in a college area where it was difficult to find tenants. To be a manager in this college building, a person might drink. Whenever the building was fully rented, I would buy the manager a bottle of vodka. The manager was happy. The owner was happy. I was happy.

You can give flowers, a cash bonus, a house gift, a gift certificate, time off, a trip, etc. Two ideas worth considering are giving managers something for their children or buying a present for which they have a special interest. If a gift illustrates that you had to give time, thought and effort, the recipient will like it more. At Thanksgiving or Christmas, turkeys or hams are a good idea. In the past, for exceptional managers, we have paid for a one-day, getaway vacation at a good resort.

GET RID OF BAD MANAGERS

The above ideas are for a good manager. If you have a bad manager, take action to remove the problem. Poor managers seldom get better. It is a mental strain and quite a job to recruit another manager, but it will be worth it. A bad manager is like a sore tooth. It can feel good for a while, and then it hurts again. Each time the pain gets worse. Finally, the pain becomes unbearable and you must have the tooth extracted. Have regular building checkups and when a problem arises, act quickly. If the manager must be extracted, do it at the first sign of "unbearable pain."

SAMPLE JOB DESCRIPTION

The manager of this building shall perform the following duties:

1. Handle phone calls with courtesy and attempt to get an appointment to show an apartment to anyone calling for a vacancy.

2. Show prospects any vacancies, and rent to qualified people.

3. Complete deposit forms and rental applications, and submit them with recommendations.

4. When an application is approved, fill out a rental agreement and have the prospect sign.

5. Collect all rents due and use diplomacy and diligence in following up on slow payers. Maintain proper records of rental payments.

6. Deposit all monies collected in the building bank account and submit a monthly report on all rents collected.

7. Make recommendations on which tenants should receive 3-day notices to pay or quit or 30-day notices to quit. Prepare and serve these notices when approval is given.

8. Schedule and supervise the preparation of apartments for showing and keep them clean during any vacancy.

9. Every day walk the building's general areas. Perform or supervise the necessary clean-up work. Establish a schedule for carport, laundry room and general area cleaning.

10. Schedule and supervise the work of any gardener, pool person, maintenance person, painters, cleaners, other repair people and suppliers. Report any unsatisfactory or outstanding work. When work is completed to your satisfaction, sign their bills or work orders and mail them to the proper person.

11. Make periodic inspections of water heaters, pool equipment, air conditioners, heating units, roofs, sump pumps, etc. to allow preventative maintenance to be done.

12. Handle the maintenance requests of tenants and do minor maintenance jobs such as repairing leaky faucets and other minor plumbing, fixing light switches,

replacing light bulbs, keeping timers properly set, doing minor building repairs, fixing windows and screens. Forward information on major maintenance jobs to the owner or property manager for approval.

13. Receive no kickback or other unauthorized payments from suppliers or repair people.

14. Visit competitive buildings periodically to better understand your area and to allow you to make recommendations on rental rates, terms or service.

15. Be friendly with everyone but do not socialize with tenants.

16. Sign a bond application when hired.

17. Listen attentively to complaints and suggestions of tenants and handle them to the best of your ability. Forward pertinent items to the owner.

18. Be alert and observant but not nosy. Enforce building rules with tact and consistency.

19. Function as an agent of the owner and conduct business as if the building were yours and as if the owner were standing beside you. This is a profit- oriented business so learn the words *"no", "maybe" and "wait."*

20. Submit complete and accurate time sheets.

21. Purchase minor supplies and pay other miscellaneous charges out of petty cash. Purchase other supplies at authorized charge account locations.

22. Never discriminate in any unlawful manner. Be alert to all possible problems.

23. Constantly check security requirements and make recommendations for improvement.

24. Do any other reasonable tasks requested by the owner or property manager.

25. Treat the tenants as how you would like to be treated. Practice the golden rule.

26. And above all keep smiling.

Chapter 3
Rental Policies

Now that you have your personnel selected, your next step is to find some tenants. It would be nice not to be bothered by tenants. I have this dream where I own a building and have no tenants. I have no late payers, complainers, property damage or other problems. I would love to have the IRS or any other agency audit my building. Then, I would watch their reaction when I tell them I have no net income or even any gross income – just a beautiful, clean and well-maintained building.

Alas, you must have tenants. You want people who pay their rent early, remain forever, never complain, maintain their unit as a showplace and have no pets. They are models of conduct, friendly, attractive, professional and travel a lot. They willingly pay large deposits and are a pleasure to be around. In short, they are people that anyone would want as a neighbor or tenant. There is one problem. These people are in short supply. Instead, you will have to settle for actual, live, breathing tenants.

Since you can't have the perfect tenants, you must compromise your standards. If you have a well-constructed, secure and soundproof building with great floor plans in an outstanding location that is impeccably managed with a reasonable rental schedule, you may not have to compromise too much. Most of us will have to compromise.

RENTAL POLICY LETTER

Your first step is to write a Rental Policy Letter for your manager. It is important to know what type of tenants you wish to find. Our decision on this subject will be based on several considerations:

1. ***General area in which the apartment is located:*** Areas of a community normally attract similar type tenants. Professional people cluster in one area, and low-income people migrate to another neighborhood. It is difficult to fight any strong trend of this type in your area.

2. **Location of this building:** Is it in a quiet section or on a busy commercial street? Are there factories nearby or any other noise problem? Is the location considered safe? What other types of tenants are in the immediate area (ages, income level, family composition, furnished or unfurnished renters)? Are any recreational facilities, job sources, shopping centers, schools, etc. nearby?

3. **Mix of this building:** What types of units does the building have and the number of each?

4. **Amenities of the building:** What age is the building? Does it compare to other competitive projects in number of benefits: Central or window air conditioning, patios, pools, recreation rooms, quality of carpets and drapes, garbage disposals, dishwashers, self-defrosting refrigerators, self-cleaning ovens, apartment size, floor plan, fireplaces, sauna, gymnasiums, jacuzzi, tennis courts, fenced yard, garage or carports, storage areas, soundproofing, security features (dead-bolt locks, locked parking, TV surveillance of visitors, intercoms), quality of wallpaper or paint, studio or split-level design, views, elevators, beach, jogging trails, in-house music systems, cable or digital TV, beam ceilings, quality of floor tile, laundry facilities, cabinets, views, nearby shopping, etc.

5. **Services provided:** Quality of furniture, switchboard service, maids, linens and dishes, utilities paid by owner, recreation director, doorman, 24-hour hotel type management, security patrol, babysitting, nursery school, lifeguards, elevator operator, free classes, tennis lessons, parking, etc.

6. **Condition of building:** Level of maintenance on landscaping, general areas, pools and inside of the apartments.

7. **Management:** Is the building well managed? If not, can it be improved?

SAMPLE POLICY LETTER

After evaluating the previous factors, we decide on the rental policy for our building. A sample policy follows.

RENTAL POLICY FOR "ABC" APARTMENT – Effective July 1, 2012

1. The rents will be as on the attached rental schedule. If a manager believes that certain circumstances warrant an increase or decrease to the scheduled rent of an apartment, they should contact the owner at once.

2. The apartments will not be leased, but an agreement not to raise rents for six months can be given with the approval of the owner.

3. The applicants are to leave at least a $500 deposit with their application.

4. Upon approval of their application, the prospects must pay the remaining money due within three days.

5. The security deposit will be $1,500.

6. All fees are included in the security deposit.

7. The first month's rent and charges listed in items 5 and 6 must be paid before the tenant is given a key or allowed to move anything into an apartment or storage area.

8. The tenants' monthly gross income must be at least $3,200 per month.

9. Children will be accepted as tenants.

10. No pets other than goldfish or small caged birds will be accepted.

11. Children must be supervised.

12. ***There is to be no discrimination of any type or manner, either overt or subtle, as to a prospect's race, creed, religion, age, color, national origin, sex, source of income, marital status, physical handicaps, life styles, etc.*** **This building adheres to Fair Housing Principles**.

13. There are to be no tenants who conduct illegal activities such as prostitution, use or sale of illegal drugs, gambling or conducting a commercial business from the apartment.

14. Prospects currently being evicted will not be accepted.

15. Credit and personal references will be checked to insure suitable character.

16. No waterbeds will be allowed unless a tenant shows a certificate of waterbed insurance.

17. The number of tenants in any unit will meet local laws.

18. A late charge on rentals will be charged.

19. Musicians will not be allowed to practice at any time.

20. All prospects must complete applications before approval to rent will be given, and future tenants must complete rental agreements before moving in.

Manager	**Owner**
Date	**Date**

This rental policy letter may seem too simple. However, it is important to give some definite guidelines to your personnel. To put your ideas in writing makes them more concrete and easier to follow. Doing this type of letter for your own building helps you to formulate your own thinking on this subject. The letter is important in case you ever turn anyone down. Suppose you turn four young men down for a studio apartment, and they claim that you are discriminating against them because they are of a minority race. If you have followed your policy letter since its effective date and rented no studio apartment to more than two people, it is hard for anyone to prove discrimination because you have not discriminated. Many times, discrimination is charged when your reason for refusal is in no way discriminatory. A policy letter is a valuable tool anytime you refuse an apartment for any reason. Remember, you can reject applicants due to low income, credit problems or bad recommendations from prior owners.

POLICY LETTER EXPLANATIONS

If managers are going to be adjusting rents, as an owner you want to know. Tenants soon find out what others are paying. If two tenants are paying different rents for identical apartments and both rented at the same time, they will be angry. Tenants need to be treated fairly, equally and with consistency.

In California, leases are of great help to a tenant. A landlord has a problem when evicting lessees for misconduct. If a person skips out on a lease, it is next to impossible to collect damages. In Beverly Hills, Palos Verdes, Newport Beach, and other expensive areas, leases are used extensively as the tenants are wealthy and less mobile. In San Gabriel Valley, San Fernando Valley and other suburban areas, leases are not used as much, although their use is increasing. It would be difficult to obtain a lease in an area when none of your competition requires leases. If the market is so strong that you can get a lease, you might not want one, as you will be stopped from raising rents for a set period. If tenants are afraid that they will move in and get an immediate rent raise, you could give them a simple written statement that you will not raise their rent for a certain period of time. This is a valuable tool in closing prospects. Another good close is to pay interest on their deposit. It is not much money.

SET TERMS

The terms of any deposits and fees should be set. This alleviates any possible misunderstanding. In California, you can no longer say that the security deposit will not be returned if a tenant moves out before six months or any other period of time. The security deposit has to be returned minus any costs for damages above normal wear and tear. Any deductions should be itemized and evidence held to help settle any future claims. The tenant has the right to the return of his or her security deposit and can't sign away this right. California has a law that states that the security deposit must be returned within twenty-one days after move-out with an accounting of charges or there are penalties. Some states and cities have laws that interest must be paid on these deposits when they are returned.

Cleaning fees can no longer be considered non-refundable in California. To retain this fee you must show that the money was used to get the apartment ready for the next tenant. In our application we do not mention a cleaning fee. We only have a security deposit. Any cleaning charges will be deducted from the security deposit

Keep an accurate record of all money spent. If you can't get a job done on time, try to get an estimate and use that figure. Make an accurate report and mail it to the moving tenant as soon as possible. Remember, be very careful in your handling of deposits and charges against them. You could be in small claims court explaining your poor record keeping to an unsympathetic judge.

A California law on deposits is that the total amount of deposits on an unfurnished apartment can be no more than two months rent and on a furnished apartment no more than three months rent. This includes cleaning fees and pet deposits.

There is a minimum salary requirement to rent an apartment. This is an excellent requirement. It eliminates people who could not meet the monthly rent payments. Also, it is good evidence that you are not abusing Fair Housing Regulations. Yes, you can still discriminate on income.

DISCRIMINATION

Be sure that you know Federal, State and Local Laws and Court Cases about renting to people with children. You should never discriminate as it can lead to many types of trouble. Talk to your attorney before you act. Not renting to people with children is illegal in many jurisdictions because there is a shortage of family units available.

Many of my most successful buildings were family units. A family building can often charge higher rents than an adult building. Although there may be an increase in maintenance or other problems (often from a lack of parental supervision), many times the added income is worth the extra trouble.

Our policy letter states there are to be no pets except for fish and birds. It would be prudent to speak with an attorney who understands property units for your area. Regulations differ by city and for different types of properties.

It should be stressed to your manager that they are not to discriminate against prospects because of religion, color, age, national origin, race, creed, source of income, marital status, physical handicaps, and life style. It is not legal, or moral, and it can be financially damaging. You should have all employees sign a statement that they will not discriminate.

The remainder of the conditions listed are self-explanatory. The requirements do give your leasing agent or manager an excellent frame of reference when considering a prospect's desirability. It is a good idea to have the manager sign and date the policy letter. This will make certain that the manager reads and absorbs the conditions listed, and at a later time a manager can't say that he or she didn't know your requirements.

MIX OF THE BUILDING

It is a major decision to decide what type of tenant you want. This determination establishes how you will promote and advertise your building. Different categories include income level, children, pets, family size, etc.

The "mix" of your building could give you some problems. A project with many three and four bedroom apartments may have trouble finding couples without children to rent the larger units. One time in a high vacancy period our management company opened a thirty-seven unit building on a secluded side street. The building had studio, one, two and three bedroom apartments. It was difficult to rent because of this mix. If we rented to people with children, no adults-only tenants would want to rent the small apartments. The owners wanted to sell the building.

Our entire advertising and promotion campaign was directed to dogs and their owners. The building was filled in three weeks with over fifty dogs coming in. The building was suitable for dogs as there were vacant lots on all sides. The building sold within a short time and the owners were happy. The pet owners were happy as they found a new building for their dogs and all of their neighbors in the building had dogs so everyone understood the problems of dog owners. Living with other pet owners was relaxing. The new owners were happy because they had a steady income stream. The nearby neighbors were probably not happy because of the arrival of these animals in the area, but with one successful building operating, they soon sold their homes at excellent prices to make way for more new apartments.

ABOVE AND BEYOND

The buildings and their location and design cannot be changed. However, there are some ideas that could be used to make your building a more desirable rental. Some ideas to be considered are:

1. Furnish soft water to the tenants by getting a soft water service contract.

2. Place an icemaker in the building for tenants' use.

3. Put in outdoor barbecues.

4. Hire a recreation or social director or have your manager do these functions.

5. Distribute a monthly newsletter or e-mail for better communication.

6. Change to self-defrosting refrigerators and self-cleaning ovens.

7. In furnished apartments, use colors instead of off-white; put up wallpaper, paneling and pictures, furnish bedspreads, plants, etc.

8. Change rental terms such as deposits, etc. if you are losing good prospects because of strict terms.

9. Brighten up the laundry room and furnish lockers, soap, etc.

10. Provide more secure parking by putting in gates, key locks, video, etc.

11. Furnish mirrors on suitable walls

12. Change locks to deadbolts and get a method of locking windows and sliding doors.

13. Put a lock on the master bedroom door in a family building. The parents will appreciate it.

14. Provide extra heaters or fans for tenants' use.

15. Provide a portable auto battery to help start stalled cars

16. Have rollaway beds available for guests.

RENTAL SURVEY

The next step is to set a proper rent schedule for the building. Schedules should be evaluated periodically. To make a proper rental survey you must learn about your competition.

Many investors purchase buildings and never research an area. Rents in a building could be high, low or correct in relation to the competition. The value of an average building is determined by the amount of net income produced. Therefore, it is imperative that the rentals be compared to other competitive buildings.

When you search for comparable projects, be sure that you have a realistic opinion of your building. If your building is an older garden apartment, the rents of a luxury high-rise nearby are not suitable for comparison purposes. Compare apples to apples and oranges to oranges. Be sure the apples you compare are similar in age, style, class and amenities.

Simply, you want to get an idea of the rental range, size and design, terms, amenities, maintenance, management standards and equally pertinent information on the other buildings. In most cases it is best to pose as a renter. You can see the vacant apartments and ask enough questions to be able to complete any survey. If you get a business card from the manager, you can call back and get further information. It is better if more than one person does the survey work, but I recommend that they go independently. A manager and owner plus both their spouses would garner four opinions. Each person should have a cover story so they can answer the questions of the manager quickly and with some conviction.

DIFFICULTIES IN SURVEYING

It is difficult to get complete data when doing a survey. If you ask too many questions as a renter, a manager may get suspicious. If she or he realizes you are not a prospect, they will not give you any more information. They could be lazy, perturbed at your lie about being a renter or afraid to tell you much because of fear that the owner would become angry.

Square footage size of competitive rentals is a valuable tool in analysis. Most of the time renters do not measure an apartment. You could pace off the overall size to get an estimation. Ask managers their opinion of the square footage.

To determine the exact number of vacant apartments is next to impossible. If you have seen a few apartments in a building, you could ask if others are available. Check mailboxes for vacant nameplates, and if you can get to the master meter box, you can see how many units have the electricity and/or gas off. At night you can drive through their parking area to see how many parking spaces are vacant. You can pose as a member of the local newspaper or apartment association and call to ask their present vacancy ratio. Remember that all of these methods of securing information gather rough approximations and have to be analyzed completely with any other pertinent data.

After you have surveyed the buildings, you must form a conclusion as to the rental value of an average apartment of the subject type in this market area. In our example, we had only two-bedroom apartments so your survey would only consider that type.

DETERMINE AVERAGE RENT

After careful consideration and discussion between all the parties, we establish an average rent of $1,500.00. After evaluating our own building, we concluded that the location, design, terms, size, services provided, etc. are average. However, the additional amenity of cable TV reception, which the others do not have, exceptionally beautiful landscaping, plus the open-air feeling of our grounds are worth $150.00 a month. Therefore, our average two-bedroom is worth $1,650.00.

Next, we must compare our units. We want to price them correctly in relation to each other. In certain buildings, all of the apartments are so similar that they need no differentiation. However, many factors can affect an apartment's value within the same complex:

1. View – This includes different floors in a high rise and different for garden apartments. Higher units afford a better view and lower floors settings offer more convenience.

2. Location within a project – For example, the distance from the elevator in a high-rise building and proximity to desirable or undesirable features in others. In a small building being next to the pool could be a detriment due to noise, but a gorgeous setting with a quiet pool area could be worth more money. Apartments next to laundry rooms, elevators, garages, water heaters or furnaces are not desirable and I always seem to get them at hotels.

3. Lighting of the apartment and where the sun shines (good or bad).

4. Extras in some apartments and not in others such as refrigerators, extra air-conditioners, built-in ranges, extra patios or fireplaces.

5. Condition of the apartments, particularly the paint jobs, carpeting, hardwood floors, drapes and other furnished items.

6. Size and layout of each apartment.

DECISIONS VARY

All of these decisions are subject to change. In many buildings, there is no difference in apartments on either the first or second floor. However, some people may want to be on the first floor to be closer to exits. In others, people want second floor apartments so they have no noise from people living above them. Often, upstairs apartments have higher ceilings. The elderly as well as parents with children and associated paraphernalia do not like to climb stairs whereas younger tenants may not care either way. In one project we set a differential of $150.00 for an apartment with a view of an attractive center court versus those with the view of another apartment house wall. When the apartments with the nice views started renting much faster, we made the differential even more.

Several rule of thumb statements might be:

1. The first floor in a garden apartment is normally more desirable.

2. The top floors in a high rise are best.

3. Townhouse apartments (upstairs and downstairs layout) are normally more desirable than units where other apartments are above or below them.

Remember, that making a rental schedule is a game. You are trying to outguess the person coming to rent. If you guess too low, you lose money because you rented at too low a figure. If you guess too high, you lose money due to excessive vacancy. It is like a Monopoly game except that this is with real money.

You might say, "Gomer, forget all of this. In my building, we never have any vacancies." If you never have any vacancies or if you always rent to the first prospect, you do have a problem. You are subsidizing people by not charging enough rent. If you want to be philanthropic with your building, you certainly are entitled to do so. However, you should evaluate the situation and determine what your generosity is costing you and your family each month. By keeping your rents low some people will stay forever. Subsequently, you will antagonize your long-term renters by raising their rents to a decent level. When you are finally forced to raise rents, these people will never remember the years that you subsidized them. You should have raised their rents periodically because any one-time large increase causes a greater reaction.

Chapter 4
Promotion and Advertising

Your sources of tenants will vary according to many factors. In an existing building, the exact sources are probably well known. A definite idea should be formed as to the basic type of tenant you want to attract. The policy letter has spelled out certain guidelines. Before starting any promotion, you should decide exactly what segment of the market you are after. Certain promotional ideas attract certain types of tenants. Use the techniques that will get you the people that you want. Some owners do no more than put up a vacancy sign and prospects appear. Other owners must be creative and imaginative in trying to get people to live in their apartments. Classified advertising is a major method of attracting tenants. Yes, Pennysaver does help rent units. Before discussing advertising other methods will be evaluated.

SIGNS

The signs that attract tenants to a project are important. It is amazing to me that developers will spend a million dollars on a building and will only buy a $15.00 "For Rent" sign to advertise their fine project.

NAME YOUR APARTMENT

Your apartment building should be given a descriptive name. Make it applicable to the project, easy for tenants to remember and a nice name. Words with a good connotation should be considered. A street name, neighborhood name or other term could be used. In certain areas Greenwood, Oakpark, Boardwalk, Beach Terrace, etc. are descriptive names. High-rise apartments might have a more elegant name, such as Park Tower or Wilshire Arms. Names that mean something to an owner, like Van-Lee Manor or Gomer's Nest Egg, do not have much advertising usage. Don't be too ridiculous and name an old four-unit Plaza Towers. Remember, that in naming a building the name can be used in marketing the building.

A logo or insignia of the building should be designed. This logo is utilized in signs, letterhead, business cards, brochures, receipts and forms. If another building is purchased, it could be called Park Plaza II. This idea of multiple stores and locations has made fast food and other businesses prosper. When a person goes into a McDonalds, they have a preconceived idea of what they will receive. This can be true in any housing effort. If two reputable projects are owned and a third is purchased, your prior good reputation can be transplanted to the new building and your operation will be easily recognized with a similar name.

NOTE: IF YOU USE A FICTIOUS NAME, BE SURE TO REGISTER THAT NAME IN THE PROPER MANNER.

PIRATING

This term may be severe. A better word might be recruiting. If an owner has a new building or wants to make a new promotion effort, direct mail to nearby buildings may be helpful.

Get apartment numbers and addresses of nearby buildings by driving by and looking at mailboxes. Another method is to use the telephone company's reverse directory. This directory lists people in an area in address order. It is simple to prepare a simple brochure with a specific offer. Costs can be verified by keeping track of the expense and checking this against any new tenants secured from the mailing. A letter mail-out can be prepared at a low price and be sent at bulk mail rates. If just one additional tenant rents for one month, the rent money has paid our costs of mailing to many nearby residents. These mail-outs can create rentals months from the time that they were first mailed.

Acquiring a new building and needing to fill the entire project need not be the only reason for sending out a mailing. If you have vacancies you can advertise about new management, a new amenity or a certain type of apartment newly up for vacancy. Remember that the people reached have already made the decision to live in our neighborhood, and we are sure to find a few who are having problems in their current living quarters.

PRESENT TENANTS

As a vacancy occurs, post the information on your building bulletin board. Existing tenants can be your best salespersons. They will become even better salespeople if they were given a monetary gift or partial rent compensation when they find a suitable tenant. When a new tenant moves into your building, give them a copy of this agreement stating rewards for referrals. Remember, that satisfied customers are a great source of referrals.

In high vacancy periods this method was used many times in our buildings. I remember an excellent example of how well it worked. Our company took over the management of a high-rent luxury unit in Sherman Oaks, California. A bank had foreclosed on the building, and it was almost empty. In explaining the ideas that we would use to fill this building, a referral reward of $200.00 was mentioned to the tenants. The bank vice-president said, "Duane, that might work in your small, low rent units but these are high priced. Try it anyway." Within a few weeks, one woman had referred two tenants, and each time this wealthy woman came to our office to pick up the money personally. She said, "This is my money, not my husband's. I want to make sure that I get it."

BROKERS AND MOTELS

This same referral fee arrangement can be made with real estate brokers in the area. I would prepare an official-looking agreement for them to sign. Give the brokers some brochures, business cards and any other advertising aids from your building. Cooperate with them and if they send a renter, pay them at once. Immediate payment of referral fees is important. Go to motels and hotels. Managers know many of their tenants who are looking for apartments. No motel manager or desk clerk ever turned down a referral fee. One clerk gave us six tenants in a one-month period.

OTHER PLACES

Personnel offices of nearby businesses will keep your information on file. When a new person is hired, they can recommend your apartment house. If they refer a tenant, give them some type of gift.

Every junior college or university has a housing office. If college age tenants are wanted, register your building with the housing office. Keep following up periodically to make sure that your listing with them is current.

Another source is nearby churches. Some ministers state that they aren't interested, but a donation to their building fund normally creates interest. Military bases and hospitals have housing assistance personnel. Delivery people and route salespeople have sent tenants to us, as have new accounts clerks at banks.

BULLETIN BOARDS

Most neighborhoods have bulletin boards. They are located in markets, laundromats, community centers, restaurants, printing shops, etc. Print up some 3x5 cards and place them in strategic locations.

Flyers can easily be printed at any printing place. These can be placed on automobiles at supermarket or neighborhood shopping centers. Distributors can hand them out at local gathering places such as movie theaters and fast food places.

OTHER BUILDINGS

There are other managers in your area who are turning prospects away. Get information on your units to them and agree to give them a referral fee for a renter. Get e-mail addresses and update them regularly.

1. Possible buildings to contact would be those that:

2. Are fully rented.

3. Do not take pets, etc.

4. Have no available three-bedroom units, etc.

5. Have too high or too low a rent.

6. Do not have a carport, pool, or any other amenity that you have.

SPECIAL EVENTS

A comprehensive program would include all of the old recruiting standards. Mail a brochure and an invitation to inspect your units to people who have had events announced in the local paper. This would include anything where a change of status might occur – weddings, births, engagements, promotions, move-ins to a new neighborhood, etc.

A large project might consider sending messages of congratulations to anyone who has achieved any success as noted in the media. A small card of congratulations to athletes, scholars, association members, or elected officers in any organization will cost little compared to the goodwill generated.

Advertising in special publications can be considered. If a building is near an airport, there are magazines and papers for pilots and flight attendants. Doctors and nurses have special interest readings. Various industries allow classified ads in their publications, as do military newspapers.

The Yellow Pages has an apartment house section. A listing of your apartment name in the white pages of the telephone directory in bold print might be helpful to prospects that recalled your "warm and easily remembered" apartment building name but can't remember the phone number. Local papers will use items of interest about a building in their news sections. If a building has something of interest happen, take publicity pictures and release a story. Ideas might include two tenants who met there and got married, evening classes being held, tenants who went on a trip or long vacation, a new addition built or some improvement made, winners of any contests announced, management change, etc.

MAINTENANCE PEOPLE

In desperate times, all methods to get tenants must be considered. Your buildings might have a continuing vacancy problem or maintenance problem. Consider advertising for maintenance workers. For example, the building is spending $400.00 for a pool maintenance person. Place an advertisement in a local paper and write to pool companies that a pool person would be given a $400.00 rental allowance for their services. If an apartment were worth $900.00, they would offer pool maintenance services and pay only $500.00 per month in rent. If a project had many vacancies, you could use this method for pool service, gardening, carpet cleaners, cleaning people, painters, security guards, etc. We have filled many vacancies in large projects with personnel supplying some needed service. The management problems increased, but so did the net profit. Be sure that you check first with your insurance carrier and owner to forestall any problems about liability and payroll accounting.

ADVERTISING

Invest your advertising money in newspapers that give the best local service. Large metropolitan dailys have wider distribution, but local newspapers are read by more rental prospects.

An advertising budget is necessary. In a small building there is no need for continual advertising coverage. In a larger building or project you must separate advertising funds into classified, display, direct mail, electronics, etc. Budgeting should take into consideration possible discounts. Newspapers will give discounts to advertisers based on payment within a certain time after receipt of bills, size of ads or continuing insertion into the papers, etc.

There must be constant comparison between the cost of advertising in certain papers versus the number of people who rent after reading about the building in their ads. Records are needed to show how many people came to look at an apartment, their comments and who rented. A dollar cost per phone call, visit and rental can be calculated. Verification of the advertising in this manner is critical. Your advertising dollar must get renters, not just lookers.

When writing ads, try to be in a secluded spot with no deadline pressure. Don't compose your ads while you are talking to the newspaper's representative. The newspapers have personnel who will help in any ad preparation – large or small. Newspapers will supply booklets with information and recommendations on ad copy and design. Learn about Fair Housing Guidelines for advertising.

AD PREPARATION

There are certain advertising rules that are common to both display and classified advertising, no matter the size of the ad involved. Visual techniques become more important with larger size ads. If experience says to use three-line ads for best results, then that is what should be used. It may appear difficult to be creative in just three lines, but creativity is not always necessary in attracting tenants. Try to refer them to your website.

With larger ads, consider the use of pictures, etchings, drawings, varied types of print styles, reversed copy where the writing is white, logos and other eye-catching techniques. The copy should be clear and have some blank space for better appearance and readability.

Ad copy should reflect the following ideas:

1. The first objective is to attract the reader's attention with the lead line.

2. After the reader's attention is secured, arouse their interest with the opening sentence.

3. The body of the ad then creates a desire for the rental.

4. The closing lines should give the reader a recommendation for action.

The following are proven lines for apartment ads:

- THE BEST IN THE CITY
- $995! We can price-advertise as this apartment is worth more than the price
- ONLY 1 vacancy – come by and you will see why – hurry!
- Happiest residents in town
- GREENWOOD – Because where you live tells more about you than anything else
- DIPLOMAT – We take pride in the maintenance of our building
- Julie Klein, Our Manager. If you want a building with a great manager, come here now
- Take a Good Look
- What a Show!
- Brand New
- Over 1,000 square feet
- Move In NOW
- Walk to Wilshire
- Children's Paradise – Notice to Parents
- If you want your child to attend a good school, our school district enjoys the finest reputation for offering the best educational facilities
- Spacious Entertainment and Social Center
- Manicured Landscaping
- Selling Your Home? Come enjoy a quiet living style at The Diplomat
- Central Heat, Central Air Conditioning, Recreation Building, Saunas, Pool, Billiard Room – What more could you ask for?
- We Call It "Luxury Living," Why Don't You Call It Home?
- Large as a House
- See It, Love It
- SUPER SPACE
- For Freedom-Loving Families
- Minutes Away from Everything, Worlds Away from It All
- The Elegant Ones
- Where the Hills Are Alive with the Sounds of Silence
- Special, No Deposit
- Squeaky Clean & Ready For You
- Live Big For Just a Little, $1,200/month
- Now Playing at the Diplomat-Tennis, Ping-Pong, Volleyball

HARD SELL TIME

In a tough rental market when your prospects must know that your building is competitive, advertise:

- Concessions of free rents will be given.
- Coupons in ads can be used for partial rent payments.
- Back to School, Vacation Time, Holiday Specials.
- Other inducements such as gifts, champagne breakfast or parties for prospects, free furniture or TV sets, etc.

- A truck and workers are available to help move the prospect.
- Free trips.
- Free use of laundry facilities.
- Free babysitting.
- Free utilities.
- Free nearby gym memberships.
- Free tickets to sporting events, plays, etc.
- Free classes at the building in adult subjects like ceramics, yoga, dancing, income tax help, etc.

All of these concessions would be tied into the rental of an apartment for a period of time. For example, the tenant would be given a new TV set and if they stayed for at least 12 months, it is theirs. On giving a concession of one month's rent on a year's lease, it increases profit greatly to give the concession for the 13th month and not the 12th. If a couple has decided to move, you still get one more month of income.

SAMPLE ADS

On the following page are four ads that were used in a rental campaign for a large new building. They illustrate ads giving specific information about the rentals; a hurry-now type, a free gift contest, and a catch-phrase ad.

When promoting a new building, consider one idea used on this same building. A full-page ad was taken and designed with excellent pictures of the building included. Other copy stressed all of the fine amenities. Then, the names of all of the subcontractors and suppliers were listed on the page with their addresses and phone numbers. The cost of the full-page ad was split among the contractors and suppliers in accordance with the dollar size of their contract at the building. This full-page ad brought in many tenants, created goodwill among the contractors, and was used successfully in mail outs.

HAPPINESS IS:

FIREPLACES
SECURE BUILDING
2 POOLS
SAUNA & RECREATION ROOM
TV SCANNER
LOW RENTS
GREAT LOCATION

HAPPINESS IS:
GREENWOOD

3724 SPENCER, TORRANCE

Near Hawthorne Blvd.   542-4252

FREE
TRIP TO
HAWAII

THIS MONTH

To a lucky tenant who rents an apartment in the most beautiful building in the South Bay Area.

GREENWOOD

Complete with fireplaces, lavish landscaping and secure building.
3724 SPENCER   TORRANCE
NEAR HAWTHORNE BLVD.

542-4252

Everything

YOU EVER WANTED IN A NEW APARTMENT AND WERE AFRAID TO EXPECT!

SECURE BUILDING – LOCKED GARAGES – INTERCOM – TV SCANNER OF VISITORS

FIREPLACES
SELF-CLEANING OVENS
WALK-IN CLOSETS
LOW RENTS
ELEVATORS
PATIOS

PLUS recreation area, saunas, outdoor gas BBQs, fountains, waterfall, fish pond, two pools, gym, 2 & 1 bedrooms

3724 SPENCER, TORRANCE

Near Hawthorne Blvd.   542-4252

60%

RENTED THE FIRST MONTH

THERE IS A REASON:
The best new building in the South Bay area.

All extras, plus:

FIREPLACES
SECURE BUILDING
TV SCANNER
SENSIBLE RENT

Greenwood Apartments

3724 SPENCER, TORRANCE   542-4252
(near Hawthorne Blvd.)

Chapter 5
Preparation of the Product

The promotion work has been done. You now have to get your building ready for the avalanche of people who will be coming. The best policy is to have the apartment ready as soon as possible. Don't force your manager to say, "Yes, it will be painted" or "It will be cleaned when we get a deposit." Few prospects can visualize what a clean place will look like. If you were going to sell a car, it would be washed and waxed. If you were out on a job interview, you would look your best. Have your apartment looking its best to attract the best tenants.

SAMPLE CHECK LIST

A preparation checklist should be used when a new vacancy occurs. Use the items listed to prepare for the new tenant.

- Front door and screens in good condition?
- Windows and walkways cleaned?
- Drapes cleaned and re-hung? (Open them when a prospect is in the apartment)
- Carpets cleaned and runners placed down if necessary?
- All walls repainted or spots removed?
- All appliances clean and working, i.e. stove, refrigerator, dishwasher, garbage disposal, air conditioner, furnaces, radiators?
- Toilet, shower, sink, tub and other plumbing fixtures working?
- Patios clean and empty?
- No refuse in apartment from previous tenant?
- Ashtrays in suitable places? (If applicable)
- Furniture in good condition? (For furnished apartments)
- All closet and cupboard doors repaired?
- Rooms are deodorized and dusted regularly?
- Locks working properly?
- Floors waxed and polished?
- Light fixtures working?
- Proper apartment temperature?
- Refrigerators are spotless and are running?

In addition:

- A good floor mat should be placed outside the door to save wear and tear on the carpeting.
- Baking soda placed inside a refrigerator will eliminate most odors.
- Have toilet tissue in bathroom, paper towels in kitchen and paper cups in the apartment.
- Have cookies baking in the oven, if it can be arranged.

MANAGERS CHECK UNITS

Have your manager look at the apartment with a critical eye. The work of the maintenance people and janitorial crew should be perfect. These workers will not be showing the apartment, the manager will. Some restaurants have a sign where the waiters pick up their orders that says, "If you are not proud of the food, don't serve it." This can be paraphrased for a manager to, "If you are not proud of it, don't show it."

Of course, there are times when an apartment must be shown before cleanup. Keep these exceptions to a minimum. If possible, show a similar apartment that is in good condition.

CLEAN AND PAINT BEFORE SHOWING

A policy of allowing any new tenants to clean the apartment before moving in or allowing new tenants a credit for painting can be damaging in the long run. Tenants are not always the best painters, and consequently your apartments will begin to look rundown. To reiterate: a good, clean, spotless apartment will attract a better class of tenant.

The manager or leasing agent should check any vacant apartments daily. This will accomplish many things. The manager will know where any keys are at all times. Going to the apartment each day assures that the manager will see the project's general areas and can correct any problems. The apartment will be dusted, vacuumed and deodorized whenever it is needed. If not maintained, an empty apartment can start looking seedy in a very short time.

GROUNDS

A good manager will keep a clean ship. It is said that the general condition of the apartment's laundry room and pool area tell a lot about the maintenance level of the building. The best prospects will be turned off by messy conditions. Prospects know that in windy, rainy or inclement weather the building may look untidy, but these conditions are not permanent.

In walking around different properties with managers, it is my impression that the better managers will stoop and pick up papers, etc. right at that time. They do not lament the fact that the tenants and pets are always ruining the looks of the property. The prospect does not want to hear the manager's problems. The prospect wants to live in a clean building.

The best route to the vacancy must be meticulously maintained and an intelligent manager will use this route when showing the apartment. Don't walk by the garbage bins to save a few seconds in contrast to walking by your lovely pool area.

CONSIDER PROSPECT PARKING

A proper parking spot has to be maintained for your prospects in any busy building. In a smaller building, prospects might have to park on the street. In this instance, signs should direct the prospect to the manager's apartment. Under certain circumstances where parking is a problem and vacancies are infrequent, managers can leave their cars in the parking spot of the vacant apartment and the prospects can be directed to the manager's regular spot near the front of the building. It is best to look at your building as a prospect would. Park where prospects would have to park and then walk to the manager's apartment. You might spot some problems that you wouldn't normally see.

LOCATE THE MANAGER

Have the manager's apartment in a proper location. It must be accessible for rental prospects and service personnel. This location can allow proper supervision of potential problem areas such as the pool, parking spaces, lobbies, etc. If an apartment unit has an inherent design or noise problem, the manager can be given that unit. Pick your location evaluating the most important factors for your building.

In some buildings, it's impossible to find the manager's apartment or renting office to get any rental information. Don't make it a game of hide and seek for the prospect. Have a scale drawing or unit layout map near the entrance for prospects and visitors to use to find apartment units.

THE BUILDING AT NIGHT

Check the building at night. Most owners and managers walk around their buildings in the daytime. Nightfall brings a different look to apartment houses. Make sure that your building has a pleasant atmosphere and is safe. Poor lighting must be improved before there is an accident. Lights could be arranged to call attention to the building's outstanding features. There may be extreme parking problems at night, and some procedures to alleviate this should be started.

Consider sensor lighting or lights on timers. Both will alleviate concern for apartment safety and should be checked and repaired as necessary. Make sure stairwells are properly lit. Check wattage to be sure you are using the correct bulbs and consider longer lasting commercial bulbs. The slightly higher cost is regained by longer usage and less maintenance time. If you change all your bulbs at once, you might save money in the long run. In addition, inaccessible fixtures require a large amount of labor time to change after a suitable period of service so consider this when appraising your lighting.

LANDSCAPING

Landscaping is of paramount importance. Good landscaping can really improve the appearance of a property.

Don't use large expanses of grass. In northern areas it looks drab in the winter months and in hotter areas grass requires cutting, edging and watering all the time.

Landscaping should look lush, not skimpy. Plants and trees native to your region should be used. Consider maintenance problems when planting. Eucalyptus and olive trees grow fast and look good, but they shed leaves and olives like a German Shepherd dog sheds hair. Bamboo trees look fine, but they can ruin paving and sidewalks faster than any other tree.

Get some color in your building. Use plants and planters in proper areas. Maintenance workers can plant colorful flowers at yearly intervals.

Utilize the natural environment whenever possible. Trees can be preserved when designing your building and an open look is appealing in garden apartments. Plants in the lobbies of apartments are inexpensive, and add a rich, full look. Plastic plants look like plastic plants. Everyone is becoming more knowledgeable in both the form and function of plants, and they are aware of the peacefulness that nature can provide in urban settings.

Gravel and wood chips can cause problems in maintenance. Gravel is excellent for color in desert regions, but keep it away from grass planted areas. Mower repairs are costly. Also, children and gravel never seem to mix well. If your project has places that are used as short cuts, don't fight it. Put in stepping-stones or some other pathway.

Trees are like a human's hair. They need pruning and cutting regularly. Find a reliable tree service and use them periodically. Fences might be necessary for security but if possible, use hedges or shrubs as your dividers. They enhance the natural open look. Sprinklers or soakers are needed in warm weather areas. Timers on them will help to insure regular watering without wasting water. Sprinklers in cold weather areas have a tendency to freeze and cause damage.

In many buildings, sidewalk vacuums and blowers are used to keep areas clean. With the current energy shortage, watering sidewalks is not an intelligent alternative. Blowers work more successfully than large vacuums. They are light, fast and efficient. Tenants thought planes were landing in the courtyard when we used larger commercial vacuums on our sidewalks.

Buildings with children have different landscaping priorities than adult-only buildings. Play areas need sand or wood chips for safety. Most parents do not appreciate asphalt, gravel and cement. Young children are often intrigued by planted areas. They have a compulsion to dig. In California, junipers have worked great in children's areas. They are attractive and take a strong beating. They are tough to kill, and they are prickly enough to discourage youngsters from playing around them. Grass in any children's areas must be strong. Small patches of grass will never make it.

PARKING AREAS

Paving can deteriorate. Once holes start appearing, repairs become expensive. Keep an eye on the asphalt and resurface whenever necessary. Painting of asphalt is not expensive and enhances the appearance considerably.

Have parking lines painted when needed and use concrete wheel stops where appropriate. Automobiles have stopped in apartment house living rooms because no concrete wheel stops were installed. Speed bumps are helpful in controlling speeds in your parking lots.

Place them intelligently or you will have drivers doing a slalom course to avoid hitting any bumps.

Junk autos should be removed. If there is an old car with flat tires, get it moved. Your rental agreement must cover this. There can be no auto repair, maintenance or washing in the parking lots. In close parking situations, recommend plastic door protectors to tenants. If old autos are left and it is impossible to ascertain to whom they belong, take the car's license number or identification number and write to your state motor vehicle department. They will give you the last registered owner. If this information is not helpful, call a local auto wrecking yard. A reputable firm can tell you how to post any notices so that the car can be removed. If an abandoned auto is parked on the street near your building, call the police to have it removed. They will take care of it. Although it is tempting to push an old auto in your parking area into the street before calling the police, it is definitely illegal.

TRASH AREAS

If a building has a central chute disposal system, your job will be to make sure that people don't leave their garbage in the hallway. Tenants often do not follow rules. This means disciplining them. Place the containers in an area away from the general traffic pattern. Also, post a sign near the containers listing the days when the trash is picked up. If you have trash bins located in different areas, use common sense and make these areas as attractive as possible. A wooden fence would improve the appearance. Smaller containers emptied more regularly are normally better than large receptacles. If the containers are covered, a light cover can make it possible for all tenants to put the rubbish inside. Daily supervision is necessary to correct any problems, and the truck drivers who pick up the containers must be neat. The containers must be washed periodically. Again, baking soda will cut down on odors.

ENTRANCES

Lobbies and entranceways have to be clean. A wastebasket here could be of service to tenants. Also, sand ashtrays are useful if placed in the lobby or general areas.

Mailbox locks are inexpensive and a supply should be kept on hand. When a lock goes bad, replace it. Names can be put on the mailboxes with some small device such as a tape machine. This can allow you to have all the mailbox names in one style and color. If there are many vacancies, place names on the boxes anyway so your building does not look extremely vacant.

A building directory of names needs to be maintained. The postal service insists on this. An up-to-date directory will help visitors find people easily without bothering anyone, and this makes your tenants happy. Some type of floor mats should be placed at the entrance. This will lower cleaning costs on carpets.

GENERAL AREAS

Swimming pools must be clean and sparkling. If you advertise a heated pool, maintain it at a set temperature. Have a thermometer in the pool. In Los Angeles we do not heat pools all year. From October to April, the heaters are shut off in many buildings. Put this information in your rental agreement to stop any arguments before they start.

Proper chemical balance, weekly vacuuming, and periodic brushing keep a pool in good condition. Give the manager a pool brush and a skimmer to retrieve any foreign matter from the pool during the period between the pool person's visits. Safety laws and common sense dictate that proper signs, safety rings and poles are located at the poolside.

Pool furniture brightens up the area. It allows an opportunity for the use of color. Chairs, umbrellas and chaise lounges look fine when they are placed around the pool.

Laundry rooms can be bright and airy. Bright colors should be used. Attractive floor tiles can be installed. There is no rule that all the machines must be white. If there is a lack of ventilation, install exhaust fans. Proper temperatures need to be maintained. Install proper locks so that your tenants feel safe when doing their laundry.

HALLWAYS

Hallways must be bright. Painting hallways is relatively inexpensive because of the ease of painting. Keep them clean. You might consider semi-gloss enamel because this type of paint can be washed easily. Put enough lights in the longer hallways. Paneling can be used in some locations to give a more luxurious look. Carpeting should be serviced regularly and shampooed periodically. If there are odors in the hallways, try to discover the source and deal with it. If it is a musty or closed odor, a ventilation fan in a corridor will help.

ELEVATORS

To prevent any damage suits from arising, have your elevators maintained and serviced by a reputable firm. Make sure that they are inspected and approved by the local public agency. Nothing will scare tenants more than the fear of being stuck between floors in an elevator or having an elevator malfunction.

If security is a problem in your building, have the elevators converted so that a key is needed to operate them. The carpeting in an elevator needs to be replaced regularly and the walls should be checked consistently for drawings or profanity. A building should have pads to place on elevator walls when anyone is moving furniture. The pads will help preserve the walls of the elevator.

MANAGER'S APPEARANCE AND APARTMENT

The prospect is coming to your building and will be ringing the manager's bell. The prospect will be standing there for a few seconds waiting. Therefore, the manager's doorway and any area nearby should be squeaky clean. The door, screen door, doorbell and floor mat should all be in proper condition.

When the manager opens the door the prospect shouldn't be taken aback. Therefore, in your training you should stress that the manager is running a commercial operation. They should appear neat and respectable.

In addition, the manager's apartment or office should illustrate some pride in appearance. The kitchen must be picked up, and all dishes should be stored away. Clutter should be kept behind closed doors. One of my managers used to keep her family clothing on her family room sofa.

Keys and forms should be in a readily accessible spot. If the manager's apartment and the manager are appealing, the prospect will be looking forward to seeing the apartment. There is no second chance to make a good first impression.

You might buy a manager some new shirts or blouses. They are tax deductible to you and your manager has to buy clothes from their taxed dollars. Building names or logos can be easily added at local embroidery or silkscreen stores.

Chapter 6
Telephone Techniques

In many instances, the prospect's first contact with your building will be by telephone. A great deal of money has been spent in promotion, advertising and preparation. Correct handling of this initial contact is vital to the success of your building.

COURTESY

All of your employees should know that courtesy is important in their professional relationships. With the impersonal atmosphere of the telephone call, courtesy becomes even more important. Telephone companies have books and movies available to you on this subject. Many of them have classes to which you can send your employees. Employees who want to improve their performance should attend these classes or read the booklets. Use this free service to educate your workers.

An overview of the telephone companies' simple guidelines is as follows:

ALERTNESS – Show that you are wide awake and ready to help the person on the line.

PLEASANTNESS – Put a smile in your voice.

NATURALNESS – Use simple, straightforward language. Avoid technical terms, acronyms and slang.

DISTINCTNESS – Speak directly into the telephone transmitter, pronouncing your words clearly and carefully.

EXPRESSIVENESS – Talk at a moderate rate and volume, but vary the tone of your voice. This will add emphasis and vitality to what you say. Match your speech to the prospects.

Managers must develop a habit of answering the phone promptly. Early in the conversation they should identify themselves. Throughout the call they have to be friendly. Interest and attentiveness should be shown so the person does not have to repeat anything said. The caller should be given the manager's complete attention. If there is some emergency or the manager is unable to speak to the caller, they should ask the caller for a number and call them back at the convenience of the caller.

Other considerations for the manager regarding phone etiquette include:

1. Politely ask the caller his or her name, and if the name is difficult to understand or pronounce, ask for the correct spelling.

2. Use his or her name in the conversation as soon as possible.

3. Use courteous words like please, thank you and you're welcome.

4. If a promise has been made to call back, do it. Forget the phrase no problem and use "it would be my pleasure".

5. Have a pencil and paper near the phone so messages can be taken quickly and efficiently. A record of phone calls is vital.

THE PROSPECT CALLS

Make sure the manager shows the above considerations to any person calling for information about any vacancy. The prospect might say, "Do you have a two bedroom vacancy?" A simple yes answer should be expanded. "Yes, we have a nice, large one that just became available. I am the manager, Mrs. Brown. What is your name?"

BE TACTFUL

Normally, a prospect will give a name and then they will want some further information. If they are obviously unqualified (have pets and you take none, want a furnished apartment and you have none, etc.), have the manager be courteous and explain your rental policies.

Try not to give too blunt an answer to the question, "How much is it?" On the phone, the manager's job is to sell an appointment to come to the building. It is impossible to close them over the phone and if too much information is given, the prospect is sure to find something to turn them off. Don't oversell on the phone.

Remember the prospect's state of mind at this time. They are probably calling a bunch of ads and trying to eliminate many of them. Then, they will go see a few apartments. They are trying to find out facts about your apartment so they can eliminate it and go on to the next call.

SELL THE APPOINTMENT

This one point is so important that it bears repeating. The main function at the time of the phone call is to sell an appointment to come to the building. When the price is brought up, have the manager say something like, "The apartment is one of the best priced values in the area. It is hard for you to realize this without seeing the unit." However, don't lead the prospect on. Let them know a price range of your apartments so that someone looking to spend only $400.00 - $500.00 does not waste their time and yours by seeing a $1200.00 apartment that they clearly would not rent, regardless of the amenities. The point of stressing seeing the apartment is because sometimes the call to your building is one of the first calls made. The prospect has set a top dollar value of $450.00. Your $600.00 price will force him or her to end the phone call with a half-hearted, "We'll drive by later." They will never see your building. A few days later when they are reconciled to the fact that they will pay a higher rent, they will not be calling you again. If they had seen your unit, they would have a visual knowledge of it and might return.

APPOINTMENT

Some helpful questions at this time might be:

- Are you in the area now?
- When do you need the unit?
- When would it be convenient for you to come by? How about 3:00 this afternoon?

Have the manager set a specific time for them to come. If it is an occupied unit that is being shown before the existing tenant vacates, explain that an appointment with the tenant would be appreciated. "We like to show all of our tenants every consideration possible." If it is vacant, have the manager say, "If you can give me some idea of when you will be by, I can be sure to be readily available and adequately show you the apartment." Get them to set in their mind a time to come. Inform the manager that by making the prospect make a commitment to see the apartment, no matter how vague, will greatly increase the chances that they will stop by. In addition, by having an idea when they will come, managers won't feel like they are watching for them all day.

GET INFORMATION

Before the conversation ends, have the manager get their present phone number in case they have to call them back. This should be written on a prospect call card so there is a record of the call. Make sure they are asked where they heard about the building for your advertising and promotion records.

If they are hesitant about setting any time and it appears that they are losing interest, have the manager tell them about any other important features of the building. It could be some amenity, some favorable terms or concessions, or a sense of urgency such as "It is our only vacancy". A features checklist for the vacancy should be near the phone as well as a copy of the present ads being run so that any questions can be answered quickly. It is helpful to know which ad the person is reading.

Keep a map of the area near the phone so that directions can be given to find the building. If the instructions are complicated, have the manager keep a copy of them by the phone. Include any instructions on where the best place to park will be if that might be a problem. End the call on a pleasant note. Good salesmen always thank someone when they leave. Use whatever courtesy words are pertinent. Your manager can ask them to check Map Quest.

HAVE PROPER EQUIPMENT

Have the manager's telephone in an area that is easily accessible. This area needs to be conducive to quiet, business-like conversations. In addition, consider giving the manager a digital/cell phone or pager for business related phone calls only. Both increase the chances a prospect will get in touch with the manager on their first try.

If this is not feasible, consider a telephone answering service or an answering machine. If a manager is out around the building showing an apartment or supervising some project, the call that is recorded can be easily returned. If your company has a Web site where messages may be left, make sure that the manager has access to a computer and regularly checks the postings. Consider installing a cable or DSL line in your manager's apartment for ease in accessing the web.

SUMMARY

Phone calls are the lifeline of the apartment business. The managers and leasing agents must understand their importance. If proper records are kept, an owner can figure out exactly what advertising cost was incurred to get a phone to ring. It might be an impressive amount, and the manager must realize this importance.

Chapter 7
Presentation of the Product

Managers must be ready for a rental prospect every time the doorbell rings. The apartment to be shown must be spotless, and the general areas of the building should be appealing. The manager's apartment must be above reproach.

If there are last minute additions that might help rent an apartment, have them added. The insides of the cabinets can be painted, and cabinet can be painted in brighter colors. Live plants placed in a furnished apartment add a cozy charm. New light fixtures, paneling and wallpaper will create a richer looking apartment.

PROPER ATTITUDE

Everything is ready. The doorbell rings. This is where the managers begin to earn their salary. The showing and renting record of a manager will separate the good manager from the outstanding manager.

The poorest managers will give the prospects a key and let them go look at the vacancy by themselves. Other managers will be upset that their daily routine has been interrupted. The thought of every manager should be: "A prospect is not an interruption to me; a prospect is the most important person in the world to my business and to my job".

When managers answer the door, they should put on a "happy face." Many times this can be difficult. There may be a problem with an outraged tenant on the phone, some important work may have been interrupted or the manager might have some personal problem. Remind your manager that the people at the door do not know about these problems. They want to be treated courteously and with respect. The manager's initial impression on the prospect can be very important.

Managers should have a clipboard kept nearby. On the board should be the necessary keys, rental schedule, brochures, rental applications, sample agreements, rental action cards, business cards, floor diagrams with measurements, a tape measure and any other helpful items. The rental application should be on top of the clipboard making it easy to close the prospect. Put a large tag on the vacancy keys and have them in the same spot at all times. If someone takes them, have them sign for them.

Have the manager refrain from smoking, drinking, eating or chewing gum while showing the apartment to the prospect. If there are a number of prospects at any one time, an area should be established where they can wait. Furnish reading material with brochures about your building in a prominent spot.

VACANT MANAGER

Any manager who is in the building but not in his or her apartment should leave a note on the door with an explanation as to where he or she can be found. Many advertising dollars are lost because a prospect appears, and the manager is not in the apartment. Managers need different notes readily available to be used whenever they must leave their apartment. The notes should be typed or printed neatly and cover all the possible reasons for the manager's absence.

If the manager is going to be gone for an extended period of time, a note should be left directing the prospect to another apartment. If this substitute manager rents the apartment to the prospect, he or she should be paid for the services. There has to be a person in every building who will do this. Even if the available person will not show the apartment, the prospect can be directed to it and the prospect's phone number and address can be secured. At this point, anything is better than the prospect being turned away. Managers need to be around most of the time when there are rental problems, but when they can't be, a "sub" manager must be ready.

THE CURTAIN RISES

The show is ready to start. The manager answers the door with a smile, "Good morning, what can I do for you?" The normal response of the prospect will be, "Do you have a two bedroom unfurnished apartment for rent?" An immediate "yes" answer should be followed with, "By the way, I'm Debbie Thompson, the manager. What is your name?" When the name is given, the manager must write it on an action card. The prospect's name is then used whenever possible. There is no more pleasant sound to anyone than the proper use of his name. One more question at this time might be, "Where did you hear about our building?" This information is important to evaluate our advertising budget.

If the price of the apartment was not listed in the advertisements, the prospect will probably inquire at this time. Have the manager keep in mind that their utmost goal is to show the apartment. If the prospect doesn't see the apartment, they can never decide on its merits later when they have exhausted all other rental possibilities. Therefore, a question directed at rental rates could be answered, "Please let me show you the apartment first. I am sure you will be surprised at how low the rent is after you see the apartment. Please follow me, Mr. Smith." Once they are in the apartment, you can give them the price.

The manager has to be friendly and take the prospects to the vacancy by the best route possible. On the way, good points about the building should be stressed, creating a friendly and positive atmosphere.

Prospects differ on how they look at a building. They differ even in their speed of walking. A manager must adapt the speed of the showing process to the speed of the prospects. Once, a manager in Ventura was doing a poor job of renting a new, large building. She was excellent in her approach. After watching her presentation to a few clients, her problem was obvious. She was hurrying ahead of the prospects so far that they felt rushed and confused. A simple suggestion, "Why don't you try letting the prospects walk ahead of you?" helped her rent more apartments.

While walking through the general area, features should be highlighted. Comments can be made on the landscaping, clean general areas, recreational facilities and other amenities. If your building has a good mixture of tenants, their occupations can be mentioned.

QUALIFY

Qualifying questions are those that begin with "who, why, where, how and when". Use leading questions that cannot be answered with one word. The questions will vary according to your type of building. For example, if you do not rent to pets, you should ask about those items early.

Some examples of qualifying questions are:

- Have you been here before?
- Where do you now live and work?
- How long have you worked and lived there?
- Why are you moving?
- When will you need the apartment?
- How did you hear about our building?
- Do you know any present tenants?
- Do you have any children? What are their names and ages?
- Do you have any hobbies, special interests, etc.?
- How long have you been in this area?
- How long have you been looking for an apartment?
- Do you live in an apartment now?
- What size?
- What are you looking for in your next apartment?
- What is wrong with your present apartment?

The manager should not form an impression too quickly. Prospects are to be considered innocent until proven guilty. For example, my youngest daughter looks about 18 years old. One wouldn't expect her to have a degree in Biology. She is a quiet, responsible tenant, a fact her youth does not suggest.

That said, if a person is definitely unqualified, the showing process can be halted. Courteously give the reason for disqualification. Say a friendly goodbye and if the person's disqualification can be changed (i.e., get rid of a pet), invite them back when they qualify.

LISTEN

As these questions are asked, make sure that the manager is listening closely to the answers. Answers to the qualifying questions can help determine how the prospect is to be handled. A person who needs an apartment like your vacancy in three days is treated differently than one who needs it in three months. A prospect new to the area needs different treatment than someone who has been looking for six months. Any answers given can lead you to ask better qualifying questions. On a busy day when there are prospects everywhere, the manager should qualify quickly. Work harder on the better prospects (those who have been there before, or must have a unit soon, or both husband and wife are present). If someone is looking in a rainstorm or blizzard, chances are this person really needs an apartment. If working people have taken time off from work, this indicates a stronger need on their part.

Impress on your manager the importance of giving equal attention to multiple prospects, i.e. a husband and wife or two roommates. You can easily turn away valuable prospects simply by favoring one over the other.

AT THE APARTMENT

When the manager reaches the apartment, he or she should quickly open the door. Fumbling for keys shows poor organization and poor organization makes a prospect think of poor building management.

As the door is opened, the manager should step back and let the prospect enter. The manager should make certain the lights are turned on and that drapes and doors are opened where necessary.

A manager should not walk through the apartment announcing that this is the kitchen, the bedroom, and the toilet. Prospects can tell the difference between standard rooms. Instead, the manager should point out something in each room that is a unique and positive quality of the apartment. Highlighted features can include room sizes, arrangement of rooms, traffic pattern, quality of furnishings, amenities such as drapes, carpets, self-cleaning ovens, frost-free refrigerators, general appearance of cleanliness, number or size of closets, new fixtures, location in building, etc.

Managers must know the strong points about their building in comparison to their competition. If there are noticeable differences, the manager can prepare a chart. On the list, write the features at your building in column form on the left side the page. Write the name of your building and comparable buildings in the area in row form along the top of the page. Use colored checkmarks to indicate the features your apartment has versus those of others. (Of course, if other nearby buildings have more features, forget your comparison charts.)

In discussing these ideas, it is important that the manager explain the advantages to the tenant and the benefit that they will derive from these features. Prospects want to know what these features mean to them. A self-cleaning oven means no more dirty, smelling oven cleaning jobs and more free time for a tenant. Don't say "fireplace." Say "cozy, intimate winter evenings." Don't say "great view." Say "relaxing, early evening hours."

Tell your managers, don't overwhelm the prospect by telling them every single amenity. Rather, tailor your approach based on what you have learned about the prospect from your previous qualifying questions.

Also, there comes a time in showing presentations when the parties want to be alone for a few minutes. If they walk together into the back room, let them go. They might want a few quiet moments to decide yes or no.

DO THE HOMEWORK

The manager should have checked the vacancies in your project to decide what questions a tenant might ask. Have the managers ask themselves, "What would I ask about in this apartment?" and get an answer ready.

For example:

1. First floor-more convenient; second floor-quieter and better view.

2. Apartment faces north - no hot sun in summer.

3. Apartment faces south - brighter on winter days.

4. Near to school - no waiting for bus and convenient for parents.

5. Bus to school - no crossing streets, home on schedule.

If a manager is prepared with an answer, a question by a prospect is welcome. When prospects ask specific questions, they are becoming interested in the apartment. We love questions.

ADVANTAGES OF RENTING

Be ready to recite the advantages of renting over buying a home.

Some advantages are:

- Freedom from maintenance and yard work.
- Better location.
- Pool and other amenities.
- Recreational facilities.
- Less cost.
- Mobility when needed.
- No investment.
- Less fear of property taxes.
- Safer for elderly and single people.
- Easier to heat and clean.

In addition, have the manager know approximately what the cost of renting is per square foot in your type of building. If you have a larger unit, use this square footage cost approach to illustrate why your unit is a bargain.

DON'T ARGUE

Although it is the 21st century, some things, such as common manners, just don't go out of style. Therefore, I've included a few points worth remembering when training your managers:

1. When showing an apartment, don't get into any arguments. This is not a debate class. If you embarrass anyone by showing how smart you are and how stupid they are, they will leave. No one likes to appear inferior.

2. Watch your language. Vulgarity is not proper. In addition, extremely poor grammar and mispronunciations are not businesslike.

3. Terminology can be a problem. While you may be familiar with rental terms, they could mean nothing to a prospect. If you mention something so matter-of-fact, the prospect may think he or she will look stupid if they ask a question. Use easy to understand terms and always explain their meaning if the prospect looks unsure.

Do not show too many apartments. Normally, three would be the most anyone should see in one showing. If a prospect sees any more, it is difficult to make a decision. Showing too many apartments can be time consuming and unrewarding.

THE SENSES

Prospects are looking at an apartment with all of their senses. The ears are listening to the presentation, and the eyes are observing the building and you. The manager must be concentrating all the time. Showing an apartment may be old stuff to a manager, but the prospect has never seen this "show." The manager should appear enthused about their job. Can you imagine how difficult it must be for an actor to give exactly the same stage performance every night for years? However, each night there is someone seeing the play for the first time.

The prospect's other senses must be used. Bad odors and musty smells have to be eliminated before an apartment is shown. One real estate broker used to recommend to his clients that they put blueberry muffins in the oven shortly before he came to show their home. The smell of home baking is a positive symbol to most people.

The prospect's sense of touch can be utilized. Have them open pantry doors, use the appliances, check equipment, etc. Getting the prospect involved in the presentation is helpful. Before doing this, make sure all the doors, appliances and equipment work. It is embarrassing to have an oven door come off in a prospect's hands.

The sense of taste is hard to implement. The manager might discuss different amenities such as gas barbecues or double ovens to illustrate how food can be prepared in this building. You can get them thinking about pleasant food tastes.

REITERATE

Good points should be repeated before the prospect leaves. If a tenant mentions a feature or the manager wants to highlight a feature, questions can be used. "Central air conditioning sure keeps this room cool, doesn't it?" "A fireplace is nice on a cold winter's evening, isn't it?" "Your children would love the pool, wouldn't they?" "A compact kitchen is great for a working couple, don't you agree?" "The hardwood floors should be easy to keep clean, don't you think so?" "You can almost smell the steaks barbecuing on the gas grill, can't you?" Reflective-type questions should be used. These questions get the prospect into the act. A prospect understands the benefits much better if he or she must answer a question about them. It starts to establish a yes pattern of answers in the presentation. Have the manager evaluate your apartments and mentally prepare some reflective questions.

It is important to remember one fact mentioned in an earlier chapter. Many tenants live where they do because of their opinion of the managers. Managers showing an apartment must remember that they are "selling" not only the apartment but also themselves. A good manager must exhibit a confident, friendly manner. There should be pride in their product and themselves. If a manager is enthusiastic, the prospect will be enthused. Enthusiasm is contagious.

Chapter 8
Conversion From Prospects to Applicants

After managers do a good job of presenting an apartment, many prospects will say, "We want it." Sometimes they will say nothing. Managers are not just order takers. They have to be salespersons in every sense of the word. They must help some prospects make up their mind. In this chapter, closing will mean helping a person make a decision that will be to the benefit of everyone.

Closing starts the minute that the prospect hears about the building. Closing continues until the person either rents an apartment in our building, another building or decides to discontinue looking for an apartment. The introduction to the building and the presentation of the apartment are parts of the entire closing process. All the parts must be done properly to help in achieving the final goal – a conversion from prospect to tenant.

Closing starts in earnest when the showing process has finished, and the prospect has not yet made a decision. There are many ideas that need to be considered about the subject of closing.

FEAR

Many people have a fear of being turned down. This fear leads them to avoid ever asking any questions that can create a situation where someone turns them down. This feeling is common in young people who are afraid to ask another certain person for a date, and young people are sometimes afraid to go out for different activities where there is competition. Managers should understand this fear. If a closing question is asked and a person says, "Hell, no. I would never live in a dump like this with a horrible manager like you." Well, you can't win them all. Forget it. A person who would talk like that has more problems than you do. What have you lost? Nothing.

You might say, "When do I ask closing question?" The answer is whenever you think you should. If the prospects are leaving and you haven't asked any closing questions, start asking them. You will never learn when to ask if you don't try.

LISTEN

An important rule in closing is to listen, listen, listen. Selling is not seeing how much you can talk. You want to find out what the other person is thinking. There has to be some reason why they are not jumping at this great value. You must find out what this reason is. If you are talking constantly, you might hit the reason. Again, you might not even come close. Psychologists and psychiatrists try to find out reasons for people's behavior. They are trained for years, and they function by asking questions that need more than a one-word answer. They concentrate on the answer and ask another question. When listening, a person should concentrate on the words of the speaker. Don't be so busy starting to formulate a reply that the speaker's words are ignored. Be a good listener – learn to concentrate your attention on what people are saying so that your response will be both appropriate and effective.

WATCH

Another important rule is to watch, watch and watch. The body and face language of a prospect can convey true feelings. If a person walks back to look at the great view from the patio, this shows interest. Prospects can look at each other and by simply raising an eyebrow or nodding, illustrate how they feel about your rental.

Questions asked by the prospects can show their interest. For example:

- When could we move in?
- How much are the deposits?
- Where would we park our car?

A prospect can show interest by making statements like, "The kids would love that pool," or "Central air conditioning sure feels good." Another way they show their interest is to talk about how their furniture would fit. Sometimes prospects start to talk in future tense as if they already were in the apartment, like "We will sure use that gas barbecue."

If any of these or other buying signals are raised, be ready to rent the apartment. Don't startle them with your quickness, but at the next possible point begin the closing procedure.

ORDER BLANK

One of the best methods is called the order blank close. When you observe some interest, questions can be asked from the rental application. This application is on the top of the clipboard that a manager carries. "I just happen to have an application handy _____."

Some examples of order blank close questions are:

- How much deposit would you like to leave?
- When would you want to move in?
- What is the exact spelling of your last name?
- What are the names of your children?

If they answer any of these questions, keep on asking questions and filling out the application. When it is done, ask them to check or approve it. Never ask them to sign, for everyone has a fear of signing documents.

ALTERNATE OF CHOICE

Another type of closing question is called an alternate-of-choice question. You can ask, "Which apartment do you like best, 204 or 208?" An answer of 204 or 208 means you start asking other questions from the application. There are many other alternative questions available. If an answer is received to one, it is easy to move on.

The above approaches can best be described as "Assumed Assent" closes. Once a manager is certain of the prospect's interest, it is assumed that the person is going to rent. I used this technique often when I was soliciting property management business.

After an interview I would take out a contract and leave it with the owners. I would state that I would go visit the buildings and check back with them tomorrow to pick up the contract. This was done with no type of pressure. It was a soft sell approach to end the interview, and it was assumed that they wanted me to property manage their buildings. This could not be used unless the clients had exhibited interest in having me do this function.

Some prospects will say, "Would the owners paint this bedroom?" If it is a reasonable request, many managers say "Yes." This is not the best reply. Our managers were instructed to answer questions of this type with this standard query, "If they would paint the bedroom, would you rent the apartment?" Our people said that this was their best closing tool. Many times, the prospect would answer, "Yes" or the prospect would bring up some other objection.

Then, our agent could clear up this next objection, which might be the prospect's main obstacle to renting.

THINK IT OVER

Another put off can be the old, "I want to think it over." Doug Edwards, the eminent sales trainer, has the best answer to this ploy. You can say, "What is it that you want to think over?" Then, don't pause so that they have time to say anything. Ask, "Is it the parking situation?" "Is it the carpeting?" "Is it the price?" etc. Keep asking "Is it" until they say, "That's the problem." Then, you can work on the now isolated objection.

Managers should not be afraid to hear objections. As long as prospects are talking, there is a chance that they will rent. It is when they quit talking and leave that you have a problem.

WILL BE BACK

Another statement used by prospects is, "I want to bring my spouse back." A manager could ask them if they would like to leave a deposit on the apartment for twenty-four hours. If a person leaves any money, they will normally come back. An apartment can't be held for too long a time, but a brief period of reservation for a small deposit could be a wise move. A definite appointment time is set for their return. If they can't give a time, ask for their phone number so that they can be called later to set an appointment.

SILENCE

Silence is a great virtue. Silence is one of the greatest pressure creators. There comes a time in many rental closing situations when you should shut up. When the proper question is asked, wait for an answer. Don't think that you have to add another word. Wait. Try it sometime. I have had many selling situations with large investors where it was important to shut up. I waited, and many times this procedure proved effective. The silence forces the prospect to make a decision. Don't be afraid of silence. Husbands and wives have used silence as a weapon for centuries. Don't make a mistake in believing that whenever there is silence, something more has to be said. Many times after a silence, the next person to speak turns out to be the loser.

KNOW THE MARKET

If a prospect objects about the price, don't be too eager to drop the rent right away. The prospects will say, "Will they lower the price?" when that is really not their major objection. If a manager thinks that the price is merely a minor objection, they can ignore it the first time it is brought up. Whenever small minor objections are brought up, it is best to ignore them. If the price question is raised again, don't give the apartment away. If it is obvious that the only problem is the price and all the other signals are go, then a manager must really understand the rental market. If the apartment has been vacant a long time and the offer is within the realm of possibility, the manager might take a deposit and fill out an application to secure the owner's approval. At this time the closing procedure has become a poker game. A manager must be able to handle this type of negotiation skillfully and attempt to get good tenants at optimum rental prices.

WHERE TO CLOSE

What is the best location for closing a prospect? Apartment buildings and prospects are different. Managers have applications with them so that the application paperwork could be done at once in the vacant apartment. It might be better to get the prospects back to the office or the manager's apartment. In this comfortable atmosphere, the prospects are more relaxed. It is important that the manager have some type of refreshments for the prospects. Stalling prospects might like it if the manager invited them back to the manager's apartment for a soft drink or other beverage. If a person has been out looking for an apartment on a hot day, nothing would taste better than a cold drink, and they would relax. On a cold day, coffee or hot chocolate would be appreciated. These refreshments are furnished by the building. Different buildings might warrant different drinks. In certain buildings a can of beer would be proper. I had older units where extremely inexpensive wine would be appropriate. In a more exclusive building, a cocktail after a hard day of apartment looking might be the proper closing tool.

Another good point to cover is the manager's attitude when money changes hands. Act like this will be a good move for the prospects. Don't ever take money in an unfriendly atmosphere - be happy.

OTHER IDEAS ON CLOSING

If your apartment has some obvious shortcomings, admit them or move onto other topics. If a bedroom is extremely small and a prospect mentions that, agree with him if it is true. If a shortcoming can't be turned into an advantage, you and the prospect both know it.

A problem that can arise is to have tenants come to you and loudly complain while you are showing a prospect around the grounds. Quickly tell the tenants that you will come and see them as soon as you have shown this prospect a vacant apartment. Don't let them get involved in any long discussion. Be assertive and move on with your rental presentation. If a person insists on continuing, ask the prospect to wait in your office and take care of the problem. I would also explain the facts of life to the complainer and if this person acted like this very often, I probably would ask them to leave. When you get back to your prospect, give a short explanation of the problem so that the prospect isn't worried about any problems in your building.

Don't use all the techniques on any one prospect. Use the procedure that you think will work best. Be yourself and work in a manner that is comfortable.

Watch the use of humor. It can backfire. Prospects have a problem that they think is serious. They have to find a new place to live. Funny stories might not be what they want to hear. Have a sense of humor but do not be too witty.

Prospects are not to be judged as to whether we like them. We have to evaluate whether they will be good tenants.

Vary any presentation according to the prospects' age, income status, occupation, life style or other factors. If a prospect appears to be wealthy, stress the amenities and not the cost saving aspects. To an older couple, you can stress the quiet atmosphere of the project.

If your building is professionally managed, describe the benefits of this situation to a prospect. They should be told that the management company's experience would ensure that the building is well managed. If the owner operates your building, tell the tenants about the benefits of this type of arrangement.

Know what units will be coming up for rent in the near future. If the current vacancy is not suitable, mention when other apartments will be available.

Ask who will be living in the apartment. The prospect looking at an apartment might not be the person who will be moving in. Don't assume they are married and say something like, "Does your wife like the view?"

If a rental market is poor and there are several vacancies, some type of concessions might be considered. Prospects could be offered:

1. A month's free rent after a year in the building.

2. No deposits to be paid.

3. Moving expenses to be paid by the building. Some larger buildings have purchased trucks for this purpose or they lease trucks.

4. Free television set for the prospect's use and the set becomes their property after a period of time.

5. Free furniture.

6. Free laundry and utilities.

7. Free babysitting.

8. Trading stamps at time of rental.

9. Free trip to Las Vegas, etc.

10. Free tickets to athletic events, plays, concerts.

Concessions that will not be used by others are best. Samples of this might be an early move-in date or lower deposit terms. Another type of concession is to give more for the same rental price, better carpeting, wallpaper instead of paint, mirrored walls, etc.

PROSPECTS WORRY

Some prospects are worried about rent raises, and they want a lease to be protected. If your building has a no lease policy and your building does not intend to raise rents for a certain period, the prospect could be given a written agreement that the rent would not be raised for a period of time. This agreement was previously mentioned, but it can be a good closing device.

Other agreements could discuss the death of a family member or a job transfer. If there is a lease required, these agreements could be important to some tenants. If a calamity occurs, they want to be free to change their residence.

WHY DO THEY RENT?

Managers need to understand the different reasons why prospects rent a particular apartment. Some prospects are price shoppers. Price is their "hot button." Appealing to other motivations would be worthless. Other shoppers want prestige. There is a little of the "snob" in a portion of the population. The phrase, "Nothing tells more about a person than where they live" is true to them. Leisure time is important to others. Recreational facilities are stressed to these prospects. Some prospects want companionship, and others want privacy. Singles apartments with involved programs for meeting people are popular in today's market. However, most people want to know that they can come back to their "space" and not have anyone hassle them.

FEARS AND APPROVAL

Prospects fear "red tape" and the "unknown." Radically different apartments and strange rental terms surprise them, and they will balk at them. People do not want to appear stupid so they will avoid anything that they don't understand. Keep everything simple. There is an old adage about presentation speeches, showings and closes that is called KISS. This stands for "Keep It Simple, Stupid."

Prospects want the approval of their friends and relatives. In today's lifestyles, certain prospects do not seem to fit this category. It may seem difficult to stress the benefits of an outstanding apartment to the young people who want to live in poverty type conditions. However, these people still want compliments from their friends. They are conforming to the standards of their peer group. In many ways, the younger set conform more than any other generation. There is conformity in hairstyle, clothes, language, automobiles, music and other phases of their life. Everyone wants a sense of worth. Their sense of worth is increased if they have an apartment that fits their self-image. A better apartment can lead to a better self-image.

Prospects want convenience and cleanliness. If these desires can be realized in your building, these facts should be stressed. Managers could discuss what other tenants have done with their apartments. Recommended decorating ideas might really impress a prospect and convince them that they can be happy here.

PROSPECTS VARY

Prospects come in all types and sizes. Some are friendly and others grouchy. Some are shy and others are verbal. Some are decisive and others are wishy-washy. Some are snobbish and others are humble. Some are positive and others are depressed. These people do not wear their labels. Prospects do not have signs around their necks announcing that they are shy, wishy-washy, humble, and that they want convenience with a low price. Managers must watch and listen. Don't form opinions too quickly and don't be afraid to change your opinion. The old clichés of "Don't judge a book by its cover" and "Prospects are innocent until proven guilty" are applicable.

Remember that some people are just not nice. If they are obnoxious, don't take it personally. They are probably obnoxious to everyone so why should you be an exception? Do your job to the best of your ability and forget those people. Be friendly with everyone, and it might surprise some prospects.

BENEFITS

When discussing the features of the building, translate them into benefits for the tenants. Instead of saying "There are two swimming pools", say "The children have one pool where they can be children and have fun while the adults have a nice, quiet, private place to swim." A tile entry hall means "less cleaning and the tile never looks shabby so your entry is impressive." Managers should sit down and write a list of all the features in the building and then next to each feature write some of the benefits to the future prospects. These benefits would jump to mind when trying to close a prospect.

Some prospects have had bad experiences with other buildings. Previous owners have withheld deposits and not completed maintenance requests. A sample of a Rental Warranty is given here. If owners are considerate, they should be able to use these warranties. A pre-rental letter like this could be reassuring to a doubting prospect.

RENTAL WARRANTY

If any persons move into our building and are reasonable tenants, we will do the following:

1. Try to insure that you have the privacy or companionship you desire.

2. Promptly complete any reasonable maintenance requests that arise.

3. Maintain the grounds, landscaping and general areas in a proper manner.

4. Listen to any pertinent recommendations, suggestions and ideas for improvement from you and other tenants.

5. Control inconsiderate tenants so that you are not disturbed by unnecessary noise or other problems.

6. Use discretion in selection of tenants so that undesirables do not move in.

7. Instruct our managers, employees and agents to be enthusiastic, empathetic, reliable, friendly, and show respect for our tenants who are our reason for existence.

8. Return any security deposit due to you within 21 days after you move out in accordance with our rental agreement.

Date:_____   Signed:_____

THEY LEAVE

When everything fails and they are leaving, thank them for coming. By this time have the prospect's phone number and address on the action card. Ask them any other questions needed to complete the action card. Courteously explain that you need this information for evaluation of the building's promotion campaign and rental structure. We know that you can't rent them all. You try to do it, but it can't be done. Some of the people coming to the door are real estate brokers looking around, other property owners and managers doing surveys, insurance inspectors, appraisers, flakes, etc. These people will never rent an apartment so you have not failed.

A last question could be, "It's obvious you don't want the apartment, so will you honestly tell me why I haven't been able to influence you to rent?" The prospect might tell the manager some facts about the building, the vacancy or the manager that would be helpful in future planning to improve the property.

BUSINESS CARDS AND FOLLOW-UP

Don't let prospects leave without receiving a business card and a brochure about the building. A double-sided business card is preferable. The apartment's name and address and the manager's name and phone number would be on one side and the other part of the fold-over card could list three or four of the most outstanding benefits of the building. Prospects will look at many buildings, and a card like this can bring back memories.

If possible, the manager should set a time when a follow-up call to the prospect can be made. Follow-up can be fruitful. Every good prospect should be called, and a letter written to them. In a strong rental market this is not necessary, but in a weak market, a follow-up call would show a prospect that the building is interested in them. It could mean another visit or rental. During this call an appointment should be established for a revisit, if possible.

If the party has rented another property, this information can be evaluated to find out why the person did not rent our apartment. Prospects seldom receive any follow-up action. If a manager does this, the property will immediately stand out as a more organized operation.

Keep a waiting list of prospects whenever an apartment is full. A waiting list can cut advertising costs, turnover down time and the workload for a manager. One phone call can do it all. Owners should check their apartments in strong rental markets to make sure waiting lists are used to help lower building turnover costs.

ONLY THE SURFACE

This short chapter is just an introduction to closing or selling. Managers and owners can do further research on this subject. Courses are offered and recorded speeches are available. No one will ever know everything about this topic, but it is important to keep trying to learn.

The entire renting process can be fun. Look at it as a challenge. Try to be the best renting manager around. Once in a while try the technique of positive affirmation and say, "I'm the best there is, and I will prove it." Good Luck.

Chapter 9
Screening the Applicants

The prospect has completed and signed your application. A deposit has been given. The prospect is told that the application will be used to check their references. If everything is satisfactory, and it is assumed that this will be true, then the prospects will be notified shortly that they have been approved to become a tenant.

NOW IS THE TIME

This is the time to make certain that a prospect will be a good tenant. In future chapters, the problems of low-rent payers will be discussed. A careful and thorough selection process will stop many of these problems before a prospect becomes a tenant.

A comprehensive application is needed. If prospects balk at filling out an application, a long look should be taken at them before giving them keys to any apartment. In an apartment rental situation, a bad tenant can cost a building a great deal of money. If an eviction case drags on into court, an owner can be out many months of rent and a bad tenant can cause considerable damage. In essence, you are lending a prospect the equivalent of $2,000.00 to $3,000.00 and before you do that, you had better check their past and present. Imagine how thoroughly a bank should check a stranger's references before lending them any money.

APPLICATION

Many apartment associations as well as other publishers have rental application forms. A prospect's income level can be useful in deciding whether they will be compatible in a building. Social security and driver's license numbers are helpful in checking out some aspects of their background. It is important to know who will be living in this apartment, their ages and relationship to the prospect and their occupations. We ask if they have any pets now or expect to get any.

FACTS TO KNOW

Other important facts we want to know concern income, unemployment, eviction, bankruptcy and current military status. Another section deals with their past three residences. Questions are directed at procuring employment information, including supervisors' names and reasons for leaving. Bank and personal references are requested, as is the name of a relative for emergency reasons.

There is a statement as to the veracity of the information, and there are blanks to be filled in about the exact unit desired with rental figures. All of this information can be evaluated when making a competent decision about a prospect's character and ability to meet rental obligations.

CHECKING THE FACTS

Once an application is in your hand, the question arises, "Who will check it?" It is possible to use a professional credit agency. Many areas have firms that specialize in this service. Costs can vary greatly. Some credit firms are not good. They run a name through a computer and if there are no derogatory comments, the person is approved.

You might like credit agencies, but in most cases I would have my manager verify the applicant's information. Later, if a tenant proves bad, we can go back and see. A manager or leasing agent checking credit should understand the importance of doing a thorough job. Mistakes here can be problems for them later.

Calls are made to the existing and the previous landlords. The comments of existing landlords must be taken with some trepidation. If a tenant is causing a present owner trouble, a good reference might be given to you to get rid of the unwanted tenant. If you feel that a proper answer hasn't been given, call back later as a person checking credit for the applicant who is asking for a loan to buy something.

Managers should take the name of the person to whom they spoke. Listen closely to what is said and closer to what is not said. A proper opening statement might be, "Hello, I'm Julie Schmidt, manager of XYZ Apartments. I'm calling to check on the tenancy of Joe Brown. Could you please tell me about him?" If there is a hesitation, ask some specific questions about their length of tenancy, payment record, living habits, etc. Ask if they would rent to them again? Do they have any bad habits? What are their good characteristics?

BE PROFESSIONAL

Many company personnel departments do not want to give out information about their workers. The best method to get results is to be professional in your approach. An opening statement might be, "I'm verifying the employment of Joe Brown, a welder who says that he has worked there for three years." Other questions will establish his approximate salary. Most companies will not give out figures on salary, but they will verify an approximate figure if you give the figure to them.

Banks, creditors and personal references are checked. Personal references are probably valueless because a person would not be listed unless a good reference will be given.

After the information on salaries, bank information, work history, monthly payments and references is collected, a decision can be made. Simple math can determine whether a person will have enough money to pay the monthly rent. Don't be like a new bride or groom and think that the person will change. If past history shows more cash out than cash in, they will be a bad risk.

A guideline is that a prospect should be making a salary about three times his rental cost, which will include his rent and utilities. This figure will probably be lower than three times in lower cost rentals as these renters use a higher percentage of their salary for rent. High monthly payments for furniture and cars could indicate a risk to you.

THE MANAGER AND SELECTION

An experienced manager's impression of the prospect can be helpful. Managers should volunteer opinions of different prospects. However, when you are doing your checking, keep a clear mind and make up a record of the information received without any editorial comment. Then, add your impressions to the data given to the person who will approve the application.

An owner should listen to these opinions and understand the motivation of the manager. Managers normally will over evaluate prospects. The managers want to fill the vacancy and stop having to show apartments. Their views could be more shortsighted than an owner who wants to stop deadbeats from getting into the project. Subconsciously, managers will normally rent to people like themselves.

Some other classes of prospects who would make excellent tenants might be downgraded because of a manager's prejudice. A prejudice could be based on age, occupation, religion, color, race, national origin, lifestyle, even length of hair, etc. The residents of a building are the prime assets of a building. Care must be taken to insure that these assets do not keep decreasing in value whenever vacancies are rented.

If a prospect is having trouble filling out an application, the manager or leasing agent should help. In fact, a manager can probably do them faster. Don't let them leave without giving you the necessary information. In certain areas, the application could be completed faster if the printed information was translated into a foreign language. Our building is not there to educate anyone to understand English. Our building wants to get complete information on our prospects.

BE CAREFUL OF

1. *The people who have to move at once.* It might be best to tell them that they will have to wait at least 24 hours until you can check their history. This is true even if they want to pay in cash. Once someone is in an apartment, it is difficult to get him or her out. If necessary, agree to pay for one night in a nearby motel, while references are checked. If they are there early in the day, perhaps a complete credit check could be done in one day.

2. *The self-employed prospect.* He or she may own a company, and their janitors are earning more money than they are. A company could be nonexistent. Business cards are easy to acquire, so don't be impressed with these self-

employed marvels. I believe in self-employment, but many self-employed have idiots for bosses.

3. **The prospect in from out of town.** Check them out. Phone calls after 5 p.m. cost very little to most spots in the United States. Make these calls. If a person really wants to rent, a call could be cost effective.

4. **The questioner** – "Can I put some items in the apartment as they are crowding my car?" Once a true deadbeat gets the keys, you are in trouble. Never give up the keys until a rental agreement is signed and all of the money is collected. I know of no circumstance for breaking that rule.

A manager's impression was mentioned as being important. Before making a final decision, the manager must see all of the future occupants. Look at them all before passing judgment on anyone. A prospect might say that it is difficult to get them all there, but it is vital to see them. Try to arrange some type of meeting. See all pets and any roommates before finalizing any agreement.

SPEED IS IMPORTANT

Don't hold apartments for a long period of time. If a prospect wants an apartment in a month, a good manager will get them to start the rent sooner. If there is a large vacancy factor in the area, an apartment can be held. It is important to know the rental market. **If** an application illustrates that a prospect is an outstanding renter (long time in each apartment, solid net worth and salary, been in the area many years, no children or pets, great recommendations), an apartment can be held longer. This person might be given a few days free rent to compensate for the loss of any rent on their other apartments. In a tight rental market, prospects are told that they will have to start their rent sooner than they wanted. This could mean paying rent for a time on two apartments, but if they really want the apartment, this is the premium that they must pay.

In many areas of the country, this is a common practice. In some cities, prospects pay large sums of money to get the keys to a subleased apartment. If you have a prize apartment, you should be strong in the negotiating of rental startup dates. In other high vacancy areas, owners will pay the last month of a new renter's lease from another building. Good tenants are sometimes hard to find.

The amount of deposits to be paid should be spelled out in the Rental Policy letter for the building. Deposits and fees vary with different factors. If the rental market becomes stronger and there are only a few vacancies in the area, make the deposits higher. This is a good form of selection. It is not foolproof, but larger deposits means less tenant skipping, and an owner has more money for repairs.

Also, if a person pays a larger deposit, chances are that they will be a more substantial tenant. At least they do have more available money at the time of renting. Deposits can vary according to how many occupants will be in the apartment. The more tenants, the harder use of the unit.

Our policy letter will list a maximum number of tenants for any unit. However, for each additional tenant up to the maximum number, fees and deposits can be increased. This is particularly true if children or pets are involved. In an exclusive building a $1,000.00 deposit requirement for a pet would not be out of line. A bad dog or cat can cause $1,000.00 of damage quickly. A deposit of this type will insure that a tenant brings in only well-trained pets.

The checking of applications should be done at once. This is fair to the prospects and if a person is turned down, your renting action can be restarted again. A sense of urgency should exist, and owners or supervisors must insist on speedy notification. If telephone numbers are outdated or wrong, have the prospects get you current information.

Be suspicious of anyone who places certain conditions on the calls, i.e., call at a specified time or ask for only one person. This could be a setup. If I am a deadbeat looking for an apartment, I could tell the manager to call a number between 3:00 p.m. and 6:00 p.m. The number could be a friend's home who would answer the phone as if it were a business or apartment house and give a glowing reference for me.

TURNDOWNS

Turndowns should be infrequent if the manager does a good job of screening at the site. If a person must be turned down, it is normally best to do this by mail. This stops arguments and long discussions. A simple form letter could be mailed saying, "We are sorry but your application has been turned down." No specifics need to be given, and giving none will work in most cases. If a person calls back and insists on knowing why, a simple answer should be given. There must be a reason for turning them down, and it should be explained.

If the tenant questions it further, send them a copy of your policy letter that shows why they were turned down. If there has been a mistake made, make more calls and get more information. Remember our rule – "A tenant is innocent until proven guilty." When applicants are approved, call them and cheerfully ask them to return to sign a rental agreement and to pay their money. Insist on their speedy compliance so that apartments are quickly occupied.

Chapter 10
Rental Agreements and Rules

The rental agreement is the most important document in apartment management. It spells out conditions about the tenancy. A proper rental agreement will help to illustrate to new tenants what you expect from them. In case of any later problems, the rental agreement is used to control the behavior of the tenants. Apartment house rules and other rules can be made a part of the rental agreement. If legal action is ever needed to enforce rent payments or to stop your tenants from violating any rules, an agreement will be helpful. Units can be rented by oral agreement. In most states, any lease for more than a year must be in writing.

In many areas, leases are not used. Still, rental agreements are strongly recommended when leases are not used. Apartment rules, swimming pool rules and a pet contract are included later in this chapter.

SOME POINTS TO CONSIDER FOR YOUR AGREEMENT

1. Parking spaces and storage spaces are listed to avoid any future problems.

2. A late charge is used to insure prompt payment of rent.

3. Tenants are told in writing to whom checks should be made payable and to whom checks should be given.

4. All of the money collected at the time of rental is listed. Deposits are to be returned within twenty-one days after move-out.

5. Who pays which utilities?

6. Who will be living in the apartment?

7. Legal terms about damages, abandonment, and condition of premises are given. The applicants agree that the apartment was in a good and clean condition when they moved in. They can't come back later and complain about move-in conditions.

8. The use of the premises is dictated by house rules, which will be given at the time of signing the application.

9. The owner's responsibility for loss and theft, defects and repairs, and right of entry and storage are given. Management reserves the right to inspect the apartments at least twice a year. This inspection can be valuable in spotting future maintenance problems. Tenants allow leaks and other problems develop and damage can become severe. If tenants know that the apartment will be checked periodically, they will take better care of the unit. The tenants know that the management is interested in keeping their apartments in good repair. Preventative maintenance can be scheduled better and preventative maintenance is less expensive than crisis maintenance.

10. Tenants are made aware that they should have insurance on their personal property. Many tenants think that the owner's insurance company will automatically reimburse any loss by them for any reason. If the loss is not due to owner's neglect, the tenant could lose a claim. For example, in a windstorm a window breaks, and a tenant's furniture is ruined. The owner could not anticipate this problem, and the break was not the owner's fault. The tenant needs insurance in this case.

11. It is advisable to put the tenant on notice that any change of employment information must be given at once to management. Tenants change jobs constantly, and it is important to know where they are presently employed.

12. If any personal property is rented, an inventory should be attached.

13. The possibility of future changes must be considered, and a space made available to list any additional agreements made.

RULES NEEDED

It would be great if tenants could be told one simple rule. "Live the Golden Rule," or to describe the rule differently, "Do unto others as you would have them do unto you."

However, a simple rule does not work. In my days as a Navy Supply Corps Officer, I became extremely familiar with the Navy Regulations. For supply problems alone, there were volumes upon volumes of regulations. Everything was done "by the book." To be a good officer, all you had to know was where to find the proper passage in some manual. Manuals were written for every probable situation. Thousands and thousands of pages were published.

In tenant management, an owner could write volumes of rules. Every possible situation could be anticipated. If any new problem arose, a regulation could be written, but it is not feasible to have too many regulations. Number one, the tenants would never take the time to read them. Secondly, a mass of rules would scare prospects away. Thirdly, tenants would never think of some violation until it was spelled out to them as a no-no. For example, to put up a sign in a young people's apartment complex that says, "Don't jump off the second floor patio into the pool" only invites them to do it.

A compromise must be struck between a large number of rules and no rules at all. When any rules or rule changes are discussed, management's position is there are rules so that the "good tenants" can enjoy their residency. The rules are present to help control the "bad tenants" and the rules are not meant to infringe on the privacy of the "good tenants." Profitable firms use discretion and common sense when enforcing rules so that the entire building profits. When a problem does arise, it is best to have a set of rules for reference. All of the rules and regulations should be reviewed constantly. Times change and rules must be changed.

Sample house rules are illustrated on the following pages. Swimming pool rules are covered. The best way to discuss living rules would be to evaluate the sample house rules.

NOISE

Noise can be a big problem in apartments. Many apartments were built with poor insulation. The buildings cannot be rebuilt. Musical instruments, stereos, televisions and radios must be controlled. Earphones are recommended to tenants who want to listen to loud music. The late or early use of dishwashers, disposals, and showers can disturb other residents.

Rules must outline the position of management on the use of the apartment for commercial or unlawful purposes. An owner does not want people coming into the apartment to buy, order, or pay for goods or services. Prostitution and drug distribution have to be eliminated.

The rules on pets, alterations, refuse, parking, signs and loitering are self-explanatory. Tenants will change any number of items in an apartment. Their choice of interior design, wallpaper, color, and workmanship can leave much to be desired. Locks are changed and management will not know this fact until an emergency occurs.

Waterbeds, pianos, organs and other heavy furniture can cause floor damage. In many cases it is reasonable to allow them, but management should be aware of the possible problems. Waterbed insurance can be secured by a tenant to pay for any damage to the property.

PARKING AND PLUMBING

Guest parking can be disturbing to your tenants. Control tenant's parking. Spaces can be assigned and no repair or washing of cars should be allowed.

Any plumbing stoppage caused by a tenant's improper action should be charged to the tenant. Have it fixed quickly yourself and then bill them. Plumbers find the strangest things in the pipes. The plumbers can write the cause of the problem on their bill, and a copy of the bill can be given to the tenant.

CHILDREN AND OTHER SITUATIONS

Rules must be established for the conduct of children. Rules are given to control problems that have occurred often in the past. The tenants should know the laundry room is run by an outside agency. Management should give tenants complete cooperation and assistance in settling problems with the laundry or vending machine companies. If the company does not do a satisfactory job, get rid of them.

A fee could be charged sometimes when tenants lose their keys. A manager could waive the payment the first time, but sometimes managers are acting as gatekeepers to tenants and their guests or offspring. Never let anyone into an apartment unless that person is known to be living there. It has happened that an ex-spouse, etc. has been let into an apartment and suddenly many valuable items are missing. A manager should be apprehensive regarding the use of master keys.

Swimming pool rules should be adapted to the situation at the building. Our sample rules cover most of the problems.

A pet contract is enclosed. This form can be completed in addition to the rental agreement. If a tenant wants a pet, they must accept the responsibility for control of the animal. A pet contract with a solid deposit will discourage the "casual" pet owners. This contract will help as a psychological tool to control the conduct of the owner in reference to their pet.

It is recommended that owners look at house rules from different buildings and then design rules suited to their own projects. One set of rules will not cover every type of building. The rules given in this chapter were established after years of operating buildings all over Southern California. Hundreds of house rules from other owners and management companies were researched so that a more comprehensive set of rules could be used. If your building exists with no written guidelines and you have problems, make up some rules and send them to all the tenants telling them that these rules are in effect after thirty days. If you are not having problems, be happy and don't worry about any rules until problems arise.

APARTMENT HOUSE RULES

Please be considerate of other people in all of your actions. If you have any questions, see the manager. Remember that we have these rules so that good tenants can enjoy their residency here. All of these rules could be summarized into "Do unto others as you would have them do unto you."

1. All activities of Tenants or those of guests or occupants are to be conducted in a quiet, dignified manner so as not to annoy or disturb other tenants or create a nuisance in any way. Boisterous activity or unnecessarily loud noises due to talking, playing of musical instruments, drums, amplified instruments, radios, stereo sets and televisions will not be permitted. Tenants are requested to be particularly careful about noise before the hour of 8:00 a.m. and after 10:00 p.m. in consideration of other tenants. This includes the early and late use of dishwashers, disposals, showers, etc.

2. Tenants agree not to use the premises for any commercial enterprise or for any purpose which is unlawful, against city ordinances, or which would injure the reputation of the building or its occupants in any way.

3. No animal, bird or pet of any kind may be kept on or about the premises without the written permission of Management or his agent.

4. No change of locks, installation of aerials, lighting fixtures or other equipment, use of nails, screws or fastening devices on walls, ceiling or woodwork, or

alteration or redecoration of the premises is to be made without prior written authorization of Management or their Agent.

5. Tenants shall keep the premises and its equipment and contents in a reasonably clean and neat condition at all times. All refuse and garbage shall be deposited by Tenants in the proper receptacles as provided, and Tenants shall cooperate in keeping the refuse area neat. Tenants shall be responsible for disposing of articles of such size or nature as is not acceptable by the rubbish hauler for the building.

6. Automobiles, motorcycles or other mechanical equipment may be parked only in such space as may be assigned and are not to be washed or disassembled on or near the general premises.

7. No signs, laundry or articles of any kind are to be hung or displayed on the exterior of the premises except for laundry in an authorized drying area.

8. Lounging or unnecessary loitering in the halls or on the front steps or public balconies in such a way as to interfere with the convenience of other tenants is prohibited.

9. No piano, organ, water furniture or item of unusual weight or dimension will be allowed on the premises without prior consent of Management.

10. No portion of said premises shall be sublet or this agreement assigned.

11. Personal items such as brooms, mops, bicycles, towels, tools, etc. must be stored inside the units.

12. Guests are not to park on the property. No boats, vans, trailers, trucks, etc. are to be parked without prior written permission from Management. Abandoned cars, cars leaking oil, or inoperable cars are to be removed from premises.

13. Management will correct any plumbing stoppage caused by Tenants at Tenant's expense.

14. Barbecuing, outside cooking, and picnicking are to be done only in approved areas.

15. Roller skates, bikes, miniature autos, skateboards, etc. are not to be used within the apartment grounds.

16. Tenants are responsible for the conduct of their guests.

17. Children under twelve years of age are to be supervised by a responsible adult.

18. Managers should be notified if you are going to be absent from the building for a considerable period of time.

19. Tenants are cautioned to lock their apartment each time they leave.

20. Tenants are not to store gasoline or other combustible materials on the premises.

21. Management should be notified at once of any building defects, breakage or maintenance problems.

22. In the event Management sets apart in the building a laundry room for the convenience of Tenants, Tenants may at their own risk and without cost, use for the purposes of laundry reasonable space therein, if such is available; that such laundry and ingress and egress thereto and there from is for the use and convenience of the respective tenants and is not operated or controlled by Management.

23. Tenants are prohibited as such from in any way moving, or handling articles in or for such laundry room, and that if any such employee does, at the request of Tenants, take part in moving, handling, opening or removing anything in or for or from such laundry room, he or she in so doing shall be the agent of the Tenant and not of Management.

24. Tenants assumes all risk of loss or damage to articles or things while in or while in transit to or from such laundry or storage room. Any loss to Tenants from use of the laundry room must be settled between Tenants and the laundry equipment rental company.

25. The Management shall not be liable or responsible for any loss, injury or damage from any cause whatever to the Tenants, any member of the Tenant's family, any guest or visitor of the Tenant or to any other person or to any property at any time within said rented apartment, or the halls, stairways, elevators or any other portion of the apartment building and adjacent property and the garage.

26. Employees of Management are prohibited as such from receiving any packages or other articles delivered to the building for Tenants or persons residing with Tenants, and that should any such employee receive any such packages or articles, he or she in so doing shall be the agent of Tenants and not of Management.

27. Management will admit Tenants who have been locked out of their unit, but the following charge can be made:

   8:00 a.m. to 6:00 p.m. $5.00
   Other Hours $10.00

28. Soliciting is not permitted without written Management approval. Tenants are requested to notify Management if solicitors bother them.

We have received a copy of these rules.

Dated _____ Signed _____   Apt # _____

                      Signed _____   Apt # _____

SWIMMING POOL RULES

The following rules and regulations are for the protection and benefit of all to assure safe and sanitary operation of the pool facilities. Your cooperation in abiding by these conditions will be appreciated by all concerned. Parents are requested to caution their children to observe all rules and regulations and obey instructions of all employees. Failure to comply with these rules shall be considered sufficient cause for any action deemed necessary by Management, including the barring of violators from the use of the pool area.

1. All persons using the pool or pool area do so at their own risk and sole responsibility. Management does not assume responsibility for any accident or injury in connection with such use.

2. Management will not be responsible for loss or damage to any personal property of any kind.

3. The use of the pools and pool area is a privilege not a right.

4. The pool may be closed at any time for cleaning or due to either breakdown or other operational difficulties.

5. Children under 14 years of age must be accompanied by an adult for admission to the pool area. Thereafter, the adult must exercise supervision over the child for safety and compliance with these rules and regulations.

6. Running, pushing, wrestling, use of profanity, ball playing or causing undue disturbance in or about the pool area is very dangerous and will not be tolerated. The game of "Marco Polo" is forbidden.

7. The pools and facilities are for the use and enjoyment of the residents. Guests are not allowed unless residents obtain prior written permission.

8. No pets are allowed within the pool area.

9. No wheeled vehicles are allowed in the pool area.

10. The pool water is chlorinated for your health and will bleach or rot the carpet in your living quarters unless you dry thoroughly before returning to the building. Slippers are required for this purpose.

11. Hairpins or bobby pins shall be removed from hair before use of the pool and there shall be no throwing of debris or other extraneous material.

12. All pool equipment must be returned to its proper place after each use Apartment furniture shall not be moved into the pool area.

13. The hours during which the pool may be used are from 10:00 a.m. to 9:00 p.m. Sunday through Thursday and 10:00 a.m. to 11:00 p.m. Friday and Saturday. Please do not violate these rules. Other tenants may wish to sleep, and we must respect their privacy.

14. No toys, inner-tubes, floats, balls or any other objects whatsoever will be allowed in the pool at any time.

15. No food is to be eaten around pool. No alcoholic beverages are to be drunk. Any beverage should be in plastic containers, not glass.

16. Pool gauges, temperature controls and water levels are not to be changed by Tenants.

17. No radios, record players and other musical instruments may be used in or around the pool area unless earphones are used.

18. Tenants and their guests are required to be properly attired at all times, going to and from and in or around the pool area.

19. Tenants and guests will please place their own towels over pool furniture when using suntan oil or other lotions.

20. Management reserves the right to close the pool in the off-season, or to stop heating the pool in bad weather. Management also reserves the right to change these swimming pool rules at any time.

21. The management reserves the right to close the pool area or to exclude any person from the pool area at any time.

Dated _____

Signed _____   Apt # _____

Signed _____   Apt # _____

PET CONTRACT

It is hereby agreed between Management and Tenants that Tenants will be able to keep a pet named _____ and described as
_____
in Apt. # _____ Address _____.

The rent of this apartment is $_____, and an additional pet deposit of $_____ must be paid before the pet will be admitted to the premises. This security deposit will be repaid to the Tenant when the pet is removed from the apartment and there is no damage or unreasonable wear and tear to the apartment. Any damage or wear and tear will be subtracted from the deposit. If the deposit amount is insufficient to cover the costs, Tenants will pay the difference immediately.

The tenant agrees that the pet will be controlled both within the apartment and on the apartment grounds.

1. Dogs will not be allowed outside an apartment without a leash.

2. Animals will not be allowed to drop waste on apartment grounds. Any "accident" will be picked up at once by Tenants.

3. Animals must be walked away from the building, and no animal waste will be left on sidewalk, building landscaping or other such area.

4. Pets will not be left unattended for unreasonable lengths of time. Excessive barking or other noise will not be permitted.

5. Any damage done by a pet must be paid by the Tenants immediately.

6. The pet owner agrees to indemnify and hold Management harmless from any and all claims made against them by reason of this admittance.

7. This pet contract may be revoked at any time by Management.

Date:_____   Date:_____

Signed:_____   Signed:_____
         Management   Tenant

Chapter 11
Simplified Accounting Systems

Few people become apartment house owners or property managers immediately upon the completion of their formal education. Most of them are active in some other profession before they start gathering experience in real estate management. Apartment owners represent a broad spectrum of professions and have varied interests in different aspects of management.

My college education centered on management, psychology, and accounting courses. My work experience before entering the field of property management involved comptroller functions, data processing, budgeting, systems analysis, and other accounting related areas. Therefore, accounting systems for management purposes is one of my major interests. I believe my company did the accounting functions for millions of dollars of property accurately and at a low cost. Money can be expended foolishly trying to prepare elaborate reports. The accounting functions for over 100 projects with over 3,700 units were done by one full-time person, a part-time person and a small service charge to a computer firm. Quicken software works great.

Accounting systems must satisfy several governmental agencies as well as property managers and owners. The procedure established must keep this fact in mind. Many owners talk glowingly about the "books" for their property. The value of any information secured must be compared to the cost expended to get that information. Complex reports that are never reviewed are worthless at any price.

Federal tax returns do not require a minute breakdown of expenses. If you review a federal income tax return, you will discover that the number of necessary expense categories is small. The government wants a simple tax return from you.

Simple principles should be outlined before discussing ideas for apartment house accounting.

1. Only necessary and valuable reports are prepared.

2. Bookkeeping work is done at the lowest employment level.

3. Files are to be maintained at the business site if possible.

4. Duplication of bookkeeping effort is not profitable.

5. Reports are prepared quickly so their information is timely.

6. Files are established so that future questions can be answered without a time-consuming search.

7. Proper cash control procedures must be present to insure that no "real" money is lost.

BE SIMPLE

It is not necessary to use complex double accounting methods on most apartment houses. Simple income and expense accounting reports are sufficient. Most taxpayers are cash basis taxpayers, so elaborate accrual accounts and impressive balance sheets are not needed. Data processing terminals at a small building might be ego-inflating to owners, but it is not intelligent to use data processing equipment as typewriters. The problems of accounting or bookkeeping are different for different size buildings. A 6-unit apartment owner does not need the same procedures as an owner of 600 units in ten locations.

The accounting function begins when rent is paid to a manager or owner. It is recommended that the rent be paid to a manager at the building, if possible. If a building has no one available, rents can be mailed to the owner. It is time consuming to keep going to a building to collect rent. Tenants are not always at home, and an owner's time has to be considered expensive. Friction can develop between the owners and the tenants through no apparent fault on either side. Tenants are not chained to their apartment.

An owner who stops by when there is no one home has to become peeved after a while. Give the tenants some stamped and addressed envelopes for their convenience. Having tenants mail in their money when there is a manager present creates work for an office. Tenants always use mail delay as their excuse for non-payment. Their checks have not been mailed, but they claim they did. Also, follow-up on late payers takes time and is costly to do from a central office.

MONTHLY BILL?

Another question to be answered is, "Should monthly bills be mailed for the rent?" This is an unnecessary expense. Every tenant knows when their rent is due. Many lenders, savings companies and other firms that require monthly payments are not sending monthly statements. Service companies who have set fees (pest control, elevator maintenance, equipment rental, rubbish collectors) could save money by sending out twelve monthly statements all at one time early in the year. If a firm has the need for many stamped return envelopes each month, they should investigate the feasibility of getting a post office permit. Then, the number of the permit could be printed on the envelopes, and the firm would be charged only for the return envelopes mailed. This procedure saves the office the time it takes to stamp the envelopes and saves the cost of stamped envelopes that are never used.

NO CASH

Many owners are insisting that the rent payments be made in check or money order. Cash is not desirable. Larger buildings might consider accepting payments by the use of credit cards such as Master Card, VISA, etc. Some people might not have the ready money, but they have their trusty little pieces of plastic. There is a cost for accepting credit cards, and this cost could outweigh the advantages. This is a decision only an owner or property manager can make.

Why not accept cash? With cash there will be no problems of checks bouncing or checks being stopped. However, there has been an unbelievable increase in the number of robberies. Apartment houses in many areas are being robbed. To me, it makes more sense from a criminal's standpoint to rob an apartment house rather than a liquor store, bank or gas station. At certain times of the month, apartment houses will have large amounts of cash around. A crook going into a liquor store, bank or gas station can get shot, killed or chased. These types of establishments have constant traffic in and out. Sometimes, the people working there are young and will grab a tire iron and start swinging. If you rob a bank, you will be filmed, there will be a substantial reward offered, and the FBI will come into the case. On the other hand, there could be money at an apartment house. In all probability, the manager will have no gun, there will be no guards, no video cameras working, no big rewards will be announced, and the FBI will not be called. Some managers would die of fright.

A period of time ago, I was eating lunch near the cashier in a nice restaurant. My back was to the cash register. Suddenly, the cashier began screaming hysterically. A man had come in, been seated, and then walked up to the front door. After seeing nothing irregular, he walked to the cashier, showed her a gun and demanded money. He grabbed the cash and took off running. About a minute later, she started screaming. The man had disappeared up the street.

This girl had been held up a few months previously. She quit right on the spot, as she was a nervous wreck. This happened in a good coffee shop in an outstanding upper middle class area. It could happen to your building. A manager who has been selected well, trained by you at some cost, and is outstanding could quit too. No one likes a gun being pointed at them. A manager could panic or annoy some crazy person and get shot.

DISCOURAGE ROBBERIES

If you post a sign "All Rent Payments Are Made by Check," robberies might be discouraged. Gas companies are using this procedure in some of their service stations, particularly during evening hours. Taxicabs are following this pattern. It is a sad commentary on the condition of today's society, but this problem is a fact of life. Another advantage of this policy is that it makes it difficult for resident managers to embezzle funds. It does not make it impossible, but having no cash around makes it less likely.

If a manager does accept cash, certain safeguards should be observed. Tenants are not to see where the cash is stored. Cash is put away after a tenant leaves. If any tenant appears suspicious, a manager can tell them to come back in a few minutes if cash has to be changed. Don't let anyone know in which room the cash is stored. For larger amounts, a small floor safe in the bedroom would be suitable. A manager should not hide money in a refrigerator. That is the first place a thief will look. Don't leave cash unguarded. One manager said that she walked out for a minute while she was in the process of making a bank deposit, and $1,900 disappeared. Of course it was never found.

BANK DEPOSITS

Bank deposits are made regularly. Cash should not accumulate. It is best, in my opinion, to let managers make their own bank deposits. It is consistent with the principle of having bookkeeping functions done at the lowest level. This procedure saves owners or property management personnel large amounts of time. Early in my management career, deposits were made by the main office. This meant that the cash and checks had to be collected or trusted to the mails. A counting and verification of the collection had to be made at the building to make sure that the managers' figures were correct. Then, a bank deposit had to be made and be delivered to the bank.

In hectic times, funds could collect at the buildings or at the office. This made robbery or loss a possible happening. One day, on a Good Friday holiday, I went to take a large deposit including thousands of dollars in cash to the bank. The bank was closed between 12:00 and 3:00 o'clock. I drove around working for the rest of the day. When I got back to the bank, I could not find the deposit. It had slipped between the seat cushions. I thought that I had lost that deposit which included much more cash than I could afford to lose. The next day, I started having the managers make bank deposits. It has worked well for many years, saving everyone large amounts of time.

Managers like this procedure as they can quickly make their own deposits and get rid of the checks and cash. Checks from the tenants will be deposited faster and this lowers the number of bounced checks or stopped payment checks. Rent discrepancies can be cleared up quickly. The managers either put the money in the bank or they didn't. In one embezzling case, a judge ruled in a manager's favor because our supervisor had not been completely thorough in giving a comprehensive receipt to the manager for the rents collected. This question could not have been raised if the manager had been making his own bank deposits.

This procedure can be done in California by making intra-branch deposits. For example, if the buildings account is in a Bank of America branch, the manager can make the deposit at any Bank of America branch. Night deposits can be arranged. If the account cannot be maintained so that the manager can make deposits into the building's account, an account can be opened in a nearby branch of any bank for the manager. The funds can be transferred to the correct management account by check by the owner or the management office.

Make it easy for the tenants. Most of them do not need a receipt, as their personal check will be their receipt. Therefore, have a spot where they can drop off the check. A slot in the manager's door can be used in most cases. If not, a strong lock box in a central location would be adequate.

ACCEPTING CHECKS

The manager should never accept third-party checks. Personal checks on out-of-state banks can be a problem, as they take so long to clear. A prospect can become a tenant and progress to deadbeat status before the first rent check clears. Payroll checks can be a nuisance if they prove uncollectible or are lost by a manager or owner. If a personal check is lost, a tenant can be told to stop payment and write another check.

It is a bad policy to cash checks for tenants. It can prove costly to allow a manager to give an owner checks for any cash collected. Manager's checks have been known to bounce and when the owner went to see them, they were no longer around.

When the manager receives a check, he or she checks to see if the tenant has made the check payable to the correct party. Then a bank endorsement stamp is used at once, so that the check is less likely to be stolen.

Checks returned by a bank must be handled quickly. For cash control purposes, these returned items must come to the owner or property manager. If the returned items went to a manager who made the deposit, false deposits could be made, and rents could be held out. If an owner was slow in making the monthly bank reconciliation, a crooked employee could embezzle for a few months. When a check is returned, the manager is called at once. The rental agreement spells out the late charge that can be collected. If an old reliable tenant has a one-time error, the charge could be waived. If it is a newer tenant, the charge must be enforced unless their bank was in error.

The manager must see the tenant at once. If no one is at home, a note stressing urgency is put on the door. The tenant has to repay the check with a cashier's check or money order. Don't re-deposit the returned check unless the tenant has a good reason. If not, they are told to pay by cashier's check or money order.

When the managers wanted to re-deposit a previously bad check, I always told them, "If the check proves to be uncollectible, you will be responsible for half of it from your next pay check." Managers normally didn't champion a tenant's request after that proposal.

A friend of mine told about how his small hometown bank handled bad checks. It was the only bank in the rural community, and the bank was located on the main street. If a bad check appeared, the bank cashier posted it to the front window where passersby could see it. People got in there fast to pay them off. In a small town, it worked wonders. In a large city, no one would care.

RENTAL DUE DATES

When should rents be due? This depends in part on the number of units in your building, the number of move-outs monthly, normal due dates in your area, management condition and other factors. If a tenant needs an apartment by the 22nd of the month, he pays rent from that date. The entire first month's rent and all deposits are to be paid before he moves in. If the building has a policy stating that all rents are due on the first of the month, then the rental amount due after one month must be adjusted. At that time, the new tenant should pay for the partial month to the first of the next month, and on the first he would pay an entire month of rent.

There are advantages to having all the rents due on the first. The collection and depositing of funds is easier. Follow-up on late payers is less trouble. If the rents come in during the month, it is more difficult to keep an eye on delinquent payers. The first of the month is easy for tenants to remember, and payments are normally more regular. If all of the buildings in your area have a first-of-the-month due date, transferring from another building to your building is easier.

Conversely, there are advantages to having the rents due throughout the month. If there is a certain amount of tenant turnover under the previous policy of first-of-the-month due dates, all of the monthly vacancies would have to be renovated at one time. This would put a burden on the managers, cleaners, painters, etc. Their work would be concentrated in a small period. If apartments were vacated during the month, the arrival of new tenants would be staggered. Apartments would be available at different times of the month for prospects that need them sooner than the first of next month. Sometimes when tenants rent an apartment to move in, for example, on the 22nd, they will try to negotiate for a free rental period from the 22nd to the 1st. If due dates are staggered, this request is not made as often.

If your rental due dates are staggered throughout the month, large sums of money will not accumulate at the first of the month. Anytime you have large sums of money, the problems of loss, theft and embezzling are more likely to appear.

A good policy might be to compromise between the alternatives. Have rents due on the 1st and the 15th; or the 1st, 10th and 20th. In this manner, you would have some of the advantages of both methods of due date designation.

CASH FOR BILLS

Don't let a manager use rent collections to pay any bills except in the most extreme emergencies. If a sewer pipe is clogged and the only available rotor service insists on cash and the manager is broke, and the owner can't be reached, there is no petty cash available but there is some rental cash on hand, then the manager should use rent money.

Another emergency might arise where a utility company is at a building ready to shut off service. These emergencies will probably never happen. If an emergency arises and there is no cash available, I would expect a manager to pay the bill by check, and I would reimburse them. This is common sense based on trust.

PETTY CASH FUND AND CHARGE ACCOUNTS

Another idea to save an owner time is to have a petty cash fund or a petty check fund at the building. The manager could be given an amount of cash or a bank account to pay for miscellaneous supplies or services, small charges, key deposit returns, etc.

The manager is responsible for this money. An envelope, which can be purchased at any bookstore, is helpful for control of the cash and storage of receipts after payment. At all times, the amount of money on hand plus the receipts on hand must equal the total of the fund. When the bills reach a certain level, the receipts are given to the owner or supervisor, and a check is written to the manager to reimburse the fund back to its original level.

It is costly for an owner to purchase all supplies and pay all the miscellaneous bills by check. A petty cash fund is extremely helpful. The manager's expenditures are always available for audit. If they are not handling the money wisely, advise them on how to improve. Let them do some shopping and bill paying. Many times, money can be saved by paying cash to small servicemen. Smaller, less expensive servicemen will not do a job without immediate payment. Conservative owners will not let a manager buy even a light bulb. An owner will use an hour of time and fifty miles of automobile usage to save $3.00 on a small part.

Charge accounts can be established with reputable suppliers. Managers should be allowed to pick up parts and supplies at these places. A top limit on expenditures must be set. If any larger items are needed, a higher authority could give telephone approval.

At a large building, a checking account could be opened for the manager's use. This account would be utilized to pay cleaning costs, smaller maintenance charges, key deposit refund, etc. A time saving procedure would be to put cleaning deposits in a separate account. The manager would use this account to pay carpet cleaners, drape cleaners and janitorial workers. If a tenant moves out and no work is necessary, a check could be given at once by the manager. If any problem arises on a claim by an ex-tenant, the information is readily available to the manager.

This money would be taken into income, and cleaning expenses would not be recorded as expenses unless cleaning expenses exceeded the deposits collected. There is not much money involved. The amount of the fund would be kept low. Any excess deposits would be kept in an interest bearing account. A good manager isn't tempted by this amount of accessible money. The action of the account would be reviewed monthly and a transfer of funds done, if needed.

INCOME RECEIPTS

Rental income for smaller buildings can be collected using a simple receipt book, which you can buy anywhere. This can be a three or four part form in numerical sequence. Many receipt books are now available that don't require carbon paper. This is simpler and is appreciated by a manager.

A receipt is to be written for all money received even if a tenant doesn't get one. This includes the money from vending machines, miscellaneous sources, deposits, insurance refunds, etc.

Complete information must be put on the receipt. A "thank-you" added might not help in tenant relations, but I don't see how it can hurt. If a check is received, the check number of the tenant is recorded on the receipt. A record is kept of the tenant's bank and bank account number.

If a partial payment is made, specify this exactly. Relate that this is a partial payment and show the rental period. If back rent is owed, apply any payment to the back rent first. Then, calculate the balance still owing and write that amount on the receipt.

It is not recommended that a manager fill out receipts in advance. If a tenant gets his hands on a receipt signed by a manager without paying, there would be a tough legal question. A filled out receipt left in a receipt book is as valuable as cash to a tenant. The advantages of having receipts immediately available could be overshadowed by the disadvantages of having signed receipts lost.

A file is maintained for each tenant. When a rent payment is received, information is recorded on this card. The date of payment and the check number of the tenant are important. This file does not have to be too fancy for a small building. It can be a sheet of paper with the tenant's name and rent listed, and a place to check off the rent each month as it is paid. One sheet of paper can last a year or more.

BANK DEPOSITS

The manager receives the payment, records it on the card, and puts the bank stamp on the back of any check. Periodically, a bank deposit is made. The bank deposit slip is made in triplicate. The copy stamped by the bank must be mailed at once to the owner or property manager. The second copy of the rental receipt has to be sent in with this deposit verification. If any receipts were voided, they are to be forwarded so the receipts are always in numerical sequence.

The bank deposit must equal the total of the rental receipts from the tenants. If these two items are not the same, any difference must be found immediately. The supervisory person will now know the size of the deposit and which tenants have paid. The manager keeps the third copy of each rental receipt in numerical order in his possession.

MONTHLY REPORTS

At the end of the month, the manager will send in a report showing the amounts received from each apartment. A columnar pad can be used for this. The manager can use a column for each month. The total of the monthly column has to equal the total of the deposits placed in the bank. With these two checkpoints (receipts and monthly report), plus a weekly call to each manager asking for amounts deposited, vacancies and delinquent tenants, duplicate records do not have to be kept by an owner.

SMALL BUILDINGS

For a small building, this is enough information. It is simple to calculate delinquency, vacancy and collection loss percentages. All of the governmental agencies (IRS, County Business Tax, State Income Tax, etc.) want to know how much you brought in. For audit purposes of your manager, you insist that:

1. All money has to be receipted.

2. Receipts are used in numerical order.

3. Voided receipts are sent into your office.

4. Bank deposits balance to the amount of the money collected.

MEDIUM SIZE

Medium size projects present different problems. Different procedures have to be considered. There are many types of "write it once" systems that are excellent for apartment house income collection. Nicknamed "pegboard systems", managers like these methods.

Receipts can be pre-printed in numerical order with the building's name on them. The receipt, cash receipts journal, and tenant rental cards are written at the same time. The three forms are lined up correctly on the pegs and the receipt is written. As this is done, the same notations will appear on the tenant's card and on two copies of the cash receipt journal.

Forms can be purchased that have the bank deposit slips attached to the cash journal so another process can be done at this time.

This description might be confusing to someone who has never seen a "pegboard" system. The pegs simply line up the individual receipts for the tenant, two forms that list the rent received and a card for each tenant so that all four items are written at once. As the tenant's receipt is written, a copy of the amount received goes on two copies of the receipt form, and the record of the payment is put on the tenant's card. A new tenant comes to pay, and his card is inserted in the proper spot on the pegs. The next receipt is used and his payment is listed below the previous payment on the cash receipts form, and his rent card is updated. The system is simple and accurate. Managers like it, and it is an inexpensive system.

The advantages of these procedures are apparent. Anytime you write something once, you eliminate the old "transposition of numbers" error. How many times have you found out that your checkbook balance is wrong because you wrote a check for one amount and put another amount on the check stub? In school you probably learned that in reconciling any account, a transposition error is divisible by nine, but that still doesn't find the error. Also, the tenant's payment is automatically recorded so that the tenant's record is more accurate and up to date. The two cash receipt journals that are prepared at the same moment are for the manager's record and the supervisor or owner's record. There are many companies making these forms. Call any local stationary or printing shop and they can demonstrate them.

The bank deposit slips and one copy of the cash receipt journal are mailed to the supervisor after the money is placed in the bank. Again, if a supervisor wants to audit tenant payments, the tenant cards are filed at the manager's office. No duplicate file need be kept unless a supervisor seldom goes to a building. Even then, a phone call can answer most questions.

MONTHLY REPORTS

At the end of the month the manager should make a report. Columnar pads can be used, as were used for the small building. There is another type of report that could be used.

Management by exception is a solid management philosophy. If everything is proceeding normally, there are no problems. As manager, we want to know about the exceptions. We have a building where there are 40 apartment units each priced $1,200.00 a month. We give a free apartment to a manager and a gardener.

We want $48,000.00 of income a month, less the manager and gardener's apartment, for a total of $45,600.00. If there were no move-outs or move-ins and the rent collected was $45,600.00, with no vacancies or delinquencies, we know all the transactions were routine rent payment. All we want to know are the exceptions and why the bank deposits weren't $45,600.00.

The cost of computers is dropping and software is becoming so user friendly that even small buildings would profit from electronic processing. A small computer using any "Quicken" software program would be adequate for most buildings. This would include recording of cash receipts and cash expenditures.

Reports would be simple for rent payments and expense accounting is very easy with the most basic programs. Computer printed checks and expense reports can be easily and quickly processed. Most accountants would be able to outline a process using a computer for management. Simple reports could include cash flow analysis, year-to-date reports, comparison to past years versus to budgeted figures, etc.

As an owner acquires more properties, specialty property management software should be evaluated. A good starting point would be to look at Yardi Systems for Property Management. This software has always received excellent reviews and Al Yardi, the owner, is a true professional.

Other ideas to consider would be electronic or on-line banking for check payments. Your bank could outline their options, and you could have them do most of your work.

FICTITIOUS NAME

When you have a building, it is preferable to have a fictitious name for the project. A checking account should be established for this name. A fictitious name will prevent people from calling you in the middle of the night after finding your name and phone number somewhere. When my company first started, it was called Duane Gomer Real Estate. Many tenants, suppliers, prospects, evictees, salesmen, servicemen, etc. would have to talk to me. After the firm grew, the management accounts were transferred to a company named Property Management Services. Then, when someone called, they would talk to a supervisor or some other party. We gave titles like Vice-President, Regional Director, etc. If a tenant called Duane Gomer Company, they would insist on talking to Duane Gomer, and it is hard for anyone else to satisfy them. If the name of the company is XYZ Properties, they would be happy talking to a Vice-President.

In certain cases, new owners could use a fictitious name even if they were going to be living on the property as resident managers. To the tenants they would be just managers, and this could relieve some problems. A tenant-owner argument can become more severe than a tenant-manager argument.

BANK ACCOUNTS

Should you have one account for each building or one account for all of your buildings? If you are one owner, it could save time to have all the deposits made into and checks written out of one account. You will have only one bank reconciliation at the end of the month. You will have to deal with only one bank. Since you own the projects, there would be no conflict of interest if one project was in a negative balance position and was "using" the other project's money to pay bills. This fact would be related on your accounting reports. If there were several accounts involved, money would have to be transferred around whenever one building was low in funds.

Many property management firms have one central trust fund for all their buildings. Advantages accrue to the firm under this procedure, but a close eye must be kept on buildings with low balances. It would be a major violation of the firm's fiduciary capacity if a building of one owner was in a negative cash situation. These are other owner's funds. I believe this problem so major that a property management firm has to evaluate their situation before combining all their buildings into one bank account. At one time, our firm's one bank account handled thousands of apartment units. This meant that a lot of money flowed through this account. With a normal balance of over $500,000.00, our account was a prime target for embezzlement or some other theft. The bank reconciliation with the many checks written and with over 100 managers making deposits all over Southern California was complex, to say the least. The monthly bank summary was like an advanced accounting review problem. Based on these experiences, I would now use one account for each owner.

PAYMENT SCHEDULES

In high vacancy periods, the amount due for mortgage payments may not be always available. The owners must have large enough balances to cover this contingency. A management person must know the late charge policies of different savings and loan associations. Ten days grace period is normal. However, some firms say that the payment must be in their head office on that date, others will allow payment in a branch office and others will consider a postmarked letter of that date sufficient.

The person reviewing expenses must be alert for any discounts that are available. Timely payments can save you money. An accounts payable clerk or an owner must know the discount policies of their suppliers. A new vendor should be questioned about a discount possibility for timely payments.

A definite payment schedule policy should be promulgated. If vendors are made aware that you pay bills on the 10th and 20th, they will know when they can expect a payment. If you pay on those dates, many problems will be eliminated. Suppliers and servicemen have been cheated out of trillions of dollars in the past. They will trust you more if they know when you pay.

A definite schedule will make your work more organized and there will be fewer headaches. A few owners will be all over a tenant who misses paying his "advance" rent by a few days, and these same owners complain when a vendor won't hurry over in an emergency when they are awaiting a past payment. This attitude doesn't make sense to me. The goodwill of vendors is an asset to an owner.

Your regular monthly bills (pest control, utilities, insurance, etc.) can be paid by a central office. However, variable charges for maintenance, repairs, carpet or drape installation, painting, cleaning, etc. need to be approved by the on-site manager. Having a manager approve a bill insures that they will be stricter in their review of a completed job. A manager will call and say that the painting job on the last two apartments was bad. The bill has been paid. It is difficult to get any correction from a paid supplier. There might be major disagreement on the extent of the discrepancy. Make it a policy that no bill is paid until the manager has approved the vendor's work order or the bill.

PURCHASE ORDERS

In a larger operation, the use of a purchase order system is recommended. Your suppliers are put on notice that your purchases will be authorized by a written purchase order. When the purchase is approved, a copy of the numbered purchase order is e-mailed to the firm. In the case of an emergency, a supplier could be told the number of the purchase order by phone and they could proceed on that basis. Before payment, the accounts payable person (clerk or owner) matches the purchase order, the manager-approved work order and the bill together before payment is approved.

ON-SITE MANAGER AND EXPENSES

Another question to be discussed is, "How much accounting report information should be given to on-site managers?" If managers are given an idea of the expenses on their building, they might help to keep costs lower. Some of my managers have been furnished copies of these reports when it was believed to be beneficial and competent managers would become critical of expenditures. Tenants would be told that painting of their apartment would have to be postponed for a few months, as painting costs had been high.

The managers look for ways to lower utility costs by adjusting times, lowering bulb wattage, checking water leaks, etc. An informed manager can do a better job than an uninformed manager. The managers should be cognizant of the comparison of expenses to budgeted figures and not to what the profit of the building is. The manager does not need to know everything about your business, but expense information could be helpful.

BUDGETING

Another valuable tool for an owner is a budget. When you buy a building, you estimate the future expenses. This is a budget. Later, after you have owned a building, you can predict expenses with a better measure of accuracy. Try preparing a budget. You don't have to wait for the first of the year. Do one for the remainder of this year or for the next twelve-month period.

In a budget for a building, all factors need to be analyzed. Inflation, price increases, maintenance needs, capital expenditure requirements, cost cutting programs and other contingencies have to be considered. Do a budget for a year and check it monthly to see how close you were. A well prepared budget can be helpful in making decisions on expenditures. Proper budgeting and comparison to expense reports can be of assistance in scheduling repairs, maintenance and capital expenditures.

Chapter 12
The Slow Rent Payer

There are a few tenants who do not pay rent. It could be a problem of a lack of money or it could be a problem of a lack of motivation. As management, you do not always know the exact situation.

One of the most important steps in eliminating your collection problems is to have a good selection process. Many of the slow or non-payers can be turned down at the time you review their application.

Government rules, laws and regulations have removed some of the power of management to decide who will live in the building. Many forms of discrimination are illegal and immoral. However, unless some government agency has passed some new law, of which I have no knowledge, you can still refuse to rent to someone if they have a bad credit rating. You must investigate the prospects thoroughly and in the same manner; but if your research shows that the prospects have a record of poor credit, you can refuse to rent to them.

It would be nice if we could eliminate the professional deadbeats by taking their belongings out of the apartment and placing them on the sidewalk. There are times that I thought "flogging" would be a good idea. However, as you are well aware, courts and judges look upon management with a probing eye and our conduct must be in accordance with the existing civil laws.

After many years of apartment management, I do believe that I could become an outstanding "deadbeat" tenant. There are so many stalling techniques available.

A SAMPLE PRO DEADBEAT

When I go to find an apartment, my appearance would be beyond reproach (suit, tie, shined shoes, neatly groomed and driving a fine new car). If comprehensive questions were asked on an application, I would keep looking. I would try to find an apartment that required no written application and no written rental agreement.

I would try to find a smaller building that had no professional managers. I would want to deal with the inexperienced or newer owner if possible. An apartment on a ground floor with a front and back door, so that I could come and go without being seen, would be great.

My first rent check would be on an out-of-state bank. However, my cover story and appearance should allay any owner fears. I would not insist on moving in that day so that the owner's suspicions would not be aroused.

An out-of-state check takes time to clear. When the check was returned as unpaid, I would pay one-half of a month's rent at once in cash. I would promise to have the rest as soon as possible. Then, I would avoid management.

THE NOTICE COMES

After a three-day notice is posted on my door, I would write a letter to the owner explaining when I would pay (giving some of the best excuses available, i.e. my check has been withheld, my boss went bankrupt, my mother died and I have to go out of town, sickness, injury, theft, anything!). This would slow an owner down a few days.

Finally, when my excuses run out, they will start an unlawful detainer action. This requires the help of an attorney in most cases. Many owners delay at this time. First, they will give me a three-day notice and even if they can't find me, they can post this notice on my door and mail me a copy. I will completely ignore this notice.

Any unlawful detainer complaint and summons has to be served on me personally. I would be unbelievably hard to find. I would park my car blocks away, and I wouldn't leave my apartment until I was sure that there was nobody waiting with the summons.

Eventually, they would try service by publication and this takes money and time. I would be alert to this step and when necessary, I would file an answer to the complaint. My answer will be simple, and I would categorically deny all of the allegations. I can get a form from any good stationary store to do this. A company named Nolo Press in Oakland provides great tenant information. Study their techniques.

A TRIAL

The owner's attorney will now have to request a trial date. Unlawful detainer actions are given priority so a trial can be set within two to three weeks in most courts. However, I would request a continuance no matter when the date was set. I would claim that I would be out of town on that date or that I have to go to the hospital.

At any step along the way, if an error were made in any form, statement of fact, service of documents, etc., I would request the court to dismiss the action. Someday, I would be brought into court, but it could be an extended period of time from the date of my move-in.

MY DEFENSE

In court, I would produce some copies of letters showing that I had requested some maintenance work to be done by the owner. The letters had never been mailed, but I show the copies. Because the repairs had never been made (how could they, the owners never knew about them), I would state that my rent had been withheld because the apartment was not habitable. I would cite the Green decision in California, Green versus Superior Court, 111 Cal R ptr 704, 517P 2d 1168, Jan 1974. This decision held that a tenant could withhold rent if an apartment was uninhabitable.

The decision goes on to state that the extent of the uninhabitability must be more than minor, but Legal Aid attorneys, deadbeat tenants, and some rightful tenants have cited this decision in answering unlawful detainer complaints. I would question any facts presented and would strive for the appearance of a nice man being persecuted by the "greedy owner." I would be gentle and not obnoxious.

APPEAL

If the court ruled against me, I would try to appeal the case on any possible grounds. I would go to a Legal Aid office and see if one of their attorneys could find some other avenue of attack. Even when the marshal came with an eviction order, I would stall for as much time as possible. This whole procedure would take many months. It could be made even more confusing if I rented an apartment and let a friend take it over and I moved into an apartment that he had rented. Then, there is always a bankruptcy threat.

In the "good old days" the rent payment was always made first. Now the theory for many renters is to pay when you have to. I have run into some strange cases of nonpayment of rent. People can give you a sob story and look you straight in the eye and lie. I have been given payroll checks that bounced, governmental checks that had fraudulent endorsements, and promises, promises, promises.

One time I made a stop and knocked on the door. A little girl answered, and I asked for the child's mother since I knew the father had disappeared. The little girl said, "My Mommy isn't here." I said, "When will she be home?" The little girl yelled back into the apartment, "Mommy, when will you be home?"

PROBLEMS OF NO COLLECTIONS

Several problems arise when someone doesn't pay his rent:

1. Other tenants hear about it, and they decide not to pay.

2. Your bills can't be paid and discounts are missed.

3. You are doing the tenants a disservice by allowing them to get deeper in debt. A good rule to remember is, "If a tenant can't pay one month's rent, they sure aren't going to be able to pay two months' rent." Soon, the tenants will owe you so much that you have made it profitable for them to pack up, rent a trailer, and

move on to another place. Some tenants have no assets so moving is no problem.

4. You are hurting your good tenants. If you have bad collection ratios, the rents of other tenants will have to be raised.

5. You are not doing your job satisfactorily. If you are a manager or property manager, you are not being fair to the owner. If you are an owner, you are not being fair to your family. Your family might have a good use for $2,000.00 of rent money that some tenant forgot to pay.

Tenants must be taught early that rents are due when they are due. A manager should have written guidelines to follow when considering late payers. Their guidelines can be flexible. If tenants have been long-time, good-paying persons and they are late one month, more empathy should be extended than for the new tenant who is late on the first payment due after move in. Apartments with fast turnover, like furnished singles, have to be evaluated differently than family units where each tenant has a lot of furniture.

A sample guideline for rental collection is given here. Remember, this is a sample guideline for an average apartment under average conditions in an average neighborhood with average tenants.

Remember, rents are due in advance. Legal notices could be given to all tenants who have not paid by 12:01 a.m. on the first of the month.

SCHEDULE

1st Day – All rents due.

3rd Day – A note is given to the tenant in their mailbox or under their door that their rent is due and payable. If there is any problem, they are to see the manager. Remember that you are not supposed to put notes, etc. into mailboxes. Also, posting a late-pay note on the tenant's door might antagonize them.

4th Day – The manager goes in person to see the tenant. If no rent is received, the following form should be completed. A tenant will make any promise to get rid of the manager. When the manager comes back later, the tenants say that they do not remember the promise made. If they said that they would pay the rent, they might pay only a portion.

This form puts their promise into writing. If tenants will not sign such a statement and will not tell you where they are now working, eviction action can be started right away. They are obviously not being fair to you.

TO: Owner of _____

My rent for apartment _ at the above address is not current. At this time, I owe

_____ to pay my rent up to _____.

I agree to pay in the following manner:

Date _____   Amount ____

Date _____   Amount ____

Date _____   Amount ____

My present phone number is _____.

I am now working at _____,

Phone _____, and my spouse is working at _____

_____, phone _____.

Date _____   Signed _____

BE SURE TO NAME ALL PERSONS WHO ARE IN POSSESSION OF ANY RENTAL ON ALL NOTICES, EVEN IF THEY ARE SELDOM THERE.

5th Day – If it has been impossible to see them or to get a written promise to pay, a higher authority could call them. A personal letter from the owner or a letter on your attorney's letterhead might start some action.

6th Day – A three-day notice to quit or pay rent should be served on the tenant. You could leave some blank three-day notices with your managers, and they could fill them out. This gets the job done faster. If you have had trouble in the past with a tenant, you could serve the three-day notice on the first of the month or any day thereafter. Don't wait until the sixth day for people with a history of slow paying.

A question can be asked, "Is it better to have a Marshal serve the notice or to have your manager serve it?" If the tenant is not hard to find, a uniformed man with a gun serving the paper would appear more official. However, true deadbeats are not impressed with anything like that. Also, a Marshal will come at odd hours, and if the tenant is not around or the tenant will not answer the door, the Marshal can't serve the notice. A manager on the premises could watch for the culprit and be ready to serve them at anytime.

METHODS OF SERVICE

There are three methods of serving the notice:

1. In person to each of the people named in the notice. It is best if you can serve a husband and wife or two parties to the agreement. You could end up evicting the husband, and the wife won't go.

2. Leave copies with a responsible person (over the age of 14) at the premises and mail copies to each of the parties.

3. Post copies on the door of the unit and mail copies.

Any adult, including an owner, can serve the three-day notice. One manager once called in a panic. He had tried to give a notice to a tenant and the tenant wouldn't take it. I told the manager to say to the tenant that it was a legal notice for her and to just leave it there. The manager saw the tenant again in the laundry room. He made his announcement and put the notice on a table nearby. The tenant left the notice there, but she had been served. If you state what the notice is, attempt to give it to them, and leave it on a table, the steps, the ground or whatever, you have indeed served them in the eyes of most courts.

9th Day – It is best to secure legal assistance at this point unless you want to struggle along by yourself. An attorney should be found who specializes in unlawful detainer. You should ask him/her up front what the attorney's fees and costs might be. An attorney could quote you costs and fees based upon the following situations that could happen:

1. Complaint is filed and tenant vacates.

2. Complaint is filed; no answer by tenant and attorney secures for you a default judgment.

3. Complaint is answered by tenant and a trial is held.

SETTLEMENT

Sometimes, we have used another procedure at this time to get the tenant to move or to negotiate a settlement. We give the information on the problem to the attorney. The attorney then sends a form letter to the tenant. It states that he/she will file an action within forty-eight hours unless satisfaction is gained. A tenant might move out upon receipt of such a letter or might call the attorney and make a reasonable offer to settle the claim. This saves court costs and fees.

Our main purpose is to get possession of the apartment as soon as possible. Then, we can make a claim for the rent. Most non-payers don't have any money, and any judgment secured is worthless.

As I am not an attorney, I cannot advise you on any legal matters. I again recommend that you find a good attorney. However, if you want to file your own actions, it is not impossible. I have done hundreds of them myself. Court clerks and judges are helpful to people doing their own legal work. A good suggestion might be to use an attorney for your first unlawful detainer action. You then would have the copies of your attorney's form to assist you.

FORMS NEEDED

Complaint – A document giving all the facts about the problem requesting the money owed you and the peaceful possession of the unit.

Summons – A form listing the names of the parties and the basic information of the action taken. It gives the tenant five days to answer the summons. A copy is given to the tenant with the complaint and the original is returned to the court, giving the information about when, where and by whom the defendant was served.

These two documents start the process. They must be filed with the county clerk. You, the plaintiff, cannot serve these papers. Have either a Marshal, process server, friend or your manager serve the papers.

If the defendant answers the complaint by filing an answer to the complaint with the court, you must go to the clerk and get the proper forms to request a trial date. You must give the information about the trial date to the defendant.

JUDGMENT DAY

If you go to trial and win, you will get a judgment giving you the right to the possession of the unit and the amount of money due you. This document must be taken to the clerk to receive a writ of execution. The writ of execution is taken to the Marshal's office to have the person evicted. The Marshal will normally go to the house to serve or post this writ. They will give the tenant five days or more to vacate. If they come back and the tenant is still there, the Marshal will escort the people out and allow you to lock up the apartment.

If there is any furniture or personal property in the apartment, you must store it in accordance with local laws, and then you can advertise it for sale. In the instances where complete units of furniture were left (tenants had no funds to move, tenants disappeared, tenants tried to stall the Marshal for more time), we just locked the furniture up for a month in the unit and then advertised it for sale. When you get to this step, reread the current law closely. You must advertise correctly and follow the law to the letter. Normally, the furniture is worthless or a lender has a lien on it.

OTHER STEPS

With your judgment in hand, you can try to garnish the wages of a tenant. This is done through the Marshal's office. Another worthwhile step is to get an abstract of judgment from the clerk and have it recorded. This will stay on the tenant's record and if they try to buy a house or some other large item, any new lender will discover it. We have had people come back and pay off judgments years later because they wanted to buy a house.

In some cases, I have requested a Judgment Debtor Review. In this action, the defendant must come into court where you can ask any questions about his financial status. If you discover any assets, you can go after them.

The defendant has five days to answer the complaint. If he does not do so, you can request a default judgment. You can check with the clerk and find out when you can appear in front of the judge. Have all of the facts ready even though the tenant will not be there. You should bring your rental records on the building to show the tenant's rental record and when you were last paid. Also, a copy of the rental agreement is necessary. The judge will probably ask you questions about the amount of the deposits, etc.

This procedure can be accomplished without appearing in court by preparing the form entitled Request to Enter Default and Judgment Default Unlawful Detainer. You must also furnish a Declaration of Plaintiff in Support of Judgment. The clerk gets the judgment signed by the judge, and you can keep moving forward.

IN TRIAL

Most people think that a non-payment of rent situation is so simple that going to court will be a lark. This is not always the case.

I have seen actions dismissed because the amount of rent due (that was stated in the complaint) was off a few dollars. Other defendants have been excused because some notice filed was not quite correct. One time a five-month delinquent tenant was let off because the plaintiff had not mailed a copy of the three-day notice after posting it.

Another plaintiff had problems because a tenant claimed that he never received a copy of the Request to Enter Default. On the backside of this form there is a declaration of mailing, which states a copy must be mailed to each defendant. The plaintiff's attorney had not done this, and the default judgment was dismissed and a trial ordered.

Whenever some true deadbeat gets an Unlawful Detainer Summons, they go to Legal Aid. Legal Aid, with their vast experience in this field can normally find some point to argue in court. If your aim is possession of the apartment, work with Legal Aid to get the tenant to move as soon as possible. You can get them to argue to a Stipulated Judgment that will not be used unless the defendant fails to live up to the agreement made.

You and I both know that the Legal Aid attorney does not want to be bothered by going to court. They want to work out a settlement. Have the tenant agree to give you a judgment that will be postponed if certain conditions are met. Then, if the conditions are not met, you can get a Writ of Execution quicker.

Also, remember that a defendant will lie. They will sit there, appear innocent and tell the largest untruths you have ever heard. Be prepared for this. Have as many facts as you can gather. Bring your managers for witnesses.

If photographs will illustrate a contention, get them. Do everything to get the judge to see your side and above all, don't lose your temper. If you do, you may lose more than your temper.

It may sound like a lot of trouble to get possession of an apartment. These extreme situations do not happen very often. If you move quickly, many of these problems can be eliminated early. If you should run into any trouble, get an experienced attorney and pay them to worry about it. I repeat that I am not an attorney. I am not giving you any legal assistance. If you have any problems, see a good real estate attorney.

PARTIAL PAYMENTS

Sometimes you will be asked to make a decision about whether to take a partial payment or none at all. My feeling is to take what you can get. After you get a partial payment, you can still start any action that you should feel is necessary. Five hundred in the hand is worth $1,000.00 in the bush. If a tenant tries to pay partial payments regularly and you do not want this, you can remove this by taking a partial payment and starting an unlawful detainer action for the balance. If you give a three-day notice for a certain amount, you can still take some money and give another three-day notice immediately. If you have filed an unlawful detainer action, you should know that when you take any partial amount of money after the filing, you will have to start all over again with another three-day notice.

MOTIVATION OF MANAGER

If you believe that your manager is not collecting rents with enough vigor, you could make the manager's salary payments when all of the rents are collected or three-day notices are delivered. Managers normally are paid on the first and fifteenth of the month. You could set the payday as the tenth and twenty-fifth of the month, or earlier, if all rents are in.

In California, an employer can hold wages ten days from the last day of work, when the employee is paid twice a month. Remember, it is illegal to say that your payday is the first and I will withhold it until the rents are in or three-day notices are delivered. You can say that your work period ends on the first and the fifteenth. Your paydays will be the tenth and twenty-fifth or sooner if all rents are in.

EDUCATION

Dr. Jon S. Baily of Florida State University conducted an interesting experiment at several large apartment units. Different methods were tried to get the tenants to pay their rent on time. Some of the methods included:

1. Late charges for late payments.

2. Prizes to people paying on time. (All on-time tenants have their names put in a pot for a drawing to award merchandise prizes.)

The methods all had some effect on improving performance. The study group came to the conclusion that the cause of non-payment was not lack of desire but more often a lack of money.

Next, they tried a technique of budget counseling. Financial advisors met with the tenants individually and collectively and established goals and budgets for them. This method had tremendous results in increasing on-time rent payments. If an owner could obtain the services of some outside advisor, it could help to achieve the result of no collection loss.

ENTERING AN APARTMENT

A manager can waste a lot of time waiting to see a tenant. If a tenant does not answer a door, you could check to see if the property has been abandoned. To stop any problems from arising, I would recommend that you first post a notice on their door asking them to see the manager. If they don't show up, then consider looking in their unit. When the manager or owner opens the apartment, they should have a witness with them (not a husband or wife). Knock loudly, and knock again and again. When you open the door, announce yourself. Leave the outside door open all the time that you are in the apartment.

You might have a "Workman Inside" sign that you hang on the door. You don't want a tenant coming in and being shocked to see you in the apartment. You don't want any tenant claiming that you took any valuables or that you were poking around their apartment. One quick look can determine whether the tenant has abandoned the apartment or as might be the case, the tenant has passed away. In elderly housing, a manager might make a verbal agreement with single tenants to check periodically on other tenants who have not been seen.

BUY THEM OUT

There comes a time when you will realize that the person in your building is a "true deadbeat." A judgment will be worthless. For example, a husband runs away from a wife with two kids. He took the car, and their household furnishings are worthless. She can't work because of the children, and it will take awhile for welfare payments to start. You really want "possession."

I have had good luck by giving a small amount of money to them to get out at once. If they are truly broke, $100.00 or $200.00 in cash might mean the difference between eating and not eating. If you don't offer them some inducement, they will just sit in the apartment. It will take a long time and lots of money to get them out. Have cash in your hand and be ready to bargain.

THE PRO

If the person holding the apartment is an experienced deadbeat, you can really talk to them. You both understand each other's positions. You might say, "The principle is the thing, not one cent will I give up." At times, principles can be an expensive luxury. Your position should be to get them out as soon as possible and to improve your selection process so that it doesn't happen again.

Whenever you encounter collection problems, check back to see how these problem tenants slipped through your application review. You might discover some shortcoming in your methods.

I have had some great talks with non-payers. When I used to visit my own buildings to collect rent, I didn't want to drive up in a Mercedes wearing a new suit. Early in my ownership days I drove up to a low-rent, four-unit building to collect some back rent in a new car and in a suit. All the tenants smelled money and started requesting repairs. I have had non-payers say, "You look loaded; you don't need the money as much as I do." Deadbeats know how long it takes to get them out, and you know that they need the money. You can threaten to ruin their credit, but that is not a concern to them. They say that they can always declare bankruptcy. You counter, "But you can only do that every seven years, and is this the right time? Let's talk."

REGULAR LATE PAYER

If tenants are late regularly, and they have no lease you can get rid of them by giving them a thirty-day notice to move. You do not have to state any reason, and if they don't move at the end of the period, you start an Unlawful Detainer Action even if they are current in their rent.

ILLEGAL MEANS

In certain cases you might threaten to throw them out bodily. In some apartments this might work. However, you could run into a real deadbeat who will sue you for an illegal eviction. The non-payer could go to Legal Aid and tell them that you moved all their furniture out and put it on the street. I hate to think of the possible repercussions.

It is illegal to have any of the utilities shut off. It appears unfair that you must continue to pay the utilities for an apartment when the tenant is paying you nothing. In California, there is a set penalty for action of this type. It is $100.00 per day. Two owners had penalties assessed over $14,000.00 each.

There is a Baggage Lien Law. However, expert attorneys have advised me against confiscating any baggage in an apartment house. They advise being a little cowardly in this regard. The advantages that you gain can really be wiped out by one disadvantage. So many items of personal belongings are exempt from being held that the law is just about worthless except in the case of motels and weekly rentals.

Forms of lock covers can be bought and put over the doorknob so that a person cannot enter the apartment. You can be sure that you will get to see the person quickly if you do this. A real bad actor might just break a window. Again, this is a type of illegal action and a judge would look upon you with an unfavorable eye. In the "old days" we had one building where we used a technique similar to this.

We took a key for the apartment and cut it in two pieces. Both halves were inserted into the lock. The top half would then be slid out. The bottom half would not come out until that same top half was reinserted. When the tenant came running into the office, the manager would say that we just wanted to discuss the rent payment. We knew in that building no one would go to any legal official, and after talking to the people, we opened the apartments at once.

CALL THE REFERENCES

If a young couple lists parents as their references, you could call them and see if the parents would take the responsibility for payment. There is a chance that you will antagonize the tenant when you do this, but you may not care about their feelings, as you merely want money or possession.

LIGHTER SIDE

A friend of mine ran several low cost rooming houses at a major university. He was the wrestling coach at school. Whenever he had some student behind in the rent, he would have a heavyweight wrestler or football lineman go to the unit. The new visitor would have a paid receipt for the room. He would tell the non-payer, "You are in my room, get out now." It worked, as none of the late payers wanted to test the visitor.

Years ago, in a three-unit building that I owned, I had a real problem with a non-paying woman who was in and out of a state mental hospital. Finally, one day she kicked holes in a wall and did other damage, and when she was done, she called the Health Department. The Inspector told me to fix the damage or the apartment would be condemned. I asked, "Do you condemn all three units or just the one?" "Just the one," was the answer. "Fine, condemn, and you kick her out." The County of Milwaukee had to remove her, and it took less time than a contested trial action would have taken.

In a book, "Apartment Management: Proven Methods," E.C. Christenson mentions an owner who used to go to the non-payer and say, "When can I show your apartment to my tenants?" The non-payers would say, "We aren't moving." The owner would reply, "Oh, I thought you must be going to move as you hadn't paid any rent."

I used to write a weekly column on real estate. A reader wrote to tell me an idea that he had used. He had rented a single-family house to a young married couple. When the rent was not paid, he called and said that he couldn't afford to make two house payments himself and he couldn't throw the man out bodily, so he would have to move back and live with them. The rent came immediately.

SUMMARY

We should try to eliminate these problems before they happen. A good selection process and high security deposits will help to keep any losses low. When a problem arises, act quickly and unemotionally. Treat a proven non-payer like a snakebite. If you let it go too long, it can be fatal. Treat it quickly, even if the initial treatment may hurt a little. You may lose a little flesh and a little blood, but you will soon be on the road to recovery.

The latest move of some "deadbeats" is to file a bankruptcy action in a Federal Court. This action is taken by tenants who do not have severe financial problems, and they file the action pending later filing of assets and liabilities. The action stops any eviction action.

An owner's only move is to get good legal advice if this should ever happen. Immediately, a hearing date must be requested from the Bankruptcy Court. At this hearing, a request must be made to remove the eviction from the Bankruptcy proceeding. Only when this is done, can a trial date be requested from our regular court. Your attorney requests a release from the Stage of Execution and shows that the tenant has equity in the property.

It is hoped that this procedure does not become too widespread. When it happens to you, don't wait. Move at once, for the procedure can become time-consuming and aggravating.

Chapter 13
Supervision Principles and Methods

The word "Supervision" is derived from two Latin words, "super" which means over and vision which means to see. "To oversee" is to supervise, i.e., to direct and correct subordinates, not just observe them.

A whole section of this book discussed the importance of selecting the correct person for your position. It is difficult to train the untrainable, to teach the unteachable, to correct the uncorrectable and to supervise the unsupervisable. So hire the right people and supervising is easy.

You should establish some guidelines for your buildings. You have to decide what your overall aim is from the ownership of this property. To do this, you must define your objectives. This is called Management by Objectives.

SETTING YOUR OBJECTIVES

Your long-range goals must be evaluated and defined in your mind. Then, put them down on paper. A long-range goal might be to do the best job possible managing this project and to create the highest amount of net profit and at the same time to maintain the building in such a manner that the resale value will be at a maximum. An estimated period of ownership would be for five to six years at which time it would be traded upwards for a bigger building; but there will be flexibility so that any outstanding opportunity for financial advancement during this period will be considered.

Another person owning a building may want to hold it for a lifetime. Another owner might want to sell it at once for a profit. Different objectives will mean different plans.

To operate a business without an objective is like starting out on an auto trip with no map. You could be making great headway, but are you going in the direction you want to go? You must know where you want to be and when you want to get there before you start planning and working.

Everyone should have long-range objectives. You should have them for your personal, family and business life. You could have different long-range objectives for different buildings that you own. I believe that it is helpful if your key management employees know your long-range objectives. If they are to function in your best interest, they must have some idea of what you want in the long run.

SHORT RANGE GOALS

After the long-range programs are established, shorter-term goals or plans must be made. For example, your goals for the next twelve months period might be "to increase the net income of the building to $2,800 a month before loan payments, and to redesign the parking area and make it more secure." Goals can be made for even shorter periods. It is understood that conditions may change and goals have to be reviewed and changed but goals give you a good frame of reference for planning.

An important phase of management is the establishment of priorities. You must know at all times what is most important to you. In a business sense you must have your goals so that you can evaluate different plans of action.

For example, many times football coaches will insist that football must be the most important thing in a player's life. A priority system for them would be football, God, country, family, and self. My own priority system puts family in the first spot ahead of self, business, God, country, etc. My decisions are based on what is most important to me (my family) while another person might have business interests as his number one priority. It is obvious that some people put business ahead of family and even ahead of their own health.

PLAN TO ACHIEVE YOUR GOALS

After the goals are set, plans must be made. To achieve the listed short-range goals from the previous section we will:

1. Resurvey the area and establish a new rental schedule with a goal of raising rents 10%-12% overall and 15% in the one bedroom apartments as they have had the highest occupancy rate in the past two years.

2. Lower expenses by 5% over the previous year's average with extra attention to be given to utilities, apartment painting and petty cash supplies. These were the items that were increasing the fastest.

3. Decrease the combined vacancy and collection losses to 3% of the gross projected rents.

4. Retain more tenants and cut move outs by keeping better records why tenants are moving and correcting any problems that are causing these movements.

5. Increase the discipline of the young children in the building:
   A. Letter to parents
   B. Gifts and parties for children
   C. Better communication

6. Make the parking lot more secure.
   A. Assign parking spaces to each tenant.
   B. Give tenants parking stickers with their parking space number on them.
   C. Put up a sign, citing city parking ordinances and instructing guests to park on the street.
   D. Investigate the costs of installing an automatic gate, which would be opened by a beeper in each tenant's car.
   E. Install new locks and closers on elevators and doors from parking spaces to apartment hallways.
   F. Evaluate the cost of having a security patrol check the parking area periodically.
   G. Check the prices for mass purchasing of car alarms for the tenants.
   H. Allow no visitors, friends or tenants to loiter in parking areas. Enlist aid of residents in helping in this phase.
   I. Recommend the tenants join a "Hot Car" club to help stop car theft.

If goals are set in this manner, employees will have a concise idea of how to perform. Many times poor results are the result of poor planning by the "boss." In this job, if you are the owner, you are the boss. If you own an apartment house, you are the chairman of the board and the "buck" stops there.

DIRECTION

Several examples of direction, instructions and procedures have already been discussed. A manager's employment contract, which allows duties, is a type of directive. A job description is another helpful tool. The policy letters that have been mentioned in previous chapters give the personnel a focal point for any decision. These letters should cover the topics of renting, accounting, collection from late payers, and rules of conduct for the tenants. A manual to assist the manager would also be beneficial. It would save the manager the time and trouble of experimentation and would save you money and time as the manager would work with less direction.

COMMUNICATION

In any relationship-personal, family, romantic, business, recreation, etc.-communication is important. There must be free flow of communication both up and down in any employee-employer situation. Systems for downward flow of information must be established but don't restrict the upward flow of communication.

SOME SIMPLE RECOMMENDATIONS

Whenever something can be written down, do so. "The strongest memory is weaker than the palest ink." When I managed many buildings, I used a Property Inspection Record form, a sample of which follows. This is helpful if you only have one building or if you have several.

A major complaint of apartment managers is that owners promise to do something, and then the owners forget. A Property Inspection Record form helps a great deal. When you walk around the property, you can note the condition of the pertinent areas. The late paying tenants and the condition of the vacancies are highlighted. A section is set-aside for *Work to Be Done* by the manager and by the owner. The final three sections are self-explanatory.

This form accomplishes many things

1. The owner or supervisor has the current information available on the building.

2. The condition of the building will be checked more regularly.

3. The owner must do his work before he comes back to the building. This form makes him more organized, as he knows the form will be looked at during the next inspection. It makes *you* do a better job.

4. Conversely, the manager has a list of things to do and he should get those items done. If there is any problem with the general areas, it has been listed and will be checked again at the time of the next visit. The form allows a review of problem circumstances without the appearance of excess nagging. Sometimes it is easier to write down a shortcoming than to verbalize it to the manager.

5. If you are a property manager, a copy of one of these weekly reports could be sent to the owner with your monthly report. It would give the owner an insight into what is happening.

If the manager knows that you will be making a written report, there is more of a chance that she will have all of the building's problems written down. If she has a written list, you can quickly evaluate her problems and make your decisions. It is not good procedure to spend too much time at your buildings. Long coffee drinking sessions can lead to trouble. You should present the appearance and attitude of being organized and decisive and that your time is valuable. The longer you stay at a building, the greater the opportunity for minor problems to appear. If you have a fine manager who has a sense of priority, she will tell you the important problems first. I do not mean to imply that you are to be curt or unfriendly. You can be friendly and still be decisive.

If a building is having problems, you will spend more time there. If the manager is new, there needs to be more time spent on giving them additional detailed instructions and correction.

OTHER IDEAS

Managers are often of the opinion that some owners do not make the phone calls that are necessary to run a building. Let's say the owner is to call a carpet man to discuss the replacement of the carpeting in apartment 101. You call the carpet man and he never shows up. The manager thinks that you never called the carpet man and the tenant is complaining to the manager. The manager becomes angry with you but he is afraid to mention it.

I try to make these phone calls from the manager's phone if possible. The call is made, and I don't have to worry about it. If there are any questions, they can be answered quickly as the manager is standing there. The manager knows that I care about her position, as I am quick about solving her problems. The manager knows that I made the call and if the carpet man doesn't come, she gets on the phone herself and instead of calling me, she calls the carpet man and straightens it out. This small change in my normal procedure saved me a lot of time and made the managers and tenants more satisfied.

PROPERTY INSPECTION RECORD

Building _____   Date _____

Condition of Property

General Areas _____

Laundry Rooms _____

Pool _____

Landscaping _____

Garages/Carports _____

Miscellaneous _____

Stairways _____

Rubbish Area _____

Windows _____

Elevator _____

Manager's Apt. _____

Rec Room _____

Vacancies _____

TENANTS OVER FIVE DAYS LATE _____

WORK TO BE DONE BY MANAGER	BY OWNER

ACTION DURING PAST WEEK AND SOURCES _____

_____

_____

Any Manager Suggestions, Complaints or Recommendations, Tenant Problems:

Signed _____   _____
                   Manager   Supervisor/Owner

Maintenance Records:

The manager should keep a record of the maintenance done on each apartment. These service request forms should be kept. This information is invaluable when you must decide what to do in an apartment. Tenants will claim that their paint job is five years old and that their carpet is pre-war unless you maintain service records that show what has been done and when.

Support Manager:

Some managers complain that the tenants can go over their heads and get sympathy and better results from the owner and/or supervisor. If the tenant can get to the supervisor by phone or visit, they will try to play the manager against you and vice versa. Another rule you might consider is that you never visit a tenant's apartment or discuss a tenant's problem without the manager present. If you do this, many possible problems will be solved and you will not destroy the manager's position. If a tenant wants to talk to me about a problem, I have the manager set an appointment at my convenience. I come to the building and talk with the manager before going to the tenant's apartment. Then, the manager and I go to the apartment together. Normally, if the work request can be done, we will schedule it then. If further research needs to be done, I will have the manager relay the final ruling to the tenant if it is favorable. If the ruling is unfavorable, I might send a letter to the tenant, call them, or have the manager deliver the message. You do not want to destroy the manager's authority in the eyes of the tenants.

AUTHORITY/RESPONSIBILITY

If you expect a manager to do a good job, you have to give them the proper authority. If you want them to be responsible for the work performance of the pool man, painter, gardener, etc., they have to be given the authority to "oversee" the work of these people. These servicemen and vendors need to know that the manager has this authority. In this vein, the manager should be involved in the hiring and firing of these assistants.

If you expect the manager to control the tenants, you have to support the manager's action in these areas. The old management saying, "If you give someone the responsibility for something, you must also give them the authority," is a true statement.

There are many decisions that can be made by the manager. Encourage your personnel to take some responsibility. If a decision was made that differs from the one you would have made, but there is no problem involved, let the decision stand. Ask them if they considered these other possibilities.

When an employee calls or mentions a problem, use a questioning approach. Ask the manager enough questions so that you both have the same understanding of the problem. Then ask the manager, "What do you think we should do?" This is a good procedure to get the manager involved and to increase his capabilities. Try to see how they think. If their solutions are plausible, adapt them whenever possible. Make them feel that they are important.

For example, let's say that you and the manager are discussing when you are to start to reheat the swimming pool. You ask the manager, "When do you think we should start?" The manager thinks and says, "The Saturday before Easter." That sounds good to you and is probably the time you would have recommended. However, it is now the manager's recommendation and if nay tenant complains the manger will explain the reasoning behind the decision.

If their answers are not sound, keep asking more questions and perhaps they will understand the problem better and come up with a better answer. Get them to think their answers through to a suitable conclusion. When you make a decision, the results of the decision must be evaluated. Whom does it affect? How will they react? What are their choices of action? When might a problem arise? Etc. I like to consider different alternatives and "think" about them and consider all the side effects.

Use the abilities of your managers. They are at the project. They know the situations first-hand. Guide and direct them. Give them the feeling that you will listen and you should listen. Stress that they are being paid to manage - they are not just an answering service. To earn their money they must make some decisions.

MANAGER'S CALLS

How often should a manager call you? Whenever something important happens that you should know. Who decides what is important? The managers must do so as they are at the job site. They have to know your feelings on this subject. If they call too much, it is a nuisance and all the calls can't be important and your time is wasted. However, if they never call, you will miss some important information. Try to strike a proper medium.

One way to handle the calls is the procedure used by a Navy Supply Base Commander I met in the service. He instructed his wife early in his career that she was only to call him on extremely urgent calls if he was at work. Extremely urgent to him was defined as "if anyone in the family died." She said, "No, but…" He hung up the phone. She tried one other time with the same results, and then she never called again.

MANAGER'S MANAGE

My feeling is that if you are paying an employee to manage, they should manage. They should analyze their calls and see if the calls are really that important to bother the owner. Many times the call is made to relay a minor tenant complaint or to let the owner know the manager's problems. The owners don't need to hear all the problems; they have enough of their own.

However, managers should keep the owner informed about complaints and pending problems. If a problem does not require immediate action, perhaps it could be held until some other problems arise and a call can be made when several problems can be discussed. If a tenant asks for some service or brings up a problem, the manager should do some preliminary checking before any call is made to you. If a person wants new carpet and the manager relays this request, my first question would be, "How bad is the carpet?" You would be amazed how many times a manager says, "I've not seen it." They should have looked at the carpet, checked the maintenance records to verify the age, found out when it was last cleaned and talked to the tenant to see how strongly the tenants feel about their need for a new carpet.

SCHEDULE

Your managers and suppliers should know when they could reach you. If they know that you are available at 2:00 each afternoon, a majority of your calls will come during that time. It will make your work easier.

I have always tried to call every manager once a week at a set time. Monday morning was a great time. If I established a pattern of doing this, the managers would expect the call and have the information I wanted readily available. This way, I would find out about vacancies, rentals, notices of moving, deposits made and late payers very quickly. If there were any problems, they would be covered. The managers knew approximately when I would be calling so if anything came up over the weekend, they would wait until the Monday morning call. For some reason I have always found it easier to maintain a positive attitude if I got the problems on a phone call I made, than if the manager called me at some inopportune time.

My schedule was set so that anyone could call me early in the morning. The calls would come in if anyone had a problem. If I called the managers regularly once a week, the number of managers' calls to me was reduced greatly.

My visits to the property were not scheduled. I wanted to see how the manager ran the building at all times. If they knew I always came on Wednesday afternoon, the property might not look as sharp at other times. Go to a building in the evening, on weekends, mornings and at other odd times.

RELATIONS TO OWNERS, ETC.

If I were a property manager, I insisted that the manager be honest with me. I would not talk to tenants without the manager present, and I did not want the manager to ever call the owner of the property.

On my management contract, I liked to include a condition that the owner would not go to the building without me. The reason for this is obvious. If an owner keeps going to the building and talks to managers and tenants, it can create chaos. Of course, an owner has every right to go to his own building despite what any contract might say. If he goes, then I have a right to cancel the management agreement. If an owner has the time and desires to go to the project often, then he should run his own building.

MESSAGES

As a supervisor or owner, I wanted the managers to give my secretary some reason for their call if I was not there. So many times they would call and say, "Have Mr. Gomer call me, I want to talk to him." If they would say, "Apartment 101 wants to give me $100. What is the status of the legal action against them? Should I take the money?" I now know the urgency of the call and if I call in from the field, I can even have my secretary call back quickly with an answer.

Managers sometimes act as if these problems are deep secrets. Messages, if they can be given, are helpful in saving you and the manager time.

ERRORS

As an owner or a supervisor, you are not always right. As a person, you are not always right. I have made some real errors in judgment. Some of mine were classic.

If you really do something that turns out wrong, admit it. It clears the air and can create an atmosphere of cooperation. If your employees realize that you know that you can be wrong, they now know that they can occasionally be wrong. If they know that, they will start to accept responsibility and authority.

If a person is afraid of making an error, many times they will do nothing. To accomplish anything, you must try something. The great Babe Ruth did not get a hit every time he batted. In fact, he set records for the number of times he struck out. In baseball, if you could get a hit just four times out of ten, you could make millions. In the latest free agent baseball drafts .280 hitters were becoming instant millionaires. A .280 batting average means a man gets a hit less than 3 times out of 10. We want a great batting average with many good decisions, but we can't be perfect.

PRAISE

Nothing does as much good and costs so little as praise. If a person is doing a good job, let them know. A spoken word here, a written memo there, a bonus now and a raise periodically. These are ways of saying, "Hey, thanks for doing a good job for me."

There are so many sincere compliments that can be given to your people. People are interesting if you give them the chance to be. Managers of mine have been artists, handicraft experts, grandparents, film contest winners, musicians, dancers, horsemen, athletes, bowlers, deputy police, ham radio operators, bankers, fishermen, salesmen, motorcycle racers, writers, actors, gourmet cooks, etc. If you can say something good, say it. It could be new plants that have been planted, good rental work, quick handling of a problem, new clothes, cleaner general areas, organized parking program, quick reporting, etc. Sincere praise is valuable.

EVALUATION FORM

You should consider using a periodic evaluation form on your employees. This is a common practice in the business community, but it is not used in apartment management.

Any type of form could be used, or a simple memo or letter could be written. If a manager is doing a super job, this is a good opportunity to give the manager a written, formal acknowledgment of your approval. If a manager is doing a poor job, certain areas can be highlighted where the manager should try to improve. It is easier sometimes to put these corrective ideas in writing as part of a formal review program. The person being admonished might take the suggestions to heart and try to improve.

A manager could be doing an outstanding job except the accounting reports are slow or the manager bothers you with too many phone calls. An outstanding letter could be written mentioning the weak areas. Periodically a review and discussion of your opinion in conference with the employee could be helpful in improving the performance level of your workers.

Industries have been doing this for years; why shouldn't apartment owners and supervisors do it?

WORK SAMPLING

If you have many buildings to manage, the technique of work sampling might be useful in evaluating your employees' work performance. This technique gives you an idea of how consistent your workers are.

Simply stated, work sampling is done when you periodically check your workers and keep records on what they were doing when you checked them. It works best in factories where you can check many times in a day and develop percentages showing what the person was doing when he was observed. If you checked fifty times in a week and the worker was working forty times, he would be 80% effective. Another worker might be 60% or 90% effective. This of course does not mean that the one man is more valuable, but it is one technique of checking on performance.

When you travel around, keep a record of what the person was doing as you came to the building. After several visits, a record and a percentage would evolve that could be used to measure the performance of different managers. If one person appears to be loafing too much, tell them about your survey. A great number of inspections have to be done so that any percentage would be representative.

MANAGERS COMMUNICATION WITH TENANTS

Tenants should feel that they can give recommendations to the manager. The manager has to be receptive. A proper attitude is important.

If you are a leader of a committee and you want recommendations from the committee, you can use a technique called "brainstorming." An important part of brainstorming is that no criticism is given of the ideas when they are presented. If a person wants to present an opinion or idea, he does so. No one is to make any negative or positive comment at that time. The ideas are just to be discussed later. Sometimes conference members will make verbal, or even non-verbal signs of disapproval. If comments are made when ideas are given, the free flow of ideas is hampered. As a leader of a group, it is difficult to sit there and hear some crazy, unworkable scheme presented. This new member does not know that experience in the past has shown the recommendation to be worthless. Still, no comments should be made by anyone.

As a manager, if you want recommendations, be a "brainstorm" leader. Listen and just list the ideas. A suggestion box for tenants could be started. In a large building an award could be given for good ideas.

An owner should do the same for manager suggestions. If someone comes up with a good idea, reward them. Publicity and money are great inducements to start people trying to create some ideas. In a property management company, a manager could give a new idea for a form. Give them cash awards and acknowledge their ideas in your next letter to the managers. You should get other suggestions soon.

BILL PAYING

If an owner pays bills slowly, the manager can be inconvenienced. The suppliers or workers can harass the manager. This is never pleasant. Also, if you get a reputation as a slow payer, the good workmen will stop coming to your project. A good business philosophy is to pay bills like a reasonable, prudent businessman. If they know you pay bills on the 10th and 20th of the month and they do work for you knowing this, they will wait for the payment. Be sure you follow through on your schedule that is, in essence, a promise to pay at a certain time.

Some of the workmen need the money right after the work is done. Many times these hand-to-mouth people give the best prices and do quality work. Apartment owners have cheated many suppliers out of money so they are wary about extending any credit. If your manager agreed the check would be coming, get it going.

It might be a good idea to take a checkbook with you when you go to a building. You can write some of the pertinent checks at the manager's office. If some checks are needed, they can be left with the manager. If the managers have any checks due them, such as petty cash or cleaning, they will appreciate getting their money immediately.

Many owners have large bank balances, and they hate to write outgoing checks. They forget their early, struggling years when checks were really needed for necessities. Remember the days when you got a check and you ran it to the payer's bank to get cash on the same day you got it. If you can remember your struggling days, show some consideration for the struggling people giving you good service now.

SHOPPERS, SPIES, INSPECTORS

If you own a building, do you know how good a job your rental people are doing when they show your property? You may think you do know-but do you really?

Some managers are hypocrites. By this I mean that they are pleasant and smiling when they see you, but prospects do not see this same person. Since you work, your only trips to your building are on weekends or in the evenings. By that time, your manager's appearance and conduct are reasonable. The prospect that comes in the morning or early afternoon meets a different character.

If you don't know how good your manager is doing in this regard or if you believe she is good, but you want to check, do something about it. Have a person whose judgment you respect go to the building and ask to see an apartment. In a larger company we had people who did this regularly.

You would be surprised by some of the stories our checkers told us:

A. Manager still in a bathrobe at 11:30 a.m.
B. Manager handed them the key and asked them to go to look at the apartment themselves.
C. A strong odor of beer, liquor, etc. was prevalent in the manager's apartment.
D. The manager's office or apartment, and the manager were a mess.
E. Vulgar language was used.
F. A bored or obnoxious attitude was exhibited.

G. Someone other than the manager did the showing

H. The manager did an outstanding job.

Where would your apartment fit in among the above alternatives? This checking on your manager is so important I cannot stress it enough.

Once an owner hired me to do a consulting job on several of his buildings. One of the managers did not impress me although the owner was satisfied with her. I recommended that he send another person to the building to check on the rental job being done. He sent his son-in-law. The "prospect" asked, "Would the owners paint this one bedroom?" The manager said, "I don't think so; these owners are the biggest cheapskates I have ever known." After hearing this, a few more people were sent to the building, and they came away with the same impression of the manager. The manager was changed and the building flourished.

As an owner, you should consider going to several competitive apartments in your area. This will show you the present rental schedules, and you will see how other people are showing apartments to the prospects who might visit your apartment. Some subtle comment like "I was considering the ABC apartments up the street" could solicit some statements from your competition about your building. The person might tell you some of the shortcomings of your building and this information would be valuable.

NEWSLETTERS AND OTHER MEANS

Certain owners have a lot of success with the use of a periodical newsletter to the tenants. Done properly, a newsletter can be worthwhile as a device to communicate news to the residents.

1. Problems can be brought to light and procedures to correct them could be listed.

2. New building policies are discussed.

3. Tidbits about the residents are interesting to most residents (marriages, honors, transfers, new tenants).

4. Neighborhood news of interest can be highlighted.

5. Important notices about children's parties, forthcoming water heater shutdowns, change in maintenance schedules, etc. might be included.

Any newsletter must be reviewed constantly to see if it is accomplishing any worthwhile results. If you do one, be sure to meet publication deadlines, as a late newsletter is worse than no newsletter. The cost of a newsletter is small. The only cost is typing and printing. A couple of residents might help out, and a local merchant might print it for you in return for a one-line ad.

Other types of communication are memos or letters and posters. These methods should be done as needed but not overdone. Posters to announce forthcoming events can be helpful, but constant posting of negative signs (don't do this, stop this, you must, etc.) are not helpful to good resident-management relations.

PERSONAL BELIEFS OF MANAGEMENT

Managers and owners should not use their positions to attempt to influence the behavior and opinions of their residents. Management personnel must not spend time trying to convert non-believers to their religion. Some managers that I had working for me use to preach the gospel and the ideas of conversion to the residents. Managers have the complete right to their religious freedom and what they do away from their job is their own affair, but they are not to hold religious confabs with tenants who are not interested. Another topic not to be argued is politics. Can you imagine the problems that could arise if a staunch Republican tenant had to be evicted after he had had some long bitter arguments with a staunch Democratic manager? Even though his eviction was not due to the political disagreement, it would be difficult to convince him of that.

Management personnel are not to take advantage of their status to try to sell any products to the tenants. The manager believes that he was making a low-key presentation and the tenant believes that he was being high-pressured. If a manager or owner earns money by sales work, they must really study their situation before doing any soliciting in their buildings.

WORDS

Good management personnel will try to use proper language. Vulgarity, poor grammar and slang are not businesslike. The use of the tenants' names is important. There is no sweeter sound to anyone than the pleasant proper use of his or her name. A "Good morning, Mrs. Brown, is Timmy over his cold?" costs nothing and is much better than a curt "Hi." Work at this. It is one quality of a good manager that anyone can acquire.

Some "better-sounding" words can be used to replace some other words that have a bad connotation. For example, "service request" instead of complaint, a "situation" instead of a problem, "owner" not landlord or they said, "policy" not rule, "staff" not employees, and the word "home" to describe the tenant's apartment could be used as in "How do you like your new home?"

INSTRUCTIONS

When instructions are given to the staff or the residents, be sure that the instructions are understood. First, the instructions should be given both verbally and in writing. If possible, the communication should be followed with a demonstration and finally have the person do the task.

Many times something that is simple to the instructor is not so simple to the student. If you were dealing with material out of your field, you would be amazed at how difficult simple things appear. For example, men who have never cooked would really have trouble doing some perfunctory chores that any housewife can do blindfolded. When my wife had major surgery, I was called upon to prepare meals for five. Getting anything done right for children who have been spoiled by exposure to all-star level cooking for years is difficult and then to get everything done at the same time is impossible. If spouses reversed roles completely for about a month, I believe they would appreciate each other much more.

Therefore, have the student use his ears (hear you), his eyes (to read instructions and to watch the demonstration), his hands (to try it himself) and his mouth (to ask questions). There is an old saying, "If a person hears it, they forget it. If they see it, they understand it. And if they do it, they remember it." When the entire instructing process is done, ask questions. You will not believe how many times a person will say they understand what you told them, but they can't answer the easiest question about the subject. Go back and start over. There is nothing wrong in explaining a subject more than once.

Let's assume for the moment that you have selected good employees. You are an outstanding supervisor so if they were not good, you would replace them. Therefore, if these good employees are given instructions and they do poorly, there must be some trouble with the instructions. A supervisor should look at himself when instructions are misunderstood (and not place the blame solely on the employee). Part of the trouble could be with the supervisor and not the employee. If a good employee messes up, perhaps the instructions were poor, the procedures were poor, or you did not anticipate the situation that arose.

When a mistake occurs, a few supervisors or managers want to fix the blame. This is a poor use of time. On an overall view, the blame for inflation could be placed on the politicians, the poor local economy on businessmen, high construction costs on labor unions and material suppliers, high energy costs on the Arabs and other suppliers, poor tenant behavior on society, poor employee work standards on their parents, you own lack of intelligence and energy on heredity, etc., etc. Now all the blame is fixed. Is that going to help us in settling the current problems? Use your blame-fixing time to get started creating a workable plan of action.

DELEGATION

There comes a time in just about every owner's life when he or she must delegate some functions to other people. Don't be afraid to let other people have some freedom in their work life. Let them make decisions within the framework developed. If you do not do this, you will still be making all the decisions. If this happens, your future growth will be stymied. You can never be free from work detail. Vacations will be few and far between.

As an owner, you want to rule on the exceptions to the ordinary routine of business. By proper supervision and training your employees will learn what exceptions are important enough to bring to your attention. When delegating these functions to the lower levels, you must give these people the authority to make the decisions. When these people have the authority to make the decisions, they will become responsible for their actions.

CRISIS

Too much of the management done by apartment owners and employees can be labeled "crisis" management. This means that the only time any action is taken is when a crisis has developed. If you find that too many of these crisis decisions are being made, evaluate your whole system.

Perhaps the problems are not so great. Discuss the problems that have arisen in the part months. Then, start a program of "preventive" management. Solve all your problems before they become "real" problems.

Preventive management would mean:

1. Constant review of policies and objectives.

2. Be on the lookout for possible trouble spots.

3. Stay ahead of all maintenance and do periodic inspections of the entire project.

4. If trends in tenant behavior are starting that could cause trouble, act quickly.

5. Be alert, sensitive, probing, and try to develop a sixth sense that allows you to spot trouble before it happens.

6. Get rid of the attitude "Let's wait and see if the trouble goes away." It hardly ever does. Procrastination has ruined more people than any other disease.

7. Remember that a supervisor's work is never done. It is similar to studying for an important final examination in school. If there were more time, you could always find more things to do. Keep busy. Do your best. Work your hardest on the highest priority items. What more can you do? Nothing.

PERSONAL PROBLEMS

A manager can be outstanding in so many ways and suddenly develop some personal problems. These could be:

A. Financial
B. Physical-Health
C. Marriage
D. Family or Friends
E. Drinking or some other addiction

A supervisor has to walk a narrow line when he becomes involved in a person's personal problems. The difference between helping and interfering is so narrow.

I believe that a supervisor should try to help his employees if he can. Some troubles are going to pop up. If an employee can be helped in a personal situation, they probably will be able to do a much better job for you. Just as long as the personal problems don't appear too regularly.

If a manager is having some financial problems, see if an advance of pay can be arranged, a budget can be prepared, a loan secured from a lender, negotiations could be handled with the people who are owed money, etc., etc. Be interested in any problems that they have, but be careful when you are giving advice. Advice is cheap to give. People ask for it and don't want it when it is received. I have been most successful when I have discussed several different alternatives of action with the employee. You can act as a devil's advocate and ask questions and direct any discussion. The final decision is up to the person involved. However, you have been helpful in bringing up some alternatives that they would not have considered and in directing evaluation of these different possibilities. When the employee makes the final decision, you cannot be held accountable. I believe that it is a compliment to you when a subordinate comes to you for advice and assistance. The subordinate respects your opinion and if you can help, do so.

SOME MANAGEMENT WORDS

EMPATHY:

The word is best described by an old Indian proverb; "Grant that I may not criticize my neighbor until I have walked a mile in his moccasins." Try to understand the other person' position, whether an employee or a tenant.

Your manager at the building has a tough relationship to maintain. He functions as a representative of the owner and lives with all the tenants. When you are making rules and plans, remember his position.

Occasionally, tenants will have legitimate complaints. Look at the problem from their point of view. For example, let's imagine that during a rainstorm many apartments start to experience leaks. There is little a person can do about a bad roof until the weather clears and a roofer can be found. However, do everything that can be done. Show your concern for your residents. It is difficult to go to the building and visit with the rained-out tenants, but you must do it. You might be able to think of some temporary solution such as rental of a water pump, placement of plastic rain covers, use of some roof sealer even in the rain, etc. A few times a situation has been alleviated by drilling a small hole in a ceiling. Prior to this action the rainwater would be running onto the ceiling and dripping in many places. By drilling a hole in the lowest part of the ceiling, the water comes out in one spot. In times of severe problems you should show some concern for your "people."

Psychologists say that empathy can even be developed. If you and a manager are having some troubles, try a role-playing situation where you take the manager's point of view and the manager assumes your views. When you discuss a situation in this vein, people start to realize the validity of other points of view. This is supposed to work in a family disagreement. However, every time I have tried it, my children say that they can't do it for they cannot come up with any pertinent, persuasive points when they are supporting "the parent's" view. It does work better in a boss-associate type arrangement.

INTEGRITY:

A supervisor must be honest in all his dealings. You can't try to use people and expect them to do their best job. Deceit and idle promises can work for the short run, but sooner or later a dishonest person will be revealed for what he is. There is no memory strong enough to allow a person to lie. You have to keep track of so many lies after a session of lie telling that it is impossible. The ole axiom, "Honesty is the best policy" is true in supervising. Be truthful and stress and strain is removed.

DECISIVE:

If a decision needs to be made, make it. Don't put a decision off. Do today what needs to be done today. Remember that if you do not make any decision, you have inadvertently made a decision. A "don't do anything yet" move is a decision and in most instances, it is not the best move. I recall a story about an interviewer asking a job prospect, "Are you decisive?" The prospect answered, "Well, yes and no."

Stress and strain are increased for all the parties when you delay. For example, you are asked to carpet number 201 and the person will renew his lease. The manager has looked at the carpet and has told you that a new carpet is needed, and that a good rent increase can be levied for a new lease. Your records show that the carpeting is over five years old, and this is old for the style of carpeting used. You procrastinate on what you intend to do. You are short of cash and might have to make arrangements to buy carpet on credit, for as you know, when 201 gets new carpet, everyone in the building will see the carpet layers coming and going. Make your move and then don't look back.

Since you are dealing with people, any delayed decision affects more than just you. Get all the information available and then make your decision. Don't be hurried into any half-considered decision. However, most supervisors know when they are stalling and when they are investigating alternatives of action. When you know you should decide, decide. Many times we duffer over what we consider a crucial decision. Later action reveals that these decisions were not as crucial as we thought them to be at the prior time.

APPROVAL:
No matter what you do in life, someone will not like it. You can't please everybody all the time. As a supervisor, you must realize this. Even in the most lopsided of elections, there is a percentage of people voting against the great favorite. You can try to do everything for people, and they will still find something about which they can complain.

If you had some tenants and you decided to do everything for them, you could not please them all of the time. In an apartment management relationship you just can't afford to try to please everyone: tenants, associates, employees, suppliers or the government agencies.

You must develop a thicker skin. Don't let other people manipulate you by expressing their disapproval of you. They will call you names that you don't deserve, but this is part of the price you pay for being a supervisor.

Remember that your manager can be doing an outstanding job and still there will be vociferous tenants. They will appeal to you and when they do, they will seem so nice and elegant. However, they could be asking for too much and your manager knows this and has incurred their wrath by telling them that their requests cannot be met. In one building of over one hundred families there was an unofficial group of advisors. They would be talking around the pool, and they would get on the manager that the building should be painted. The building did not look that bad, and it would cost about $25,000 to paint it. My stock answer for the manager was to tell him that they could paint it whenever they wanted and whatever color they wanted whenever they either:

1. Found somebody who would do it for nothing.

2. Bought the building.

3. Took up a collection and got $250 from each tenant.

I had considered painting as part of an upgrading process, but there were other more important uses for our money and the tenants knew this.

Years ago, I used to write a weekly article for a local newspaper. Mail was received from the readers about the columns. A few readers would disagree and complain. The first time that anybody complained, my feelings were hurt and I was concerned. The Real Estate Editor said that the publisher thought the mail response was great, and he hoped there would be some disagreement. It was an expected return, and illustrated that the articles were being read by a cross section of people.

Previously, I discussed a procedure where you mailed a form to tenants and asked for their comments on the operation of the building. Managers are apprehensive about this, as they know complaints will be received. Tell them that you know certain people will complain. If you have a building where no one ever complains, you obviously have a problem. Either you are giving way too much service or your rents are so low everyone is afraid to complain. Check out a never-complain building thoroughly to find out why this is happening.

CONSISTENCY:

A true mark of any good supervisor is consistency. You should function on as even a keel as possible. This can be difficult.

One day, you are visiting a building after just having argued with your wife and children, the IRS has called to schedule an audit, the Health Department wants to discuss many problems, you have a head cold and got to bed late, and your sweet manager wants to discuss the parking arrangements at the building. Your first reaction might be to explode.

Now, suppose the same day you just had a great lunch date with your wife and had a superb filet of sole with some wine, the children's report cards came with all the best of grades, you are celebrating a large sale that has given you many dollars, it's a beautiful sunny day, and no business clouds are on the horizon; if the manager brought up some situation, your reaction might be a little different. When employees, residents or associates want to discuss some idea, they don't know your personal situation at the moment or your frame of mind. Personally, I have to tone down my highs and tone up my lows. When I am high or low, I should know where I'm at and not let it affect my relationships or my decisions. The vast majority of the time I am high. I am optimistic to a fault, but there are times that the pressures get to anyone. If I go home, run a few miles, get in the Jacuzzi and have a glass of wine, the pressures always disappear. That is hard to work into a schedule at 10:15 in the morning so we have to understand our emotions and try to keep them out of our relationships and our decisions.

UNIQUE:

People are the total of all their past experiences. No one person has the same past experiences. Therefore, each person is a unique individual. This is important when you are analyzing any idea. Since people are unique, you can never know how they will react. You can make a decision and one person will not like it. Understanding human nature is an impossible task at best. Just do the best job you can. Remember that you are unique. No one will do a job exactly like you. You cannot copy the actions of another person. When you are supervising, don't change your complete personality. You will not be comfortable, and you will not do a good job. Try to improve as a supervisor, but don't try to be someone you aren't.

CHAIN OF COMMAND

In a small, one owner operation, there is not much need for an official chain of command. There is only a manager and one owner. However, as more people become involved, there might be a need for a written form to explain the chain of command.

An organization chart could be used with a pyramid type of command display. Consider putting the workers on the top and the top men at the bottom. Most charts start the other way with the big mogul on top and the tenants, our most valuable commodity, at the bottom.

Managers should know to whom they are to report. If a problem arises in this person's absence, the managers should have another person to call. The manager should know about the functions of central office personnel and where these people fit in the scheme of things. What authority do the clerks and bookkeepers have? The managers should know that maintenance men, leasing agents, suppliers and servicemen are placed under their control. Managers can and must supervise these people.

If a chain of command is drawn and understood, you will have less animosity between on-site personnel and office personnel. If people know that the managers are responsible for the tenants, office personnel and maintenance, people will know that they must go through the manager when dealing with tenants unless the situations have been cleared beforehand.

OVERSUPERVISING

Don't try to do too much. If you are a good planner, organizer and controller, you should not have to be too involved in daily details. Your employees will do a great job without your looking over their shoulders and you can use your time on more valuable projects.

In business you should be training a person as your replacement for when you move upward. If you are doing a fine job, you should have no worry about the employee working to take your job away. In sports, it is testimony to a coach's ability when his assistants are selected for other head coaching jobs. The same idea is true in business.

Some people feel that certain traits of a good manager (closing ability, human relations, common sense) cannot be taught no matter how great a supervisor you are. All we can hope for is recognition of those talents when they do appear. In many functions the ability to recognize talent and to utilize these gifts to the best degree is paramount to success.

MANAGEMENT "LAWS"

Parkinson's Law:
This law states, "Any job will expand to meet the size of the work force." This means that if you have a landscaping job and three regular men are too busy doing it, when you hire two additional men, all five will be busy. This same law is true of accounting, office and other functions. In my visits to property management offices I am surprised at the size of the staffs involved when I am told how many projects are handled. There are instances of dynasty building in large companies, but a management firm should try to hold overhead as low as possible. If you own the company, the size of the dynasty may be flattering to you, but that is your money you are wasting. Cut off deadwood and the work still gets out.

Peter Principle:
Dr. Laurence Peter of USC has a theory that every worker gets promoted to his level of incompetence and there he stays. To explain: A salesman does well in the field and is promoted to supervisor. He does well at supervision and after awhile he is promoted to regional director. Now, as a deskman in a regional office he does poorly. His talents were in eyeball-to-eyeball meetings. Since he is doing poorly, he does not get any more promotions and so there he sits. He has raised his standard of living to a point where he can't go back into the field, so he has to stay.

In another example, a bookkeeper is good and becomes an accountant. He is a good accountant and moves to supervisor. He is a good supervisor and moves to controller. There he fails and there he stays.

I recommend that you read Dr. Peter's books. They are thought provoking. If a person is a great manager and he or she is happy there, you don't have to shove them upstairs unless you believe that they will make a greater worker at a higher level. Use people where they are productive and happy. Conversely, if a person is happy and is a good carpenter or accountant, no one should force them into a higher position. My generation was the one that was competitive, goal-oriented and promotion hungry. Today's generation seems to have a better grasp of how to be happy even when they are not at the top of the heap.

Murphy's Law:
Paraphrased this law says that in any building anything that has to be done will take longer and cost more than you thought, and if anything *can* go wrong, it *will* and at the worst possible moment.

O'Toole's Law:
Says: "Murphy was an optimist."

Sense of Humor:
Have one!

WORRY

People are hindered more by worry than any other characteristic. People worry about the past, the present and the future. Worrying about the past can't change anything. Analyzing the past to benefit from the experience is productive, but what good did worry ever do?

There are so many things about which we worry that we can't change. For example, there is not too much we can do about the ultimate prospect of death. True, we can watch our diets, our health and our physical safety, etc. and help postpone death. But worrying about it is not going to achieve anything.

It is true that many of the subjects about which we worry never happen. To test your memory, try to remember what you were worried about twelve months ago. It is difficult to recall unless there were some major milestone problems. How about twelve years ago? We were all worrying then.

Normally, you worry about choosing one course of action over another. Doesn't it appear true after many years of looking back that those "critical" decisions were really not so "critical" after all? If a decision proved to be right, it doesn't necessarily mean the other decision would have been wrong. You will never know. Worrying about it isn't going to change it, and it is just about impossible to go back to that same spot and choose the other road.

WORRY HOUR

Worry time is lost time. I have one recommendation for you about worrying. Give yourself a "worry hour" one day a week. Let's say that it is Tuesday, at 8:00 p.m. Now, whenever anything comes to your mind to worry about, (business, building, tenant, employee, family, marriage, pollution, government, human nature, inflation, foreign affairs, athletics, etc.) write it down on a piece of paper. Save these papers until Tuesday. Once you write it down, you tell yourself to forget the subject until the "worry hour."

When the "worry hour" comes, you take your papers, go to a quiet place and worry. If anyone tries to interrupt, tell them to please wait, for you are worrying. At nine o'clock you are done for one week. You have gotten some good concentrated worrying out of the way. After a few months of this process, you will have a record of your worries. You can analyze them to see that worrying is really a waste of time.

PLAN OF ATTACK

One of the major times that worrying enters your mind is when you are in bed and not yet asleep. In the quiet dark your mind can just flit from worry to worry and very often the major topic of concern is all the things you have to do tomorrow. Before you go to bed, make a list of the projects that you have to do tomorrow. List them and grade them in importance. Assign them priorities by number. The list can include many more items than you can accomplish in a day.

The next day you start on item one and get it done and go on to two, etc. You are now working on the most important items. You know you are not going to finish them all so you don't "worry" about it. You are secure in the knowledge that you are working on the most important. What more can you do?

That evening you look at your unfinished list and make another list just before going to bed. Put your list aside and you will be surprised how much more rested your mind is and how much easier it is to go to sleep. Sometimes you will be fumbling for your pencil in the dark to write another item on the list after you have been lying there for awhile, or maybe even in the middle of the night. These scribblings are hard to decipher in the morning, but you will be resting better and you will be more organized the next day. I know some people who keep a tape recorder handy to get their ideas on tape when they awake in the middle of the night.

OLD PROVERBS

A grand old proverb says it best: "God grant me the Serenity to accept things I cannot change, Courage to change the things I can and Wisdom to know the difference."

Another proverb I have always liked says:

The six most important words are: I admit I made a mistake
The five most important words are: You did a good job.
The four most important words are: What is your opinion?
The three most important words are: If you please.
The two most important words are: Thank you.
The most important word is: We
The least important word is "I"

Chapter 14
Retention of the Good People

If we have a good tenant, we want to keep the person. It is much easier to keep a good tenant than to find a new good tenant. You must consider the importance of keeping good tenants.

Bad tenants have to be removed quickly, but the loss of any tenant costs money. Consider the possible cost of one turnover in an apartment renting for $1,200 a month. The existing resident had lived there three years. The carpeting and drapes will not need replacing, but they will need cleaning. A complete paint job is needed. It will take one week to get the work scheduled and completed. Another week is needed to rent the apartment. Our rental market is not exceptionally good and we have to wait two weeks for the new prospect to move into the building. The vacancy loss alone on the turnover is $1,200 and there will be some advertising costs. If the paint work had been done for the existing tenant, some of the work (inside cabinets and closets) might have been eliminated.

TURNOVER COSTS

Turnover involves extra work by building personnel. The showing and renting of the apartments and any move-in follow-up take time. These factors should be considered when a tenant requests some fix-up work. You have to know what the requester wants, what it will cost, how much of the request you can turn down, and at what point a tenant will move out. It is much easier to deal with the existing resident. You know that tenants request more than they hope to get. This is a very important game - "Ask and Let's See What We Receive." To be a successful manager or owner you have to learn how to play this game well. If you don't give the tenants enough, you will suffer through turnover expense and if you give the tenants too much, you will have a smaller cash flow and a lower building evaluation. The game is a combination of poker, monopoly and debating. Quick thinking, knowledge of real estate market and your building, confidence in yourself and your abilities, lack of emotion, sensitivity, empathy, etc. are good characteristics to have during the negotiation.

Don't be afraid to say "no" when a "no" is needed. It is not that hard. You don't have to argue, just maintain good eye contact and say that you are sorry, but the redecoration can't be done.

Another technique that can be used is to tell the resident that the work will be done, but that due to other projects it has to be scheduled for the month of April. Give them this promise in writing and they will probably wait and be happy. You might say, "My word is my bond," and the tenant might know this, "so I don't have to write it down." However, we both know that tenants have received many unkept promises from other owners so a written promise might keep them happy while an unwritten one won't.

If you decide to do something, do it quickly. Call the painter, carpet man or serviceman from their apartment. You will create a good image.

SIGN-UP TIME

A good policy of retention starts the minute the person decides to rent your apartment. Since we have selected only the good prospects, we must assume that the new tenant will be a good one. Show them immediately that your building is the greatest.

With them along, check the apartment thoroughly. Try the plumbing and mechanical items. It is easier to fix an item in a vacant apartment, and fixing the deficiencies before the moving date will make any tenant happy.

Every person has many needs. A tenant wants shelter at a reasonable price with no inconveniences. When a person's physical needs are met, the psychological needs come into play. Everyone likes to feel important. This can mean different things to different people. As a manager or owner you can illustrate that you want the tenant to remain and that you consider him more than just a rent check.

When the prospects have signed the application, give them an information sheet to help them move from their present address. The sheet would show what they must do to have utilities connected, a list of recommended moving companies, the number of the telephone company, newspaper delivery information, recommendations on the easiest way to move items into the apartment, location of dollies or other moving aids, any rules of the building about move-ins (elevator pads to be used), the exact mailing address of the building, location and information on local schools, etc. Ask the tenant to let you know the estimated time of their arrival on moving day so you can plan to be available.

MOVE-IN DAY

Someone from the management staff should be present when the tenant starts their move-in. There are sure to be many questions. As a small-added feature, you could place toilet, paper cups, light bulbs and other small items in the apartment. One building uses prestigious keys and gives them to the tenant in a decorative box. It is an elegant building and the keys to the building give an elegant impression.

A gift to celebrate move-in day is given by many owners. There is a wide range of possibilities. A bottle of wine or champagne, flowers, a plant, candy for their children, or even some food for the first evening in the apartment would be appreciated. One owner has a catered meal brought into the apartment, and another gives the new tenant a gift certificate to eat that night at a nearby restaurant.

It would not take too much work to design a "Welcome Wagon" type book for the new arrivals. You visit the different retailers in your area and request a gift or discount to be given to your new tenants. A booklet showing all the items is given to the tenant. Each retailer furnishes a letter explaining his or her services and outlining the gift available to the new resident. Retailers who will cooperate include restaurants, department stores, gas stations, fast food franchises, dry cleaners, hair salons, specialty stores, theaters, and other people with items to sell or services to provide. It is an inexpensive method for these vendors to get a message to the new people in the area. The tenants profit by receiving some gifts of appreciation for their patronage.

RESIDENTS' HANDBOOK

The new tenant should be given a Resident's Handbook when they move in. This booklet would include:

1. Their rental agreement or lease.

2. Copy of the house rules.

3. Copy of maintenance service request and instructions on how to use it.

4. Instructions on use of the appliances in the apartment.

5. List of all the important phone numbers for your area - police, fire, ambulance, manager.

6. List of any items of information - schools, churches, businesses, newspapers, retailers, banks, savings and loans, auto repair.

CARDS OR LETTERS

Periodically, a card or letter could be sent to a tenant on a special occasion. This might be on a birthday, wedding, anniversary, graduation, addition to family, sickness or death, or after some award like a child gaining recognition, business promotion, etc. Another good time to send a card is on the yearly anniversary of the move-in date. This card can thank them for their cooperation and consideration during their tenancy.

GIFTS

We have gotten good results in achieving a solid relationship with tenants by giving small gifts at appropriate times. These appropriate times might be at the holiday seasons, New Years, move-in anniversary, wedding anniversary, children's birthday, or after a building has become fully rented. Some of the gifts were bottles of wine or champagne, candy, plants, a party, children's candy, gift certificates, etc.

DEPOSITS

One of the major complaints from "good " tenants is that the "greedy" owners have their security deposits and are earning interest on this amount. Several states have now ruled that owners must pay interest on these deposits to the tenants.

There are a couple of ways to eliminate this gripe and achieve a better spirit of cooperation in your building. First, you can explain to the tenant that by law now (at least in California) the deposit must be retained only for damage to the unit and has to be returned within 21 days after move out. To show good faith you could pay the tenant the interest on the money once a year. On a $1,200 amount that would be $24 at 2% interest. Technically, it is the tenant's money and this small payment might impress them. You could return the money to the tenants after a year or so, but this would leave you open to some damage loss. The payment of interest would stop tenants' complaining.

There are many companies that will give a security deposit bond to an owner. The tenant pays a fee to the company, and the company gives a "bond" to the owner. The tenant might have to pay $30-$40 one time, but he knows that he won't be fighting for the return of his money after move out. The owner is happy for he does not have to do all the deposit accounting in and out, and he knows that the tenant will not demand that his security deposit be considered his last month of rent.

AFTER A MOVEOUT NOTICE

Retention of good tenants is important. If a good tenant fills out a notice of moving, a representative from your company, not involved in the normal routine of operation, could call them. In a one owner, one manager operation, this call will be made after the manager has asked the reason for the move out and tried to settle any problems. The objective of this call is to see if any action can be taken to convince the person not to move. A little interest shown at this time might lower your turnover expense. Anytime a manager gets an unexpected move-out notice, quick action must be taken to see if the tenant can be convinced to stay.

POSSIBLE AMENITIES TO BE ADDED

Some small buildings do not have the resources, the space or the need to give many amenities to their tenants. Several of the amenities listed here have been mentioned before. As a helpful reminder, I have listed them again here.

- Mail service
- Porter service
- Manned guard gate
- Telephone message service
- Car wash area or service
- Doorman
- Check cashing
- Secretarial or notary service
- Valet parking
- Newsletter
- Travel Service
- Youth center
- Toddlers' program/pre-school operation
- Laundry area
  a. free service
  b. carpeted and paneled

    c.   individual lockers

    d.   free supplies

- Dry cleaning and laundry service
- Closed-circuit TV scanner
- Tennis lessons
- Vending machines or small store in bigger buildings
- Interior design service
- Linens and dishes
- Hair salon
- Exercise room
- Masseur
- Jacuzzi, steam room
- Bike or boat rental
- Tennis courts
- Indoor golf range
- Swimming pool
- Exercise classes and self-defense classes
- Sports outings
- Sports clubs
- Billiards
- Athletic tournaments
- Bridge and backgammon classes and play
- Mixed parties
- Feature films
- Classes on any subject (at the building)
- Bingo
- Parties
- Photo lab or hobby shop
- Banquet room for use by tenants/catering consultant
- Expensive shower heads
- Free car starting service (heavy duty battery and jumper cable)
- Vacuum sweepers, floor scrubbers, rug shampooers available
- Babysitting list
- Closed circuit TV service for films and special programs
- Gardening space
- Extra garage space for rent
- Rollaway beds for guests
- Vacant apartments for guests
- Wall paneled, mirrored or wallpapered
- Picture postcards of building
- Use of color in apartments
- Secure bicycle and motorcycle racks
- Self-defrosting refrigerators
- Silent light switches
- Air conditioning
- Dishwashers (could be portable)
- Garbage compactors
- Ranges with self-cleaning ovens

- Fireplaces (new non-wood burning available for easy insertion)
- Vinyl tile or ceramic tile for richer look
- New lighting fixtures
- Silent bathroom fixtures
- Richer carpeting
- Up-graded drapes
- Blackout drapes (drapes hung between regular drapes and window-keep out heat, cold and light and save wear on drapes. Loved by tenants, not expensive)
- Larger storage areas
- Individual washers and dryers
- Outdoor gas barbecues
- Picnic area
- Soft water service
- Lifeguard service
- Children's supervisor
- Fitted bedspreads in furnished apartments
- Loan of appliances
- Coin hair dryers
- Rental TV's
- Furnished apartments (Pictures on wall, plants, etc.)
- In hard times, anything for which a tenant will pay more than it costs to provide

PROPERTY MANAGEMENT SUCCESS PRACTICE QUESTIONS:

True or False?

CHAPTER 1

1. President Grover Cleveland recommended real estate investing.

2. Tax benefits of real estate should not be considered.

3. Duane Gomer recommends apartment house investments.

4. Real estate investments have few problems.

CHAPTER 2

5. A job description is an important first step in personnel selection.

6. Preparing a job profile is a waste of time.

7. You should determine the characteristics you consider important .

8. In a manager search you should never consider present tenants.

9. Interviewing and making a personnel selection is an important job.

10. References do not need to be checked.

11. You should complete a contract with your manager.

12. Rules of thumb on compensation are easy to follow.

13. Minimum wage laws must be followed.

14. Bonuses are not recommended for apartment managers.

15. Job descriptions should cover many possible situations.

16. Paying managers on an hourly basis is against wage laws.

CHAPTER 3

17. A rental policy letter is an important first step in management.

18. Discrimination should not be discussed in a policy letter.

19. Terms of rentals and deposits should be set in the policy letter.

20. It is illegal to set a minimum income requirement for your building.

21. Amenities should be considered to help increase rent.

22. Rental surveys are not recommended when setting prices.

23. Decisions on rents are always subject to change.

CHAPTER 4

24. Pirating or recruiting tenants from other buildings is illegal.

25. Present tenants can be a great source of new tenants.

26. Motels are never a source or tenants.

27. Local papers are more apt to be read by rental prospects.

28. In hard times concessions should not be used.

29. The first objective of advertising is to get the reader's attention.

CHAPTER 5

30. It is best to wait to do painting until a prospect makes a deposit.

31. A preparation checklist should be prepared for each vacancy.

32. A manager has no responsibility for the property condition.

33. A manager's appearance is of paramount importance.

CHAPTER 6

34. The main function of the first phone call is to get a time to move in.

35. Phone calls can be the lifeline of many projects.

CHAPTER 7

36. Prospects should be allowed to view units for about two hours a day.

37. Managers begin to really earn their salary when they are showing & renting.

38. Talking is more important than listening in the selling process.

39. Freedom from yard work is a benefit of an apartment dweller.

CHAPTER 8

40. Managers should work as order takers.

41. When would you like to move in, is an order blank close.

42. Silence is not a good tactic for a manager.

43. Closing a prospect can be done anywhere.

44. A waiting list when you have no vacancies, should not be used.

45. Don't let prospects leave without something in their hand.

CHAPTER 9

46. Previous landlords should not be called for tenant's background information.

47. Be careful of people who have to move in immediately.

48. Mail or an email would not be a better way to give a "refusal to rent".

CHAPTER 10

49. The rental agreement is a most important document in management.

50. Pets should never be allowed under any condition.

51. Many times problems can be abated if there are good building rules.

52. Parking spaces should not be assigned.

53. Violations of swimming pool rules could be a cause for eviction.

54. It is not necessary to get the tenants to sign a copy of the house rules.

CHAPTER 11

55. Simple principles should be followed in establishing accounting procedures.

56. Rental bills should be sent monthly to all tenants.

57. A "No Cash" rule is desirable to avoid embezzling or burglary.

58. All managers despise making bank deposits for the building.

59. Third party checks can be a real problem.

60. All buildings should collect all rents on the first of the month.

61. Allowing the manger to have a petty fund could be desirable.

62. Purchase orders should be used only on very small projects.

CHAPTER 12

63. A step to avoid non- paying tenants is a good qualification step.

64. Shutting off utilities to remove a tenant is legal and recommended.

65. Many tenants know eviction law better than owners.

66. Tenants should always be allowed to be at least 15 days late.

67. Promises to pay rent when late should be put in writing.

68. The three day Notice to Quit must be delivered in person.

69. When you win your "Trial", you get a judgment.

70. It is illegal to offer a tenant money to move out faster.

71. Be careful of using any illegal means to force a tenant to move.

CHAPTER 13

72. Short term unwritten flexible goals are best.

73. The Latin word for supervision translates to "oversee".

74. Plans are not necessary to achieve goals.

75. A manager's contract is a type of directive.

76. All forms must be comprehensive and complicated.

77. A simple form to list comments and needed follow up could be extremely helpful.

78. Managers should be given responsibility but not authority.

79. A questioning approach with managers could get them more involved.

80. Good managers should call owners often.

81. Owners should call the manager regularly.

82. You should not leave tenant information on a message service.

83. Managers should be given periodic evaluations.

84. You should never use shoppers or testers to check on managers.

85. Managers should keep their personal beliefs to themselves.

86. Personal problems of a manger are not the concern of the owner.

87. Good words for supervisors and owners to live by are empathy and integrity.

88. Parkinson Law doesn't apply to apartment projects.

89. Worry time is lost time.

90. The most important word in management is "I".

CHAPTER 14

91. Turnover cost is expensive to an owner.

92. Gifts to tenants are not good business

93. Adding amenities could help retain good tenants.

94. Tenants must be paid interest on security deposits in all cases.

Practice Questions designed to prepare you to pass the final exams are available. New BRE Regulations do not allow us to give the answers to the quizzes in the book so the questions and answers are presented online. This makes the test taking very easy as you get the answers immediately.

To access the practice quizzes please visit http://www.DuaneGomer.com/after . Check on the proper link for the course you desire.

NOTE: Do not use Google, Yahoo, Bing etc. They are Search Engines. You must put the above URL link in your address bar or you won't get there.

You may request the questions by email to info@DuaneGomer.com, fax at 949-455-9931, or phone 800-439-4909. You will receive only the practice questions. You may FAX back your answers to Duane Gomer, Inc., at (949) 455-9931 and we will FAX your results to you within 24 business hours. Our recommendation is find a computer even if it's a friend or relatives it makes everything so easy under the new BRE rules.
t

MAKE MONEY IN CALIFORNIA FORECLOSURES

Chapter 1
Introduction

One question many people ask me about today's market is, "Is it possible to make money in foreclosures?" We have seen many experts giving programs in the foreclosure field and exciting the public about the possibilities in foreclosures. These seminars have been publicized in the newspapers, radio and television. Some seminars have attracted crowds of 10,000 or more. With this type of interest, you might think that it is impossible to still make any money in the foreclosure market. But this is not true.

It is my opinion that it will be possible to make money in the foreclosure field for many years to come. There will always be foreclosures because they are caused by many factors. Even in a good economy, there are foreclosures.

What causes foreclosures? The biggest causes are the 3 D's: divorce, drugs and death. People get divorced or separated. When they are forced to pay for two households, it becomes impossible to maintain their debt, and they lose their property. Alcohol and cocaine are frequently the drugs used today. These dangerous drugs cause many financial problems, and foreclosures are often the result. The death of a spouse or a loved one can disrupt financial planning, so there will always be foreclosures.

BANKRUPTCIES TODAY

In today's market, another word has become important. The word is "bankruptcy." The laws of the United States make it easy to file bankruptcy. This has caused many people to simply walk away from their properties. Bankruptcy is so common that people are talking about Chapter 11s, Chapter 13s and Chapter 7s.

The ease of credit has also caused many foreclosures. People can borrow on anything. Credit card companies are sending credit cards out to anyone. One person I spoke to received six credit card applications in one day, each with a $5,000 limit. He returned all of the applications and got six new credit cards. Although he was in financial trouble at the time, the next day he went out and borrowed $30,000 on the credit cards and bought a property.

A few years ago I read an advertisement for a book, which said, "Get $200,000 in one day with no trouble." So I mailed away for it. I received a small report that said, "Apply for 20 credit cards one day and then keep applying for 20 credit cards every day with a $2,000 limit on each credit card. After five days, you will have one hundred new credit cards. You could then borrow $200,000 in one day."

Another thing that has happened in today's economy is that many families have two members working, even though there are still young children at home. This is a change from the past, when there was usually only one wage earner. If the one wage earner became ill or incapacitated, the loss of income would cause a credit crunch. There could be a foreclosure, trustee sale or bankruptcy problem.

Today, there are many two-wage earner families and if either person becomes ill or unemployed, a credit crunch and financial problems will result. The possibilities of money problems in a family unit have doubled.

In addition, a higher percentage of a family's earnings today will be going toward maintaining a home. When I first started in real estate, the normal situation was that approximately 25% of earnings went for housing costs. Today, this percentage is higher. Families have burdened themselves with mortgage payments or credit payments that take up to 50% of both working partners' income. With this higher percentage, financial problems of any type can cause a foreclosure.

TOO MANY "EXPERT" CLASSES

Another factor that has caused foreclosures is the proliferation of many real estate classes discussed earlier. Many of the classes have stressed "nothing-down financing", "cash-to-buyer financing", or many of the other creative or alternative methods of financing.

There is an expression that has become common in real estate: "negative cash flow." There are ways to stop negative cash flow, but sooner or later, if you buy property and it's overvalued, you're going to have a lot of problems. This is what has happened with many of these nothing-down or cash-to-buyer people. Without experience, they have found that the real world is tougher than the seminar world. When negative cash flow meets low experience investors, foreclosures have resulted.

Another expression that has come into the American vocabulary is, "balloon payment." When balloon payments come due, some owners can't find the money to pay them. In the last decade, a lot of people felt there was no problem with balloon payments. You could buy a house worth $100,000 and guarantee that you would pay a balloon payment of $30,000 in three years. It was hoped or expected that the property would increase in value and in three years you would be able to refinance.

In some areas of the country, housing prices have flattened. Prices have not increased at the volatile rates of the past, and as a result, one of the major problems has been that the balloon payments could not be paid. Many of the foreclosures are "installment type" foreclosures where the homeowner has gotten behind on their monthly payment. Lately, more and more of the foreclosures are called "balloon foreclosures." In these cases the whole note is due, and the people have not been able to pay this balloon, so the lenders have had to foreclose.

Many owners have Adjustable Rate Mortgages with low beginning payments and a small down payment. When the payments increase after a few years, owners can't keep up.

ONE-SECOND REVIEW

As mentioned earlier, foreclosures are caused in today's market by divorce (and divorce is increasing at an extremely high rate), drugs and the death of spouses or loved ones. The ease of bankruptcy has caused an additional amount of foreclosures, as has the ease of getting credit. Moreover, two members in many families are working and a higher percentage of the couples' monthly income is going toward housing costs. Furthermore, the nothing-down classes and the cash-to-buyer classes are causing problems, as is the flat inflation. There will still be a chance to make money in foreclosures. That is why you should continue to get more education, to read, listen and go out and work in the field to acquire knowledge. When your opportunity does arrive, you will be ready with the needed knowledge. It is too late to become educated when opportunity is knocking at your door.

THIS IS A CALIFORNIA BOOK

In looking at the other books available in the field, I noticed that there was a problem. They were "generic books." The books were written so that they could be sold all over the United States. The rules on foreclosures are different in each state. That is the reason this book is called, "Make Money in California Foreclosures."

This book has been designed specifically for people in the State of California. All of the rules and laws that will be discussed will cover California foreclosures. California foreclosures are governed by the California Civil Code, and if you become an expert in this one code, you can be an expert in California foreclosures.

California is a trust deed state. Almost all of the notes that are used to purchase real estate are secured by trust deeds, not mortgages. Mortgages are used in many other states, but not in California.

In a mortgage there are two parties, the mortgagor and the mortgagee. If there is a problem with nonpayment, the only action available to the mortgagee, the holder of the note, is to go through a judicial foreclosure. In many states, this takes an extremely long period of time because you must go to a court, and a judge must hear the case.

In California, if you have a mortgage or if you have a trust deed, you can judiciously foreclose on it by going to court. The time frames are very long. A judicial foreclosure normally takes over one year. Then, the owner has a one-year right of redemption: that is, they have one year after the court action to redeem the property. This makes a total of over two years from the time that the action is started until the lender can get the property back. During the one-year period of redemption, the owner of the property can continue to live in the property and will pay a rent determined by the judge.

Because of these problems, almost all of the notes in California are foreclosed by the use of a trust deed sale. A trust deed sale, which is commonly referred to as foreclosure, is in essence a nonjudicial foreclosure. You do not go to court. A trustee holds the sale.

There are three parties to a trust deed. One party is the trustor, the owner of the real estate. The lender is called the beneficiary, and the third party is called the trustee. The trustee holds title to the property until the beneficiary has been paid off, or a Trustee Sales is held.

This system is comparable to a person holding a pink slip on an automobile until the loan is completely paid off. California is a trust deed state and has had many court cases and judicial decisions. California foreclosures are a field unto themselves. That is why this book has been written specifically for California foreclosures.

EVERYONE CAN'T MAKE MONEY

You hear statements by different experts claiming that anyone can become a millionaire in 20 minutes. I have a different opinion. There are many people who cannot make money in the foreclosure market or in any type of investment market. There are some people who are just not capable. Now, this may be a small percentage, but there are certain people who will always be thinking of becoming rich instead of doing anything about it. They have a tremendous desire to be rich, but they do not have the ability.

What qualities do you need? Some people are too lazy. They just do not have the initiative to get out and do the work. There is some work involved. You have to have some ability and a desire to work.

Other people will never get started. They are "seminar junkies." They keep going to seminar after seminar. If they are without a seminar or a cassette tape for more than two weeks, they get withdrawal pains. They have to be buoyed up. They are getting more and more prepared. They have terrific files on what they are going to do. They have set their goals. They are ready. They just never take that first step.

To make money, you have to do some reading and listening. If a person lacks intelligence or can't read, I think that they will have problems trying to do anything.

One serious problem some people have is a negative attitude. Their attitude is so pessimistic that they think nothing can ever be done. If you go through life thinking that everything is going to turn out wrong, the chances are that everything will turn out wrong. In real estate particularly, there are many times when you will have emotional ups and downs and if you have the wrong attitude, you will be handicapped. You have to be optimistic. Some recent government studies verified that optimistic people even live longer than pessimists.

In addition, it's very important to have proper peer groups. You should associate with people who are optimistic, intelligent, ambitious and motivated. Being associated with failures has ruined many people. If you want to be a success, you have to be around people who are successful. If you are in a negative group, it will be difficult for you to have an optimistic outlook about investment real estate.

Another thing people lack is confidence. You're going to need self-confidence because you have to make many important decisions. This is not just deciding when to buy or when to sell. These obviously are important decisions, but you will make many decisions on which tenant to pick out of five. If you pick the wrong one, it could cause tremendous problems. You will have many decisions to make on whether to fix-up, repair or replace. If you lack confidence, this will be reflected in your decisions.

Some people have had a problem about deciding when to sell. Real estate is not a real liquid situation, but if you price it properly, it will sell. The decision of when to sell often determines whether or not the entire project will be successful.

In summary, almost anyone can make money in the field of real estate. If you have a bad attitude, if you are lazy, if you're associating with a bunch of losers, or if you lack confidence, you may have problems.

How important is money? Money is helpful, but many people have made money in real estate investments without having any finances at all. It is possible. Some of the stories that you hear about people making tremendous amounts of money are true. Many of them are not true. In fact, many of the so-called experts have had bankruptcies in their lives. It is not all sweetness and light. Nevertheless, many people have made money in this field.

WHAT DOES IT TAKE?

What does it take? It takes some education. You have to acquire knowledge from some place. You can acquire this knowledge by going to meetings, talking to experts, reading, or using any other method. You have to get some basic background information before you go rushing into the field.

You must have some desire. There has to be some motivation and a competitive nature. You have to want this badly. If you do not want the rewards enough, it will be very hard to put up with many of the problems that occur as you start out.

You have to be willing to work. James Downs, a famous real estate economist from Chicago, has a term that he uses – "sweat equity". It is his belief that a lot of money that will be made in the next few years will not be the so-called "steals." It will be made by using your own sweat, buying a property at wholesale, fixing it up, and putting it back on the market or renting it.

Another thing that you must have is confidence and courage. If you do not have the courage to get started, you will not ever have the courage to make it big. Courage and confidence are very important for you to get started in this field.

MANY RETURNS IN REAL ESTATE

Why should anyone want to go into real estate? There are many reasons. One of the biggest is financial freedom. If you can become successful in real estate, it is possible to become free from debt and to live off your investments. This is one of the most important desires for people who are investing in real estate of any type. One of the other returns that you get is cash flow when your properties are purchased wisely and managed properly.

You can get the benefit of capital gains. If you buy a property and it increases in value, you can sell it later. Real estate is one of the investments that is inflation proof. That means that real estate does move up with the inflation spiral better than most investments.

Let's say you lived in a city and you owned more real estate than anyone else in that city. You would hope that the inflationary spiral would be very high, because this would give you more return than anybody else. If you own an extremely large amount of real estate, you are not completely dismayed when the inflationary spiral does start to climb because you profit. You will be amazed that in many areas of the world, prices are even rising faster and higher than in California.

Another of the reasons for buying real estate is tax benefits. Tax benefits accrue when you own real estate. You can depreciate a property and write off from your normal income amounts that really are not a loss but a loss only on paper. By using these write-offs, your normal income taxes will be lowered. The years of life of rental buildings have been increased which lowered depreciation rates, but real estate still has great tax advantages. Check with your accountant.

There are talks of reform, tax changes, and new tax bills, but no one has ever attacked the sanctity of investing in real estate for a tax reason. Improved real estate has substantial benefits and if you are paying too much in income taxes, you should be investigating this portion of the real estate investment market closely.

One of the other advantages of owning real estate is "psychological return." Owning real estate can make you feel confident about yourself, secure and confident about your future. It is an extremely good way to achieve financial independence and is becoming more and more popular because of the two main benefits of owning real estate.

1. The possibility of getting an increase in value if there is inflation.
2. The possibility of realizing cash flow in a normal market.

BACKGROUND OF THE AUTHOR

Some of you might be wondering about my background. If you're going to be reading my ideas, it is important that you understand how these ideas were acquired.

I'm originally from Wisconsin and earned a Bachelor of Science degree from Indiana University. After graduation I received a teaching assistantship appointment in the field of management at UCLA. I became a teaching instructor and received my Masters of Business Administration degree from UCLA. I went into the Navy as an Ensign and attended some Navy postgraduate accounting schools.

My one tour of duty was at the Rhine River Patrol in Germany. I spent two years as the Accounting and Assistant Supply Officer of the Rhine River Patrol until it was closed and returned to the Germans. At that time I was discharged from the Navy and stayed on one year in Germany as Director of Athletics for the 17th Air Force, traveling around Europe running athletic events for the military bases. I stayed another two years as director of Data Processing for the PX Services in Europe. Then I was promoted to their worldwide headquarters in New York City.

I had been teaching management and accounting classes for the University of Maryland in Europe and had saved some money. I read a book by a man named William Nickerson, "How I Turned One Hundred Dollars Into a Million in Real Estate in My Spare Time." This was in the early 60s. The book was the first of a long series of self-help books in the real estate field. In my opinion, it is still the best book on the subject. I read it and was excited. I went back to Wisconsin on a leave of absence, where I purchased four small investment properties in Milwaukee.

While in New York City, I decided to move back to California. I became Director of Property Management for the Forest Olson Company. Later, I started my own company, doing property management and syndication of real estate. To increase my credibility and for publicity, I began writing a weekly column in a Van Nuys newspaper and became an instructor in the UCLA Extension Program. My property management business grew until we were managing approximately 3,700 units. At the same time I became a general partner in many investment groups.

Later, I started doing real estate seminars full time in California. I have a seminar company that has had more than 300,000 students during the past 27+ years. We have become one of the largest companies in California giving live seminars to real estate licensees, investors, managers, notaries, attorneys, accountants, lenders, etc. in the State of California.

MY FORECLOSURE BACKGROUND

California had a tremendous amount of foreclosures in rental properties during my management career. Since I was a Certified Property Manager, some attorneys came to me and asked if I would be a court-appointed receiver for their lenders when the lenders foreclosed on different properties. If a lender foreclosed on a property that was rented during the foreclosure period the person who owned the property would collect all the rents and not pay the lenders. The lenders wanted a receiver appointed to handle the property during this period of the foreclosure. I did hundreds of foreclosures in the counties of Kern, Los Angeles, Ventura, Santa Barbara, San Bernardino and Orange.

What I would do was take over the property, pay the bills and collect all of the rents. When the foreclosure ended, the court would rule that my period of watching the building was over. I would go to the court and make an accounting of the money that I had collected. The judge or commissioner would tell me to whom to pay the money I had acquired and set my fee.

It was an extremely lucrative field because there were foreclosures on many rental properties. The rents were high, and the fees were high. Fortunately, I got to work with many of the better legal firms in Southern California and acquired a thorough background in foreclosure procedures from the perspective of the lenders.

SEMINAR BACKGROUND

While conducting real estate seminars, I have faced many crowds. In many of these crowds there have been attorneys, CPAs, trustees, lenders, presidents of Savings and Loans, as well as investors, and with all these people listening to me over the years, I have learned a great deal. Hundreds of great ideas came from the people who have attended my seminars, and are passed on to you in this book.

The ideas presented have been criticized, critiqued and corrected so that I am confident that these ideas are current and valuable. Because this seminar has been presented so many times, we have learned many of the important things that should be covered.

Most of our courses have been approved by the State of California for presentation to real estate brokers for their Continuing Education credit. The courses are at a higher level than many of the beginning investor seminars. We do think that beginners and experienced investors both should read the laws and regulations that will be discussed in this book.

This book is a transcript of the seminars that we have presented. It will be an informative, conversational-type of presentation. If after reading this book you have any questions or comments, please write to us and we'll be happy to answer any of your queries that do not constitute unauthorized practice of law. When you become an investor, legal and accounting fees will be one of your most important expenditures. You need legal and tax advise for your individual circumstances. I have studied many years and I'm still learning but I know one thing for sure, you should find good advisors.

THE FIELD IS NOT ALL SWEETNESS AND LIGHT

There is another thing that I'd like to clear up right from the start. Real estate has been good to me. I have bought property from REOs and in foreclosure. I have put together syndications, and, without any of my own money, have controlled large projects. I do not want to give anyone the idea, however, that everything I ever did turned out perfectly. I have made many, many errors in the real estate field. But I believe that the errors I have made are helpful to you because I will counsel you. Thus, you will not make the same errors that I did. I am dismayed many times by people who try to insinuate that they have always been perfect in every endeavor and know everything there is to know.

Chapter 2
Laws and Regulations

How will I present this book on foreclosures? I believe it is very important for anyone considering the foreclosure field to know foreclosure law fully. In addition, I will give you myriad pieces of other information. After you have learned about the laws and the forms, then I will illustrate a step-by-step approach to be used to investigate foreclosures in different areas. I recommend that you pick one area of specialization and become an expert in that area, rather than trying to branch out into every area of foreclosure at once.

Knowledge in the foreclosure business is important. For example, in California, you could buy a house from an equity seller as an investment and if you did not give the equity seller a five-day cancellation right, you would be committing a felony. If you were buying the home to live in, and you did exactly the same thing, no five-day cancellation right is needed. If you did not know the law and the procedures at a trustee sale, you could buy a property and learn there is another trustee sale scheduled in three days by a senior lender. You have to know how to check these items so you aren't penalized due to of lack of knowledge.

You might spend a lot of time investigating a property. You look at the property, investigate it, visit neighbors, check prices and estimate renovation costs. You try to buy the property from the owner or at a trustee sale only to discover a bankruptcy has been filed. The bankruptcy has stopped all legal action and you have been wasting your time. A simple phone call to the right party at the beginning would have saved you time and money.

YOU HAVE TO KNOW THE LAW

You have to understand you must know the laws first. As you are reading these laws, remember there are many different areas in which you can function. For example, you could buy from the trustor before the Notice of Default is filed when they are having trouble with their payments. You could buy from a trustor after a Notice of Default is filed. You could buy from a trustor after a Notice of Sale has been published.

You could buy from a junior lien holder. You could buy from the beneficiary who is foreclosing before the sale subject to them acquiring title. You could buy at the Trustee Sale. You could buy from the beneficiary who is foreclosing after the sale. The beneficiaries could be private parties, institution, the VA or FHA.

When institutional lenders take a property back, it is put into their Real Estate Owned Department. That is an expression you'll hear many times in the foreclosure industry. Buying REO's is another way to secure reasonably priced properties.

MANY DIFFERENT WAYS

There are different ways of buying property from a trustor. You could buy the property from a trustor and rent it back to them on a sale-and-lease-back arrangement. You could lend a trustor money and let them pay off the money owed. You'd have a note against the property. You would become a lender on the property and make a substantial cash return because of the risk involved.

There are many different ways you can buy in all these areas, but first you must know the rules. Remember as you are reading, there is not just one way to succeed, there are many. According to your status, your time, your money, your experience, your education and your goals, you should pick one of these ways.

You might say, "As I am reading these laws, I'm really learning more than I need to know." I think you need to know more than you will ever imagine. You need to know more than the other person in the negotiation process. California regulations are different from other states and you should know them. You should throw away a lot of your presumptions and your assumptions of what the laws are. Don't think that what is fair is going to be the law. The law in many of these cases is not fair, often not reasonable, and in most cases, not simple. Furthermore, the law changes all the time.

EVERYTHING STARTS WITH THE LOAN

The California Foreclosure process starts when somebody borrows money against any property. When they borrow this money, they sign a promissory note. This note states that somebody borrowed money, agreed to pay a certain interest and to pay it back at a certain time.

In California mortgages are not used. A trust deed is prepared. The note is secured by a deed of trust that will be recorded in the county in which the property is situated. The lender is the beneficiary. The borrower is the trustor and there is a third party, the trustee. Remember this terminology. Earlier it was mentioned that the biggest reason Trust Deeds are used in California is the speed of the Non-Judicial Foreclosure Trustee Sale. If everything moved smoothly with no problems, a Trustee Sale could be held in about four months. There is a three month Notice Period and then there is a required twenty-one day advertising period.

Lenders want to have this speedy no-court involved method of foreclosing. When the lenders received this benefit, they did give up aspects of foreclosure. If a lender uses the Trustee Sale Auction method, they cannot get a Judgment Deficiency against the owner. They can only take the property.

In my experience I have never seen a Judicial Foreclosure used on a home to get a judgment against the owner. The public is not aware of this facet of the Trustee Sale. In simple terms "They can't come after your other assets."

Technically, the beneficiary picks the third party trustee. In most cases in California it is the escrow officer who prepares the trust deeds who names the trustee. Most people do not know who the trustees are on their own notes. Most of the people reading this book do not know the trustees on many of their properties. Trustees are not important until something goes wrong. If something goes wrong, the beneficiary will notify the trustee there has been a late payment or some other problem has arisen. The trustee will start the trustee sale action by filing a Notice of Default. If nothing goes wrong and a loan is paid off, the trustee will transfer title back to the trustor. This is accomplished by the use of a Deed of Reconveyance.

THE BENEFICIARY AND A TRUSTEE

It might be good to discuss this trustee situation from the beneficiary standpoint. The beneficiary can substitute trustees at any time. There might be several reasons for doing this. The trustee may be conservative or an expensive trustee and the beneficiary could save money by appointing a different trustee. In many areas private escrow companies are used. Many of the people who work with the private escrow companies find out they are often easier to work with than conservative institutions. This could be a reason for substituting a trustee.

A Beneficiary might lose a note that is the cause of the action. If the note is lost and you go to a conservative trustee, you might have to post a bond before there could be any reconveyance. With another trustee you could substitute your attorney as trustee or even yourself. It is possible to be your own trustee. Sometimes functioning as your own trustee is to your advantage. You should really know what you're doing before you attempt this action. It is my recommendation that the beneficiary considers substituting trustees but use someone who's experienced. An inexperienced trustee could cause serious problems.

WHAT'S A TRUST DEED

The trust deed names the trustor, the beneficiary, and the trustee. The trust deed makes a statement that this instrument is for the purpose of securing a note. On the front page of the trust deed there is a list of the different counties in the State of California. Fictitious trust deeds have been filed in every county and the book and page reference of where the trust deed is filed in that county is given on the front page. When this trust deed is noted as a reference on your trust deed, the provision of the fictitious trust deed will pertain to the trust deed in question.

There are other parts of the trust deed worth discussing. Most are standard. For example, owners must keep their property in good repair. If they don't, they are violating the contract. If the owner is neglecting the property, the beneficiary could start an action to have a Notice of Default filed and start a trustee sale. In California, owners must cultivate, irrigate, fertilize, fumigate, prune and do other acts that may be reasonable and necessary. Owners must maintain fire insurance. Another provision states that owners have to defend any action or proceedings that could affect the beneficiary's interest. The owner agrees to pay all taxes and assessments on the property. If the trustor fails to make any of these payments, the beneficiary could start a trustee sale.

Trustors must pay immediately all sums expended by the beneficiary, with interest, and if there are any awards or damage in connection with any condemnation for public use, the beneficiary will be paid first. Another provision is that the beneficiary can accept a late payment but this acceptance doesn't waive any rights. Also, the beneficiary can reconvey certain parts.

Another provision allows the beneficiary to order the trustee to reconvey, while another gives the beneficiary rights to rents, issues, and profits of property. This is commonly called an "Assignment of Rents". The beneficiary has the right to request any rents be paid to the beneficiary if there is any default under the note. This is an important clause if there is rental housing, commercial property or industrial property involved.

There is another clause that gives the trustee the right to hold a trustee sale if all the costs are not paid. You should check your own trust deeds because there are some variations between the trust deeds on different properties. When you are examining a property to see if you should purchase it, one of the things you should check is the trust deed filed for that property. There could be major problems. The trust deed has been recorded in the county in which the property is situated. If you contact the county recorder's office, you can get a copy and read it at your convenience.

LATE PAYMENTS CAUSE PROBLEMS

The most common problem that leads to a Notice of Default being filed involves note payments. Either the trustor is late or the trustor fails to come up with the entire amount due.

The first type of late payment is called an installment type of payment. This means a payment on the loan is late, and the beneficiary has started an action. The second type of foreclosure starts when the entire amount is not paid when due. This is called a balloon foreclosure. In an installment type of foreclosure, there is a certain period of time during which you can bring the note current.

Some notices of default are filed one day after a payment is due, and some have not been filed for years after the payment was late. This late time can vary greatly. The person who makes the decisions as to how long this late period will be is the beneficiary who has to notify the trustee that payments are late.

DECLARATION BY THE BENEFICIARY

The first step in this Notice of Default process is a Declaration by the Beneficiary to the Trustee that there is a problem. Most of the time the problem is nonpayment of money, but it could also be for nonpayment of a senior loan on the property, property taxes, or insurance. It could be the property has been wasted (neglected), the due date of the loan has arrived, or it could be there is a Due on Sale Clause that has been activated. If the property is sold, the due date on the note that is secured by any trust deed with this clause will be accelerated and will have to be paid.

The beneficiary must notify the Trustee. The trustee will ask the beneficiary to make a Declaration. The Declaration of Default is simple. It gives the pertinent information concerning the property, the deeds of trust, the notes recorded, and a statement that a breach has occurred. The beneficiary must give information on the unpaid principal, the unpaid advances, and any other costs incurred. This statement is given to the trustee.

The trustee's first function is to record with the County Recorder a Notice of Default. This starts the entire action. This is an important date. If you are ever involved in any foreclosure, be sure you check to see the exact date the Notice of Default was recorded. This starts the whole action, and time frames are calculated from that date.

THE MOST IMPORTANT DATE

The reason this is an important date and one you should remember is that if three months pass with no reinstatement, the Trustee can start to advertise a Trustee Sale. Many people use the phrase ninety days to describe this period, but ninety days is not the correct number. It is three months. The trustor has until five days before the sale to reinstate the loan by paying all that is due, including foreclosing costs. After that day, the trustor has to pay the loan in full to retain ownership.

The first thing you should do is check the notice to find the exact date of recording. Go forward three months from that day. On that day the beneficiary will have the right to schedule the trustee's sale. The beneficiary can extend this notice period, and many beneficiaries who do not want the property back will do so.

In many cases there is a definite possibility the beneficiary will extend, but if the loan has a low interest rate and other good terms, the beneficiary might want to change some of those terms. You can see why it is important for you to know the time at which this right of reinstatement ends (five days from the date the Trustee Sale is scheduled).

Before any professional trustee would file a Notice of Default, they would first request the declaration from the beneficiary. They would need the original note, the original trust deed, and copies of any assignments or power of attorney involving this transaction.

TRUSTEE SALE GUARANTEE POLICY

The next step for the Trustee is to purchase a Trustee Sale Guarantee Policy from a title company. The trustee has specific responsibilities and obligations. There are certain rules that must be followed. Certain people must be given notification and certain other items must be recorded. Therefore, the trustee has to know the exact condition of the title when they file the Notice of Default.

The trustee will contact a title company and get a title policy. This title policy will cost approximately eighty percent of an average title policy on a sale. This title policy will not be for the entire value of the property. The title policy will be for the amount of the note that is being foreclosed plus an additional amount to cover advances, costs, fees, late payments, and other costs that might be advanced.

It is called a Trustee Sale Guarantee Policy because the title company guarantees to the trustee the condition of the title at that moment. The trustee can start the trustee sale action, knowing the condition of the title is as the title company warrants it. If there is any problem, the title company would have the responsibility of protecting the beneficiary and the trustees because they have told the trustees they will be protected. The Trustee Sale Guarantee policy is not for the benefit of the beneficiary or the trustor, and it is not for the benefit of anybody who buys at the trustee sale or from the trustor.

THE NOTICE OF DEFAULT

Who gets a copy of this Notice of Default that has been recorded? It must be recorded with the County Recorder. Within ten days after the recording, it must be mailed by certified mail, postage prepaid, to all persons who have filed a request for Notice of Default. A request for a Notice of Default is a document that can be filed by any party having an interest in a property.

It is a simple procedure to get a copy of a Request for Notice of Default and file it with the County Recorder. Then, if a Notice of Default is ever filed, the party who has filed this form will receive notice of the default within ten days of the filing. For example, a holder of a note junior to any foreclosing note would definitely want a Request for Notice of Default filed.

The Notice of Default is sent to the last known address of any party, so it is important, if you move to keep your Requests for Notices of Default up-to-date. The mail service will not forward them after a certain period of time, and the Trustee is not responsible if addresses are not current.

If the trust deed does not contain the address of the trustor, the Notice of Default must be published once a week for at least four weeks in a newspaper of general circulation with the first publication to begin within ten days after recording the Notice of Default. This is another function of the trustee. If you are ever a trustor or beneficiary, it behooves you to keep all of these addresses current so that you are given proper and quick notice of any problem.

Furthermore, within one month, the trustee must mail a copy with the recorded information on it to any successor in interest as of the recording date of the Notice of Default. The beneficiary of any trust deed that is recorded subsequent to the one being foreclosed or recorded prior to such trust deed must be given notification within one month. If there are any assignees of any interest on this note, they get the one-month notice, as does any vendee of any contract sale, and the successor in interest to any vendee. Any lessee who has had their lease recorded will be given the same thirty-day notification, as does the State Controller, when there is any Notice of Lien for postponed property taxes.

THE NOTICE PERIOD

Let's discuss this period of Notice from the eyes of the three parties involved. The three parties are the trustee, beneficiary, and trustor. The trustee's function during this period is to monitor the entire operation. If the problem is settled by the trustor paying all the amounts due, then the trustee must file a rescission. A rescission is an end to the Notice of Default. This is what happens in most actions. I would estimate that out of every ten Notices of Default, about eight of them will be paid up or the property will be sold during the period of reinstatement. If the trustee is not notified of a paid-up situation by the end of the three-month period, it is the trustee's function to notify the beneficiary and to ask for instructions as to how to proceed.

Let's discuss what the beneficiary should be doing during this time. We may seem to be getting a little away from how you want to deal with foreclosures, but we think most of you will sometime become the beneficiary of notes. Therefore, you should know the problems that can arise from the beneficiary viewpoint.

The beneficiary should do some thinking before filing the Notice of Default. In California when you file a Notice of Default, it starts a trustee sale action. If you have a trustee sale action, according to California law, you cannot get a judgment deficiency against the party. That means if the party owes you $20,000 and you have a trustee sale to get the property back, the action of using the trustee sale means you agree not to ask for any judgment deficiency. If you are owed $20,000 and you take the property back, resell it, and lose $10,000 when you use the trustee sale vehicle, you are making an agreement that you will not proceed with any judgment against the party. Not only are you unable to proceed, the law says you will not be able to get any judgment even if you do proceed. So the biggest question you must answer is, "Do you want the property back if all else fails?" That is your only threat to the owner.

If you don't want the property back, you should try some other attack. With some of the poor loans that are made, the threat of taking the property back is not a big threat. Keeping this in mind I recommend that a beneficiary communicate with a borrower and maintain a good relationship. I think communication is important in all phases of real estate, but it is extremely important between the beneficiary and the trustor when there are payment problems. Beneficiaries may become obstinate and arguments might start, but this is not a good time to become emotional. The problem should be addressed with a view to solving it. Don't let emotion enter into the situation. By maintaining a good relationship with the borrower, the beneficiary may be able to work out a solution without having to incur the cost of a trustee sale.

DEEDS-IN-LIEU OF FORECLOSURE

For example, one of the solutions might be a deed-in-lieu of foreclosure. A deed-in-lieu of foreclosure is similar to a quitclaim deed. It is a deed given by the owner to the beneficiary for not using a trustee sale action. What are the advantages to a beneficiary? They do not have to go through all the costs of the trustee sale. They do not have to pay for the Trustee Sale Guarantee Policy and any trustee fees. The trustee sale policy will cost real money and must be paid by the beneficiary if a trustee action is started. If a Notice of Default is filed, a fee will have to be paid to the trustee. This fee is set by State statute and increases with the size of the loan.

If the beneficiary can get a deed-in-lieu from the owner, time is saved. You don't have to go through the whole four-month procedure and can get the property back sooner.

PROBLEMS WITH A DEED-IN-LIEU

What are the problems with a deed-in-lieu? If an owner gives a deed-in-lieu to the beneficiary, the beneficiary owns the property. But if there have been any loans or liens placed on the property after the beneficiary's note has been recorded, these notes will not be cleared off by taking a deed-in-lieu. Keep in mind that if a second trust deed forecloses with a third and fourth trust deed on the property, and the trustee sale is held, the third and fourth loans are removed from the property and the owners of those notes lose all their equity. But if the beneficiary takes back a deed-in-lieu, those notes are not removed. This is a problem that should be considered by a beneficiary who is thinking about taking back a deed-in-lieu.

A deed-in-lieu can be a great weapon for a beneficiary. The beneficiary should get legal advice before taking one and should make certain there are no junior liens. This can be accomplished with a title report, etc.

NEGOTIATE, NEGOTIATE, NEGOTIATE

The beneficiary should negotiate all these points. Negotiation is important. Few people benefit from a foreclosure sale. The costs can be huge, and the time problems are unbelievable. If anything can be negotiated, it should be tried.

There are times when a beneficiary might give the owner money to move out. Rather than get involved in a long eviction process, it is sometimes best to give tenants some money and have them move out. The trustee sale action could be a long costly process and if, for a small amount, you could get a deed to the property with the owner or tenants gone you might be way ahead. However, don't give any of this money to a tenant or an owner until everything they own is sitting on the sidewalk, and you have a locksmith standing next to you ready to change the lock. If something can be negotiated at the beginning, it might be beneficial for all parties.

When you're doing all this negotiating, I recommend you put everything in writing. Putting information in written form is one of the best ways of eliminating misunderstandings. If you're going to make an offer to an owner or you're going to agree to some other payment schedule, make sure it is done in writing. If you do give the owner a few extra days or another payment schedule, make certain it is in writing and it looks like a formal document. It is worth the effort to visit a secretarial service and have something typed up so that there will be no problems later. A lot of people depend on word-of-mouth and on handwritten documents that are later lost. I believe everything should be in writing and should be accurate and businesslike.

Another idea you might consider before starting an expensive action of foreclosure is to have a letter from your attorney mailed to the borrower. This might help solve your problem. Many times we have asked our attorney to send a letter to the tenant before filing an eviction action. In response, the tenant, the tenant's attorney, or legal aid would contact our attorney and would help solve the problem if communication had stopped between the tenant and our manager. Put everything in writing and use a letter from your attorney when it seems necessary.

IT'S TIME TO REACT

Suppose negotiating has failed, and you have to start with your foreclosure action. My recommendation is to have all your documents ready, so when you go to start the action you have the note, the original trust deed, any assignments, an accurate record of exactly what's owed, and a copy of the payment records to show exactly how much you've received over the period of time. If you do this, you will solve the trustee's problems, and you won't have a time delay.

Be sure you have the correct legal description. Have any item that will help a trustee file the action. Have your money for fees ready. Understand when you file a Notice of Default, you are going to pay trustee fees, recording fees, and for a Trustee Sale Guarantee Policy. By having funds ready, the action can be started promptly.

If you make a decision to go ahead with a Notice of Default, move quickly. I'm not telling you always to move to a Notice of Default because you may want to negotiate first, but when you make the decision to move, move quickly and decisively.

You should know the problems of the trustees. If you can be more accurate and have all the documents ready, they will be better able to serve you. Be aware that the trustees are involved in a tremendous amount of actions, and they don't make a lot of money from any of them. Be sure you consider the problems of the trustee and help them in every way possible.

Again, I would recommend to beneficiaries that they maintain communication. Many beneficiaries do not want the property back. They would rather have their note reinstated or be paid off. They file a Notice of Default but do not say anything to the trustee, and so the trustee will not give any information to any parties who are calling.

IF YOU DON'T WANT THE PROPERTY

I would tell the trustee that I was not interested in having the property back saying, "If anyone calls, please give out any information you can". In fact, I would probably prepare a set-up sheet or an information sheet on the property and give it to the trustee. If somebody called for information on the property, the trustee could simply send out the information. In this way more people would have accurate information on the property. The result could be more interest in buying my position, in paying off the trustor and taking over the property, or in coming to the trustee sale and buying it at that time.

A big mistake I see many beneficiaries make is not realizing that their trustee could be giving out information. Most trustees do not give out information unless they are specifically instructed to do so by a beneficiary. Therefore, I would work with a trustee who is very aware of this. If I were not interested in getting the property back, the trustee could give out all the information possible to callers. If I were interested in getting the property back, I would instruct the trustee not to give out any information.

Another recommendation for the beneficiary to consider is to bring the senior loans and property taxes current. If you think there is equity in the property and you want it back, but don't want problems with the trustee sale action, it is my recommendation that you pay up all senior loans, any property taxes due and any fire insurance policies. If there were a fire on your property, you could lose the whole property. You do not want a senior loan holder to start a foreclosure action if you have filed a Notice of Default on a junior note.

If you do not bring any senior loans current, they can file their own Notice of Default after yours. You would have filed your Notice of Default first, and you would get ownership of the property first. However, you will have to pay off the other loans sooner or later or they can hold a trustee sale. If you let them start an action, they pay trustee fees and other costs and you will have to pay them off to secure the property. To summarize, if you are a beneficiary foreclosing, you should consider bringing senior loans current and paying any fire insurance or property taxes.

PARTIAL PAYMENT PROCESS

If you accept a partial payment from a delinquent tenant, you have to start again with your three-day notice. A partial payment from an owner does not automatically stop a foreclosure action unless, and this is a big unless, the owner thinks the payment stopped it. If you ever accept a partial payment, the owner is going to "think" the payment stopped the action. This does not mean you cannot accept a partial payment. As the beneficiary, I would consider accepting a partial payment. I would make certain, however, the trustor knows this does not stop the action. The best way to do this is to have the trustor sign a statement to specify that they are making a partial payment to you with the understanding that this does not stop the action.

Who would ever pay this? I have seen many cases where trustors have wanted to pay some money to the beneficiary because they know they're going to cure this action in the long run. For example, you are starting a foreclosure action for $4,000 in late payments. The owner of the property has $2,000 in the bank earning only five- percent interest. The interest on your note is fourteen percent. The owner would be happy to pay you the $2,000 to avoid the fourteen- percent interest cost. I would certainly accept the money as long as the trustor knows the partial payment will not stop the action.

RECEIVERSHIP OR NOT

A further consideration is whether to appoint a receiver or not. A receiver can be appointed to collect rents. Earlier, we mentioned that an assignment-of-rents clause is in most trust deeds. The courts do not always enforce this assignment of rents. I have seen many cases where the lender sends out an assignment of rents to the tenant and the owner counters with a letter to the tenant saying, "If you pay any money to the lender on the assignment of rents an eviction action will be started." Thus, the tenant many times does not pay anybody. In this instance, it would be a benefit to the beneficiary to go into court and have a receiver appointed.

Some attorneys are afraid of getting receivers appointed. If rent is being paid on a property, the beneficiary should get this money instead of the owner. The appointment of a receiver is not extremely expensive, and you can talk to different receivers to see what their fees are. A receiver could be an experienced property manager, an experienced real estate broker, or an experienced attorney. They would collect the rents during the foreclosure period. On a 10-unit building that is renting for $5,000 total per month, that's approximately $20,000 over a four-month period. I recommend, on any of these actions where rental income is involved a beneficiary contact an attorney to discuss having a receiver appointed.

THE TRUSTOR'S VIEW

Let's look at the reinstatement period from the position of the trustor or the owner. It is a completely different situation. There are many good books on this subject. One of the best is, "How to Stop a Foreclosure," by Hal Morris.

Remember that we are completely changing our viewpoint. First, we discussed the reinstatement period from the trustee's position, then from the beneficiary's situation, and now we will look at it from the trustor's situation.

One of the first tips I would give any trustor is to communicate constantly and frequently with the lender. Don't wait too long and get yourself in so much trouble the lender has no possible way of helping.

I attended a seminar given by a well-known attorney, and he made a good recommendation to trustors who are in trouble. He recommended that you get dressed up in your best clothes, take your spouse or friend and your children, get into the car and drive to the bank that is handling your loan. Go in and talk to the manager. Don't talk to a teller. Wait for the manager. If it means sitting outside and waiting thirty or forty minutes or calling ahead for an appointment, make certain you do this. Don't leave until you talk to someone in authority. If you take the initiative in this type of confrontation, you will usually get yourself more time.

What you have done is taken a situation where you're a mere loan number and translated it into a personal situation. In many instances with an institutional lender, you can get extra days before any action could be started. Of course, a personal meeting with some lenders will not get you any additional time. They feel strongly about the situation, move quickly, have certain rules and will not budge.

Private parties may not respond to a personal meeting either but try it. You have nothing to lose but some time. Load your family in the car and drive down to communicate with the lender personally. This idea is recommended by many people who believe it will get you more time.

An old foreclosure story involves a man who followed this plan. He couldn't get the proper person to return his phone calls so he went to the lender's main office with a book to read and a lunch basket. He was going to wait days if necessary. The proper person came out quickly.

SELL OR REFINANCE?

Borrowers can consider collateralizing their equity, selling part of their equity, or refinancing. It is best to refinance before any Notice of Default is filed. If someone is going to give you a loan, one of the first things they will do is investigate the property. If they find a Notice of Default has been filed, they will look at the property from a much different viewpoint. If you are trying to save the property, look at your life insurance values. A lot of people do not understand their life insurance policies have cash values. I know many people whose families have grown, their income is at a high level, and yet they never investigate using the low interest loans from insurance companies.

One of the other things you should consider doing at this time is trying to supplement your income. This might mean getting a part-time job or doing some other type of work. By doing this you are showing the lender you are making an effort, and they might work with you.

As a last resort, you might go to relatives for a loan or you could even try to sell the property. You could go to the lender and offer a change of terms. Tell the lender you have a problem, and you will try to make up the difference by increasing your monthly payment. Or tell them you have a cash flow problem, and you will be able to work it out in a short time.

You could ask for a moratorium on payments. The word moratorium means stop. You could ask the lender to give you a six-month moratorium during which time you would not make any payments. Most lenders will not do this, but it does not hurt to ask.

If you have a first trust deed on the property that is near foreclosure, and there are other loans, these junior lenders might not want their equity damaged. They might be interested in advancing you some money and adding it to the amount owed. You might say, "Who would want to throw some good money after bad?" But junior lenders might prove helpful if you can show them your setback is temporary and things will improve, so don't be afraid to call. What have you got to lose? Only the cost of a phone call.

YOUR ATTORNEY AND YOUR BROKER

At this time you should talk to an attorney and a real estate advisor. If there has been confusion, a legal problem, or some other difficulty on the property, an attorney might be able to get you an injunction. For example, the delinquent amount on the Notice of Default is $8,000, but you believe it is a much lower amount. You obviously have a point of contention and should get an attorney to file an injunction to stop the action. Of course, you wouldn't do this if the figure were only fifty cents off.

OTHER TIPS FOR TRUSTORS

You should keep good records and keep track of all payments. In case there is any problem you should have canceled checks and any agreements that have been made.

During this period you should file a homestead on the property. Someone might say, "According to California law a homestead is not affected by a secured note." That is true. It is not going to harm anything to file a homestead, particularly if it's a residence. Consider filing a homestead and sending a copy to the trustee. At least this illustrates something is happening. It might delay a trustee from starting an action. When you are the trustor/owner, you want to do anything to confuse a trustee and a lender.

You could open an escrow and send a copy of the escrow instructions to the trustee. This would show you were trying to sell the property. You should put all these offers in writing. If you make a promise to somebody and you sincerely mean it, be sure to put it in writing. Put any promise in writing and pay a few dollars to have it notarized so everyone knows you mean business. Lenders hear over and over, "The check is in the mail." It ruins their faith in people. Putting agreements in writing and notarizing them increases your chance of being believed.

DEEDS-IN-LIEU AGAIN

There are times as a trustor when you should advance the idea of using a deed-in-lieu of foreclosure. We discussed why a beneficiary should take one, now let's discuss why an owner or trustor would want to give one. Many times giving a deed-in-lieu to a lender will save a trustor's credit. If you let the foreclosure proceed and it later appears on your credit report, you may find it hard to get a loan in the future. You want to make certain your credit is saved and giving a deed-in-lieu could accomplish that.

Sometimes, there are psychological reasons for a deed-in-lieu. For example, supposed you borrowed money from friends, and you can't repay it. Should you force your friends to go through a long, costly foreclosure process to get the property back? The decent thing to do is to give the property to your friends by giving them a deed-in-lieu.

Someone may ask, "Why not use a quit-claim deed?" Some of the title companies with whom I've talked believe a quitclaim deed should not be used when a deed-in-lieu is indicated. A deed-in-lieu has a lot of different caveats and statements that make it a better choice, in most cases, to stop a foreclosure action. <u>Never use a deed-in-lieu of foreclosure or a quitclaim deed without talking to an attorney first.</u>

LAST STOP: BANKRUPTCY

One of the last actions to consider when someone is having financial difficulty is bankruptcy. A bankruptcy will slow down a foreclosure action. In fact, it stops a foreclosure action in mid-sentence. If you're in a reinstatement period and a bankruptcy is filed, the clock stops running on that foreclosure sale. A stay is placed on all actions pertaining to the person who filed bankruptcy. To continue the foreclosure, the beneficiary's attorney must go into bankruptcy court and get a release from this stay of execution. It is going to take time and money and definitely slows down a foreclosure.

One of the most common types of bankruptcy to be filed is a Chapter 13. This is generally called a "Wage Earner's Plan." A borrower will submit a plan to the court, and the court will either approve or modify the plan. This plan will be used to try to get the person who is filing bankruptcy out of financial trouble. Certain payments may be lowered, other adjustments may be made, moratoriums may be requested on certain debts, debts may be paid back cents on the dollar and other actions may be taken to allow the person to remove the bankruptcy.

Bankruptcy can stop a foreclosure for a period of time. Before any person considers filing a bankruptcy they should explore all other possibilities and use bankruptcy only as a last resort. More and more people are using it, and bankruptcy is a well-known word in the foreclosure field. You may be investigating a property or trying to buy it and a bankruptcy will be filed. All action is stopped on the property for an undetermined period of time. It affects everyone: trustees, beneficiaries, junior lenders, and any investors considering the property.

A trustor should not use a bankruptcy in a frivolous fashion. It will affect credit for a long period of time. It could affect your confidence and your self-esteem to know you've had to file for bankruptcy. Of course, there are cases when you should file bankruptcy, but don't do it without a great deal of thought about the ramifications of this action. When you decided to do it, don't look back. Go forward as soon as feasible.

IT'S TIME FOR A SALE

The three-month reinstatement period has ended, and nothing has been done. It is up to the trustee to notify the beneficiary the period has ended and to ask for new directions. In most cases, the beneficiary will tell the trustee to go ahead with the trustee sale and the trustee will request additional information. The next stop for the trustee is to call the title company. They ask for what is called a date down. This is a term that is used in the title industry. If there are any new actions against this property, they will be given to the trustee at this time. If there are bankruptcies or other problems, the trustee has to take suitable action.

The trustee will learn by getting the date down as to when a trustee sale could be held. When it is clear that a trustee sale can be held and the date is cleared with the title company, the trustee will file a Notice of Trustee Sale with the County Recorder.

THE NOTICE OF SALE

The Notice must be accurate. The trustee has to be accurate in determining the amounts owed. The Notice must show the street address of the property or a common designation. If the property has no street address, then the legal description will be inserted. The Notice must contain the name and address of the beneficiary at whose request the sale is to be conducted. The Notice must contain the name, street address, and telephone number of the trustee or the person conducting the sale.

The Notice of Sale must contain a statement of the total amount of the unpaid balance of the obligation and a reasonable estimate of the cost and expenses, in advance, at the time of the initial publication. Included are costs like the Trustee Sale Guarantee Policy, trustee fees, any back-payments and any payments made by the beneficiary to other parties. This amount could be larger than the face amount of the original note.

The Notice must contain the date, time and place for the sale. The sale must be conducted in the county where the property is situated and at a specific location and in the judicial district where the property is situated if it is a large county. If a public building or a large office complex is named, the exact location must be specific such as, The North Court House Steps, so it is easy for people to find.

For many years, Court House Steps and City Halls were locations for most trustee sales. Presently, more and more sales are being conducted by the trustee or by a trustee service agency at their own location. Many times you will see an office location for the trustee sale.

PUBLICATION OF THE NOTICE

The Notice of Trustee Sale must be recorded at least fourteen days prior to the date of the sale. It doesn't have to be immediately recorded the minute it is written. At least twenty days prior to the date of the sale, the notice must be posted in a public place, usually the bulletin board of the County Court House or City Hall.

A copy of the Notice of Sale must be posted at some conspicuous place on the property to be sold. This is normally the front door. If there is no front door, it has to be posted in some other conspicuous location. A copy of the Notice of Sale must be published at least once a week in a newspaper of general circulation for at least twenty days prior to the date of sale.

A copy of the Notice must be mailed at least twenty days prior to the sale to all persons who've requested special notice and to all other people who have an interest in the property. Normally, these are the same people to whom the Notice of Default was sent.

During this period of time before the sale, the trustee has other functions. If the trustors want to pay off the note, they will make a demand request to the beneficiary and then the trustee will calculate exactly the amount that is needed to close the account. If the trustor pays the trustee this amount, the trustee will stop the Notice of Sale Action and will send a reconveyance of the note to the trustor. Since the entire note has been paid, the trustee will simply reconvey the entire note. The entire amount of the money due will go to the beneficiary.

The trustor could ask if the note might be brought current again. If the trustee gets this request after the reinstatement period has ended, the trustee will normally notify the beneficiary and ask what action should be taken. Many times, even though the reinstatement period is ended and the sale is pending, the beneficiary would be happy to reinstate the loan. Such a reinstatement might be contingent upon raising the interest rate, collecting a sum, or collecting an additional payment, but the trustee should notify the beneficiary.

JUST BEFORE THE SALE

Suppose nothing is done and the day of the Trustee Sale approaches. At the time of the trustee sale, the trustee will calculate the exact amount owed the beneficiary. This will be done accurately taking into account all interest on amounts advanced, trustee fees, Trustee Sales Guaranty cost, closing fees, estimated closing costs, any money advanced to other lenders or to pay notes, all the money due on late payments, the entire face amount of the note and every other figure owed the beneficiary. The trustee will calculate this amount, which will normally be the opening bid of the beneficiary or, as it is also called, the credit bid.

On the day of the sale, the trustee will appear at the time and spot designated. More than one sale could be scheduled at the same time. The normal pattern is that the trustee will call out the sales that have been postponed to a later time and then will start and complete the first sale, continuing consecutively until all the sales are done.

THE SALE ITSELF

For each Trustee Sale, the trustee will read the Trustee Sale Notice and ask if there are any bidders. The bidders will be qualified and will have to show enough money to bid. Civil Code Section 2924H states, "At the trustee sale, the trustee shall have the right to require every bidder to show evidence of his ability to deposit with the trustee the full amount of his bid in cash: a cashier's check drawn on a state or national bank, a state or federal credit union, or a state or federal savings and loan association domiciled in this state."

The trustee writes down the amount each bidder shows. The trustee will not announce this amount to the other people. The trustee will be the only person who knows the amount of money each person possesses. Some trustees will take the funds and hold them, but in most cases in California, the trustee takes a look at the check, writes down the amount, returns the check to its owner, and then maintains a journal showing how much money each person has shown.

After qualifying the bidders, the trustee will read the opening bid. An example would be, "I am authorized by (name of beneficiary) to bid so many dollars. Are there any other bids?" The beneficiary does not have to be at the sale and does not have to have any money. But if the beneficiary would like to bid above this amount against other bidders, the beneficiary could show up. The beneficiary would have to show funds to go above any opening bid.

UNDERBIDDING

There's one thing I'd like to cover at this time and that is underbidding by a beneficiary. In many cases, underbidding by a beneficiary might be a smart thing to do. The beneficiary is able to bid the entire amount due but should consider underbidding in certain instances.

As an example, the note the beneficiary is foreclosing on is an installment sale note, and some funds were received as a down payment. When the sale was made as an installment sale, the beneficiary had paid some tax on the amount that had been collected. But the beneficiary has to foreclose on the note and bids the entire amount due on the note. There is a possibility that, although the beneficiary took the property back, some more tax would have to be paid. This is covered in Section 1038 of the Internal Revenue Code. If a beneficiary is foreclosing on an installment sale note, a CPA should be contacted to see if it would be advantageous to lower the bid and not have any tax liability for the year of the sale. This is normally done when the beneficiary does not expect anybody else to come to the sale.

There is another example of when the beneficiary might consider lowering the bid. This would be a case in which the beneficiary's opening bid could be $27,000, but they would be happy to get $10,000 in cash and not have to worry about taking the property back. There is little value in the property. In this case, the beneficiary might consider bidding only $10,000. This might mean too, that more people would come to the sale if the opening bid were lowered. It could be a benefit to a beneficiary to lower a bid if there is not much value in the property.

The underbidding process has been common for a very long time. Many years ago in an issue of the <u>Los Angeles Bar Bulletin</u>, there was article entitled, "The Beneficiary's Underbid – A Neglected Tool," by Ben S. Crocker, Attorney for Lincoln Savings and Loan Association. Ben was a member of the firm of Halstead & Crocker, and I worked with him on many receiverships. I found him to be one of the most competent attorneys I've ever met and a most outstanding young man. In his article on underbidding, he included some other reasons for a beneficiary to consider underbidding.

One reason would be if there were any money left in the receiver's account. If a beneficiary bid the entire amount due, there is a possibility the court might hold that the note had been completely paid off. If, months later, a receiver came into court with money that was left over from a receivership, the judgment may be that the money should go to the trustor. In the case of receiverships, Ben Crocker would always call me a few days before he was going to file his bid and if there was money in the receivership account, he would lower the bid at the sale so this cash would come to Lincoln Savings.

Underbidding would also allow room for a miscalculation of the closing bid by a trustee and for a lower assessment where the bid might be used to question any assessment by a County Assessor. An underbid could be used when you want to prove fraud and damages.

IT'S TIME TO BID OR SHUT UP

After the people have qualified by showing their money, the sales officer, the crier or auctioneer- whatever you want to call them, will hold the sale as a simple auction. In most cases, the bid to be accepted will have to be a certain amount over the prior bid. Trustees do not want you raising bids by a penny at a time, so perhaps each bid must be $100 over the old bid. At the end, when the bids are slowing down and the auctioneer thinks they have gotten their final bid they will say, "Going, going, gone." The hammer will fall and the sale will be over.

The trustee will take the money from the person who had the top bid. If the person who made the bid brought a check for $30,000 and the final bid was $27,800, they would give the check to the trustee and the trustee would return the balance the next day or within a short period of time after they had done their calculations. The trustee will also give a Trustee's Deed to the person buying. This title is not guaranteed at this time. The person buying at the Trustee Sale is simply taking the position of the beneficiary who started the foreclosing action. The trustee will take the money, check all the claims and will use the money to pay the claims. If the beneficiary takes the property back, the trustee will give the beneficiary a trustee's deed and the beneficiary will become the owner of the property.

If there were a higher bid, the trustee will pay the beneficiary and check the priority of the following claims and will pay them in order. If there is money, they will pay a second claim until the extent of the money is used and if there is still money left over, then a third priority loan will be paid and then any other secured liens in order. If any money is left over, it will be given to the trustor.

IF THE PEOPLE DON'T MOVE

This is the process from beginning to end. But most times, it does not end here. The new owner goes out to the property and the renter or the former owner is in the property. What should the new owner do?

An eviction action must be taken just like an eviction action for a tenant in any rental property. The only change is the form used is not a Notice to Pay Rent or Quit but a Notice to Quit. The person does not have the right to pay any money. A Notice to Quit is served on the party who is still sitting in the property. If they do not move, an Unlawful Detainer action must be started.

Now, you know a little bit about the law. It is time to start discussing different ways to work in the foreclosure market. Keep reading.

Chapter 3
Starting in the Field

When starting to work in the foreclosure market, a question arises as to whether you should subscribe to a service or a legal newspaper to get information about foreclosure notices. When you're first starting out, you should use the newspapers for current information on foreclosures. The newspapers are inexpensive and will furnish you with more than adequate information. When you become more experienced, you might find that a service would be preferable because they are more detailed and give more information.

Here is another action item. Your first action item was to buy the California Civil Code (see Chapter 2). Your second action item is to call a legal newspaper in your area and ask them for subscription information. Most of them will give you a free sample subscription for a period of time. You can use this free subscription and see if the paper meets your needs. In most cases it will. Call today to get a subscription.

TRANSCRIPTS OF DEFAULT NOTICES

Transcripts of Default Notices in legal newspapers and in the Foreclosure Service's Information are not always accurate. These facts cannot be relied upon in many cases and must be verified. However, you have to start somewhere.

Most transcripts will have the following information:
- SITUS (City & Address)
- Legal Description
- Trustor's Name
- Assessed Values
- Trust Deed Account Number
- Date of the Trust Deed
- Trust Deed Recording Date
- Amount Due & Date Calculated
- Default Date & Recording Number
- Trustees' Names

- Trustees' Record #
- Beneficiary's Name

Some of the items you should understand:

1. If the address of the trustor is different than the SITUS address, the property is probably a rental and the owner is not at the property.

2. The recording date of the note foreclosing could give you an indication of how long the trustor has owned the property.

3. If the amount due is extremely large, the entire note might be due.

4. The assessed evaluations are an indication sometimes as to the value of the property or the type of property (single family or larger).

5. If only a small amount is due, it might be cured quickly by the trustor and would be a waste of time to investigate the property immediately.

6. Is the beneficiary, a private party, primary lender, large savings & loan, or a small hard-money lender?

7. The default notice doesn't cite whether the loan foreclosing is first in priority or a junior loan.

OUT OF STATE LENDER

There are different things you check when you're reading transcripts. One thing to check is out-of-state beneficiaries. Out-of-state beneficiaries often do not know the property, and a better bargain can be made. It might even be possible to make an offer subject to them acquiring title to the property at a trustor sale.

How can you do that? They don't own the property at the moment. Make your offer subject to them getting title. If the out-of-staters knew that there was a party who was ready, willing, and able to buy the property at a certain price, they might attack the foreclosure more aggressively.

EMOTIONS INVOLVED

When a person is going through a foreclosure, there is a tremendous amount of emotion involved. If somebody has serious financial problems and is going to lose a home or an investment property, they could be angry.

Years ago I read some books on death and dying. Most of them generally agreed that in terminal illness there are five stages that a patient goes through during the course of an illness.

The first step is denial that there is a problem. The second step is anger. The person will get angry at everything. The third step is rational thinking and the person will try to solve the problem. They will try to get different opinions or try to take different treatments. The fourth stage is desperation and depression. The fifth stage is acceptance. These stages aren't the same for everybody, and the time frames vary greatly. Some people go to the doctor, hear that they have a problem, and immediately go into acceptance or resignation.

My impression from working in foreclosures is that the emotional stages of a person undergoing a foreclosure occur in the same manner. One of the first stages is denial. The owner will deny that there is a problem. You'll find that there is a lack of communication, or there's some bargaining, or there's some poker playing going on. You'll go out and try to talk to them and they will say, "We have no problem."

The second stage, corresponding to the second state of terminal illness, is anger. Investors knock on doors, and the anger they meet surprises them. They do not understand the emotions. I want to stress to you specifically to understand that there are a lot of emotions present during a foreclosure and anger can be one of them. Do not take it personally. Be prepared for these people to react in anger. You've come to talk to them and they will say things like "Get the hell out of here. I don't want to talk to another person. The vultures are coming all around." They may use even stronger language.

After the anger subsides, many will take action. This is the third stage – rational thinking. The people finally will get into problem solving and bargaining, and they might say, "Bring me any offer." You'd be amazed at how many people sitting in their houses with foreclosure notices think that they have no problem because no Notice of Sale has been filed. But when that reinstatement period ends five days before the sale. The person sitting in the house does have a problem. He or she will not be able to refinance in a five-day period and get new funds. Even if they sell, the chances of getting a new loan to bail them out of trouble will be unlikely. It is very difficult to save a property when someone allows too much time to pass.

The last stage is acceptance. This is when the people finally just say, "It's over. I'm either going to file bankruptcy and get out of this, or I'm just going to let the property go back. There's nothing we can do, so let's just sit here as long as we can."

If you start working the first day the notice is in the paper, you could be wasting time. If you have nothing else to do, you may want to contact the owner early and see if something can be done. But if your time is short and you're a busy person, I wouldn't recommend starting in the early days of the Notice of Default. Some of the experts I've heard have said that they file the Notices of Default away in a tickler file and won't do anything on them until at least sixty days have passed.

PICK AN AREA

The first thing you should do is select an area in which you are interested. Do not try to cover the entire world. It is impossible to cover the entire world and know it in detail. Pick an area that you know and in which you can specialize. Make the area big enough so that there are some properties in foreclosure but don't try to cover too much space.

Val Cabot, in a book called "Gold Mining for Foreclosures" uses the term "between two houses." He will pick two houses he knows. He will become knowledgeable about the area between those houses. He knows the properties and can make a good decision about properties quickly.

There's an old play called "The Music Man," which had a scene where the salesmen were on the train discussing what you had to do to become a successful salesman. They kept saying, "You've got to know the territory, you've got to know the territory." This is one of the best pieces of advice you can follow. "You've got to know the territory."

One time I went to hear a speaker in one of the "Become a Millionaire in 20 Minutes" type of seminars. The speaker was telling everybody how he went to many cities and made offers on properties. He would see a sign and automatically make an offer. I was not surprised to hear later that the gentleman did not have a cent to his name after losing all his properties. Specialize and learn a territory.

SEND A LETTER OR A POST CARD

When you get started, consider sending something the day you see the notice. Don't spend a lot of time on this step. Send a letter to the trustor, in which you say you have funds for a loan, or could arrange for a loan, or would make a cash offer for the home. There would be no real estate commission involved, and the owner could make a decision and move quickly. This is a number's game and isn't easy. You have to do some work. Get a letter or a post card out to the trustor and send a letter to the beneficiary. The beneficiary may not want to take the property back at a trustee sale.

If it's a private lender or an out-of-state lender, send a letter. If it's a lender who has a whole series of foreclosures, send a letter. Don't send a letter to every beneficiary. Tell private and out-of-state lenders you'd be interested in discussing their problems and possibly buying their interest or taking some other type of action.

Send a letter to the trustee. This letter should ask for information. In most cases the trustee will not give anyone any information, so you have to form your letter accurately and use some thought. What I would say is, "It might be to the benefit of the beneficiary and trustor if the trustee would send me information on the property. I might be able to solve their problems and get them out of this situation. I am a professional individual dealing in the field of foreclosures and would be happy to receive whatever information they have available to construct an offer for the property." It won't always work, but you can try.

These letters should not be too formal or too long. When you are first starting, go to a local stationery store and get some memos. These would be two-part memos where you would simply write the letter on the memo. If it is handwritten with a hand-addressed envelope and a first class stamp, you will get a better response than if you put out a form letter. Don't make it too formal. Don't put it on legal stationery or formal stationery. Don't use a form and fill in the blanks.

Do write a hand-written note saying, "I would be happy to discuss your problem at this time. You might be having financial difficulties, but this does not mean that there is not a solution." You could say, "You may have problems and we could get you cash funds at this time" or, "We could get you a cash offer for your home" or, "We would like to send you some information on foreclosures." Just write the letter in your own words, because your own words will be more sincere than copying my words.

A NUMBER'S GAME

File the notes away. You've got your first mailings out. If you get any answers from these parties, don't try to work properties where you're running into antagonism. Life is too short to try to investigate properties where you're running into antagonism. Life is too short to try to solve somebody's anger problems. If they're angry at the moment, find somebody who isn't. Your time on earth is not so long that you should be spending it in unpleasant situations. Don't go out and try to solve every problem. Some people have problems that nobody is ever going to solve.

If they write back and give you good information, then of course you will take steps in line with their response. Go visit any beneficiary or any trustor who has replied to your memo.

Suppose nothing happens. In approximately sixty days, you might send a second copy of your memo and then follow in two or three days with a phone call. A reason you send this letter the second time (before you make the phone call) is so that you have a good opening to start the phone call. One of the best ways to start a phone conversation is, "Did you receive a letter that I just mailed to you about the Notice of Default? My name is Duane Gomer and I am talking about the Notice of Default that has been filed on your property." What you're doing, is trying to set up an appointment.

Don't try to buy the property over the phone. That's the biggest error in direct phone work. You must never try to buy it over the phone or try to close over the phone. The thing that you're trying to do is close for an appointment. So you say, "Do you have any interest? What is your situation at this time?" Ask some questions to which they cannot answer yes or no. Try to get an appointment, but if it's going nowhere, go to the next call. Think how you react when someone interrupts your dinner.

When you send your second letter to the trustor, you could send another copy to the beneficiary. Phone in four days and see if you can get an appointment. Many times you cannot find either the trustor or any phone numbers or don't get any response at all. This doesn't necessarily mean that the situation is impossible. It just means that you go to the next steps.

THE NEXT STEPS

Following are the steps to take after the opening letters. These steps will probably be taken after sixty days. If you've heard nothing and you're still interested in the property, your move at this time would be to look at the multiple sheets from the local real estate offices. When you're inexperienced in this field, you'll go running out to the property to find a broker's sign. It's listed in the multiple sheets or on the Association's web site. If you're licensed by the State of California to sell real estate and you're a member of a local Board of Realtors, you can begin by looking at the "multiple records" to see if this property is listed. This is one of the reasons anybody who is investing in real estate should be licensed. Also, you can check web sites like Realtor.com to see if any of the properties are listed.

If you discover the property is listed, you will have to deal with the broker who will have all the information. If you want to make an offer at this time, you are going to have to work with this broker.

PROPERTY PROFILES

If you like the property and it's not listed in the multiple listing sheets, your next step is to get a property profile. You can get this from a title company. Pick a good title company in your area and ask them for a Property Profile, which provides information on the property. Profiles vary from one title company to another, but basically they give the assessed valuations, the note, the trustor of record, and other information that might be useful to you. You might learn from the property profile whether the loan that's being foreclosed is a first, second, or third, and other valuable information.

If you use a title company for the property profile, show loyalty to them and use them when you buy or sell any property. This is the best way to get good service when you request property profiles. Don't request property profiles indiscriminately because you'll create animosity with the title company and they will resent your overuse of their property profiles service.

Now, it's time to look at the property. Before you get in your car, you should have certain items. First, you should have the actual printed transcript pasted on a form. This would be your preliminary information form. Of course you should always have a city map in your car. I recommend that you have a camera and other supplies.

You should have a hand-held recorder. A recorder is extremely valuable because it will save you time when you're driving, and when you're looking at a property. You can walk around the property and not have to be carrying note pads and pencils. You will discover that if you speak into a recorder, your notes are much more understandable when compared to written notes.

Keep a recorder in your car whether you're looking for foreclosures or not, because you will often find that when you're driving, some of your best ideas will come to you. Buy yourself a little hand-held recorder that you can use for recording your ideas. Many times when you're driving along you will get a great idea or more than one great idea. If you wait until you get home to make a note, it will be forgotten. When you have it on tape, you'll not forget it.

PROPER SUPPLIES

To look at the property you should have a preliminary information form, a city map, a camera, and a hand-held audio recorder. For this preliminary trip, have a legal pad. Why a legal pad? Keep a legal pad in your car all the time because there are many times when you're going to need to write some information. It doesn't necessarily mean that to be successful you must have a legal pad, but every successful real estate investor I know always seems to be writing on legal pads. I don't know if they're successful because they use legal pads or vice-versa. Perhaps, it's just a coincidence.

When you're going to the property, look at the neighborhood and the condition of the property. Are there indications that it might be rented? Is somebody moving? Does it look owner-occupied? What does the landscaping look like? Is mail piled up, along with newspapers, or debris? How can I tell this from the street? Well, walk up to the door and simply say again, "Did you receive the letter I mailed to you at such and such and so and so?" This is your approach at the door -- the same as your approach on the phone.

When you go to the property, do not wear your Gucci shoes and your expensive suit, your fancy pinky rings, and do not put on all your jewelry. Dress simply and neatly. The owners might think that you're a process server and process servers never get the door opened. Don't look too formal and don't carry a briefcase.

LOOK AT THE PROPERTY

When you come to these properties, look for names. Many times people researching properties record license plate numbers of cars. Why? If you see somebody is getting a magazine subscription or have their name on the mailbox, you can use that name when you're searching county records. You search the county records not by address but by name. If you search the county records, you need as many names as you can get.

Suppose there isn't anybody at the property. How can we find the person? There are two ways. One is to check telephone information to see if there are any new telephone numbers in the trustor's name. Another method that we have found successful is to use the Postal Service. Go to the local post office, pay a fee, and ask them what the forwarding address is for parties who have lived in that house. We have found that the postal service works best for locating people. There are now Websites where you can get addresses and phone numbers of people all over the United States.

Look at other homes in the area and other types of owners. Get a feeling of the area. Decide whether it's on the way up or down. You don't want to buy a property in a distressed area. You want to buy a distressed property in a good area. It is important that you look at the area.

There are other sources of information to consider. When you get a copy of the property profile, it will probably tell you if there are any other junior loans against the property. These lenders are people you should do your utmost to contact. I call the junior lien holders the "Maytag Repairman" of this business, because they are so lonely. Nobody ever contacts these people. Sometimes junior lenders don't have the money to cure the foreclosure, and they are the first people you should visit.

GO TO THE NEIGHBORS

Another source of information is neighbors. In most cases, neighbors should not be visited if the property is occupied. You're not going to be able to deal with a trustor if the trustor hears from a next-door neighbor that somebody's running around the neighborhood saying there is a default. But, if you have talked to the trustor and have been completely turned down or if you have not been able to find the trustor at home, I recommend going next door to the neighbors. Will the neighbors be helpful? Sometimes yes, sometimes no. It's a number's game. So you visit several neighbors.

Your first statement could be something like, "Hi, I'm Duane Gomer and I'm interested in the house next door. I can see that it's vacant and I'm interested in it because there has been a Notice of Default filed against the property." At this time you might reach in your back pocket and pull out a copy of the transcript that you have and hold it up. You would be amazed at how many times a neighbor wants to see the information on the Notice of Default.

You can tell them on the phone and you can tell them in person, but when you hold up the transcript, you'd be amazed at how many times they want to see the Notice of Default information. You're not going to force your way in at this time. You want to start talking to them. The neighbors are often great sources of information and might tell you where the trustors have gone if the house is empty.

COUNTY RECORDER'S OFFICE

Another source of information is the County Recorder's office. This is used when the trustor has not been helpful. At the County Recorder's office you can find out about the trust deeds that have been recorded. You can take a look at the actual trust deeds that have been recorded to see if there are any tricky clauses that might cause you a problem. You'd be amazed sometimes at what's in trust deeds.

Once, I was voted in as a general partner to replace a general partner in a syndication. He had combined five doctors together to buy a sixty-unit apartment house in Hollywood. The note came due, and we were being pressured to pay off an all-inclusive trust deed. This would have meant the end of the partnership, because it would have been impossible to refinance at that time. The building was leased on a net-net lease to the Church of Scientology, and we were getting a rental check each month. We didn't want to lose the property.

I asked the Partners if they had a copy of the original trust deed. Because of the confusion, none could be found, so I got a copy from the County Recorder's office. On the deed was a statement that at the expiration of the note, it would be renewed for five years if financing could not be found. At that time financing could not be found for an old Hollywood brick building that would need earthquake correction. The note had to be extended for five years by the beneficiary and this meant that we received the income for another five years. Researching the trust deed in this case made a tremendous difference. As a footnote to this story, we sold the building for a profit before the end of the five-year renewal because of an Earthquake Financing plan begun by the City of Los Angeles.

COMMON SENSE ABOVE ALL

What you're going to do from this point on is to use as much common sense as you can. Common sense in real estate can be intuitive – a feeling based on knowledge. Common sense is knowing what rents should be, what expenses should be, or what a selling price should be. This is the basis of the expertise of real estate. Important decisions are made long before the facts ever go into a computer.

The only way you will develop your common sense is to get more information. Go to the properties and seek every source so you can learn as much as you can, so that you are armed with as much information as possible. When you start negotiating a price, you need to have all the background information available so that you can negotiate most profitably.

Chapter 4
Buying From the Owner

Section 1695 of the California Civil Code covers Home Equity Sales Contracts. This legislation was passed in 1979 to protect homeowners from unscrupulous people who were preying on them. "Foreclosure saviors" were cheating the poor out of their homes. The legislature's mood is reflected in the first sentence of the regulation, "The legislation finds and declares that homeowners whose residences are in foreclosure had been subject to fraud, deception, and unfair dealings by home equity purchasers."

Further, the lawmakers say, "The intent of this chapter is to provide each homeowner with information necessary to make an informed and intelligent decision regarding the sale of a home to an equity purchaser, and to require the sales agreement be expressed in writing to safeguard the public against deceit and financial hardship. To insure, foster and encourage fair dealing in the sale and purchase of the homes in foreclosure. To prohibit representation that tends to mislead. To prohibit or restrict unfair contract terms. To afford homeowners a reasonable and meaningful opportunity to rescind sales to equity purchasers and to preserve and protect home equities for the homeowners of this state. This chapter shall be liberally construed to effectuate this intent and achieve these purposes."

Therefore, you can understand what might happen if you ever get called into court. You must realize any judge will be ruling against any purchaser in a foreclosure case unless the evidence is overwhelmingly in his or her favor.

CODE SECTION 1695

This code states that every contract shall be written in letters of ten-point bold type and in the language principally used to negotiate the sale of the residence. That refers to whether it's in English, Spanish, Chinese, etc. Moreover, every contract has to include certain items, such as the name, business address, and telephone number of the equity purchaser, the address of the property, the total consideration to be given by the equity purchaser, and a complete description of the terms of payment.

Two additional points in this requirement are the exact time at which possession is to be transferred to the equity purchaser and the terms of any rental agreement must be expressed in writing. Also, sellers must be given a "Notice Required by California Law." The heading of this Notice must be in fourteen-point type if it's printed or in capital letters if it's typed. This Notice must state the Equity Purchaser or no one working for the Equity Purchaser can ask the seller to sign any deeds or any other documents until the right to cancel a contract has ended.

A Right of Cancellation has to be included with the contract, the Notice of Cancellation heading must be in twelve-point type, and the remainder must be in ten-point type. The Notice of Cancellation gives the equity seller the right to cancel for five business days. It must be worded, "You may cancel this contract for the sale of your house without any penalty or obligation at any time before _(insert date)_. To cancel this transaction, personally deliver a signed and dated copy of this cancellation notice, or send a telegram." The name and the street address of the buyer must appear on the Notice of Cancellation so the seller can cancel.

RIGHTS OF CANCELLATION

The Right of Cancellation for the equity seller must read, "The equity seller has the right to cancel any contract with an equity purchaser until midnight of the 5th business day following the day on which the equity seller signs any contract or until 8:00 a.m. on the day scheduled for the sale of the property." A business day is defined in the code as any calendar day except Sunday or the following business holidays: New Year's Day, Martin Luther King's Birthday, President's Birthday, Memorial Day, Independence Day, Labor Day, Columbus Day, Veteran's Day, Thanksgiving Day, and Christmas Day. Since the seller has five business days to cancel, if a Sunday or holiday is included, there would be six days to cancel. Saturday is a business day for this code.

This period of time has to expire before the contract is actually valid. If you're buying from an equity seller until the time passes, you as the equity purchaser shall not do any of the following: You can't accept from the equity seller any execution or induce any equity seller to execute any instrument of conveyance; the equity seller cannot give any document that can be recorded; no County Recording can be done until the period of cancellation has run; you can't transfer, encumber, or purport to transfer or encumber any interest in the residence foreclosure to any third party; and the equity seller cannot be paid any consideration until this cancellation period has run out.

Within ten days following receipt of a Notice of Cancellation, the equity buyer shall return, without condition, any original contract and any document signed by the equity seller. Some other pertinent rules that are in the Civil Code are, "An equity purchaser shall make no untrue or misleading statements regarding the value of the residence in foreclosure, the amount of proceeds the equity seller will receive after a foreclosure sale, any contract term, the equity seller's rights or obligations incident to, or arising out of, the sale transaction, the nature of any document which the equity purchaser induces the equity seller to sign, or any other untrue or misleading statements concerning the sale of the residence in foreclosure."

MORE CONDITIONS

Another part of the code states, "Whenever any equity purchaser purports to hold title as a result of any transaction in which the equity seller grants the residence in foreclosure by any instrument which purports to be an absolute conveyance and reserves or is given by the equity purchaser an option to repurchase such residence, the equity purchaser shall not cause any encumbrance or encumbrances to be placed on such property or grant any interest in such property to any other person without the written consent of the equity seller."

This statement means that if you buy a property and give the seller the right to repurchase, before you can refinance or do anything to that property, you must get the written consent of the equity seller. If the equity seller brings any action, they can recover damages or other equitable relief. They can get actual damages plus reasonable attorney's fees and costs, exemplary damages or equitable relief or both. Triple damages could be awarded. Any action brought pursuant to this section shall be commenced within four years after the date of the alleged violations.

If there's a violation by an equity purchaser, according to Code Section (1695.8), the penalty is $25,000 or imprisonment in the County Jail for not more than one year or to be punished by both such fine and imprisonment for each violation. The equity seller can't waive any of these rights. For example, you can't give the equity seller an additional $25,000 in exchange for the equity seller waiving the right to later sue you or waiving the right to the five business days right of cancellation. If you're ever going to buy a piece of property from an equity seller, get good legal advice. If you are going to give the equity seller the right to repurchase, it could be construed to be a loan transaction and cause you tremendous problems. Be sure you know this code section completely if you give an option to repurchase. The IRS could call you a lender.

ANOTHER SET OF RULES

There's another prohibitive act, which reads, "It is unlawful for any person to initiate, enter into, negotiate or consummate any transaction involving residential real property in foreclosure as defined in Section 1695, if such person by the terms of such transaction takes unconscionable advantage of the property owner in foreclosure." This means if the equity sellers believe that unconscionable advantage had been taken of them, they have the right to rescind the contract any time within two years. Even if you follow all of the Civil Code Regulations, if it is decided by a judge or jury that you have taken unconscionable advantage of the property owner in foreclosure, your contract can be rescinded within a two-year period.

What should you do? I believe if you're being honest, you have nothing to fear regarding this section of the Civil Code. The people who have to worry are the crooks.

The words "unconscionable advantage" are not defined anywhere in the code. If there is a question, it will be up to a trial judge to determine whether "unconscionable advantage" was taken. Most of the trial judges are using 75-80% of value as a benchmark. If you paid 75-80% of value when you were purchasing from someone in foreclosure, you'll probably never have any problem with this law. If you are trying to cheat someone, then you might have some problem if a court action is ever filed.

THERE ARE EXCEPTIONS

There are some exceptions to the Civil Code Section 1695. If you're buying from an equity seller whose "residence is in foreclosure", you must follow Code Section 1695 unless you fit one of the exceptions. The definition of a "residence in foreclosure" is a person or persons living in a property of 1 to 4 units they own. Commercial buildings, rental properties, or rental houses do not come under this code section. This code section was initiated to protect homeowners, not rental property owners, etc.

There are six exceptions to this code. If your transaction fits one of these six exceptions, then you do not have to follow the code section or do not have the problems of unconscionable advantage, rescission or rights of cancellation.

1. Equity purchasers who are going to use the house as a personal residence do not come under this code. This legislation was designed to stop the people who have cheated the poor. The person buying just one property for a home does not come under this section. To use a home means to use as a residence, not to move in and stay one or two days or stay on weekends. If a question ever comes up and you're put on the witness stand, they'll ask you questions like; "Did you change all your magazine subscriptions? Did your children change schools? Did you change your driver's license address? Did you sell the other residence in which you lived? Did you change churches? Did you change your IRS address? Could we see your utility and phone bills to see where you were most of the time?" If they get the wrong answers to these questions a court could rule against you. You will become involved in all kinds of problems including being convicted of a felony. If you're a real estate licensee and are convicted of a felony, you will lose your license and go to jail.

2. Others who are not subject to this law are people who get the property by a deed-in-lieu of foreclosure of any voluntary lien or encumbrance.

3. If you buy at a trustee sale, you do not come under Code Section 1695.

4. Another exception is if you buy the property at a sale authorized by a state statute.

5. It is an exception if you buy by order of judgment of any court. The legislature removed certain sales from the regulations. What they tried to do was, stop the swindlers who go to a trustor's house, sit down at the kitchen table, write up a contract, get a grant deed, and immediately rush down and record it.

6. And the last exception is if you buy from a blood relative.

As exception number one stated, many people do not come under this law because they are buying the foreclosed property to live in. As a real estate salesperson, this becomes an important question when you're showing any property in default: "Are you going to live on the property?" If a Notice of Default has been filed on the property and somebody is buying it as a rental income property, the sale comes under this law. Anyone working in the foreclosure market must be aware of the exceptions to Civil Code 1695.

USE AN ADDENDUM

What should you do to eliminate problems when you're trying to buy from a trustor? First, you should have a good contract. Use a professional deposit receipt. You should prepare an addendum to be used with your contract. On the addendum you will list the items that are peculiar to this law. What are those items? The notice required by California Law and the Notice of Cancellation.

What type of rental agreement should be used? It must be a complete rental agreement. This is a lot of work. It is best to discuss everything ahead of time, put all agreements in writing and have them signed. This will protect you against having a rescission problem or other types of problems with your contract. If the property is going to be purchased and a right of repurchase is to be given to the equity seller, it could be construed as a loan transaction by the State and the IRS. Before doing this, get legal advice from an attorney who knows real estate. Let me repeat. If you are buying from an equity seller (a person who has a Notice of Default filed on his residence) and you are going to give that person the right to repurchase the property, get legal advice from a real estate attorney. It will prevent problems in the future.

RECOMMENDATIONS

Some other procedures are recommended. Number one - use an escrow company. For a small fee, you have somebody else look at your documentation to make certain there is no problem. Make it clear to the escrow officer you are buying this property under Civil Code Section 1695, and do not intend to live in it. This will make a difference in how the transaction should be handled. Be sure to find an escrow company experienced in handling foreclosures.

Number two - use a title company. Some title companies might not want to insure your purchase from a trustor because of possible lawsuits. If that is the case, discuss it with other title companies. Have your escrow company contact other title companies and make certain your title policy does not include any exceptions. A title company might give you protection against all claims, except a claim under Section 1695.13 (unconscionable advantage, etc.). This policy would be worthless to you. If a title company gives you a standard title policy with no exceptions, and if there's any problem later about unconscionable advantage, rescission or cancellation, it would be the responsibility of the title company. Use both escrow and title companies.

If you believe there might be a problem later about whether you took unconscionable advantage of the sellers, get an appraisal by an outside party. Attach the appraisal to the rest of your documentation. You might have the seller initial the appraisal you obtained. Why should you do that? To stay out of trouble and avoid a future lawsuit.

An idea from a seminar speaker and investor, Herb Lewis, is to give money to the equity seller to have the documentation checked by an attorney during the five-business day cancellation period. Often, an attorney can be helpful. This idea would be implemented when you're talking with the equity seller. An appointment is made and the equity sellers go to an attorney they choose and have the documentation reviewed. If an attorney looks at the documentation and approves it for them you would be in a stronger position in a court case.

You should write a statement about why your offer is good for the seller. The seller would take this to the lawyer. For example, you should state that the trustee sale would be coming in a few days. If nothing is done, the lender will have the right to insist on the redemption of the loan, and the loan will have to be paid off. It could be sold at a trustee sale, so you believe this offer is a valid offer. You prepare this explanation to make certain the attorney is not told facts solely by the seller. Write down your facts in a short note the seller will take to the attorney.

LET'S GO NOW

It is time to see the trustor or the owner. One of the biggest misconceptions fostered by many of the real estate seminar experts is that they make this process appear easy. It is not easy. It can be very profitable but do not think it is a piece of cake.

Do not be disturbed if you are somewhat nervous the first time you are going out or if you feel you're somewhat unprepared. The best time to go is now, and the best time to start is now. Do not wait any longer. Get ready to go.

When you call for the appointment to see the trustor, right from the start you should establish that you are a busy, professional person and your time is valuable. You do not want to create the impression that your whole life revolves around this one property. When some real estate brokers call for an appointment, they say, "When would be a better time to come and see you, tonight at 7:00 or tomorrow at 9:00?" This alternate choice of time is not a good close. It implies your time is not valuable. You should close on a specific time by saying, "I would like to come and talk to you. Would tonight at 7:00 p.m. be convenient?" If that's not convenient for them, they will tell you and then you might say, "What time would be convenient for you?" Perhaps their recommendation fits into your schedule.

THE IMPRESSION YOU GIVE IS IMPORTANT

Your personal appearance is going to be eminently important. Go to the property looking good, but not too wealthy. Do not try to overpower the trustor with your symbols of wealth. This is particularly true with some real estate brokers who will drive up in their Lexus or limo with diamonds, rubies and Rolex watches, etc., and think this will make the correct impression. It is important that you do not give the impression that you are independently wealthy. It will hurt you later in negotiations.

When you go to meet with the people, be friendly; be relaxed, but not humorous. This situation is not humorous to them.

Do not talk quickly, and notice the pace at which they speak and try to mirror them. If they talk quickly, you know they're used to this type of conversation, so you can talk a little more quickly. If they speak slowly, do not respond to them with a nervous, staccato type of talking. Be friendly and try to get them into a situation where you can sit down and discuss the property. Perhaps, you can get them into a room that does not have a lot of distractions such as a television or a telephone ringing. Many times you should make the appointment in your own office. If the property needs to be inspected, it's obvious your first meeting should be at the property.

You have to get the owner to believe you are professional. To look professional and organized, you should have data and information about this situation and the foreclosure process. First ask to look at their copy of the Notice of Default. Check the date on which the Notice of Default was recorded and immediately say, "Well, the three-month period will end on such and such date." Count another twenty-one days from that date and say this is the earliest time at which the trustee can hold the auction. Write these figures down for them.

GET LOAN INFORMATION FIRST

Loan information is needed, such as the names of the lenders in order of priority; loan numbers; addresses and phone numbers; what the monthly payment is; the interest rate (whether it is a variable interest rate or fixed is important); the amount that would be necessary at this time to bring the loan current; the date the loan was written; the due date of the loan; the original amount, and the due-on-sale position (Is this loan assumable or will this loan have the possibility of being called by the lender if there is a sale?). Get this information on all the different loans. Find out what the payoffs would be at this time. Ask if there's any possibility that these lenders might discount their values.

After you've gotten the loan information, walk the property. You should not be giving a complete history of yourself. You should be listening, watching and being alert to the conversation. Many times, glances between couples who are in foreclosure will tell you a great deal about what's going on. The reactions of one spouse to the other will be more meaningful than numbers. Even though you might know the property, walk the property and walk it slowly. Have a form or pad with you or use a hand-held tape recorder.

AFTER WALKING THE PROPERTY

The next step is to comment on different items that need repair. The owners know which items need repair. They have been living in the house and know the problems better than you do. As you walk through the home, make comments. Don't be derogatory. Be pleasant. Many times you don't even have to say anything. If a faucet is running and obviously needs washers, just turn it on and off. Your action indicates you've noticed it. You don't have to say, "Look at this faucet! It's going to cost so much money to fix!" One of the things you might say is, "The faucet seems to be running. Do you have any idea what a new faucet would cost if we had to put one in?" If you accept some of their figures, you're talking only about a few dollars and you're negotiating for thousands of dollars. So, if they say the faucet will cost $20.00 to repair and you know it might cost $25.00, do not argue at this point for the $5.00. Simply put down $20.00 to show that you're accepting some of their figures.

To argue at this time for one or two dollars is ridiculous. In that regard, I can remember one of my first sales as a real estate broker. The price was over $600,000 and the buyer made an as-listed offer two hours after he saw the property on the first day the property was listed. This buyer was an intelligent CPA, and he was a brilliant individual in analyzing properties. We inspected the building. He was a good decision-maker and had done his research so well that even though this was the first day the property was on the market, he made an offer.
A few days later, we did the inspection, and found some problems with toilets and leakage. We calculated that this was going to cost something like $1,500. After his inspections, he said he would go ahead with the offer to buy the property, but the bathrooms must be fixed. The whole transaction would have been lost for $1,500, when beforehand, he had agreed readily to the

listed price of more than $600,000 with no hesitation. Nothing would persuade him to change his mind. He had had problems with bathrooms in a previous building and wanted the owner to fix the bathrooms.

This listing had several backup offers. It was listed with another broker, so if our offer were changed in any way, the other broker would immediately have an offer that he would happily submit. You know who paid the $1,500. My broker and I shared the costs and closed the escrow. The point I make here is sometimes even brilliant people do not understand the situation and get involved in, "The Principle of the Thing," for a few dollars.

TAKE PROPER TOOLS AND SUPPLIES

When you visit a property, be prepared. Again, you should have your camera, tape recorder, tape measure and small calculator. If you need measurements, it can be done quickly and you look organized. Some people recommend a flashlight and a marble (you might want to put a marble on the floor to see if it's smooth or if there is any major problem with it shifting or moving). John Reid in his "Apartment Investing Check List," does a great job of telling you how to inspect an apartment. He recommends that you take a large kit containing certain items including a flashlight, a marble and an ice pick to check for dry rot. He recommends a stud finder, so you can check the walls to see if the studs were installed properly.

While walking around, you should check any water heaters. Many times, heaters need to be replaced. Look at the date on the installation tag. Another thing I've always done as a habit is to lift up the cover to the tank on the toilet. Normally, this will be stamped with the date when the building was built. If the bathroom has been modernized this shows when the modernization was done.

Have a form to estimate what it will cost to fix the property. You may or may not bring this out right away, depending on how things are going. You might think, "I'm going to need a great big truck." No, you can get a briefcase or catalog case. When you look organized, you become more organized, and this is an impression you want to create.

WHAT WILL IT COST TO FIX-UP?

Estimate all your repair costs. This includes landscaping, painting, and a new water heater. Check the garbage disposal, dishwasher and the trash compactor. Flush every toilet and try every faucet inside and outside. Check the gates, the pool heater, skimmer, etc. If there are some items for which you need more information, obviously you cannot make a decision at this time. If large repairs are needed, you should get a written estimate.

Sellers sometimes say, "I have to sell right now." Don't be pressured. This is the seller's property. If it is a residence in foreclosure, it is probably their only property. But it is not the only property to you. It is not the end of the world if you don't get it. You can be more casual.

Sellers may put pressure on you and say, "Hey, look, I've got somebody else coming tonight at 9:00." That's fine. If you think you can make a good decision and everything looks fine, go ahead. Have the courage to make an offer, but make it subject to getting an approval of any repairs pending. Write the approval open-ended. "This offer is subject to getting an approved estimate for the backyard magnesite." If I was selling to you and you wrote an open-ended contingency, I definitely would not accept it. Most people only know what to do when they are buying a property. But when you sell, it's quite a bit different. You make an offer subject to the repair. Write, "This offer is approved if an estimate can be received for less than $2,000 within 48 hours."

Many people will try to bluff you. This is a poker game. The poker game starts the minute you meet the trustor or the first time you talk on the phone. There are times when you should just call any bluff. Know when to hold and know when to fold them and know when to run.

CALCULATING "YOUR PRICE"

One of the next forms you have to complete is a form calculating the price at which you think the property is a good value. A sample form is in the last chapter of this book.

When you get to this point, you might have to excuse yourself and go somewhere else to calculate your price before you go back and make an offer. If you were working for me in the field of investment real estate and you were going out to list somebody's rental property, I would insist you do not give the owner a price on your first discussion. If you walk into a property and give a price out of mid-air immediately, you have no basis for your opinion. Doing a firm calculation makes your price more valid.

START WITH FUTURE VALUE

On the Trustee Sale Down Payment worksheet, one of the items that may be unusual is that we start out with future value. This might mean that you'll fix-up the property and put it back on the market. This may mean you will repair and rent the home. It could be repaired for you to live in. Start with the future value of the property to get the present equity. What will the property be worth, when it is ready for future resale or for you to occupy?

Put different data on this future value form. An item listed is carrying costs. This is an important item that many buyers forget; particularly people who are going to fix-up a property and either move into it or resell it. If you're fixing up a property in bad condition, it's going to take two months or more to fix the property. If you're going to sell the unit, it could take another four months or more. In this case, you would have six months of carrying costs in your calculations.

If the property is worth $500,000, it's going to cost at least $3,000 to $4,000 a month to carry it. You're going to have to make payments. You say, "Well, I'm going to put a large amount of money in it, so it isn't going to cost me anything." That's unrealistic thinking. If you're going to put $300,000 to $400,000 in this property, you could make a certain amount having that money in some other investment. If you're making 12% or 15% on that money in some other real estate investment or discounted second trust deed, you have to calculate the cost of the lost interest on your money. A possible rule of thumb for carrying costs is 1% of the future value per month.

BACK TO FIX-UP COSTS

Another item on the form is fix-up costs. What will it cost you to fix-up this property? Let's say that one of the items on your sheet is painting the inside of the house, at a cost of $3,000 if we hired a painter. But you decide that you and your spouse are going to do the painting and save that $3,000. This is called, "sweat equity." Do not subtract the $3,000 from the fix-up costs. You deserve this money.

Put down selling commissions if you're going to resell or "flip" this property. If you're going to lease it, the leasing commissions should be listed. What would a leasing commission be? Probably 6% to 10% of the income for leasing a house. If the home will rent for $3,000 a month; the commission would be at least $2,160 for a year's lease. An easier way to calculate this amount is to take 72% of the $3,000 monthly rent, which would give you the same answer.

If you're going to sell, and you're in an area where a 7% commission is charged on selling homes, you'd have to consider the 7% in addition to other costs. You may have some title costs as well as other selling costs. As an estimate, use 8% to 10% for selling costs in normal transactions.

If you're a real estate licensee include the entire amount charged for selling it. If you're a real estate broker and going to get a 4% commission, I would not lower the selling costs. This is like sweat equity. This is money you're going to earn from performing another function. You might list and sell it, but that's money you're going to make from your real estate operation. It's not going to be a function of the investment. If the price is $500,000 and you're going to get a listing commission, there's approximately $20,000 you're going to receive. Adding that to the $3,000 you're going to make for painting and you've got a $23,000 return, in addition to any profit.

The next item would be miscellaneous costs. You never know what's going to come up. Even when you consider everything in your fix-up cost calculations, allow an amount for contingencies. There could be a bankruptcy, an eviction problem, or unexpected repairs.

DON'T FORGET PROFIT

The last item is profit. There is nothing objectionable about profit. You deserve some profit. If you're going to spend time and effort and risk money, you deserve a profit. You're buying and selling high-ticket items with no guarantee.

What should it be? Some experts will give you a percentage. They say you should never make less than 30% on any property, or you should always buy at 60% of value. There are experts who contend that you can buy at $.03 or $.04 on the dollar. I've been in real estate over 30 years. I associate with knowledgeable investors. We have yet to find these three cents on the dollar buys. Many of these investment gurus or flippers are filing bankruptcies.

One of the most famous gurus, who has written a best-selling book, went out with a reporter and bought many houses with no money. Later, lenders took all of those houses back. I'm not saying this person is not an expert. His book is outstanding. The point I'm making is it isn't as easy as it looks. You're going to find you don't get property at pennies on the dollar, but you should make a profit if you buy wisely.

A percentage should not be used when calculating profit. Every profit situation is different. For example, you have a property under consideration. You're going to fix it up, put it back on the market and sell it. You estimate it's going to take you about four months. The fix-up costs are $32,000, a large amount of money for you. There is a lot of work you're going to have to supervise. Supervising the rehabilitation of a building can be time-consuming and hard work. If it's going to take you 4 months to do this and there's a high risk involved because you're going to resell it, you should make a larger profit. If the unit is a low-end type of property and in a poor area, there is even more risk involved. In this case, you should make a higher profit.

For example, you are considering another property with a future value of $600,000. You're not licensed in real estate so you're not going to make any commission return. $30,000 would be a decent profit figure. However, you know this house and have been negotiating with the owner. You're coming down to the final figures and you already have a contract with a prospective buyer. You will pay a certain amount.

Being a smart person, you have already pre-sold this building to somebody else, subject to you getting title. You are trying to get a $30,000 profit, which would mean you would not want to go any higher than the equivalent of $570,000 to the seller. Your buyers are unique. They want this particular property and you've got the offer in your back pocket. There won't be any fix-up work or any other expenses. You know the minute you get the property, you're going to be able to resell it and close escrow at once. Will you take less than the $30,000? Maybe. This sale is already made and if you don't own it soon, you're going to lose that possibility.

DON'T USE PERCENTAGES

Your profit estimate should be different on every property, depending upon the risk, the money involved and the work you have to do. It's based on what other returns you'll get from this property, such as sweat equity, commission return, and other factors. Don't just pick a percentage.

Would I recommend a guideline? No. It depends on your situation. If you're a wealthy doctor and you're making $200,000 every six months and that's net income, you're not going to run around for $13,000 and do a lot of work. But if you're an unemployed person and have a chance to make $13,000, you're in a different circumstance. Everything is judged by the value and condition of the particular property as well as your financial condition at the time.

TALK TO THE SENIOR LENDERS

Another thing you should do before you make your offer, is to contact the senior lenders to see what they will do if you buy this property. Obviously, you're buying the property from a trustor. Such a sale would be a transfer, and if there's a due-on-sale clause, the lenders may cite it and say the entire loan has to be paid off. A few lenders are doing this. Some lenders are difficult on any transfers.

Be alert, listen and watch. Another habit I'd recommend you try to learn when you're negotiating with people is, after the person finishes speaking or after you finish a thought make a mental count to three. Just "one, two, three," before you start to speak again. Take your time before you speak.

Most of the time, people will continue speaking. They don't want that little bit of silence, so they keep talking. You're going to learn more when they're talking than when you're talking. Learn this habit of counting. Don't interrupt them. Let them finish their thoughts. Let them ramble. You're trying to make money not dominate a debate. You may win the debate and lose the whole game. An example that illustrates this point is a study of Yale graduates. A survey showed pipe smokers made more money than non-smokers did and non-smokers averaged more money than cigarette smokers did. What this seems to indicate is the pipe smokers often appear to be more intellectual because they have this ability to dominate a conversation by putting the pipe to their mouth, lighting a match, and providing periods of silence.

Another technique is when you make your offer, make it in an uneven dollar amount. Mark McCormack, in his book, *"What They Don't Teach You at Harvard Business School,"* made several good points on negotiation. Mark McCormack is an agent for many famous athletes and has one of the greatest management companies in the United States. He does a lot of negotiating with famous figures and companies like ABC and NBC. One of the points he made was to use silence. Another point he made is to always make your offer uneven, and have a reason for that amount. A lot of people will make an offer and always round it off to $100,000 or $50,000 or $85,000. Make your offer an uneven amount. It illustrates you have worked hard on your offer.

I learned this in real estate a long time ago. For example, a seller would have a house for sale, listed at $100,000 and someone would make an offer at $90,000. Many times a counter-offer would split the difference and come back at an even $95,000. If you think the counter-offer should be about $95,000, don't make it an even $95,000. A person made the $90,000 offer, handed it to the broker who took it to the seller. The seller came back with a $95,000 offer. The person who made the $90,000 offer has had a long period of time to consider any counter. They've been saying, "I'm probably going to get a counter of $95,000." They've had a couple of days to think up all their reasons why $95,000 is no good. What you want to do is surprise them.

According to McCormack, you come back with an offer, not of $95,000, but $95,287 or $94,816. By doing it this way, the first words out of the recipient's mouth are, "Where'd you get that figure?" It could change the negotiation a little bit. Many times it won't make any difference at all. However, it livens up negotiations. If you're going to go through life negotiating and spending a lot of time negotiating, then negotiating should be fun to you.

One other idea on this subject came from a brilliant attorney in Encino named Norton Karno. I was interviewing Norton, and he said something very pertinent: "When you give that uneven offer of $94,816, have a reason for it." Whether the reason is so much per square foot or minus so much for fix-up costs or something, come up with an uneven amount. If you come up with a solid reason when they say, "Where'd you get that figure?" it's going to help you a lot in the long run.

PERSONAL PROPERTY AND RENTAL STATEMENTS

There are a couple of other items you should consider when you're making an offer. If any personal property is going to be involved, you should have a personal property inventory that lists everything being sold. If a refrigerator is involved, don't just write down one refrigerator. You may return to the property after the sale and find an old refrigerator has replaced the new refrigerator that had been there. Don't get caught in the trap of writing "a refrigerator." Write Frigidaire, Serial Number such and such; Magic Chef stove, Serial Number such and such. Don't make this too simple. Getting down on your hands and knees and writing down serial numbers will save you a lot of trouble in the long run.

If there is a rental on the property, you should demand an Estoppel Certificate. This is a statement signed by the tenants listing the monthly rent, deposits, due dates, services and furniture included, parking spaces and any other agreements. I don't want the owner telling me the rent is $3,000 and later I find that's incorrect. I have never sold an apartment house in my life where the deposits and the rents ever came out the same for both the buyer and seller unless an Estoppel Certificate was used. Errors will be made most of the time in the amount of deposits and due dates.

For example, there are cases where the owner listed a tenant's deposit as $2,500 and the tenant had made an additional deposit of $500 (for a pet deposit). The tenant had signed receipts from the owner for $3,000, but you got only $2,500 from the owner's rental statement. When the tenant moves you say, "I didn't get that money, I'm not paying it. Go after the owner." If the tenant goes to Small Claims Court, you're going to pay.

If you ever buy rental property, remember the words "Estoppel Certificate." Get a statement signed by the tenant stating what the rent is, what the deposits are, due date, security deposits, advance rents, utilities they pay, and if they have been given any concessions. If they have been paying $3,000 a month, but they were given the first two months free on a one-year lease, they're not paying $3,000 because they were given one sixth of their rent-free for the whole years. Be sure to ask about concessions.

IT'S TIME TO CLOSE

You might try the following two closes with the seller. One is, "I'm going to save your credit." If you can say, "Sure you can slow down the action with a bankruptcy, but that will hurt your credit for a long time and the foreclosure is going to hurt your credit score for a long time. Every time you sign a loan application for the rest of your life, they're going to ask you if you've ever experienced a foreclosure or bankruptcy. If you lie, it's perjury and a lender could cancel a loan."

Another idea is that you can save them time. They can go ahead with the rest of their life. If they list the property, it takes listing time, showing time, refinance time, escrow time and all the other items. You're saving them both time and credit.

No "scripts" are included in this book. I disagree with the people who give you planned scripts. A planned script is fantastic for the person who wrote it. You should write your own. You know what you're going to talk about and have some idea of what you want to cover. Write your ideas down and cover them from a checklist. Don't try to take somebody else's words and use them. It doesn't work.

When I first got into selling, I tried to learn the scripts my bosses recommended, and I knew all my lines. When I was going through a script, the clients didn't know their lines and we didn't get anywhere. Every case is different. You'll know what to do and how to change your presentation when needed.

If you feel there's something going on and you're indecisive as to whether to ask them to do something or not, ask for action. They're either going to say no, or you're going to keep talking. Ask for the action. If you want to offer $505,000 right now, ask them, "If you got the $505,000 now, would you sell?" or "When would you like to move?" or "When would you like to meet at the escrow office?" You will learn more closes as you work in the field. But as I said before, if in doubt, ask for action.

That's one of the reasons children are such good closers. Children will always ask and they'll keep asking and asking and even though they're obnoxious, they win. Don't be afraid to ask, but don't be pushy. Sometimes you should just try to find out what's going on. If they say "No," then say, "What is your biggest objection to this?" Listen, listen, listen. Silence is a great close. Spouses have been using it for centuries.

MAKE IT WIN-WIN

Don't drive for the last penny. Make your negotiation a win-win situation and move on to the next sale. You won't have many sales fall out of escrow and won't have as many problems later. If you squeeze for the last penny, you're going to have problems sometime.

Don't try to be a philanthropist. Don't try to solve the problems of the world. You're going to run into problems. The sellers have them at this time or they wouldn't be in default and you can't save everyone.

You can help them find solutions, which will make you feel good, but if it starts affecting your business sense, you should not get involved in this situation. Many people should not be dealing with trustors. I do not deal well with trustors. I deal better with REO's and junior lenders. If you feel you can deal well with trustors, it's one of the more lucrative areas. As I said before, be fair but business-like. Try to get the sale at the best possible price so you both benefit, then you can move on to your next property.

Chapter 5
Junior Lenders

Earlier in this book, I referred to junior lenders as the Maytag repairmen of this whole process. They are the lonely ones. Many people visit the Real Estate Owned Departments of Lenders. Trustors are visited by many people. Many people go to Trustee Sales, but hardly anybody ever calls on a junior lender. I know this to be true because in my seminars I have asked a lot of people who have had junior loans on a property, "What happened when a senior loan foreclosed on a property and the Notice of Default had been put in the paper?" No one ever called them, and their equity was wiped out unless they had taken control of the situation.

Suppose a real estate licensee has worked extremely hard on a listed property. A second loan is foreclosing, and the real estate licensee is trying to sell this house with a third and fourth trust deed on the property. Perhaps there's equity in the property. But nobody ever contacts the third and fourth holders to see if they would discount their notes.

Work with junior lenders. Junior lenders are intelligent when it comes to lending money and are intelligent on collecting money, but maybe a junior lender does not know anything about foreclosures. Many of these loans were created as purchase money loans when a sale was closed. The lenders might even think they have the right to foreclose and get a judgment. If it's a purchase money deed of trust where somebody carried a note back from a sale of a piece of property, the chance of getting any money is slight. I have never heard of anyone getting a personal judgment when a purchase money deed of trust is defaulted. It just isn't going to happen. According to the California Civil Code, the only thing the lender can do is look to the property. Junior lenders do not know their situation. Help them.

Explain the procedures to them; educate them and try to do it eyeball to eyeball. Use the phone to get an appointment, but don't close over the phone. Use the phone only to get the appointment, then go eyeball to eyeball and remember our good impression rule: You don't get a second chance to make a first impression.

JUNIOR LENDERS HAVE DIFFERENT OUTLOOKS

There are some good points about dealing with junior lenders. They are less emotional, when compared to a person who's going to lose their home. Many times a junior lender will be more sophisticated. It is easier to explain the procedures of trustee sales to them.

As a junior lender, they have the right to request beneficiary statements from senior lenders. If you're dealing with junior lenders, you can get accurate dollar amounts as to what is owed, rather than trying to guess.

When you're dealing with junior lenders, consider trading notes with them. They have a note. They know the note is in foreclosure because a Notice of Default has been filed. They don't know exactly what this means. You might give them information from your California Civil Codebook to show them what it does mean. There is a definite period of time in which the trustor has the right to bring the senior loan current. If the note isn't brought current and there is a trustee sale, the junior lender loses everything. Consider trading their note for a note on a property that is not in foreclosure. Their note is an "I-don't-want-it-note."

Consider an idea from Herb Lewis. He recommends that you go out and buy other notes. Go to a note holder from whom you can buy a note at a discount. Notes on properties that are secured by real estate often can be discounted.

For example, a junior lender's note is $80,000. You ask, "Look, you have a note in default, so therefore your note has to be discounted 40%. A 40% discount is $32,000, so your note is only worth $48,000." Now, you go out and try to find a note for around $48,000. It may not be a good note and you can discount it 40%, so you pay only 60% or $28,800. You take this note and trade it to the junior lender. Because the junior lenders are worried at this time that they might lose all their equity, they might consider a note on another piece of property.

USE AN ATTORNEY

When you agree on a price, enter into a contract approved by an attorney. You ask, "What kind of an attorney?" A real estate attorney. Call the local Real Estate Association or Board of Realtors and ask them who their attorney is. They might be able to refer you to a real estate attorney. Be sure you get a real estate attorney and not an attorney who specializes in other areas. This field is complex, so find somebody who knows it.

After the contract has been signed and consummated, you'll get an assignment of the rights of this party. You take your assignment and record it with the County Recorder. You are now the holder of a recorded note. There is a Notice of Default pending filed by a first trust deed holder, and you have purchased the second trust deed. You now foreclose on your note. How do you do that? You pay the default amount due on the first loan and bring it current. You start your own foreclosure for the amount the second is owed, plus the amount you advanced to the other lenders and any costs incurred to start your own foreclosure.

One of the advantages of doing this, is that you're going to gain control of the property at a trustee sale and not come under Civil Code Section 1695. In an earlier chapter our discussion was about buying from a trustor. If you were buying from a trustor and were not going to live on the property, you have all those strict rules to follow. By doing your own foreclosure you avoid those rules. You would not come under the two-year rule or the four-year limit on damages rule, or the unconscionable advantage rule of rescission.

After you've purchased the junior note in this situation, you could visit the trustor. You're now a third trust deed holder, and there is nothing to lose by talking to the trustor unless you think there's a possibility of violence. Of course, if you're buying from a junior lender and you call the trustor and say, "By the way, I'm buying the junior lender's note so I can foreclose myself," you are not going to be welcomed with open arms at the house. You'll have to make your decision in each case, based on your feelings.

YOU CAN GO TO THE OWNER

Contact the trustors and ask if they will give you a deed-in-lieu and take over the property. Of course, if there's a recorded note junior to yours, you may want to go ahead with your foreclosure to clear off that trust deed. You should get a preliminary title report long before you enter into this situation. You would not accept a deed-in-lieu without a preliminary title report, and you would not have bought the note without a preliminary title report. This is what any good attorney would have mentioned.

When you are the junior lender, you can contact the trustors and offer them some money to move. They may need the money to move. They may be completely broke and can't get away. Remember our previous rule: "Don't hand them the money until they're on the street and you're standing there with the locksmith next to you."

The situation on evaluating the property will be exactly the same as with the trustor. You have to evaluate the property from the same standpoint and use the same workup sheet. Your down payment is the amount you're going to be paying the third note holder, not what you'd be paying the trustor.

You have to contact the senior lenders to see what they will do. Suppose you called them and said, "I am buying a third trust deed on a property upon which you have a loan. What is your policy?" You'll find in most cases if somebody forecloses and has a foreclosure sale and takes the property back, lenders will not call their loan "due on sale." If you, as a beneficiary, take over at a trustee sale, you are in a much safer position with most lenders.

Do not forget the Maytag repairman of the foreclosure business, the junior lienholders on a property. You can be doing them a favor; you're not being a vulture. If you do not contact them, they will get nothing. It is a win-win situation. The junior lenders would have let the property go to a foreclosure sale and would have lost their equity. You don't have to feel that you're a vulture or a snake or a shark or a weasel. You can believe that you've done people a service and given them something. The reason you made money is because you have a better knowledge of the foreclosure system.

Chapter 6
Trustee Sales

Some advisors will tell you to never buy at a trustee sale. You just never buy at a trustee sale; you buy before the actual auction. You buy from the trustor or you buy from the junior lender, but in no way, do you go to a trustee sale.

I don't agree with that idea. There are times when you should go to a trustee sale. For example, you don't receive information in time about the default notice. You can't find the trustor. Trustors might be uncooperative.

The property could be listed with a broker. In order to buy the property you would have had to go through a broker, which might make it unprofitable, so you wait for the trustee sale. Sometimes there are such large amounts of loans on the property that it is impossible to buy from the trustor. If the property has excessive financing, it might be a good buy only at a trustee sale.

LACK OF KNOWLEDGE

Trustee sales are a topic that most of the public does not understand. In classes, I give some evaluation problems, not to expose the student's lack of knowledge, but to show the licensees that they do not understand trustee sales. The question is, "How much money would you take to a sale, based on these facts?" I'd give them the loan amounts, opening bids, present value, etc. You'd be amazed at their answers. Five years ago one or two percent of the class would get the right answer. Today, more people get it right because they have attended foreclosure seminars. However, less than twenty percent of licensed real estate agents get the correct answers. They have been in the field of real estate many years and do not know the answers to questions about trustee sales.

GET YOUR INFORMATION

Where do we find out about trustee sales? We read about them in newspaper transcripts or from a service to which we subscribe. Also title company websites have information. The trustee sales transcripts are similar to default sales transcripts, but they don't give an extensive amount of information. Most of them will show:

- Address
- Legal Description
- Estimated Opening Bid
- Place & Time of the Auction
- Recorded Trustee Sale Number and Date of Record
- Name and Telephone Number of Trustee
- Trustor
- Beneficiary

You should visit a trustee sale before you ever go to one to bid. You should not go to your first trustee sale intending to bid on a property. You should go to at least one sale for a practice run so that you will be more confident and prepared when you are ready to bid. It costs nothing to be a spectator at a sale.

START SLOWLY

What do you do? The sale is thirty-five days in the future. I recommend you do not do anything for a period of time. It may take you approximately fifteen to twenty days to find out about the property and to get ready for the trustee sale. So don't do anything until approximately fifteen days before the sale, because you may spend a whole lot of time working on a sale to no avail. The owner may file bankruptcy, the sale be postponed, the note paid off, or the beneficiary may allow the borrower to reinstate. These are just a few of the possibilities. Don't waste your time until about fifteen days before the sale.

What do you do then? You call the trustee and ask, "Is the sale on Blank Street still scheduled to be held?" They'll either tell you "yes", or the sale has been postponed, or the default has been cured. If it's still scheduled, then do your analysis. You will do the same calculation of present value that you did when you were talking to the trustor.

There is one other caveat that you should consider. The person in the property will probably not move out, and you're going to have to allow eviction time plus the cost of an eviction. There is the possibility the person might claim bankruptcy, and it will take even longer for you to get possession. Estimate that you're going to have at least one extra month of carrying costs because of the eviction problem that's almost sure to arise.

In most cases, you probably will not get in to see the property because you're not talking to the trustor. So drive by, get as good a look as you can, and then estimate your costs. You ask, "You actually expect me to buy a property without seeing the inside of the property?" My answer to that question is a statement, "I have seen many, many, many people make a lot of money at Trustee Sales, and they have never been inside any of the properties before they buy at the trustee sale." It's the way the game is played.

THE DAY OF THE SALE

The day of the sale has come. You call the trustee early on the morning of the sale and ask five questions.

Number 1: "Is the sale on Blank Street still on?"

Number 2: "What is the opening bid going to be?" The opening bid that was listed in the paper may have changed due to many factors.

Number 3: "What will overbids have to be?" If the opening bid is $270,000 and a penny and the next person says $270,000 and 2 pennies or 3 pennies or 4 pennies, trustees will not allow this type of bidding. They might say $100 or $500 for overbids, depending upon the size of the bid. This will be the minimum amount that you would have to take to bid.

Number 4: "What type of funds do you accept?" You have read the Civil Code and know the answer, but you want to check to prevent any problems. If they say something that isn't in accordance with the Code, you can say "Hey, this doesn't sound right, because here, under trustee sales in the Civil Code, it says I can bring a cashier's check from a Federal Savings and Loan or a Credit Union." Ask them, so that you do not have any problems at the sale.

Number 5: "To whom must the checks be made payable?" The possibility that this would be a problem is probably remote, but lately trustees, who work for beneficiaries who want the property back, have insisted that the checks be made payable to them. Most people who go to a trustee sale will carry cashier's checks made payable to themselves. The reason that you have the check made payable to yourself is that in the case that you do not get the property, you will still have the money in checks made payable to yourself. If you wanted to go to another sale later or to a sale the next day, you could still carry those checks with you. If you wanted to put the money back in the bank, this would be no problem. If the checks were made payable to XYZ Title Company and you didn't get the bid, you'd have to take the checks back to your bank to cash them and this is time-consuming. You want to take $400,000 to the sale. That's what you've calculated. The opening bid is $270,000. You might take one check of $270,100 and then another check for $75,000 and another check for the remainder of the amount. If you get the bid of $27,000 you don't have to give the trustor a check for $400,000 and wait to get your money back. Remember, all the costs involved are figured in the trustee sales bid for the beneficiary, so if the bid is $270,000 and you bid $270,100 and get the property, that's all you have to pay at that time. But if the bids go up to $330,000, you'll give the $75,000. If the final bid is $380,000 and you have only the checks for $400,000, you would give the $400,000 and get any extra money back within a few days.

CHECK WITH SENIOR LENDERS

Long before you went to the trustee sale, you should have checked with any senior lenders. This is important. Many people go to the sales without checking with the senior lenders. To worry about it might be unnecessary, but I still recommend that you ask the senior lenders what they would do if you purchase a property.

Many lenders do not want the property back and are happy if someone will bring their loans current. If it's a loan with great terms, they may want one point, a loan processing fee, or an interest rate increase. They may want to blend a new interest rate based on the existing interest rate and the current market rate. Many investors do not talk to senior lenders, and they have no problems, but it's wise to talk to senior lenders to prevent later problems.

HOW MUCH MONEY TO TAKE

The next step is to calculate how much money to take with you to the sale. This is important because it is another question to which most people don't know the answer. It is a simple calculation, but many people become confused.

This is how you should do your calculating. You find out what the present value of the property is to you. To do this, you start with the future value and subtract the fix-up costs, carrying costs, and costs of vacating; add in some profit for yourself and all of the other costs involved in doing the transaction. Take this figure and subtract it from the future value. By doing this, you find out what the value of the property is at this moment to you. You take this figure, the present value to you, and put it aside. Then research any other obligations against the property.

Are there any back property taxes? If there are any, they do not have to be paid off at the trustee sale. But if you buy the property at the trustee sale those taxes are never wiped off. Real estate taxes are the most senior lien on any property. No matter who forecloses, the real estate taxes stay there. You don't have to take any money to the sale to pay them, but they have to be considered a loan to any buyer because later you are going to have to pay them.

List the other loans that are senior to the loan foreclosing. In your calculations, you should list all of the loans on the property. You figure out which loans will still be on the property after the trustee sale is completed. Obviously, the loans that are junior to the loan foreclosing are removed and do not have to be considered.

If the final bid is higher than the opening bid, any overage will go to any junior lien holder in order of priority. If there is still money left over, it would go to the next loan. If there is still money left over and there were no other liens or loans, the remainder would go to the trustor. The senior loans and their arrearages do not have to be paid at the time of the sale.

Write the loan amounts down and determine which loan is foreclosing (which one is making the opening bid). Remove the foreclosing loans and any junior loans from your list. Completely disregard the opening bid, the foreclosing loan amount and all the junior loans. They are of no consequence to you as a buyer at a trustee sale when you are calculating what you think the property is worth.

In rare instances, the junior lienholders might show up at the trustee sale and bid, but to you, they are like strangers from the street. Disregard the opening bid at this time. You will do your calculations as to what you think the property is worth. The opening bid is of no consequence to you at this time. It does not indicate value.

If a lender had made a really stupid loan and put a tremendous amount of money into this property in excess of the value of the property, you should not have to worry about their poor evaluation. Therefore, you look at the loans that will be on the property after the trustee sale. If you add the opening bid to the senior loans outstanding after the trustee sale, you get an amount that would be like a listed price in a real estate listing. It could be high or low when compared to our evaluation.

PRESENT VALUE – OBLIGATIONS TOMORROW

Take the present value of the property to you at this time and subtract the obligations that will be on the property tomorrow (senior loans or senior liens to the loan foreclosing and any delinquent real estate taxes). That is the amount of money you would take to the sale, and the highest amount you would bid. After you have completed this calculation, you then look at the opening bid. If your amount is larger than the opening bid, you go to the sale. If your calculation is lower than the opening bid (and it may be in many cases), you do not go to the sale, and you let the beneficiary take the property back.

This does not mean that you couldn't possibly call the beneficiary later and see if they would take a reduction. If your calculation shows the value is $210,000 and the opening bid is $270,000, then you stay home. If you go to a sale where the opening bid is $270,000 and you yell out $210,000, you're not going to buy many properties.

Don't ever take too much money to the sale. If you take too much, you will get caught up in the emotions of the situation. If you think the property is worth only $400,000 to you, then take only $400,000. Do not take $600,000 to see what happens.

This reminds me of a sale in Northridge, California years ago. The house was owned by CALTRANS. CALTRANS was going to sell this house to the public by auction. The beginning bid was only $40,000. The house was worth about $60,000. (Hard for you young people to understand.) CALTRANS auctions were fun because to bid you only needed a personal check for $1,000. You could bid whatever you wanted to. In fact, you could bid without even showing your money. If I could have bought the property for the amount of the opening bid, it would have been an excellent buy.

Half the population of Northridge was at this property. Even though there was no chance of getting the property at the opening bid, I thought I'd stay to see what happened at the sale. The bidding started at $40,000 and went by $60,000 quickly. The value was $60,000 to me as an investment, so I just watched. All of a sudden the bidding was going 61, 62, 63, getting up near 70, 71 and now the bidding is being done by only two couples.

These two couples separated from the remainder of the group and inched towards the auctioneer. A woman was making one of the bids, and she wasn't even looking at the auctioneer anymore. She was just turning to the other woman as if to say, "Take that - $71,000!" The other woman, after the bidding increased even more, turned to her husband and said, "John, don't let that #@%*# get my house." Now, we're not talking value anymore, we're talking emotion – pure and simple. Obviously someone was going to pay much more for the house than it was worth. Probably John.

TAKE THE RIGHT AMOUNT

By the same token, do not take too little money. A woman at one of my meetings interrupted the class and kept insisting you should never take more than one dollar over the opening bid. She had heard this was the only way to go to a trustee sale.

Suppose, you think a property is worth $40,000 above the obligations that will be there tomorrow. The opening bid is $20,000. You go to the auction with $20,100. That would be a good move if no one else showed up to bid. You could then hand the auctioneer $20,100 and walk away with the property and have a fine profit. However, you would like it even at a bid of $40,000, because you've already done your present value calculations and you have allowed profit in the $40,000 bid. You'd be happy to give the auctioneer the $40,000 and walk away with the title to the property.

If you take only $20,100, somebody could show up with a few dollars more and they'll make a great profit because they knew how much money to take to a trustee sale. Don't get caught up in the theory that you only take a few dollars more than the opening bid because good buys do not come along that regularly. Properties are not like subways where a train comes along every few minutes. Properties are hard to find. If you go through all the calculations and take the time to go to the sale, then you may find that you're wasting a great deal of time if you don't take enough money. Remember, take enough money, but don't take too much money.

KNOW WHAT YOU'RE DOING

When you're at the sale, be alert. This is not tea and crumpets time. This is business, and there are people standing around who'd love to get that property away from you. One time a naïve bidder was standing next to two very experienced bidders. The two experienced bidders looked over at the naïve bidder and, without even stopping for breath, one man said to the other, "You're a cement contractor, John. What are you going to do about that great big old cracked foundation? Did you notice how cracked that foundation was in back?" John says, "Yeah, I figure about $50,000." The inexperienced bidder heard this and became confused. He didn't lower his bid and the other men got the property.

Be alert. Stand and observe what the people are doing. Watch the body language and everything that you possibly can. Don't be intrigued by how the people are dressed. Don't be impressed by what type of car they drive. The fact that someone drives up in a Mercedes simply means that they had enough money to make the lease payment at one time or they borrowed the car. This does not necessarily mean the person is wealthy. Many times the people who are dressed the poorest have the biggest amounts of money in their pockets. Learn to watch, look and listen, and do not give out too much information. Keep your eyes and ears open and your mouth shut.

The State of California passed a law because of something that was happening at trustee sales. Let's say there's value in the property at a trustee sale. The opening bid is going to be $40,000 and two people show up. One is experienced and the other is not. In the past, the experienced bidder would walk over to the inexperienced bidder and say, "Look, we're both standing here and the opening bid is going to be $40,000 and both of us know that." (There's probably another $30,000 of true value and so a reasonable, rational person would be there with $70,000. So let's assume that this inexperienced person is reasonable and rational, and might have anywhere from $40,000 to $70,000).

The experienced bidder would reach in a pocket and show an extremely large amount of money, something like $110,000 in cashier's checks. He or she would show the money and say, "This is how much money I have - $110,000. I'm not asking you how much you have, but I am telling you that I have enough to buy this property. If you don't have that much money, I will give you $1,000 or $2,000 to leave the sale at this time. If you have more than that, simply show it to me and I'll leave right now." If the inexperienced person saw that kind of money and knew he or she would not be able to get the property, they might take the $1,000 or $2,000 and walk away. Then, since they were the only two bidders at the sale, the experienced bidder would bid $100 over the $40,000 and get the property.

ANYTHING CAN HAPPEN

You say that couldn't happen in the US of A. It happened so often in California that the State passed a law making it a criminal offense to offer anybody money not to bid at a sale. In fact, I have a friend who said he knew of someone who used to dress up in a suit and tie and go to some of these sales and stand around hoping that someone would hand him money to walk away.

The sale is like an auction. To qualify for the bidding, people must show their money. You show the money only to the trustee. In some areas the trustee takes the money and holds it. In other areas they just check if you have enough money to bid and how much money you have. If the opening bid is $20,000 and you have $40,000, they will let you bid up to $40,000. The trustor will keep track of the bids and when you go over $40,000, they will interrupt the bidding and say you cannot bid. Obviously, the trustees don't tell anyone how much money each bidder holds.

In certain counties, the trustees tell the bidders that they must give all the money that they hope to bid at the beginning. This would be like table stakes in poker. Every area is different. In some areas the trustees will hold the money, and some will just look at the amount. You must have the money. You cannot use a Letter of Credit or anything like that.

WATCH, LOOK AND LISTEN

Do not be too verbal. Do not give away anything. At a trustee sale one time, the opening bid was $200,000 and several bidders were there. One man was experienced, while an effervescent young couple seemed very inexperienced. The opening bid was $200,000 and the trustee said, "All bidders who would like to qualify step forward and show their funds." So the young couple, led by the wife, walked up and said loudly, "Oh, we have $260,000", and showed the money to the trustee, who wrote down $260,000.

This trustee had said that any bids would have to be $500 over the previous bid, so the experienced bidder looked at the situation and analyzed it. He knew that if this young couple had $260,000, they were ready to bid that amount. He thought the property was worth much more and so rather than let them bid $260,000, which would mean he would have to bid $260,500, the first bid out of his mouth was $260,000. Therefore, the young couple could not bid, and the buyer saved $500.

A person in Torrance told me a story of a sale where the bidding was getting spirited. One bidder bid $29,000 and the next bidder bid $30,000. Then the trustee said to the man who had bid $30,000. Your bid has to be erased. Do you have any more money?" The man had no more money, so the trustee said, "I have $29,000," reacting back to the prior bid. The person who had bid $29,000 became so excited that he yelled out, "$30,000, and overbid himself." Do not get caught up in the emotions of the situation.

OTHER WAYS TO DO IT

One step that you could take would be to borrow money on any equity that you have. People forget that if they have Certificates of Deposit, they can borrow against them. I know someone that had a Certificate of Deposit, which he could have used, but instead he used a credit card for a large amount of money at 18%. What a waste! What you can do is, take the Certificate of Deposit to the bank at which you deposited it and in most cases get a loan at no more than 2% above the face interest of the Certificate of Deposit. So borrow against something.

There are some banks that have revolving credit on property that you own. You go to the bank and get approval of a 2nd trust deed on your home, and they approve you to a certain level. If you need money to go to a trustee sale, you borrow against this equity line of credit. They will lend you money to go to the trustee sale. If you win at the trustee sale and get the property, you will fix the property up, resell it, and pay the loan back. If you don't get the property, you take the money back to the bank. You pay a one-time processing fee when you start.

Another idea is to get some partners to equity share this type of property. Perhaps, you can find somebody who might even like it as a home and share with you. We don't have the time to get involved in this book but remember the term, "equity share." You get somebody to move into the property and help with the payments; they get the residence and you get the tax benefits and a share of the profit.

Another method is to find a partner. You could form a partnership with an attorney, CPA, or doctor, etc. You would find the property, and they would put up the money. The property would be sold later, and the profits split by prearranged agreement.

You could function as a buyer's agent. In this case, you'd find buyers and take them out to the property. I strongly recommend that you become licensed. But even if you're not, you can make an agreement with somebody to take them to the sale in exchange for a share of future profit instead of a commission.

Put away any idea of not going to a trustee sale. Remember, many times this is the last chance you will have to buy that property, because you couldn't find the trustor, or the trustor was uncooperative, or the property had high financing, or it's listed with a real estate broker and it has not been possible to create a sale, or you happen to hear about the property late. So get out there, look at some properties and go to a trustee sale right away; and start to make some changes in your life.

EXTRA INFORMATION

Included on the following pages are some forms to illustrate points made in the book. They are: an Addendum to Deposit Receipt for Equity Purchase, Owner's Equity in Property, Amount of Cash to Take to Sale, and Trustee Sale Problems and Answers.

ADDENDUM TO DEPOSIT RECEIPT FOR EQUITY PURCHASERS

Property:_____

Date:_____

Buyers:_____

Sellers:_____

"NOTICE REQUIRED BY CALIFORNIA LAW" Until your right to cancel this contract has ended

_____ or anyone working for
        (Name of Equity Purchaser)

_____ CANNOT ask you to sign
        (Name of Equity Purchaser)

or have you sign any deed or any document."

NOTICE OF CANCELLATION_____
                       (Enter date contract signed)

You may cancel this contract for the sale of your house, without any penalty or obligation,
at any time before_____
    (Enter date and time of day)

TIME OF POSSESSION (to be transferred to buyer at_____

Property is to be rented to seller. Yes_____ No_____

If yes is checked, a completed rental agreement is attached.

_____   _____
   (Buyer)   (Seller)

_____   _____
   (Buyer)   (Seller)

_____   _____
   (Buyer)   (Seller)

Date and time signed _____   Date and time signed_____

EQUITY IN PROPERTY – TRUSTOR SALE

Address: _____

Date: _____

Date of Default: _____

Value of Property $_____

Less:

    Loans
    1st $_____

       2nd   _____

    3rd   _____

    Other   _____

    Taxes & Lien   _____

Fix-up Costs
(include sweat equity)   _____

Carrying Costs   _____

Selling or Leasing Costs
(include your commission)   _____

New Financing Costs   _____

Contingencies   _____

Profit
(varies for each property)   _____

    Totals $_____

Present Equity of Owner $_____

TRUSTEE SALE DOWN PAYMENT OF CALCULATION

(Amount of cash to take to sale)

FUTURE VALUE OF PROPERTY $_____

Fix-up Costs
(include sweat equity) $_____

Carrying Costs   _____

Selling or Leasing costs
(include your commission)   _____

Vacating costs   _____

Other costs   _____

Contingencies   _____

Profit   _____

      PRESENT VALUE $_____

Less:

    Loans senior to
    bidding party including
    back payments:

        1st $_____

        2nd _____

        3rd _____

    Property taxes and other
    liens   _____

      LOANS AND TAXES $_____

CASH TO TAKE TO SALE $_____

OPENING BID $_____

IF OPENING BID IS HIGHER THAN THE ABOVE AMOUNT DON'T GO TO THE SALE

TRUSTEE SALE PROBLEMS

Problem No. 1

A property has a first loan of $500,000 that is current. Property taxes are current. The second loan holder has a note for $200,000 and is the beneficiary bidder at the trustee sale. The opening bid is $272,000. The trustee states any new bid must be $200 over the old bid. There is a third loan balance of $100,000 that has back interest owed of $15,000.

You are a person off the street. You have checked the first loan and it was made by a State Savings and Loan in 2000.

Your future value calculation is $1,200,000 and your present value including a good profit is $950,000.

How much cash should you take to the sale based on the above figures? *950,000?*

882? or 815,0'

Will the trustor get any money from the sale if we make our highest bid? How much?

Problem No. 2

> 1st loan - $500,000 plus $20,000 owed in back interest
> 2nd loan - $200,000 plus $12,000 owed in back interest
> 3rd loan - $100,000 – bidding $135,000 at trustee's sale
> Property taxes – $22,000 owed
> Future Value - $1,200,000
> Present Value - $987,000   *465?*
> Overbids - $1,000

> How much cash should you take to a sale?

Problem No. 3 (A small condo somewhere)

> 1st loan - $110,000 – opening bid of $118,700
> 2nd loan - $22,000 plus $3,500 behind in interest
> 3rd loan - $11,000 plus $1,100 behind in interest
> Taxes - $5,200 in arrears
> Present Value - $130,500   *don't*
> Overbids - $500

How much cash should you take to a sale?

If winning bid is $152,100, will the 3rd loan holder get any money? How much? *3900*

Problem No. 4

Same facts as number 2, but our present value is $845,000. How much should we take?

Answers to Problems

Problem No. 1

Answer is: Present Value – Obligations Remaining Tomorrow. $950,000 - $500,000 or $450,000. All of the other loans will not be there tomorrow. $450,000 is the amount to take to the sale.

The second loan holder will receive $272,000. The third loan holder will receive $115,000 leaving $63,000 for the trustor.

Problem No. 2

Present Value to me		$987,000

Less Obligations Remaining Tomorrow

1st loan	$520,000	
2nd loan	212,000	
3rd loan	erased	
Taxes	22,000	
Total	$754,000	
		$233,000

That is more than the opening bid so we go to the sale

Problem No. 3

Present Value	$130,500

Less Obligations Remaining Tomorrow

1st loan	erased
2nd loan	erased
3rd loan	erased
Taxes	$5,200
Total	$5,200
Money to take to sale	$125,300

Part No. 2 – If $152,100 is bid (obviously not our bid) the first loan holder would receive $118,700, the second would receive $25,500 leaving $7,900 for the third and nothing for the trustor.

Problem No. 4

Present Value $845,000

Less Obligations Remaining Tomorrow

1st loan	$520,000
2nd loan	212,000
Taxes	22,000

Total   754,000

Money to take to sale $91,000

That is less than opening bid so we don't to go to sale.

I don't get it at all!

Chapter 7
Questions, Answers & References

In California Real Estate Continuing Education there are these types of courses: Agency, Ethics, Trust Fund Handling, Fair Housing, and Risk Management are the required courses and are called Mandated Courses. Other courses are either Consumer Protection or Consumer Services.

Consumer Service classes are more or less designed to give consumers better service and to make licensees more money. Consumer Protection Courses, as the name implies, are supposed to educate licensees so that they can better protect their clients. The Real Estate Update Course is Consumer Protection. One way to better protect clients is to find answers to their questions even before they ask them. The best method to find answers is to go to the applicable Code Sections so you can give clients reference sources. It is not intended for you to give legal advice. That is for attorneys. However, telling a client a Civil Code reference is not practicing law. You are showing them where they can find answers to difficult questions. If they need more information or an interpretation of a Code Section, you advise them to quickly see an attorney.

Agents, Escrow Officers, Loan Officers, Notaries, etc are told time and time again to avoid "unauthorized practice of law" or you will suffer dire penalties. You can really protect clients by being aware of certain problems and knowing when to advise clients to get legal assistance.

Possible client questions will be presented in this chapter. These are questions that have been asked of me and many other licensees before you. After the question a simple or pithy answer will be given. Then when feasible the proper Civil Code Section will be given and you can read the entire code for a more complete explanation.

QUESTION: WHY ARE THERE SO MANY LAWS ABOUT PROPERTIES IN FORECLOSURE?

Answer: The State Legislature believes that dishonest investors were cheating many homeowners, so in 1979 a Code Section was written to protect homeowners.

Civil Code Section 1695 – Purpose
(a) The Legislature finds and declares that homeowners whose residences are in foreclosure have been subjected to fraud, deception, and unfair dealing by home equity purchasers. The recent rapid escalation of home values, particularly in the urban areas, has resulted in a significant increase in home equities which are usually the greatest financial asset held by the homeowners of this state. During the time period between the commencement of foreclosure proceedings and the scheduled foreclosure sale date, homeowners in financial distress, especially the poor, elderly, and financially unsophisticated, are vulnerable to the importunities of equity purchasers who induce homeowners to sell their homes for a small fraction of their fair market values through the use of schemes which often involve oral and written misrepresentations, deceit, intimidation, and other unreasonable commercial practices.
(b) The Legislature declares that it is the express policy of the state to preserve and guard the precious asset of home equity, and the social as well as the economic value of homeownership.
(c) The Legislature further finds that equity purchasers have a significant impact upon the economy and well being of this state and its local communities, and therefore the provisions of this chapter are necessary to promote the public welfare.
(d) The intent and purposes of this chapter are the following:
    1. To provide each homeowner with information necessary to make an informed and intelligent decision regarding the sale of his or her home to an equity purchaser; to require that the sales agreement be expressed in writing; to safeguard the public against deceit and financial hardship; to insure, foster, and encourage fair dealings in the sale and purchase of homes in foreclosure; to prohibit representations that tend to mislead; to prohibit or restrict unfair contract terms; to afford homeowners a reasonable and meaningful opportunity to rescind sales to equity purchasers; and to preserve and protect home equities for the homeowners of this state.
    2. This chapter shall be liberally construed to effectuate this intent and to achieve these purposes.

QUESTION: WHAT ARE THESE INVESTORS CALLED?

Answer: Purchasers of residential properties in foreclosure are called equity purchasers unless they fall under one of the six exceptions listed in Civil Code 1695.1

Civil Code Section 1695.1 Definitions
The following definitions apply to this chapter:
(a) "Equity purchaser" means any person who acquires title to any residence in foreclosure, except a person who acquires such title as follows:
    1. For the purpose of using such property as a personal residence.
    2. By a deed in lieu of foreclosure of any voluntary lien or encumbrance of record.
    3. By a deed from a trustee acting under the power of sale contained in a deed of trust or mortgage at a foreclosure sale conducted pursuant to Article 1 (commencing with Section 2920) of Chapter 2 of Title 14 of Part 4 of Division 3.

4. At any sale of property authorized by statute.
5. By order of judgment of any court.
6. From a spouse, blood relative, or blood relative of a spouse

QUESTION: WHAT PROPERTIES ARE COVERED UNDER THIS LAW?

Answer: This law covers 1-4 family dwelling units that are owner occupied and are in default.

Civil Code Section 1695.1 Definitions
(b) "Residency in foreclosure" and" residential real property in foreclosure" means residential real property consisting of one-to-four-family dwelling units, one of which the owner occupies as his or her principal place of residence, and against which there is an outstanding notice of default, recorded pursuant to Article 1 (commencing with Section 2920) of Chapter 2 of Title 14 of Part 4 of Division 3.

QUESTION: IF I WANT TO INVEST IN A "RESIDENCE IN FORECLOSURE," WHAT TYPE OF CONTRACT DO I NEED?

Answer: You need a very complete full contract with all pertinent information. It is recommended that you use a professional purchase agreement such as the California Association of Real Estate Purchase Agreement. You need two additional items when buying this type of property. They are a Notice Required by California Law and A Notice of Cancellation.

Civil Code Section 1695.2 Contract – Type Size – Language - Execution
Every contract shall be written in letters of a size equal to 10-point bold type, in the same language principally used by the equity purchaser and equity seller to negotiate the sale of the residence in foreclosure and shall be fully completed and signed and dated by the equity seller and equity purchaser prior to the execution of any instrument of conveyance of the residence in foreclosure.

1695.3 Terms of Contract
Every contract shall contain the entire agreement of the parties and shall include the following terms:
(a) The name, business address, and the telephone number of the equity purchaser.
(b) The address of the residence in foreclosure.
(c) The total consideration to be given by the equity purchaser in connection with or incident to the sale.
(d) A complete description of the terms of payment or other consideration including, but not limited to, any other consideration including, but not limited to, any services of any nature which the equity purchaser represents he will perform for the equity seller before or after the sale.
(e) The time at which possession is to be transferred to the equity purchaser.
(f) The terms of any rental agreement.
(g) A notice of cancellation as provided in subdivision (b) of Section 1695.5.
(h) The following notice in at least 14-point boldface type, if the contract is printed or in capital letters if the contract is typed, and completed with the name of the equity purchaser, immediately above the statement required by Section 1695.5(a).

```
+------------------------------------------------------------------+
|               NOTICE REQUIRED BY CALIFORNIA LAW                  |
|                                                                  |
|  Until your right to cancel this contract has ended,             |
|                                                                  |
|  _____ |
|                         (Name)                                   |
|  or anyone working for_____ CANNOT     |
|                         (Name)                                   |
|  ask you to sign or have you sign any deed or any other document.|
|                                                                  |
+------------------------------------------------------------------+
```

The contract required by this section shall survive delivery of any instrument of conveyance of the residence in foreclosure, and shall have no effect on persons other than the parties to the contract.

1695.4 Right of Cancellation - Time and Manner

(a) In addition to any other right of rescission, the equity seller has the right to cancel any contract with an equity purchaser until midnight of the fifth business day following the day on which the equity seller signs a contract that complies with this chapter or until 8 a.m. on the day scheduled for the sale of the property pursuant to a power of sale conferred in a deed of trust, whichever occurs first.

(b) Cancellation occurs when the equity seller personally delivers written notice of cancellation to the address specified in the contract or sends a telegram indicating cancellation to that address.

(c) A notice of cancellation given by the equity seller need not take the particular form as provided with the contract and, however expressed, is effective if it indicates the intention of the equity seller not to be bound by the contract.

1695.5 Cancellation Right – Time and Notice

(a) The contract shall contain in immediate proximity to the space reserved for the equity seller's signature a conspicuous statement in a size equal to at least 12-point bold type, if the contract is printed or in capital letters if the contract is typed, as follows:

"You may cancel this contract for the sale of your house without any penalty or obligation at any time before

_____
                (Date and time of day

See the attached notice of cancellation form for an explanation of this right." The equity purchaser shall accurately enter the date and time of day on which the rescission right ends.

(b) The contract shall be accompanied by a completed form in duplicate, captioned "notice of cancellation" in a size equal to 12-point bold type, if the contract is printed or in capital letters if the contract is typed, followed by a space in which the equity purchaser shall enter the date on which the equity seller executes any contract. This form shall be attached to the contract, shall be easily detachable, and shall contain in type of at least 10-point, if the contract is printed or in capital letters if the contract is typed, the following statement written in the same language as used in the contract:

NOTICE OF CANCELLATION

_____

(Enter date contract signed)

>**You may cancel this contract for the sale of your house, without any penalty or obligation, at any time before**

_____

(Enter date and time of day)

>**To cancel this transaction, personally deliver a signed and dated copy of this cancellation notice, or send a telegram**

To_____

(Name of purchaser)

at_____

(Street address of purchaser's place of business)

NOT LATER THAN_____

(Enter date and time of day)

I hereby cancel this transaction_____

(Date)

_____

(Seller's signature)

(c) The equity purchaser shall provide the equity seller with a copy of the contract and the attached notice of cancellation.

(d) Until the equity purchaser has complied with this section, the equity seller may cancel the contract.

1695.6 Responsibility of Equity Purchaser - Prohibitions

(a) The contract as required by Sections 1695.2, 1695.3 and 1695.5, shall be provided and completed in conformity with those sections by the equity purchaser.

(b) Until the time within which the equity seller may cancel the transaction has fully elapsed, the equity purchaser shall not do any of the following:

1. Accept from any equity seller an execution of, or induce any equity seller to execute, any instrument of conveyance of any interest in the residence in foreclosure.

2. Record with the county recorder any document including, but not limited to, any instrument of conveyance, signed by the equity seller.

3. Transfer or encumber or purport to transfer or encumber any interest in the residence in foreclosure to any third party, provided no grant of any interest or encumbrance shall

be defeated or affected as against a bona fide purchaser or encumbrancer for value and without notice of a violation of this chapter, and knowledge on the part of any such person or entity that the property was "residential real property in foreclosure" shall not constitute notice of a violation of this chapter. This section shall not be deemed to abrogate any duty of inquiry which exists as to rights or interests of persons in possession of the residential real property in foreclosure.

4. Pay the equity seller any consideration.

(c) Within 10 days following receipt of a notice of cancellation given in accordance with Sections 1695.4 and 1695.5 the equity purchaser shall return without condition any original contract and any other documents signed by the equity seller.

(d) An equity purchaser shall make no untrue or misleading statements regarding the value of the residence in foreclosure, the amount of proceeds the equity seller will receive after a foreclosure sale, any contract term, the equity seller's right or obligations incident to or arising out of the sale transaction, the nature of any document which the equity purchaser induces the equity seller to sign, or any other untrue or misleading statement concerning the sale of the residence in foreclosure to the equity purchaser.

(e) Whenever any equity purchaser purports to hold title as a result of any transaction in which the equity seller grants the residence in foreclosure by any instrument which purports to be an absolute conveyance and reserves or is given by the equity purchaser an option to repurchase such residence, the equity purchaser shall not cause any encumbrance or encumbrances to be placed on such property or grant any interest in such property to any other person without the written consent of the equity seller. Nothing in this subdivision shall preclude the application of paragraph (3) of subdivision (b).

QUESTION: IF SOMEONE VIOLATES THESE PROVISIONS, WHAT ARE THE POSSIBLE PENALTIES?

Answer: One item that should catch anyone's interest is that damages could be actual damages plus attorney's fees and exemplary damages not less than three times actual damages and the Statute of Limitations is four years. Also, fines of $10,000 and one year in prison are mentioned.

Civil Code Sections 1695.7-9
1695.7 Violations by Equity Purchase – Damages
An equity seller may bring an action for the recovery of damages or other equitable relief against an equity purchaser for a violation of any subdivision of Section 1695.6 or Section 1695.13. The equity seller shall recover actual damages plus reasonable attorneys' fees and costs. In addition, the court shall award exemplary damages or equitable relief, or both, if the court deems such award proper, but in any event shall award exemplary damages in an amount not less than three times the equity seller's actual damages for any violation of paragraph (3) of subdivision (b) of Section 1695.6 or Section 1695.13. Any action brought pursuant to this section shall be commenced within four years after the date of the alleged violation.

1695.8 Violation – Criminal Penalties
Any equity purchaser who violates any subdivision of Section 1695.6 or who engages in any practice which would operate as a fraud or deceit upon an equity seller shall, upon conviction, be punished by a fine of not more than twenty-five thousand dollars ($25,000), by

imprisonment in the county jail for not more than one year, or in the state prison, or by both that fine and imprisonment for each violation.

1695.9 Provisions of This Chapter Not Exclusive
The provisions of this chapter are not exclusive and are in addition to any other requirements, rights, remedies, and penalties provided by law.

QUESTION: CAN I GET A SELLER TO WAIVE THEIR RIGHTS UNDER THIS LAW BY GIVING THEM MORE MONEY?

Answer: NO

Civil Code Sections 1695.10 & 11
1695.10 Waiver Void and Unenforceable
Any waiver of the provisions of this chapter shall be void and unenforceable as contrary to the public policy.

1695.11 Severability
If any provision of this chapter, or if any application thereof to any person or circumstances is held unconstitutional, the remainder of this chapter and the application of its provisions to other persons and circumstances shall not be affected thereby.

QUESTION: CAN I BUY THE PROPERTY AND GIVE THE OWNER AN OPTION TO REPURCHASE AT A LATER TIME?

Answer: This transaction will probably be called a mortgage by any California Court and you will have another big box of problems.

Civil Code Section 1695.12 Repurchase Option – Loan Transaction
In any transaction in which an equity seller purports to grant a residence in foreclosure to an equity purchaser by any instrument which appears to be an absolute conveyance and reserves to himself or herself or is given by the equity purchaser an option to repurchase, such transaction shall create a presumption affecting the burden of proof, which may be overcome by clear and convincing evidence to the contrary that the transaction is a loan transaction, and the purported absolute conveyance is a mortgage; however, such presumption shall not apply to a bona fide purchaser or encumbrancer for value without notice of a violation of this chapter, and knowledge on the part of any such person or entity that the property was "residential real property in foreclosure" shall not constitute notice of a violation of this chapter. This section shall not be deemed to abrogate any duty of inquiry which exists as to rights or interests of persons in possession of the residential real property in foreclosure.

QUESTION: I HAVE HEARD THE TERM "TAKING UNCONSCIONABLE ADVANTAGE" OF AN "EQUITY SELLER" AND DON'T UNDERSTAND IT.

Answer: If you "really cheat" a seller a court could rule that you have been unconscionable. Then, the seller has the right to rescind the transaction within a two-year period from date of recording. By the way, two further points: There is no "safe

harbor rule" or "court or code definition" on what is unconscionable advantage so "Caveat Emptor" and you are responsible for everything your representatives do.

Civil Code Section 1695.13-17

1695.13 Prohibited Acts

It is unlawful for any person to initiate, enter into, negotiate, or consummate any transaction involving residential real property in foreclosure, as defined in Section 1695.1, if such person, by the terms of such transaction, takes unconscionable advantage of the property owner in foreclosure.

1695.14 Rescission

(a) In any transaction involving residential real property in foreclosure, as defined in Section 1695.1, which is in violation of Section 1695.13 is voidable and the transaction may be rescinded by the property owner within two years of the date of the recordation of the conveyance of the residential real property in foreclosure.

(b) Such rescission shall be effected by given written notice as provided in Section 1691 to the equity purchaser and his successor in interest, if the successor is not a bona fide purchaser or encumbrancer for value as set forth in subdivision (c), and by recording such notice with the county recorder of the county in which the property is located, within two years of the date of the recordation of the conveyance to the equity purchaser. The notice of rescission shall contain the names of the property owner and the name of the equity purchaser in addition to any successor in interest holding record title to the real property and shall particularly describe such real property. The equity purchaser and his successor in interest if the successor is not a bona fide purchaser or encumbrancer for value as set forth in subdivision (c) shall have 20 days after the delivery of the notice in which to reconvey title to the property free and clear of encumbrances created subsequent to the rescinded transaction. Upon failure to reconvey title within such time, the rescinding party may bring an action to enforce the rescission and for cancellation of the deed.

(c) The provisions of this section shall not affect the interest of a bona fide purchaser or encumbrancer for value if such purchase or encumbrance occurred prior to the recordation of the notice of rescission pursuant to subdivision (b). Knowledge that the property was residential real property in foreclosure shall not impair the status of such persons or entities as bona fide purchasers or encumbrancers for value. This subdivision shall not be deemed to abrogate any duty of inquiry that exists as to rights or interests of persons in possession of the residential real property in foreclosure.

(d) In any action brought to enforce a rescission pursuant to this section, the prevailing party shall be entitled to costs and reasonable attorney fees.

(e) The remedies provided by this section shall be in addition to any other remedies provided by law.

1695.15 Liability for Acts of Representative

(a) An equity purchaser is liable for all damages resulting from any statement made or act committed by the equity purchaser's representative in any manner connected with the equity purchaser's acquisition of a residence in foreclosure, receipt of any consideration or property from or on behalf of the equity seller, or the performance of any act prohibited by this chapter.

(b) "Representative" for the purposes of this section means a person who in any manner solicits, induces, or causes any property owner to transfer title or solicits any member of the property owner's family or household to induce or cause any property owner to transfer title to the residence in foreclosure to the equity purchaser.

1695.16 Contract Cannot Limit Liability

(a) Any provision of a contact which attempts or purports to limit the liability of the equity purchaser under Section 1695.15 shall be void and shall at the option of the equity seller render the equity purchase contract void. The equity purchaser shall be liable to the equity seller for all damages proximately caused by that provision. Any provision in a contract which attempts or purports to require arbitration of any dispute arising under this chapter shall be void at the option of the equity seller only upon grounds as exist for the revocation of any contract.

(b) This section shall apply to any contract entered into on or after January 1, 1991.

1695.17 Representative Must be Licensed and Bonded

(a) Any representative, as defined in subdivision (b) of Section 1695.15, deemed to be the agent or employee, or both the agent and the employee of the equity purchaser shall be required to provide both of the following:

1.   Written proof to the equity seller that the representative has a valid current California Real Estate Sales License and that the representative is   bonded by an admitted surety insurer in an amount equal to twice the fair market value of the real property which is the subject of the contract.

2.   A statement in writing, under penalty of perjury, that the representative has a valid current California Real Estate Sales License, is bonded by an admitted surety insurer in an amount equal to at least twice the value of the real property which is the subject of the contract and has complied with paragraph (1). The written statement required by this paragraph shall be provided to all parties to the contract prior to the transfer of any interest in the real property that is the subject of the contract.

(b) The failure to comply with subdivision (a) shall at the option of the equity seller render the equity purchase contract void and the equity purchaser shall be liable to the equity seller for all damages proximately caused by the failure to comply.

QUESTION: THE PREVIOUS QUESTIONS ALL APPLIED TO INVESTORS BUYING PROPERTIES. DIDN'T THE LEGISLATION AT THE SAME TIME DISCUSS "CONSULTANTS"?

Answer: Yes, another Civil Code Section 2945 was added to curb these problems and 2945 (a) lists why this law was passed.

Civil Code Section 2945 Legislative Findings/Intent

(a) The Legislature finds and declares that homeowners whose residences are in foreclosure are subject to fraud, deception, harassment, and unfair dealing by foreclosure consultants from the time a Notice of Default is recorded pursuant to Section 2924 until the time of the foreclosure sale. Foreclosure consultants represent that they can assist homeowners who have defaulted on obligations secured by their residences. These foreclosure consultants, however, often charge high fees, the payment of which is often secured by a deed of trust on the residence to be saved, and perform no service or essentially a worthless service. Homeowners, relying on the foreclosure consultants' promise of help, take no other action, are diverted from lawful businesses which could render beneficial services, and often lose their homes, sometimes to the foreclosure consultants who purchase homes at a fraction of their value before the sale.

(b) The Legislature further finds and declares that foreclosure consultants have a significant impact on the economy of this state and on the welfare of its citizens.

(c) The intent and purposes of this article are the following:

1. To require that foreclosure consultant service agreements be expressed in writing; to safeguard the public against deceit and financial hardship; to permit rescision of

foreclosure consultation contracts; to prohibit representations that tend to mislead; and to encourage fair dealings in the rendition of foreclosure services.

2. The provisions of this article shall be liberally construed to effectuate this intent and to achieve these purposes.

QUESTION: WHAT IS A "FORECLOSURE CONSULTANT?"

Answer: The best answer as to what a foreclosure consultant is and isn't and what are their services is in the following Section.

Civil Code Section 2945.1 Definitions
The following definitions apply to this chapter:
(a) "Foreclosure consultant" means any person who makes any solicitation, representation, or offer to any owner to perform for compensation or who, for compensation, performs any service which the person in any manner represents will in any manner do any of the following:

1. Stop or postpone the foreclosure sale.
2. Obtain any forbearance from any beneficiary or mortgagee.
3. Assist the owner to exercise the right of reinstatement provided in Section 2924c
4. Obtain any extension of the period within which the owner may reinstate his or her obligation.
5. Obtain any waiver of an acceleration clause contained in any promissory note or contract secured by a deed of trust or mortgage on a residence in foreclosure or contained in any such deed of trust or mortgage.
6. Assist the owner to obtain a loan or advance of funds.
7. Avoid or ameliorate the impairment of the owner's credit resulting from the recording of a notice of default or the conduct of a foreclosure sale.
8. Save the owner's residence from foreclosure.

(b) A foreclosure consultant does not include any of the following:

1. A person licensed to practice law in this state when the person renders service in the course of his or her practice as an attorney-at-law.
2. A person licensed under Division 3 (commencing with Section 12000) of the Financial code when the person is acting as a prorater as defined therein.
3. A person licensed under Part 1 (commencing with Section 10000) of Division 4 of the Business and Professions Code when the person makes a direct loan or when the person (A) engages in acts whose performance requires licensure under that part, (B) is entitled to compensation for the acts performed in connection with the sale of a residence in foreclosure or with the arranging of a loan secured by a lien on a residence in foreclosure, (C) does not claim, demand, charge, collect or receive any compensation until the acts have been performed or cannot be performed because of an owner's failure to make the disclosures set forth in Section 10243 of the Business and Professions Code or failure to accept an offer from a purchaser or lender ready, willing, and able to purchase a residence in foreclosure or make a loan secured by a lien on a residence in foreclosure on the terms prescribed in a listing or a loan agreement, and (D) does not acquire any interest in a residence in foreclosure directly from an owner for whom the person agreed to perform the acts other than as a trustee or beneficiary under a deed or trust given to secure the payment of a loan or that compensation. For the purposes of this paragraph, a "direct loan" means a loan of a real estate broker's own funds secured by a deed of trust on the residence in foreclosure, which loan and deed of trust the broker in good faith attempts to assign to a lender, for an amount at least sufficient to cure all of the defaults on obligations which are then subject to a recorded notice of default, provided that, if a

foreclosure sale is conducted the with respect to the deed of trust, the person conducting the foreclosure sale has no interest in the residence in foreclosure or in the outcome of the sale and is not owned, controlled, or managed by the lending broker; the lending broker does not acquire any interest in the residence in foreclosure directly from the owner other than as a beneficiary under the deed of trust; and the loan is not made for the purpose or effect of avoiding or evading the provisions of this article.

4. A person licensed under Chapter 1 (commending with Section 5000) of Division 3 of the Business and Professions Code when the person is acting in any capacity for which the person is licensed under those provisions.

5. A person or his or her authorized agent acting under the express authority or written approval of the Department of Housing and Urban Development or other department or agency of the United States or this state to provide services.

6. A person who holds or is owed an obligation secured by a lien on any residence in foreclosure when the person performs services in connection with this obligation or lien.

7. Any person licensed to make loans pursuant to Division 9 (commencing with Section 22000), 10 (commencing with Section 24000), or 11 (commencing with Section 26000) of the Financial Code, subject to the authority of the Commissioner of Corporations to terminate this exclusion, after notice and hearing, for any person licensed pursuant to any of those divisions upon a finding that the licensee is found to have engaged in practices described in subdivision (a) of Section 2945.

8. Any person or entity doing business under any law of this state, or of the United States relating to banks, trust companies, savings and loans associations, industrial loan companies, pension trusts, credit unions, insurance companies, or any person or entity authorized under the laws of this state to conduct a title or escrow business or a mortgagee which is a United States Department of Housing and Urban Development approved mortgagee and any subsidiary or affiliate of the above, and any agent or employee of the above while engaged in the business of these persons or entities.

9. A person licensed as a residential mortgage lender or servicer pursuant to Division 20 (commencing with Section 50000) of the Financial Code, when acting under the authority of that license.

(c) "Person" means any individual, partnership, corporation, limited liability company, association or other group, however organized.

(d) "Service" means and includes, but is not limited to, any of the following:

1. Debt, budget, or financial counseling of any type.

2. Receiving money for the purpose of distributing it to creditors in payment or partial payment of any obligation secured by a lien on a residence in foreclosure.

3. Contacting creditors on behalf of an owner of a residence in foreclosure.

4. Arranging or attempting to arrange for an extension of the period within which the owner of a residence in foreclosure may cure his or her default and reinstate his or her obligation pursuant to Section 2924c.

5. Arranging or attempting to arrange for any delay or postponement of the time of sale of the residence in foreclosure.

6. Advising the filing of any document or assisting in any manner in the preparation of any document for filing with any bankruptcy court.

7. Giving any advice, explanation or in instruction to an owner of a residence in foreclosure which in any manner relates to the cure of a default in or the reinstatement of an obligation secured by a lien on the residence in foreclosure, the full satisfaction of that obligation, or the postponement or avoidance of a sale of a residence in foreclosure pursuant to a power of sale contained in any deed of trust.

(e) "Residence in foreclosure" means a residence in foreclosure as defined in Section 1695.

(f) "owner" means a property owner as defined in Section 1695.1.
(g) "Contract" means any agreement, or any term thereof, between a foreclosure consultant and an owner for the rendition of any service as defined in subdivision (d).

QUESTION: CAN A CONTRACT BETWEEN AN OWNER AND A CONSULTANT BE ORAL?

Answer: No. The contract must be complete, plus dated and signed by the owner. Also there must be the NOTICE REQUIRED BY CALIFORNIA LAW and a NOTICE OF CANCELLATION.

Civil Code Sections 2945.2 & 3
2945.2 Owner's right to cancel contract with consultant; time and manner of cancellation
(a) In addition to any other right under law to rescind a contract, an owner has the right to cancel such a contract until midnight of the third "business day" as defined in subdivision (e) of Section 1689.5 after the day on which the owner signs a contact which complies with Section 2945.3.
(b) Cancellation occurs when the owner given written notice of cancellation to the foreclosure consultant at the address specified in the contract.
(c) Notice of cancellation, if given by mail, is effective when deposited in the mail properly addressed with postage prepaid.
(d) Notice of cancellation given by the owner need not take the particular form as provided with the contract and, however, expressed, is effective if it indicates the intention of the owner not to be bound by the contract.

2945.3 Written contract; contents; language, date, and signature; notice of cancellation; form
(a) Every contract shall be in writing and shall fully disclose the exact nature of the foreclosure consultant's services and the total amount and terms of compensation.
(b) The following notice, printed in at least 14-point boldface type and completed with the name of the foreclosure consultant, shall be printed immediately above the statement required by subdivision (c).

NOTICE REQUIRED BY CALIFORNIA LAW

_____ **or anyone working for him or her CANNOT**

    (Name)

(1)   take any money from you or ask you for money until

_____ **has completely**

    (Name)

finished doing everything he or she said he or she would do.

(2)   Ask you to sign or have you sign any lien, deed of trust, or deed.

(c) The contract shall be written in the same language as principally used by the foreclosure consultant to describe his services or to negotiate the contract; shall be dated and signed by the owner; and shall contain in immediate proximity to the space reserved for the owner's signature a conspicuous statement in a size equal to at least 10-point bold type, as follows: "You, the owner, may cancel this transaction at any time prior to midnight of the third business day after the date of the transaction. See the attached notice of cancellation form for an explanation of this right.

(d) The contract shall contain on the first page, in a type size no smaller than that generally used in the body of the document, each of the following:

    1. The name and address of the foreclosure consultant to which the notice or cancellation is to be mailed.

    2. The date the owner signed the contract.

(e) The contract shall be accompanied by a completed form in duplicate, captioned "notice of cancellation", which shall be attached to the contract, shall be easily detachable, and shall contain in type of at least 10-point the following statement written in the same language as used in the contract:

NOTICE OF CANCELLATION

_____ **You may cancel this transaction, without any**

  (Enter date of transaction)

penalty or obligation, within three business days from the above date.

To cancel this transaction, mail or delivery a signed and dated copy of this

cancellation notice, or any other written notice, or send a telegram.

To_____

          (Name of foreclosure consultant)

at_____

    (Address of foreclosure consultant's place of business)

NO LATER THAN MIDNIGHT OF_____

             (Date)

I hereby cancel this transaction_____

             (Date)

          _____

           (owner's signature)

(f) The foreclosure consultant shall provide the owner with a copy of the contract and the attached notice of cancellation.

(g) Until the foreclosure consultant has complied with this section, the owner may cancel the contract.

QUESTION: WHAT ARE PENALTIES FOR VIOLATION OF THIS CODE?

Answer: These are very similar to the penalties for the dishonest investors. Note the treble damages, $10,000 fine, one year in prison, no waivers and responsibility for all representatives.

Civil Code Sections 2945.5-11

2945.5 Waiver

Any waiver by an owner of the provisions of this article shall be deemed void and unenforceable as contrary to public policy. Any attempt by a foreclosure consultant to induce an owner to waive his rights shall be deemed a violation of this article.

2945.6 Action against consultant; judgment; cumulative remedies; limitation of actions

(a) An owner may bring an action against a foreclosure consultant for any violation of this chapter. Judgment shall be entered for actual damages, reasonable attorneys' fees and costs, and appropriate equitable relief. The court also may, in its discretion, award exemplary damages and shall award exemplary damages equivalent to at least three times the compensation received by the foreclosure consultant in violation of subdivision (a), (b), or (d) of Section 2945.4, and three times the owner's actual damages for any violation of subdivision (c), (e), or (g) of Section 2945.4, in addition to any other award of actual or exemplary damages.

(b) The rights and remedies provided in subdivision (a) are cumulative to, and not a limitation of, any other rights and remedies provided by law. Any action brought pursuant to this section shall be commenced within four years from the date of the alleged violation.

2945.7 Violations; punishment; cumulative remedies

Any person who commits any violation described in Section 2945.4 shall be punished by a fine of not more than ten thousand dollars ($10,000), by imprisonment in the county jail for not more than one year, or in the state prison, or by both that fine and imprisonment for each violation. These penalties are cumulative to any other remedies or penalties provided by law.

2945.8 Severability

If any provision of this article or the application thereof to any person or circumstance is held to be unconstitutional, the remainder of the article and the application of such provision to other persons and circumstances, shall not be affected thereby.

2945.9 Liability of consultant for statements or acts committed by representative

(a) A foreclosure consultant is liable for all damages resulting from any statement made or act committed by the foreclosure consultant's representative in any manner connected with the foreclosure consultant's (1) performance, offer to perform or contract to perform any of the services described in subdivision (a) of Section 1945.1, (2) receipt of any consideration or property from or on behalf of an owner, or (3) performance of any act prohibited by this article.

(b) "Representative" for the purposes of this section means a person who in any manner solicits, induces or causes (1) any owner to contract with a foreclosure consultant, (2) any owner to pay any consideration or transfer title to the residence in foreclosure to the foreclosure consultant, or (3) any member of the owner's family or household to induce or cause any owner to pay any consideration or transfer title to the residence in foreclosure to the foreclosure consultant.

2945.10 Limitation of liability under section 2945.9; voiding provision or contract; arbitration(a)
Any provision in a contract which attempts or purports to limit the liability of the foreclosure
consultant under Section 2945.9 shall be void and shall at the option of the owner render the
contract void. The foreclosure consultant shall be liable to the owner for all damages
proximately caused by that provision. Any provision in a contract which attempts or purports to
require arbitration of any dispute arising under this chapter shall be void at the option of the
owner only upon grounds as exist for the revocation of any contract.
(b) This section shall apply to any contract entered into on or after January 1, 1991

2945.11 Representative of consultant; statements to be provided to owner, remedies
(a) Any representative, as defined in subdivision (b) of Section 2945.9, deemed to be the agent
or employee or both the agent and the employee of the foreclosure consultant shall be required
to provide both of the following:

    1. Written proof to the owner that the representative has a valid current California Real
    Estate License and that the representative is bonded by an admitted surety insurer in an
    amount equal to at least twice the fair market value of the real property that is the subject of
    the contract.
    2. A statement in writing, under penalty of perjury, that the representative has a valid
    current California Real Estate Sales License, that the representative is bonded by an
    admitted surety insurer in an amount equal to at least twice the value of the real property
    that is the subject of the contract and has complied with paragraph (1). The written
    statement required by this paragraph shall be provided to all parties to the contract prior to
    the transfer of any interest in the real property that is the subject of the contract.

(b) The failure to comply with subdivision (a) shall, at the option of the owner, render the
contract void and the foreclosure consultant shall be liable to the owner for all damages
proximately caused by the failure to comply.

QUESTION: I KEEP HEARING ABOUT A NOTICE OF DEFAULT BUT HAVE NEVER SEEN ONE. WHAT MUST THEY CONTAIN?

Answer: Again, the exact wording is prescribed in the Civil Code. The notice must be in at least 12-point type and certain phrases must be in 14-point boldface.

*Civil Code Section 2924c Cure of default; payment of arrearages, costs and fees; effect on
acceleration; notice of default; trustee's or attorney's fees; reinstatement period*
(a)(1) Whenever all or a portion of the principal sum of any obligation secured by deed of trust
or mortgage on real property or an estate for years therein hereafter executed has, prior to the
maturity date fixed in that obligation, become due or been declared due by reason of default in
payment of interest or of any installment of principal, or by reason of failure of trustor or
mortgagor to pay, in accordance with the terms of that obligation or of the deed of trust or
mortgage, taxes, assessments, premiums for insurance, or advances made by beneficiary or
mortgagee in accordance with the terms of that obligation or of the deed of trust or mortgage,
the trustor or mortgagor or his or her successor in interest in the mortgaged or trust property or
any part thereof, or any beneficiary under a subordinate deed of trust or any other person having
a subordinate lien or encumbrance of record thereon, at any time within the period specified in
subdivision (e), if the power of sale therein is to be exercised, or, otherwise at any time prior to
entry of the decree of foreclosure, may pay to the beneficiary or the mortgagee or their
successor in interest, respectively, the entire amount due, at the time payment is tendered, with
respect to (A) all amounts of principal, interest, taxes, assessments, insurance premiums, or
advances actually known by the beneficiary to be, and they are, in default and shown in the

notice of default, under the terms of the deed of trust or mortgage and the obligation secured thereby, (B) all amounts in default on recurring obligations not shown in the notice of default, and (C) all reasonable costs and expenses, subject to subdivision (c), which are actually incurred in enforcing the terms of the obligation, deed of trust, or mortgage, and trustee's or attorney's fees, subject to subdivision (d), other than the portion of principal as would not then be due had no default occurred, and thereby cure the default theretofore existing, and thereupon, all proceedings theretofore had or instituted shall be dismissed or discontinued and the obligation and deed of trust or mortgage shall be reinstated and shall be and remain in force and effect, the same as if the acceleration had not occurred. This section does not apply to bonds or other evidences of indebtedness authorized or permitted to be issued by the Commissioner of Corporations or made by a public utility subject to the Public Utilities Code. For the purposes of this subdivision, the term "recurring obligation" means all amounts of principal and interest on the loan, or rents, subject to the deed of trust or mortgage in default due after the notice of default is recorded; all amounts of principal and interest or rents advanced on senior liens or leaseholds which are advanced after the recordation of the notice of default; and payments of taxes, assessments, and hazard insurance advanced after recordation of the notice of default. When the beneficiary or mortgagee has made no advances on defaults which would constitute recurring obligations, the beneficiary or mortgagee may require the trustor or mortgagor to provide reliable written evidence that the amounts have been paid prior to reinstatement.

(a)(2) If the trustor, mortgagor, or other person authorized to cure the default pursuant to this subdivision does cure the default, the beneficiary or mortgagee or the agent for the beneficiary or mortgagee shall, within 21 days following the reinstatement, execute and delivery to the trustee a notice of rescission which rescinds the declaration of default and demand for sale and advises the trustee of the date of reinstatement. The trustee shall cause the notice of rescission to be recorded within 30 days of receipt of the notice of rescission and of all allowable fees and costs.
No charge, except for the recording fee, shall be made against the trustor or mortgagor for the execution and recordation of the notice which rescinds the declaration of default and demand for sale.
(b)(1) The notice, of any default described in this section, recorded pursuant to Section 2924, and mailed to any person pursuant to Section 2924b, shall begin with the following statement, printed or typed thereon:

"IMPORTANT NOTICE (14-point boldface type if printed or in capital letters if typed)
IF YOUR PROPERTY IS IN FORECLOSURE BECAUSE YOU ARE BEHIND IN YOUR PAYMENTS, IT MAY BE SOLD WITHOUT ANY COURT ACTION, (14-point boldface type if printed or in capital letters if typed) and you may have the legal right to bring your account in good standing by paying all of your past due payments plus permitted costs and expenses within the time permitted by law for reinstatement of your account, which is normally five business days prior to the date set for the sale of your property. No sale date may be set until three months from the date this notice of default may be recorded (which date of recordation appears on this notice).

This amount is_____ as of _____
                                                        (Date)
and will increase until your account becomes current.

While your property is in foreclosure, you still must pay other obligations (such as insurance and taxes) required by your note and deed of trust or mortgage. If you fail to make future payments on the loan, pay taxes on the property, provide insurance on the property, or pay other obligations as required in the note and deed of trust or mortgage, the beneficiary or mortgagee may insist that you do so in order to reinstate your account in good standing. In addition, the beneficiary or mortgagee may require as a condition to reinstatement that you provide reliable written evidence that you paid all senior liens, property taxes, and hazard insurance premiums.

Upon your written request, the beneficiary or mortgagee will give you a written itemization of the entire amount you must pay. You may not have to pay the entire unpaid portion of your account, even though full payment was demanded, but you must pay all amounts in default at the time payment is made. However, you and your beneficiary or mortgagee may mutually agree in writing prior to the time the notice of sale is posted (which may not be earlier than the end of the three-month period stated above) to, among other things, (1) provide additional time in which to cure the default by transfer of the property or otherwise; or (2) establish a schedule of payments in order to cure your default; or both (1) and (2).

Following the expiration of the time period referred to in the first paragraph of this notice, unless the obligation being foreclosed upon or a separate written agreement between you and your creditor permits a longer period, you have only the legal right to stop the sale of your property by paying the entire amount demanded by your creditor.

To find out the amount you must pay, or to arrange for payment to stop the foreclosure, or if your property is in foreclosure for any other reason, contact:

_____
(Name of beneficiary or mortgagee)

_____
(Mailing address)

_____
(Telephone)
If you have any questions, you should contact a lawyer or the governmental agency which may have insured your loan.

Notwithstanding the fact that your property is in foreclosure, you may offer your property for sale, provided the sale is concluded prior to the conclusion of the foreclosure.

Remember: YOU MAY LOSE LEGAL RIGHTS IF YOU DO NOT TAKE PROMPT ACTION. (14-point boldface type if printed or in capital letters if typed).

Author's note: There are two Code Sections that outline the Conduct of the Sale & Bidding at the sale. The complete sections follow:

Civil Code Sections 2924 g & h
2924g Conduct of sale; time; place; interested parties; postponement; order of sale
(a) All sales of property under the power of sale contained in any deed of trust or mortgage shall be held in the county where the property or some part thereof is situated, and shall be made at auction, to the highest bidder, between the hours of 9 a.m. and 5 p.m. on any business day, Monday through Friday.

The sale shall commence at the time and location specified in the notice of sale. Any postponement shall be announced at the time and location specified in the notice of sale for commencement of the sale or pursuant to paragraph (1) of subdivision (c).

If the sale of more than one parcel of real property has been scheduled for the same time and location by the same trustee, (1) any postponement of any of the sales shall be announced at the time published in the notice of sale, (2) the first sale shall commence at the time published in the notice of sale or immediately after the announcement of any postponement, and (3) each subsequent sale shall take place as soon as possible after the preceding sale has been completed.

(b) When the property consists of several known lots or parcels they shall be sold separately unless the deed of trust or mortgage provides otherwise. When a portion of the property is claimed by a third person, who requires it to be sold separately, the portion subject to the claim may be thus sold. The trustor, if present at the sale, may also, unless the deed of trust or mortgage otherwise provides, direct the order in which property shall be sold, when the property consists of several known lots or parcels which may be sold to advantage separately, and the trustee shall follow that direction. After sufficient property has been sold to satisfy the indebtedness no more can be sold.

If the property under power of sale is in two or more counties the public auction sale of all of the property under the power of sale may take place in any one of the counties where the property or a portion thereof is located.

(c)(1) There may be a postponement or postponements of the sale proceedings, including a postponement upon instruction by the beneficiary to the trustee that the sale proceedings be postponed, at any time prior to the completion of the sale for any period of time not to exceed a total of 365 days from the date set forth in the notice of sale. The trustee shall postpone the sale in accordance with any of the following.

   (A) Upon the order of any court competent jurisdiction.
   (B) If stayed by operation of law
   (C) By mutual agreement, whether oral or in writing, of any trustor and any beneficiary or any mortgagor and any mortgagee.
   (D) At the discretion of the trustee.

(c)(2) In the event that the sale proceedings are postponed for a period or periods totaling more than 365 days, the scheduling of any further sale proceedings shall be preceded by giving a new notice of sale in the manner prescribed in Section 2924f. New fees incurred for the new notice of sale shall not exceed the amounts specified in Sections 2924c and 2924d, and shall not exceed reasonable costs that are necessary to comply with this paragraph.

(d) The notice of each postponement and the reason therefore shall be given by public declaration by the trustee at the time and place last appointed for sale. A public declaration of postponement shall also set forth the new date, time, and place of sale and the place of sale shall be the same place as originally fixed by the trustee for the sale. No other notice of postponement need be given. However, the sale shall be conducted no sooner than on the seventh day after the earlier of (1) dismissal of the action or (2) expiration of termination of the injunction, restraining order, or stay (which required postponement of the sale), whether by entry of an order by a court of competent jurisdiction, operation of law, or otherwise, unless the injunction, restraining order, or subsequent order expressly directs the conduct of the sale within that seven-day period. For purposes of this subdivision, the seven-day period shall not include the day on which the action is dismissed, or the day on which the injunction, restraining order, or stay expires or is terminated. If the sale had been scheduled to occur, but this subdivision precludes its conduct during the seven-day period, a new notice of postponement shall be given if the sale had been scheduled to occur during that seven-day period. The trustee shall maintain records of each postponement and the reason therefore.(e) Notwithstanding the time periods established under subdivision (d), if postponement of a sale is based on a stay imposed by Title 11 of the United States Code (bankruptcy), the sale shall be conducted no sooner than the expiration of the stay imposed by that title and the seven-day provision of subdivision (d) shall not apply.

2924h Bidders at sale; bid as irrevocable offer; security deposit; finality of sale; rescission for failure of consideration; delivery of payment; restraint of bidding; remedies
(a) Each and every bid made by a bidder at a trustee's sale under a power of sale contained in a deed of trust or mortgage shall be deemed to be an irrevocable offer by that bidder to purchase the property being sold by the trustee under the power of sale for the amount of the bid. Any second or subsequent bid by the same bidder or any other bidder for a higher amount shall be a cancellation of the prior bid.

(b)(1) At the trustee's sale the trustee shall have the right to require every bidder to show evidence of the bidder's ability to deposit with the trustee the full amount of his or her final bid in cash, a cashier's check drawn on a state or national bank, a check drawn by a state or federal credit union, or a check drawn by a state or federal savings and loan association, savings association, or savings bank specified in Section 5102 of the Financial Code and authorized to do business in this state, or a cash equivalent which has been designated in the notice of sale as acceptable to the trustee prior to, and as a condition to, the recognizing of the bid, and to conditionally accept and hold these amounts for the duration of the sale, and (b)(2) to require the last and highest bidder to deposit, if not deposited previously, the full amount of the bidder's final bid in cash, a cashier's check drawn on a state or national bank, a check drawn by a state or federal credit union, or a check drawn by a state or federal savings and loan association, savings association, or savings bank specified in Section 5102 of the Financial Code and authorized to do business in this state, or a cash equivalent which has been designated in the notice of sale as acceptable to the trustee, immediately prior to the completion of the sale, the completion of the sale being so announced by the fall of the hammer or in another customary manner. The present beneficiary of the deed of trust under foreclosure shall have the right to offset his or her bid(s) only to the extent of the total amount due the beneficiary including the trustee's fees and expenses.
(c) In the event the trustee accepts a check drawn by a credit union or a savings and loan association pursuant to this subdivision or a cash equivalent designated in the notice of sale, the trustee may withhold the issuance of the trustee's deed to the successful bidder submitting the check drawn by a state or federal credit union or savings and loan association or the cash equivalent until funds become available to the payee or endorsee as a matter of right.

For the purpose of this subdivision, the trustee's sale shall be deemed final upon the acceptance of the last and highest bid, and shall be deemed perfected as of 8 a.m. on the actual date of sale if the trustee's deed is recorded within 15 calendar days after the sale, or the next business day following the 15th day if the county recorder in which the property is located is closed on the 15th day. However, the sale is subject to an automatic rescission for a failure of consideration in the event the funds are not "available for withdrawal" as defined in Section 12413.1 of the Insurance Code. The trustee shall send a notice of rescission for a failure of consideration to the last and highest bidder submitting the check or alternative instrument, if the address of the last and highest bidder is known to the trustee.

If a sale results in an automatic right of rescission for failure of consideration pursuant to this subdivision, the interest of any lien holder shall be reinstated in the same priority as if the previous sale had not occurred.

(d) If the trustee has not required the last and highest bidder to deposit the cash, a cashier's check drawn on a state or national bank, a check drawn by a state or federal credit union, or a check drawn by a state or federal savings and loan association, savings association, or savings bank specified in Section 5102 of the Financial Code and authorized to do business in this state, or a cash equivalent which has been designated in the notice of sale as acceptable to the trustee in the manner set forth in paragraph (2) of subdivision (b), the trustee shall complete the sale. If the last and highest bidder then fails to delivery to the trustee, when demanded, the amount of his or her final bid in cash, a cashier's check drawn on a state or national bank, a check drawn by a state or federal credit union, or a check drawn by a state or federal savings and loan association, savings association, or savings bank specified in Section 5102 of the Financial Code and authorized to do business in this state, or a cash equivalent which has been designated in the notice of sale as acceptable to the trustee, that bidder shall be liable to the trustee for all damages which the trustee may sustain by the refusal to delivery to the trustee the amount of the final bid, including any court costs and reasonable attorneys' fees.

If the last and highest bidder willfully fails to deliver to the trustee the amount of his or her final bid in cash, a cashier's check drawn on a state or national bank, a check drawn by a state or federal savings and loan association, savings association, or savings bank specified in Section 5102 of the Financial Code and authorized to do business in this state, or a cash equivalent which has been designated in the notice of sale as acceptable to the trustee, or if the last and highest bidder cancels a cashier's check drawn on a state or national bank, a check drawn by a state or federal credit union, or a check drawn by a state or federal saving and loan, savings association, or savings bank specified in Section 5102 of the Financial Code and authorized to do business in this state, or a cash equivalent that has been designated in the notice of sale as acceptable to the trustee, that bidder shall be guilty of a misdemeanor punishable by a fine of not more than two thousand five hundred dollars ($2,500).

In the event the last and highest bidder cancels an instrument submitted to the trustee as a cash equivalent, the trustee shall provide a new notice of sale in the manner set forth in Section 2924f and shall be entitled to recover the costs of the new notice of sale as provided in Section 2924c.

(e) Any postponement or discontinuance of the sale proceedings shall be a cancellation of the last bid.

(f) In the event that this section conflicts with any other statute, then this section shall prevail.

(g) It shall be unlawful for any person, acting alone or in concert with others, (1) to offer to accept or accept from another, any consideration of any type not to bid, or (2) to fix or restrain bidding in any manner, at a sale of property conducted pursuant to a power of sale in a deed of trust or mortgage. However, it shall not be unlawful for any person, including a trustee, to state that a property subject to a recorded notice of default or subject to a sale conducted pursuant to this chapter is being sold in an "as-is" condition.

In addition to any other remedies, any person committing any act declared unlawful by this subdivision or any act which would operate as a fraud or deceit upon any beneficiary, trustor, or junior lienor shall, upon conviction, be fined not more than ten thousand dollars ($10,000) or imprisoned in the county jail for not more than one year, or be punished by both that fine and imprisonment.

MAKE MONEY IN CALIFORNIA FORECLOSURES PRACTICE QUESTIONS:

True or False?

CHAPTER 1

1. It is possible to make money in the foreclosure field.   T

2. Bankruptcies have decreased over the past 50 years.   F

3. Foreclosure laws vary greatly from state to state.   T

4. Everyone can make money in real estate.   F

5. Real estate has many types of returns.   T

6. Sweat equity is never required in real estate investing.   F

7. There are three parties to a trust deed.   T

8. The author of this textbook is Duane Gomer.   T

CHAPTER 2

1. The beneficiary picks the trustee.   T

2. The borrower can substitute the trustee at anytime.   ?

3. The trustee purchases a Trustee Sale Guarantee Policy.

4. A deed-in-lieu of foreclosure is like a quit claim deed.

5. Notices of Trustee Sales are never recorded

6. You can bid at a Trustee Sale with a credit card.

7. The Notice of Default is recorded by the Homeowner.

8. California real estate loans are mortgages.

9. Trust deeds have a trustee, a beneficiary and a trustor.

10. The first step in a foreclosure action is the sales auction.

11. A Notice of Default must be recorded with the county recorder.

12. Deeds-in-Lieu of foreclosure are illegal and never allowed.

14. It is feasible to consult with an attorney when investing in the foreclosure process.

14. Bankruptcies can never be filed to slow down a foreclosure.

15. The trustee doing the Notice of Sale must be accurate in filing.

16. The property owner conducts the trustee sale auction.

17. A beneficiary could underbid the amount owed at the sale.

18. When the trustee sale is complete, the property is always vacant.

CHAPTER 3

1. Transcripts of defaults in newspapers are not always complete.

2. You should investigate properties in several states for investment.

3. Finding a good investment is a number's game and takes effort.

4. Property profiles should never be considered.

5. The County Recorder's office could be a source of information.

6. Property investigation to determine price is a simple process.

7. In a terminal illness the first step is many times denial.

8. You should never talk to neighbors.

CHAPTER 4

1. Civil Code Section 1695 covers Foreclosure Sales.

2. An equity seller has 12 months to cancel.

3. There are exceptions to the strict rules of Civil Code 1695.

4. Walking a property when evaluating is a waste of time.

5. Fix-up costs must be calculated and considered

6. Stay away from senior lenders when considering investing.

7. Personal property must be considered when making an offer.

8. Drive for the last penny in negotiating, it's a win-lose situation.

9. Profit estimates and percentages can vary in different transactions.

10. On foreclosure purchases never use escrow companies.

11. A good contract is essential when buying from an owner.

12. Your profit is not considered when making a offer.

13. If there is a renter on the property, demand an Estoppel Certificate.

14. One thing to mention to a seller could be "I will be saving your credit."

15. Allow for contingencies when estimating repairs.

CHAPTER 5

1. If possible consider contacting junior lenders to discuss their plans.

2. Junior lenders are always more emotional than owners in foreclosure.

3. When buying a note from a junior lender you do not need to evaluate the property.

4. When you buy a note from a junior lender, you will have to foreclose to get control.

CHAPTER 6

1. Properties can sometimes be good values at Trustee Sale Auctions.

2. Determine your purchase price when the auction starts.

3. It is important to take the right amount of money to the sale.

4. The owner in foreclosure will always let you see the property.

5. Check with the trustee the day before the sale to be sure the sale is still on and it has not been cancelled.

6. All foreclosure auction properties are worth the bid price.

7. Be alert and observant at the Trustee Sale.

8. If a second trust deed is foreclosing, the first loan is wiped off.

9. Addendum to your deposit receipt are sometimes valuable.

10. Calculating how much to take to the trustee sale is simple.

11. An important calculation is "How much money to take to a Trustee Sales Auction."

12. One way to get money to go to a Trustee Sale is to get a partner.

13. It is best not to go to a sale until you have money to bid.

CHAPTER 7

1. The State of California passed several laws to keep homeowners from being cheated.

2. Purchases of residential properties in Foreclosure are called "equity purchases."

3. The Foreclosure Law (C.C. 1695) covers all properties in California.

4. A contract to meet C.C. 1695 regulations must be complete.

5. The Notice of Cancellation can be in any form.

6. Violating these rules has a maximum fine of $100.

7. Jail time of up to one year can be assessed.

8. An Equity Sales can never be rescinded.

9. Equity purchasers are responsible for their representatives' actions.

10. A contract to purchase a contract can be oral.

11. I can give an Equity Seller extra money to waive their rights under C.C. 1695.

12. There are laws covering Foreclosure Consultants.

13. The Notice of Cancellation must be in at least 10 point type.

14. The Notice of Cancellation must be always in English.

15. A Foreclosure Consultant is liable for all damages resulting from his or her statements.

16. Auctions are held on weekends.

17. It is illegal to accept money not to bid.

Practice Questions designed to prepare you to pass the final exams are available. New BRE Regulations do not allow us to give the answers to the quizzes in the book so the questions and answers are presented online. This makes the test taking very easy as you get the answers immediately.

To access the practice quizzes please visit http://www.DuaneGomer.com/after . Check on the proper link for the course you desire.

NOTE: Do not use Google, Yahoo, Bing etc. They are Search Engines. You must put the above URL link in your address bar or you won't get there.

You may request the questions by email to info@DuaneGomer.com, fax at 949-455-9931, or phone 800-439-4909. You will receive only the practice questions. You may FAX back your answers to Duane Gomer, Inc., at (949) 455-9931 and we will FAX your results to you within 24 business hours. Our recommendation is find a computer even if it's a friend or relatives it makes everything so easy under the new BRE rules.

Duane Gomer Seminars
REAL ESTATE & NOTARY EDUCATION
23312 Madero, Suite J
Mission Viejo, CA 92691
(800) 439-4909 / (949) 457-8930
Duane@DuaneGomer.com   www.DuaneGomer.com

WHY DO I SO STRONGLY BELIEVE YOU SHOULD BECOME A BROKER?

MONEY: Broker Associates make more money over the life of a career than Sales Associates. It's a fact.

FLEXIBILITY: If you ever want to become an Owner or Broker Associate in another company, you are ready. I get many calls when a Broker passes away, etc., and the partner or spouse needs to become a Broker immediately.

LIABILITY: The old theory "There is more liability if you have a Broker License" is a myth. Ask an Errors and Omissions Company if they charge higher fees for Broker Associates.

DOUBLE-DUTY: With a Broker License you can be an Associate, for example, at a Sales Office and a Management Office and a Loan Broker's Office, as long as the responsible brokers in those companies have knowledge of the arrangement.

RETIRING, ETC.: This is when you really want to be a Broker. If previous client, referral, or new friend calls you can refer them and get the entire referral fee.

STATUS: You can inform clients that you took additional courses and passed a full-day exam only 37% of prospects passed so you can probably handle their property to their satisfaction better than sales associates.

EDUCATION: Will the extra education harm you?

PASSING GRADES: Highest in history.

COURSES: If you received your Salesperson License after 1/1/1986 you have three courses done, only five to go. Also, we have an amazing crash learning course to help you pass the exam the first time.

EXPERIENCE: Only two years full-time salesperson experience in the last five years OR a four year degree from an accredited college or university with a major or minor in Real Estate may exempt you from the salesperson experience.

PAY AS YOU GO: Duane Gomer, Inc. has a payment plan.

GET STARTED: Call 800-439-4909 or go to www.DuaneGomer.com to get started.

BECOME A BROKER... *Today!*

Experience Requirements: Complete One Of The Following

- Worked full-time in California real estate for two of the last five years or worked part-time within the last five years that equals two years full time <u>OR</u>
- Worked two years full-time within the last five years in an equivalent activity such as escrow officer, title officer, loan officer, sub divider, contractor <u>OR</u>
- An applicant with a degree from an accredited four year college or university which included a major or minor in real estate may be exempt from the two-year salesperson experience requirement. <u>OR</u>
- Members of the California State Bar are exempt from the college-level course requirements; however they still need to complete the experience requirement.

Education Requirement: Complete Eight College Level Courses

Required Courses (Must take all five)

- Real Estate Appraisal
- Legal Aspects of Real Estate
- Real Estate Finance
- Real Estate Economics or Accounting
- Real Estate Practice

Elective Courses (Choose any three)

- Real Estate Principles
- Accounting or Economics
- Business Law
- Property Management
- Loan Brokering
- Escrows
- Common Interest Development
- R.E. Office Administration

- If you got your Salesperson license after 1986, you already have three courses.
- If you know anyone who has taken our courses recently, borrow their books.
- Prices include $15 for each book and the shipping.
- Contact us for "Why You Should Become A Broker" (There Are Many Reasons)

NEW PROGRAM ONLY AVAILABLE FROM DUANE GOMER
If your order is $296 or more, you can pay for the courses on a payment plan.
This option is only available by calling our office at 800-439-4909.

- To pass the exam you should order our Exam Prep course at your time of purchase so you can start studying for the full-day State Exam.
- The program from legendary attorney, John Henderson, includes comprehensive materials, practice tests, audio download, math workbook, glossary & weekly updates.
- The cost for a home study prep package is $85. For a highly recommended live presentation in Los Angeles or Orange County the cost is $150.

$$ OUR LOW PRICES $$

Add a Live Prep Course for $150 or
a Homestudy Prep Course for $85
and you can start studying for the State Exam now

1 Course - $79.50	2 Courses - $118.50
3 Courses - $177.75	4 Courses - $237.00
5 Courses - $296.25	6 Courses - $355.50
7 Courses - $414.75	8 Courses - $474.00

Duane Gomer Seminars

REAL ESTATE & NOTARY EDUCATION

23312 Madero, Suite J
Mission Viejo, CA 92691
(800) 439-4909 / (949) 457-8930
Duane@DuaneGomer.com   www.DuaneGomer.com

WHY DO I SO STRONGLY BELIEVE THAT YOU OR YOUR TEAM MEMBERS BECOME NOTARIES?

1. Getting a Notary Commission is simple and we have a successful "Become A Notary In One Day" program. It is quick and very inexpensive. All you have to do is pass a 30-question exam, pass a background check, and pay the State $40. We have extremely high passing rates.

2. With a Notary Commission you will be able to give clients better service. You are not going to get rich charging the maximum $10 per signature, but you will gain exposure. I recommend agents advertise "free" service to clients and their friends. One transaction created from Notary work would pay all the expenses for an entire Notary Career.

3. In my opinion, being a Notary and putting the information on your business card increases credibility, particularly for new or inexperienced licensees.

4. You can assist fellow associates and state law allows you to notarize your client's Grantor's and Trustor's documents. If you have a financial interest in a transaction you can't notarize, but when you are receiving a commission on a transaction, you have an agent's interest.

5. Having a commission allows you to promote yourself in different ways. You could advertise free acknowledgements once a month at a Senior Center. You could visit hospitals, rest homes, senior housing, libraries, jails etc. and offer your services and you could charge for your "time" and "travel".

6. Escrow and Title Companies need "loan document signers" to carry refinance papers. Reverse mortgage companies need Notaries with real estate knowledge to carry documents. Also, asset management companies need traveling Notaries. Foreclosure trustees need people to post sales information on properties and in a public place.

7. When you hire workers, you could have them take a Notary class, be tested and be fingerprinted. When they pass, you would know that they are above average in intelligence, ready to try something new, can work under pressure and they passed an extreme background check. That is worth the small cost and you have a Notary in your office.

8. One more thought. You have a bright young offspring going to college or looking for a job. If they apply for a job, for example, at a college or retail operation, I believe applicants who stress they are a notary (tested and fingerprinted) would move to the front of the line. Starting this year Notary applicants are checked out by the Department of Justice and the FBI. Impressive on a job application.

9. We have a six-hour live review with the state exam following, for your convenience, or we have a six-hour home study course. **New**: A three-hour home-study course for renewing Notaries. **New and exclusive from Duane Gomer**: Our six-hour review course is available on CD. Save time, travel and gas. Learn at home.

Made in the USA
San Bernardino, CA
21 January 2014